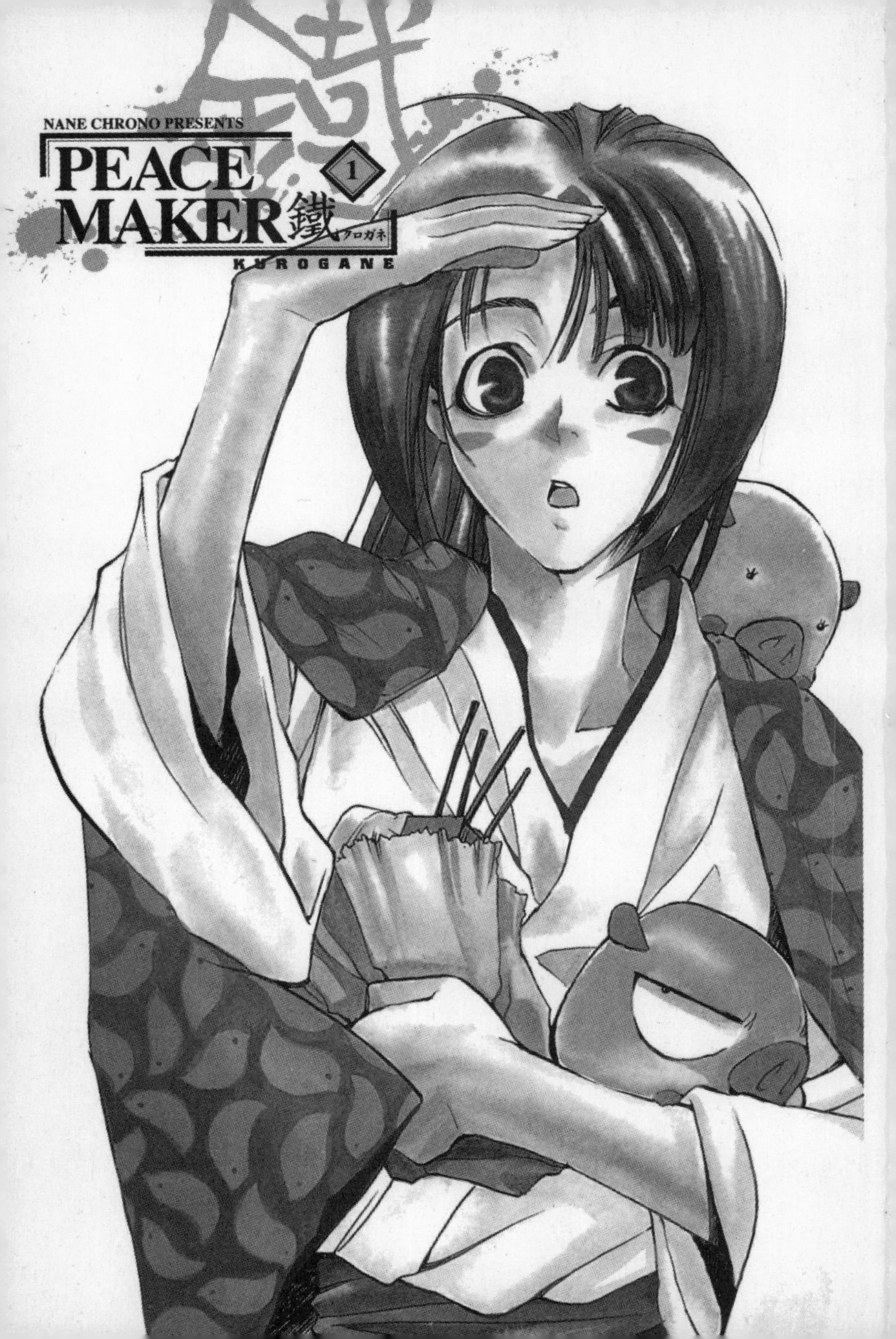
NANE CHRONO PRESENTS
PEACE MAKER 鐵
クロガネ
1
KUROGANE

CONTENTS

再龍刀一始

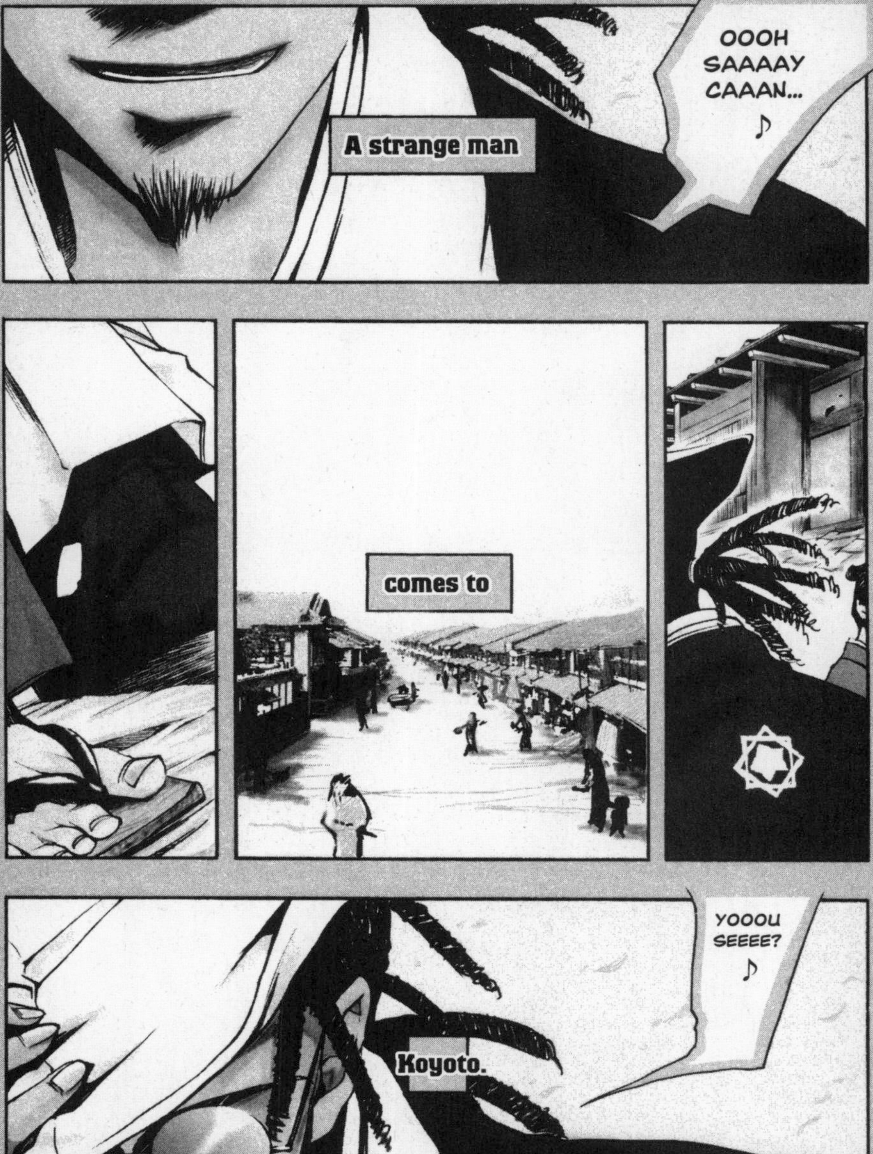
OOOH SAAAAY CAAAN... ♪
A strange man
comes to
YOOOU SEEEE? ♪
Koyoto.

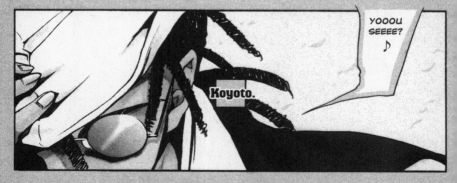

CHAPTER 1
BEGIN 鐵

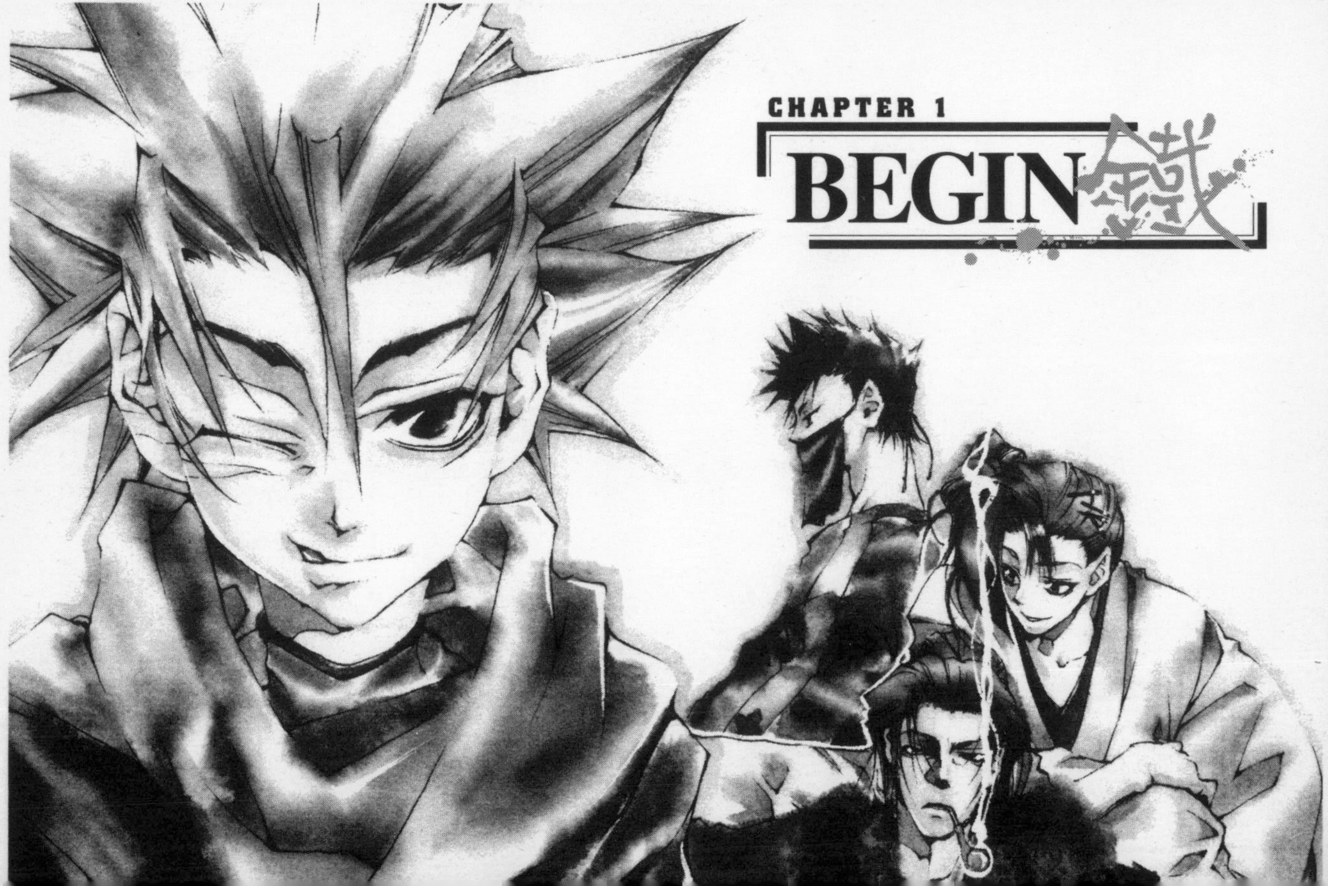

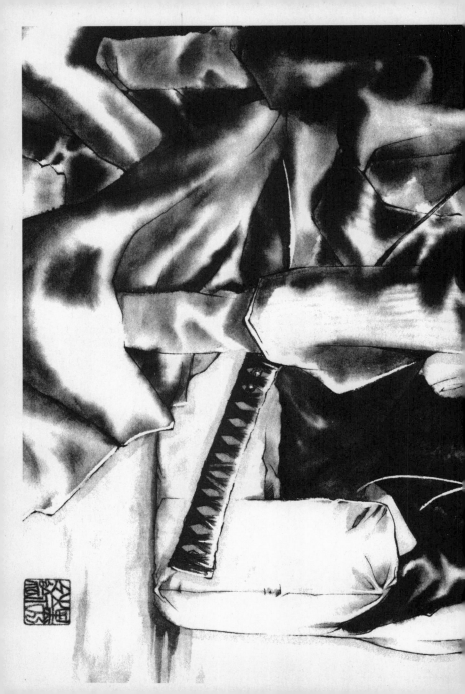

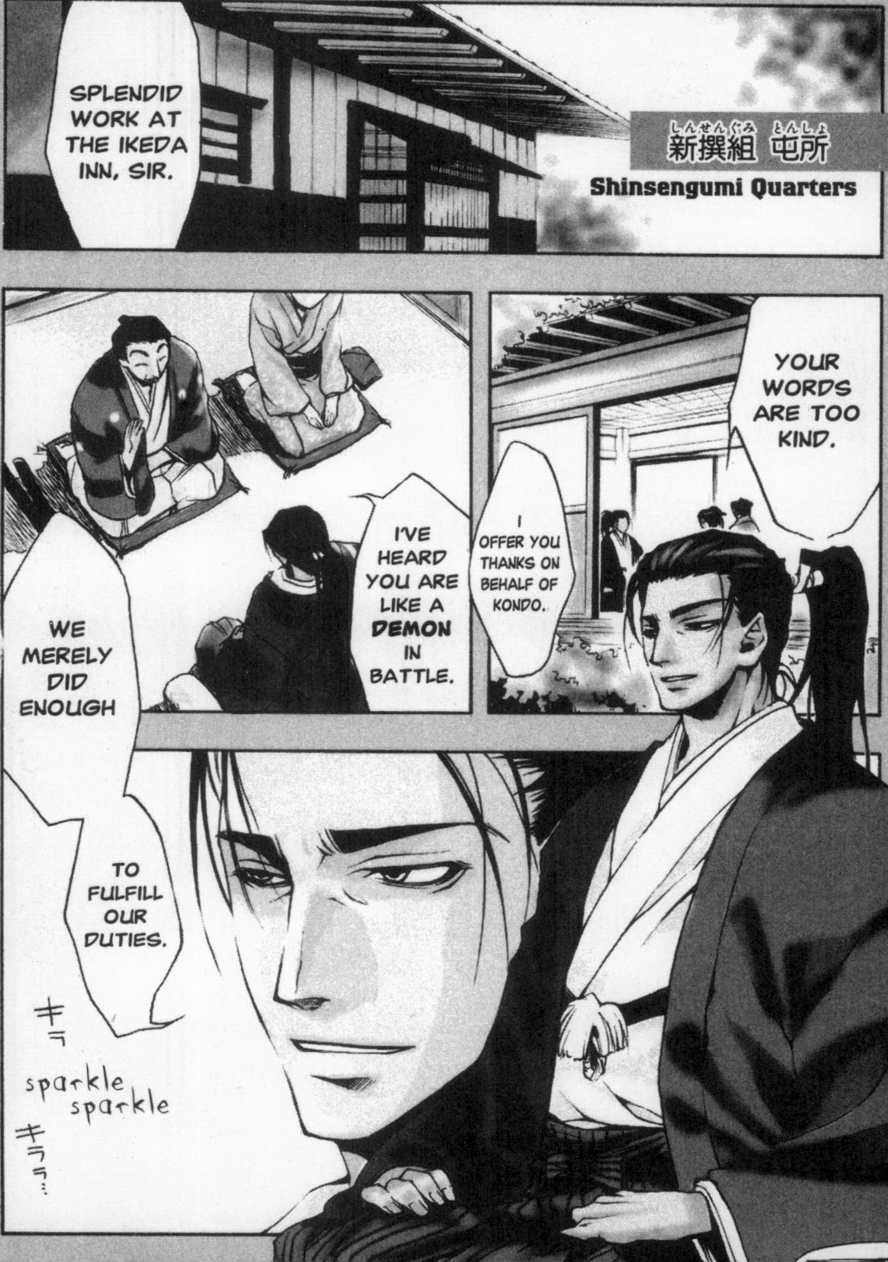
新撰組 屯所
Shinsengumi Quarters
SPLENDID WORK AT THE IKEDA INN, SIR.
YOUR WORDS ARE TOO KIND.
I OFFER YOU THANKS ON BEHALF OF KONDO.
I'VE HEARD YOU ARE LIKE A DEMON IN BATTLE.
WE MERELY DID ENOUGH
TO FULFILL OUR DUTIES.
キラ
sparkle sparkle
キラ…

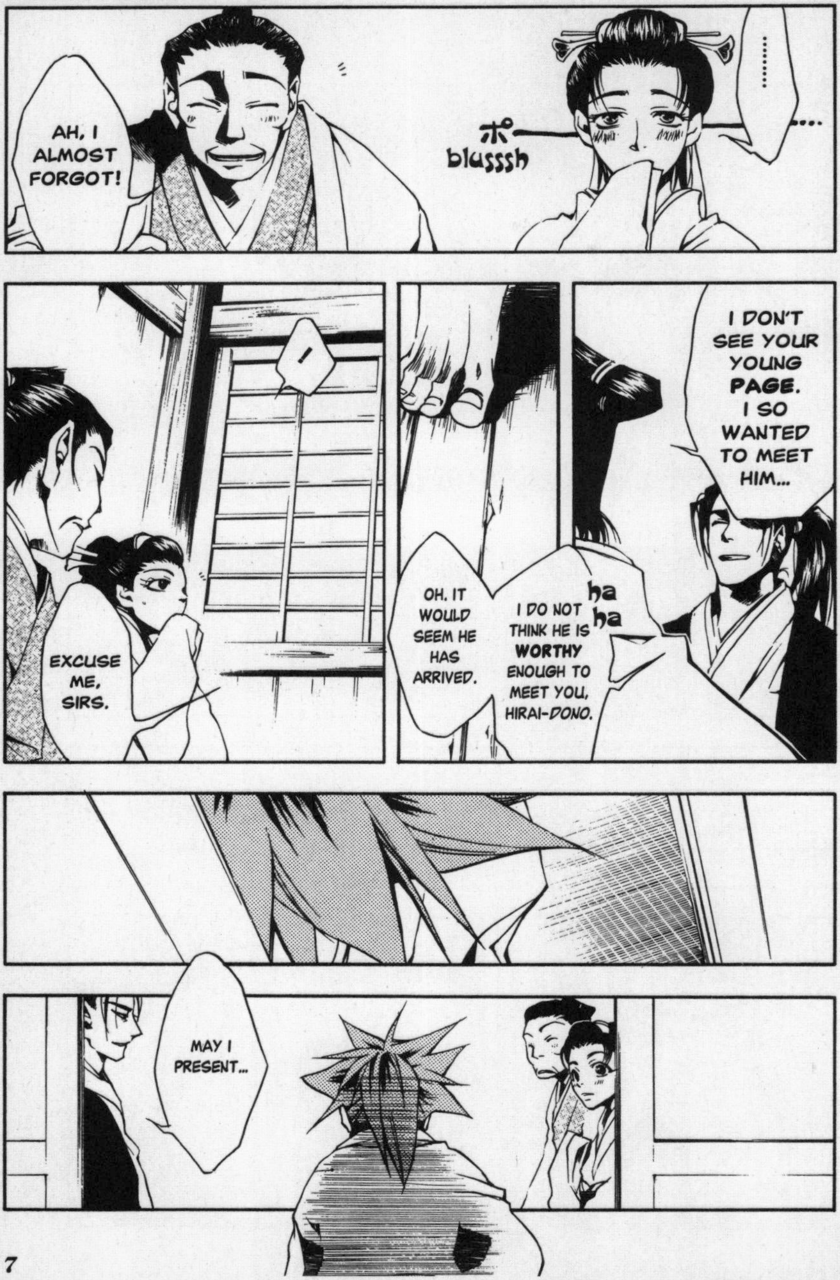
......
....
ポ
blusssh
AH, I ALMOST FORGOT!
I DON'T SEE YOUR YOUNG PAGE. I SO WANTED TO MEET HIM...
ha ha
I DO NOT THINK HE IS WORTHY ENOUGH TO MEET YOU, HIRAI-DONO.
OH. IT WOULD SEEM HE HAS ARRIVED.
!
EXCUSE ME, SIRS.
MAY I PRESENT...

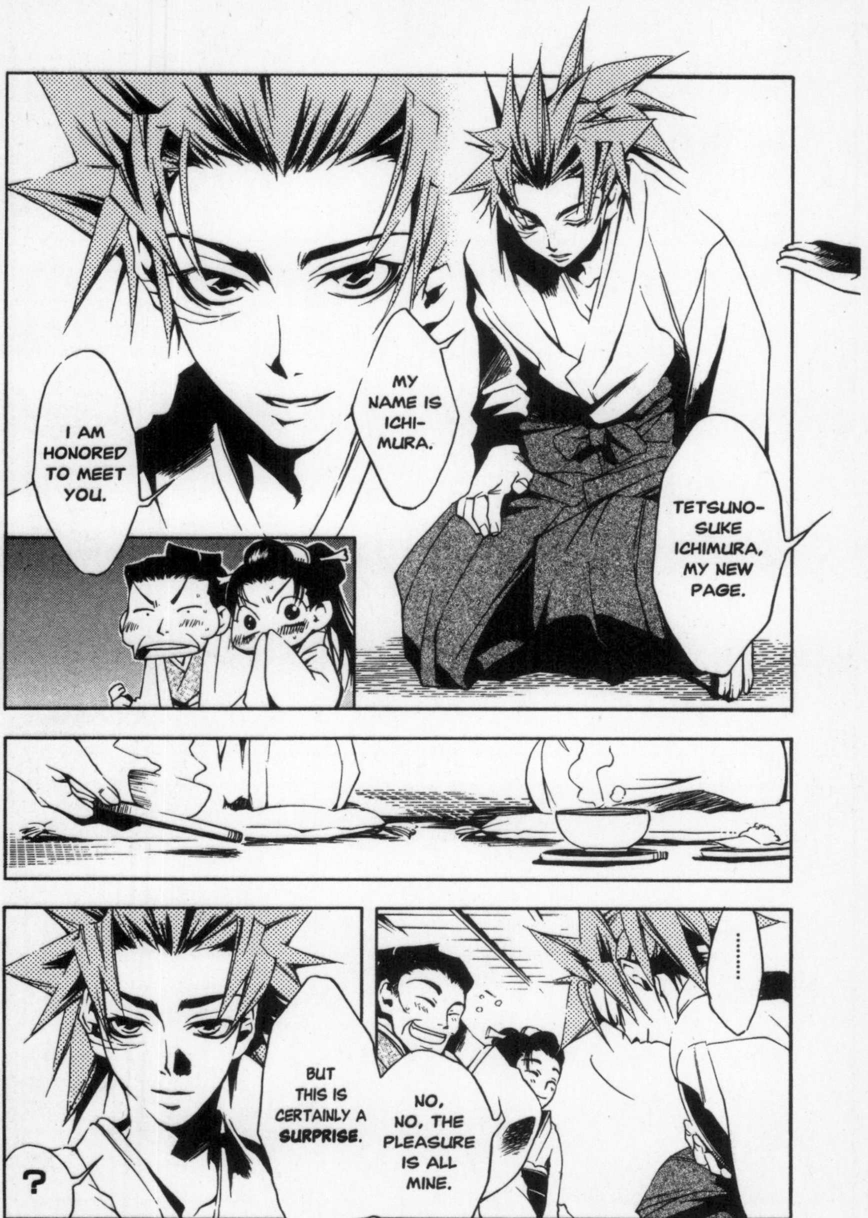
TETSUNOSUKE ICHIMURA, MY NEW PAGE.
MY NAME IS ICHIMURA.
I AM HONORED TO MEET YOU.
......
NO, NO, THE PLEASURE IS ALL MINE.
BUT THIS IS CERTAINLY A **SURPRISE**.
?

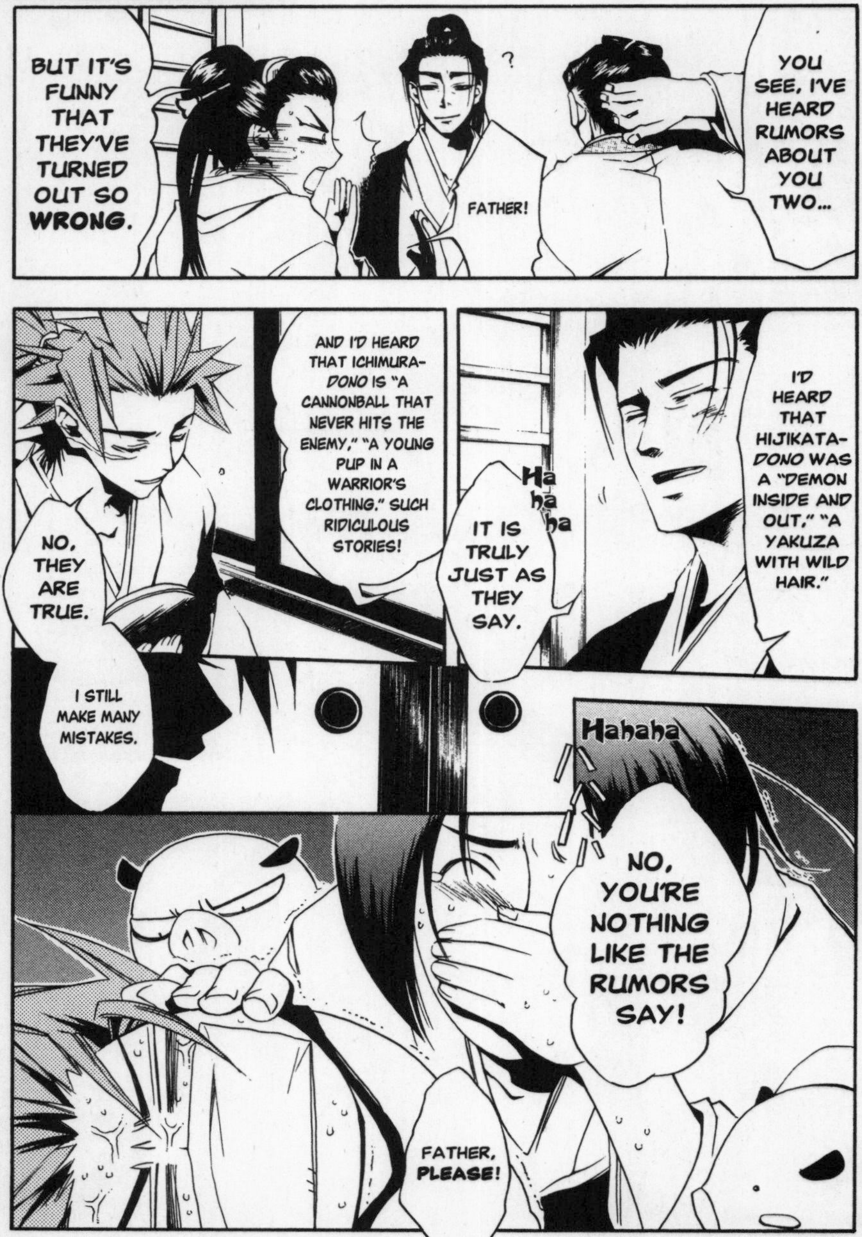
YOU SEE, I'VE HEARD RUMORS ABOUT YOU TWO...
FATHER!
BUT IT'S FUNNY THAT THEY'VE TURNED OUT SO WRONG.
I'D HEARD THAT HIJIKATA-DONO WAS A "DEMON INSIDE AND OUT," "A YAKUZA WITH WILD HAIR."
Ha ha ha
IT IS TRULY JUST AS THEY SAY.
AND I'D HEARD THAT ICHIMURA-DONO IS "A CANNONBALL THAT NEVER HITS THE ENEMY," "A YOUNG PUP IN A WARRIOR'S CLOTHING." SUCH RIDICULOUS STORIES!
NO, THEY ARE TRUE.
I STILL MAKE MANY MISTAKES.
Hahaha
NO, YOU'RE NOTHING LIKE THE RUMORS SAY!
FATHER, PLEASE!

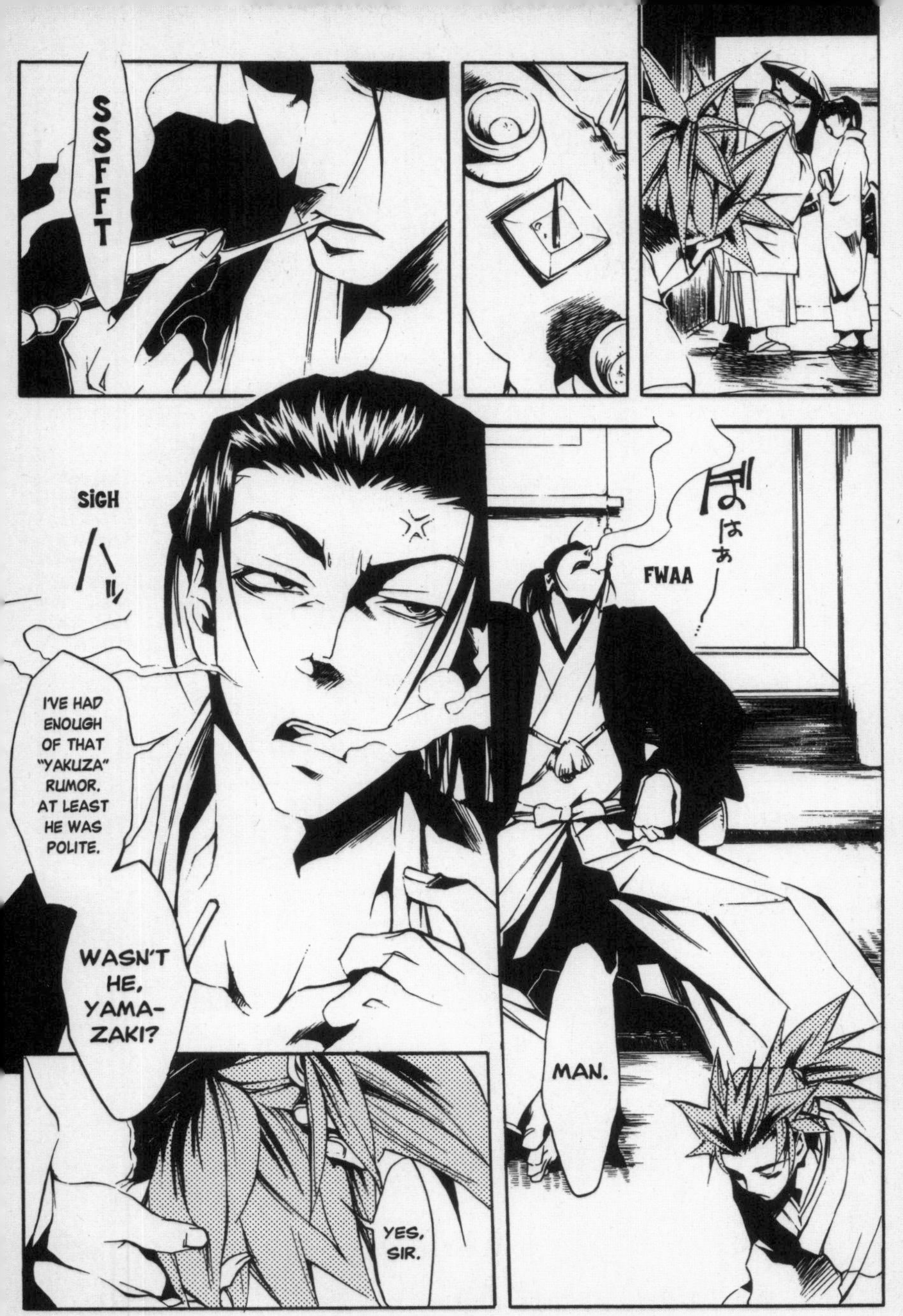
SSFFT
FWAA
ぱはぁ
MAN.
SIGH
I'VE HAD ENOUGH OF THAT "YAKUZA" RUMOR. AT LEAST HE WAS POLITE.
WASN'T HE, YAMA-ZAKI?
YES, SIR.

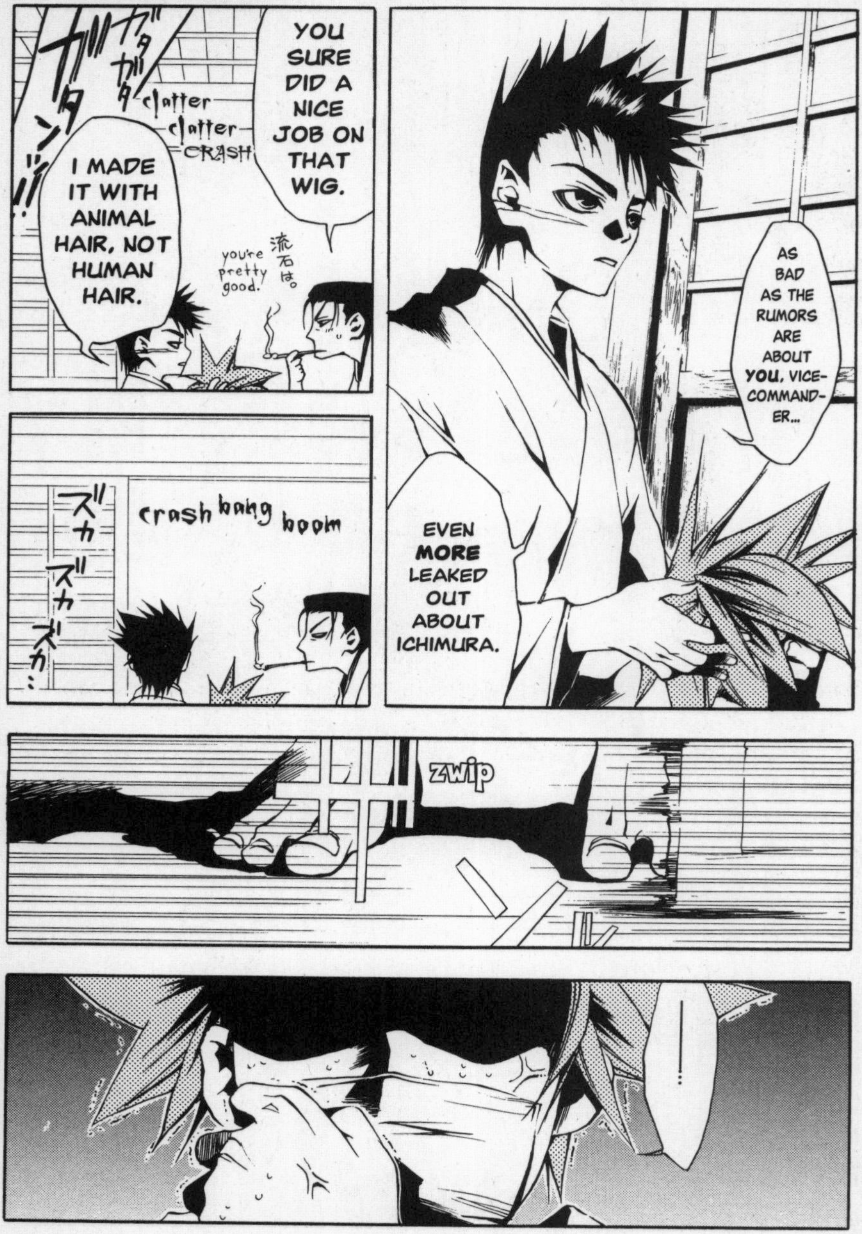
AS BAD AS THE RUMORS ARE ABOUT YOU, VICE-COMMANDER...
EVEN MORE LEAKED OUT ABOUT ICHIMURA.
YOU SURE DID A NICE JOB ON THAT WIG.
ガタガタ
clatter clatter
ガタン!!!
CRASH
I MADE IT WITH ANIMAL HAIR, NOT HUMAN HAIR.
流石は。
you're pretty good.
ズカズカズカ
crash bang boom
zwip
...!

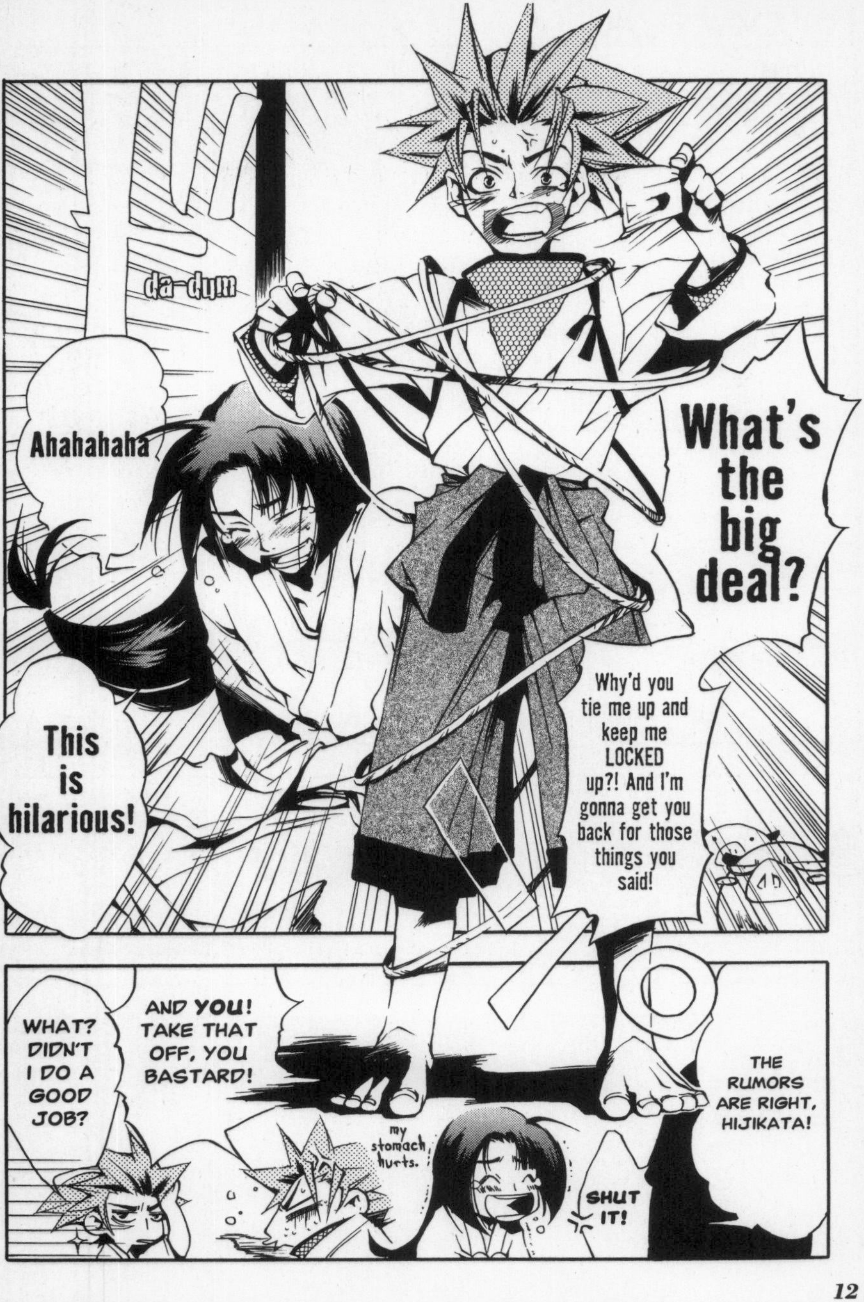
da-dum
What's the big deal?
Why'd you tie me up and keep me LOCKED up?! And I'm gonna get you back for those things you said!
Ahahahaha
This is hilarious!
THE RUMORS ARE RIGHT, HIJIKATA!
SHUT IT!
my stomach hurts.
AND YOU! TAKE THAT OFF, YOU BASTARD!
WHAT? DIDN'T I DO A GOOD JOB?

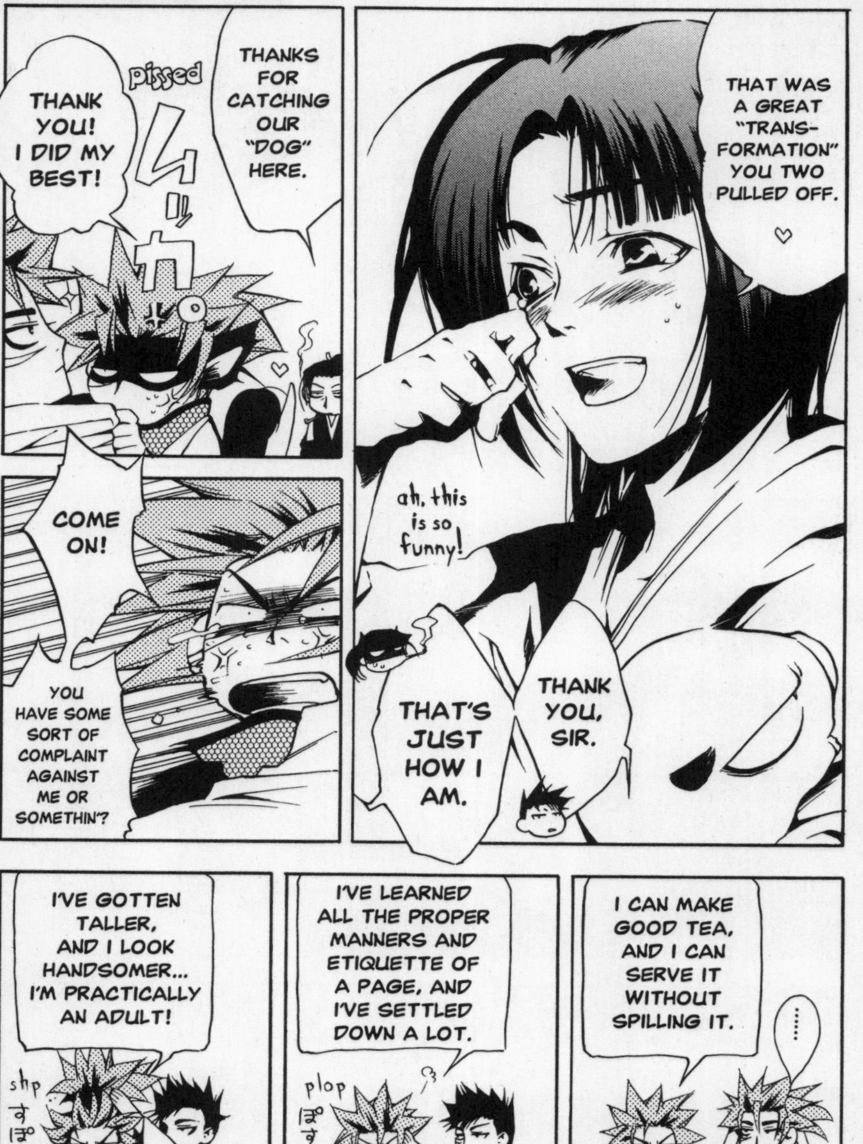
THAT WAS A GREAT "TRANS-FORMATION" YOU TWO PULLED OFF.
ah, this is so funny!
THANK YOU, SIR.
THAT'S JUST HOW I AM.
THANKS FOR CATCHING OUR "DOG" HERE.
pissed
ムッカ
THANK YOU! I DID MY BEST!
COME ON!
YOU HAVE SOME SORT OF COMPLAINT AGAINST ME OR SOMETHIN'?
I CAN MAKE GOOD TEA, AND I CAN SERVE IT WITHOUT SPILLING IT.
......
I'VE LEARNED ALL THE PROPER MANNERS AND ETIQUETTE OF A PAGE, AND I'VE SETTLED DOWN A LOT.
plop
ぽすっ
I'VE GOTTEN TALLER, AND I LOOK HANDSOMER... I'M PRACTICALLY AN ADULT!
shp
すぽっ

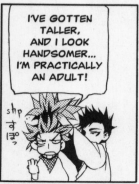

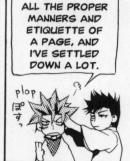

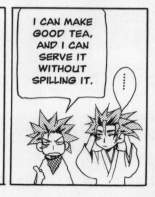

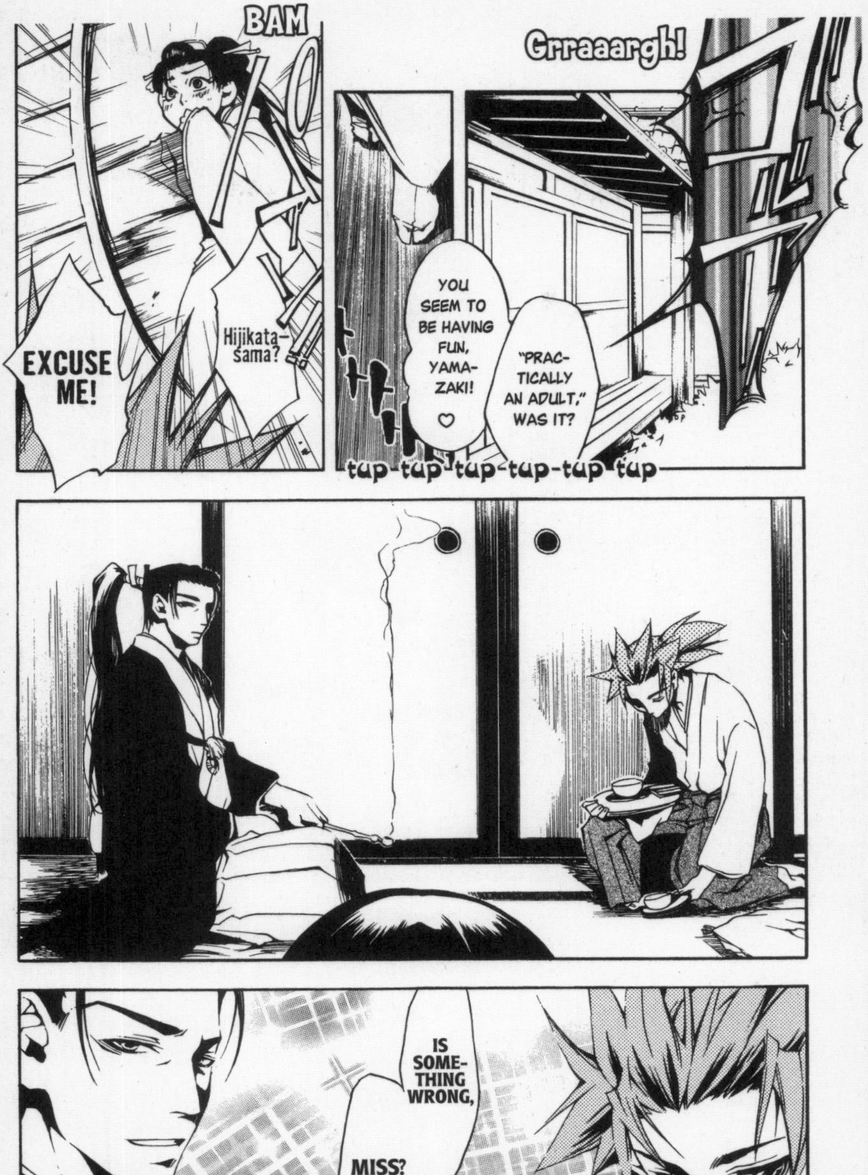
Grrraaargh!
"PRAC-TICALLY AN ADULT," WAS IT?
YOU SEEM TO BE HAVING FUN, YAMA-ZAKI! ♡
tup-tup-tup-tup-tup tup
BAM
Hijikata-sama?
EXCUSE ME!
IS SOME-THING WRONG,
MISS?

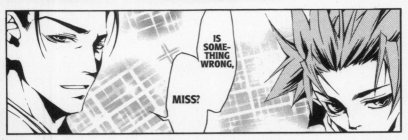

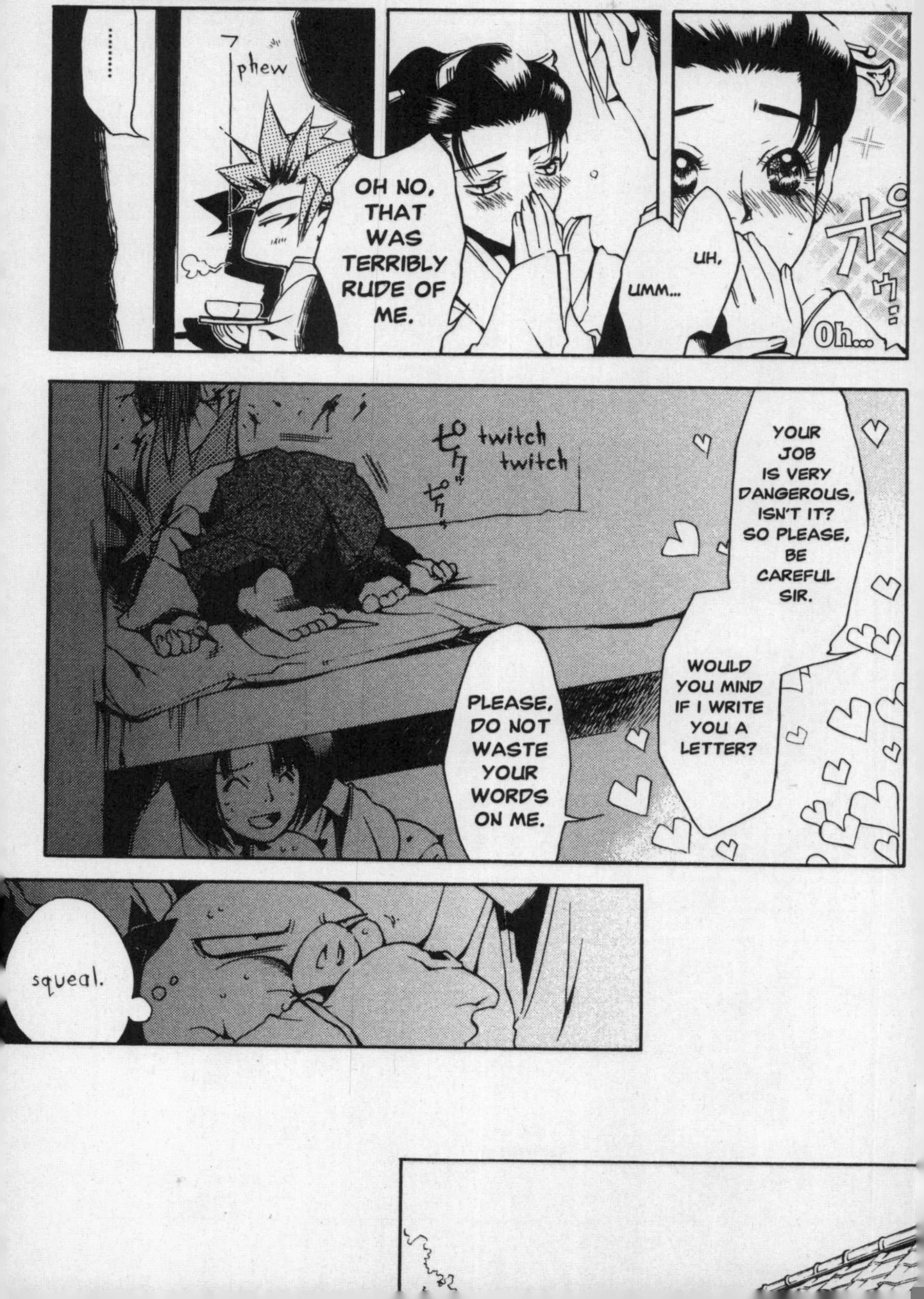
Oh...
UH, UMM...
OH NO, THAT WAS TERRIBLY RUDE OF ME.
phew
......
YOUR JOB IS VERY DANGEROUS, ISN'T IT? SO PLEASE, BE CAREFUL SIR.
WOULD YOU MIND IF I WRITE YOU A LETTER?
PLEASE, DO NOT WASTE YOUR WORDS ON ME.
twitch twitch
squeal.

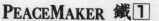

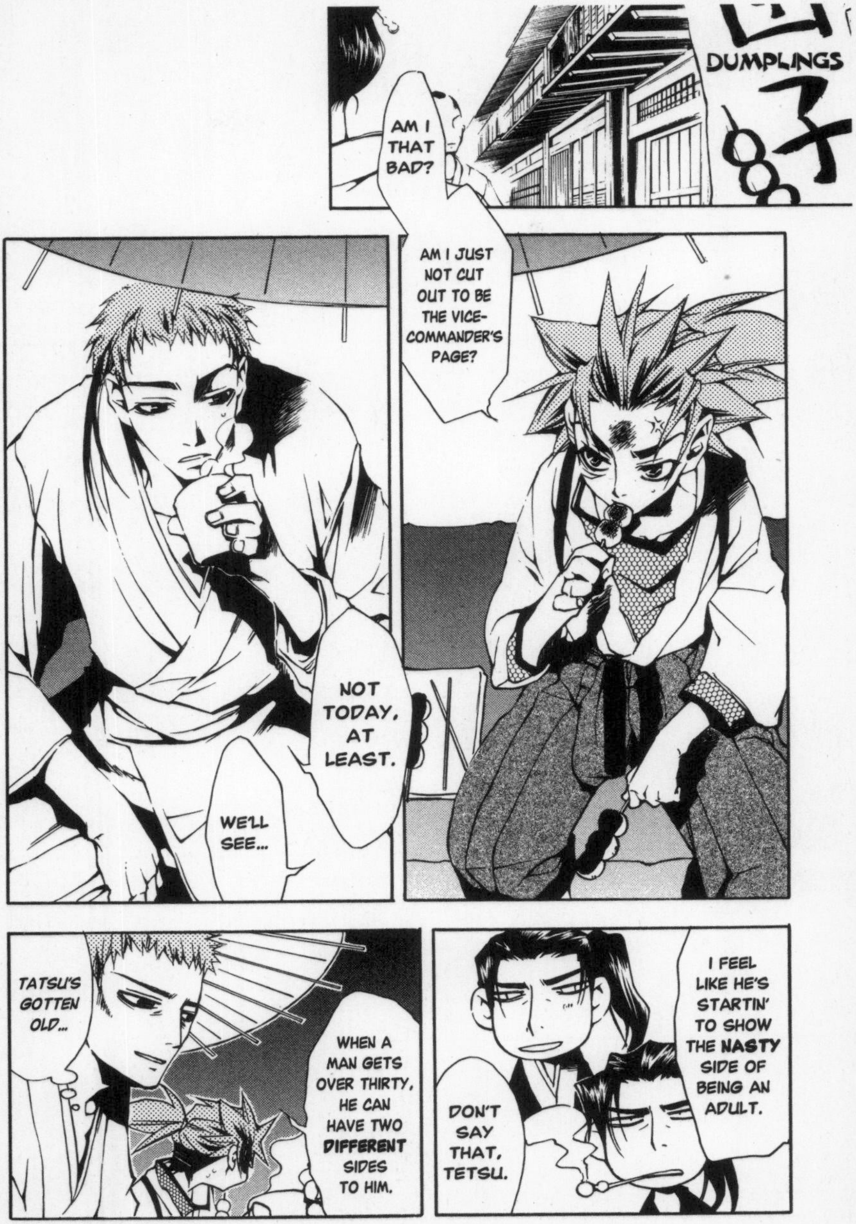
DUMPLINGS
AM I THAT BAD?
AM I JUST NOT CUT OUT TO BE THE VICE-COMMANDER'S PAGE?
NOT TODAY, AT LEAST.
WE'LL SEE...
I FEEL LIKE HE'S STARTIN' TO SHOW THE NASTY SIDE OF BEING AN ADULT.
DON'T SAY THAT, TETSU.
TATSU'S GOTTEN OLD...
WHEN A MAN GETS OVER THIRTY, HE CAN HAVE TWO DIFFERENT SIDES TO HIM.

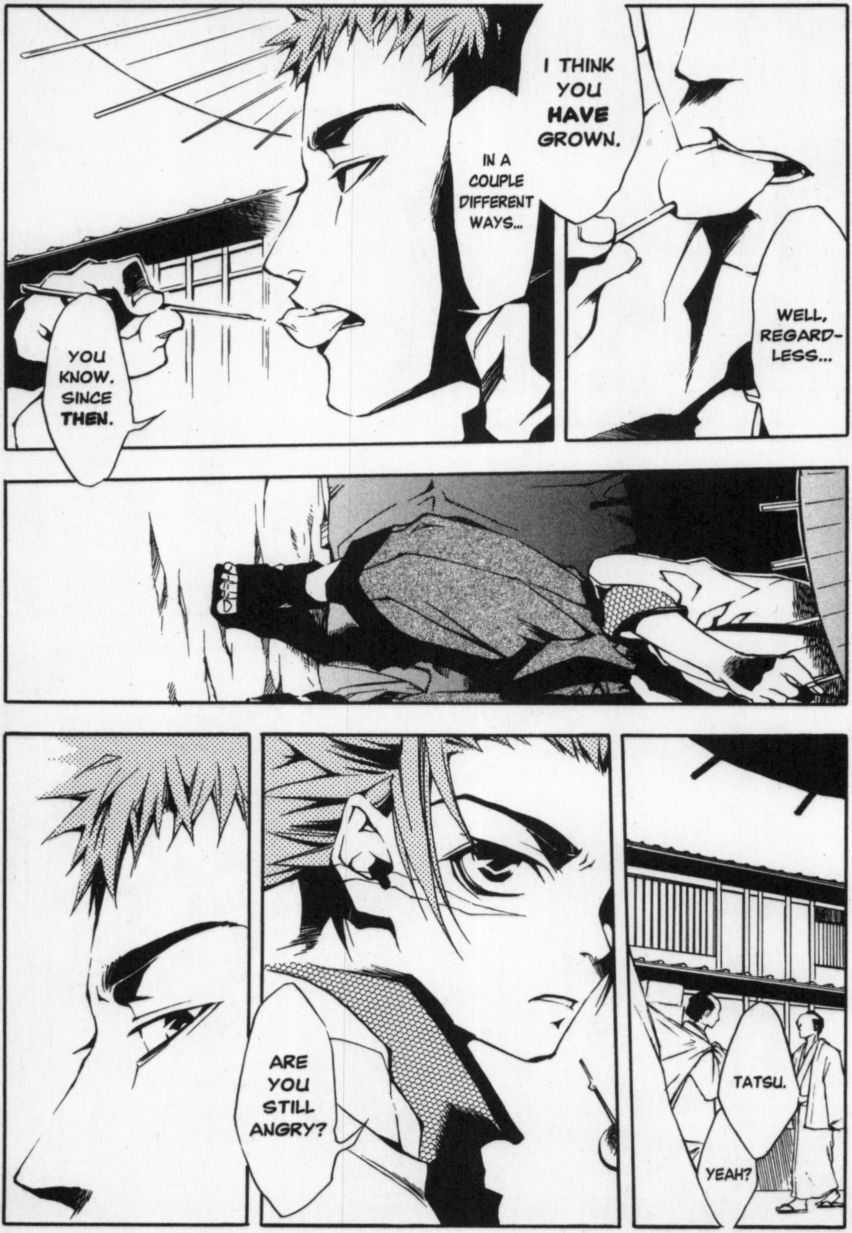
I THINK YOU HAVE GROWN.
WELL, REGARDLESS...
IN A COUPLE DIFFERENT WAYS...
YOU KNOW. SINCE THEN.
TATSU.
YEAH?
ARE YOU STILL ANGRY?

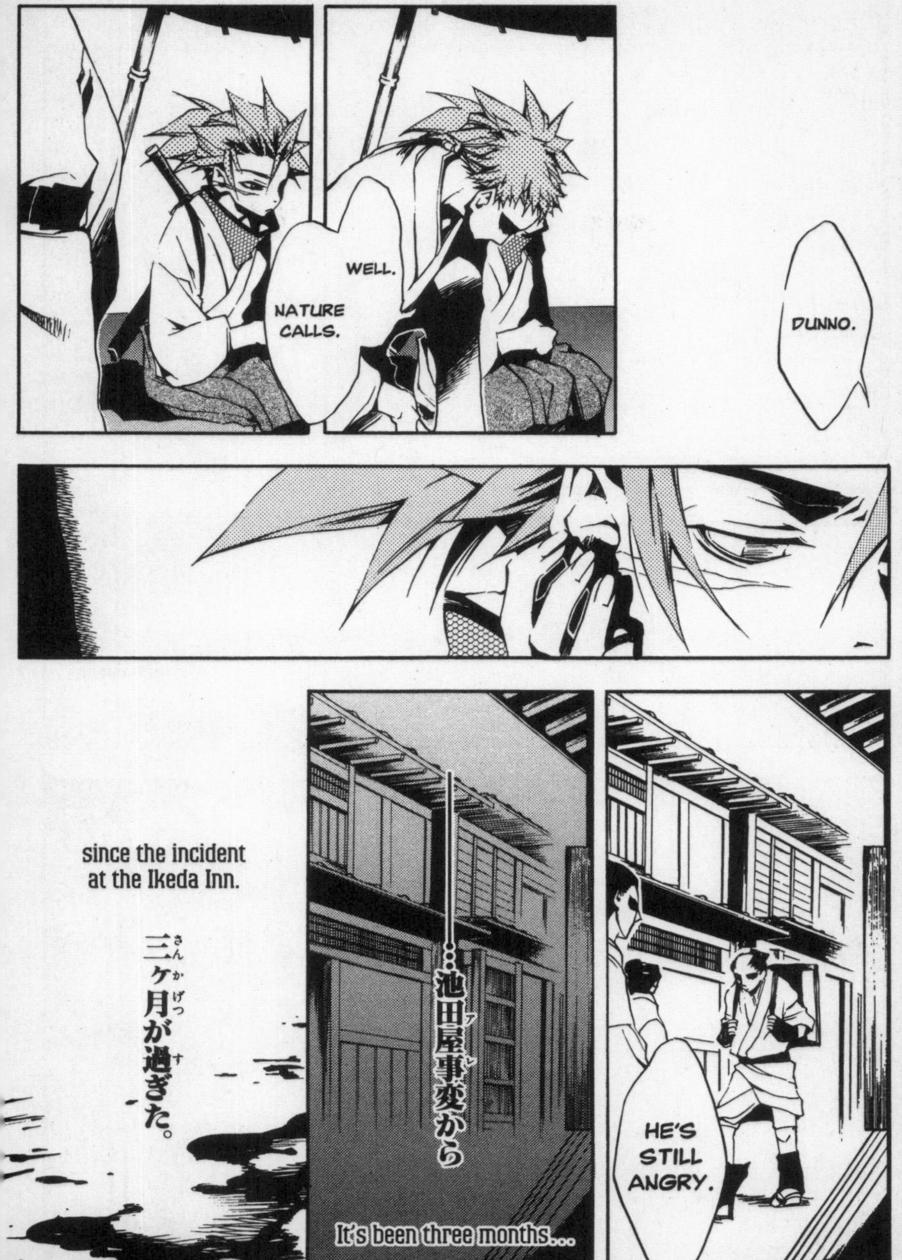
DUNNO.
WELL. NATURE CALLS.
HE'S STILL ANGRY.
池田屋事変から
It's been three months...
三ヶ月が過ぎた。
since the incident at the Ikeda Inn.

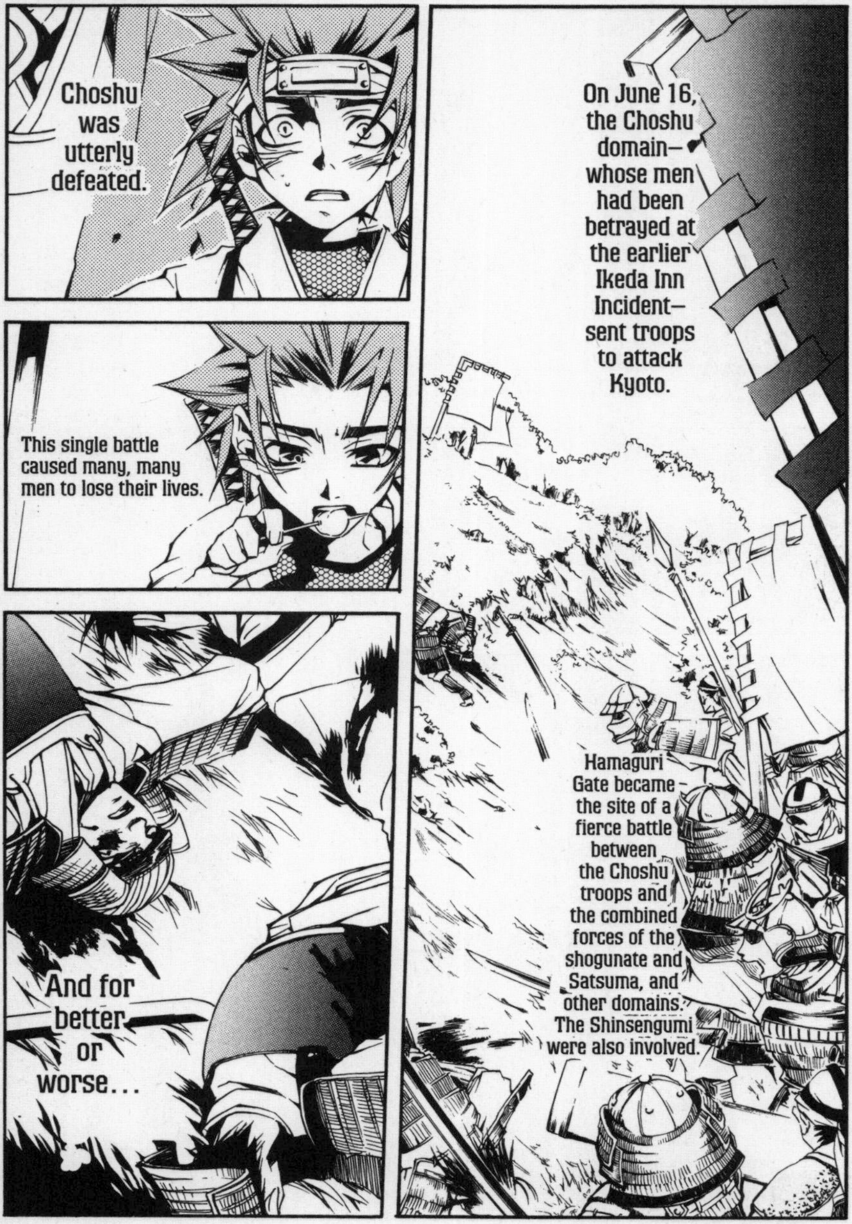
On June 16, the Choshu domain—whose men had been betrayed at the earlier Ikeda Inn Incident—sent troops to attack Kyoto.
Hamaguri Gate became the site of a fierce battle between the Choshu troops and the combined forces of the shogunate and Satsuma, and other domains. The Shinsengumi were also involved.
Choshu was utterly defeated.
This single battle caused many, many men to lose their lives.
And for better or worse...

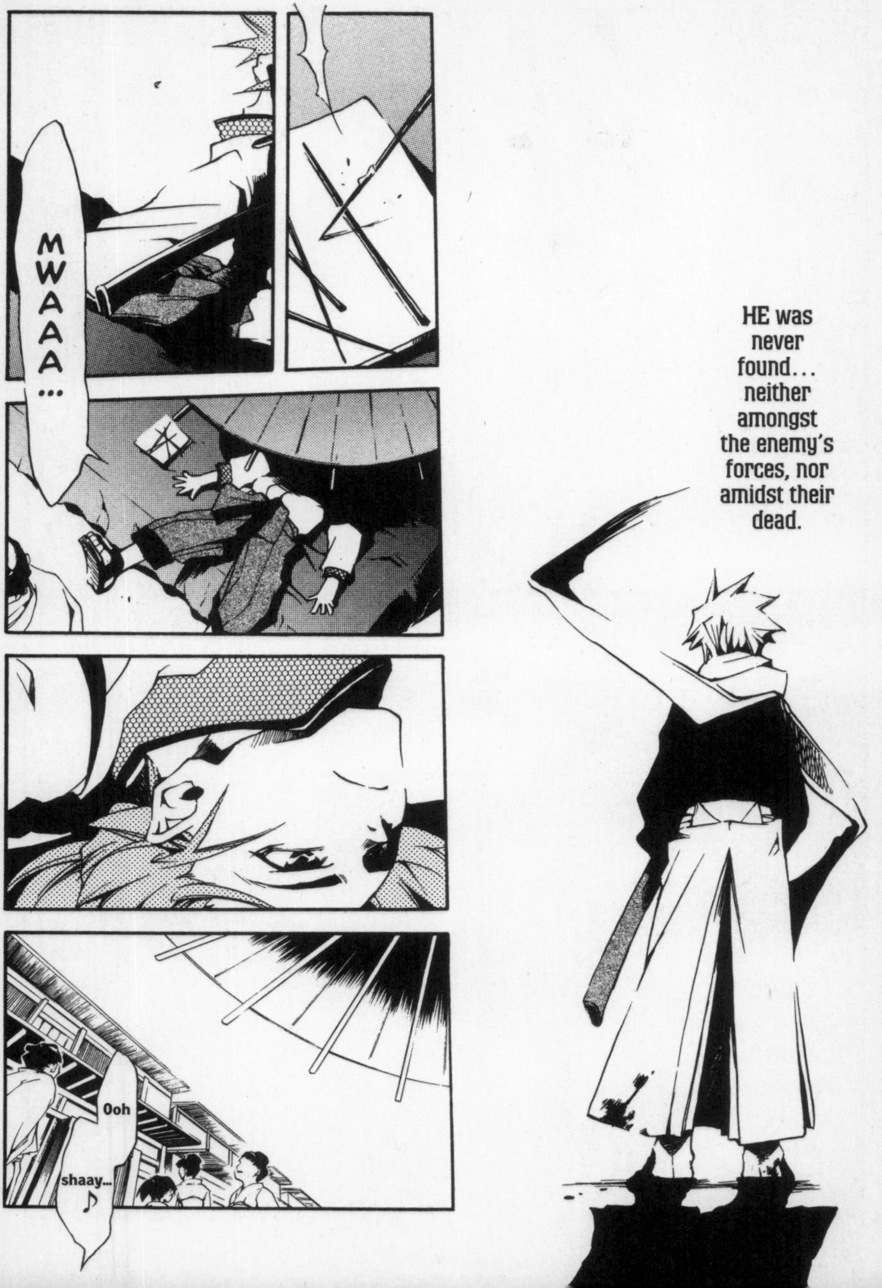
HE was never found... neither amongst the enemy's forces, nor amidst their dead.
MWAAAA...
Ooh shaay...♪

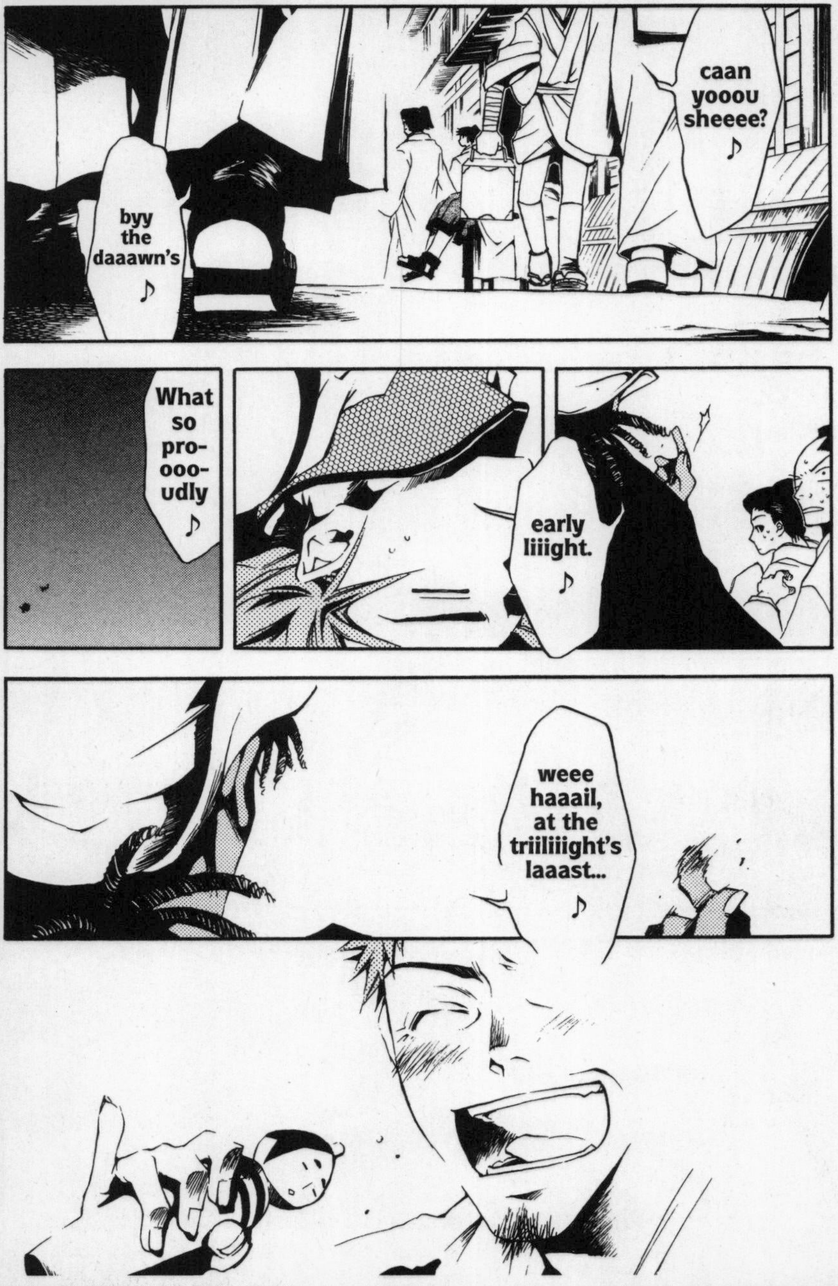
caan yoooou sheeee? ♪
byy the daaawn's ♪
early liiight. ♪
What so pro-ooo-udly ♪
weee haaail, at the triiliiight's laaast... ♪

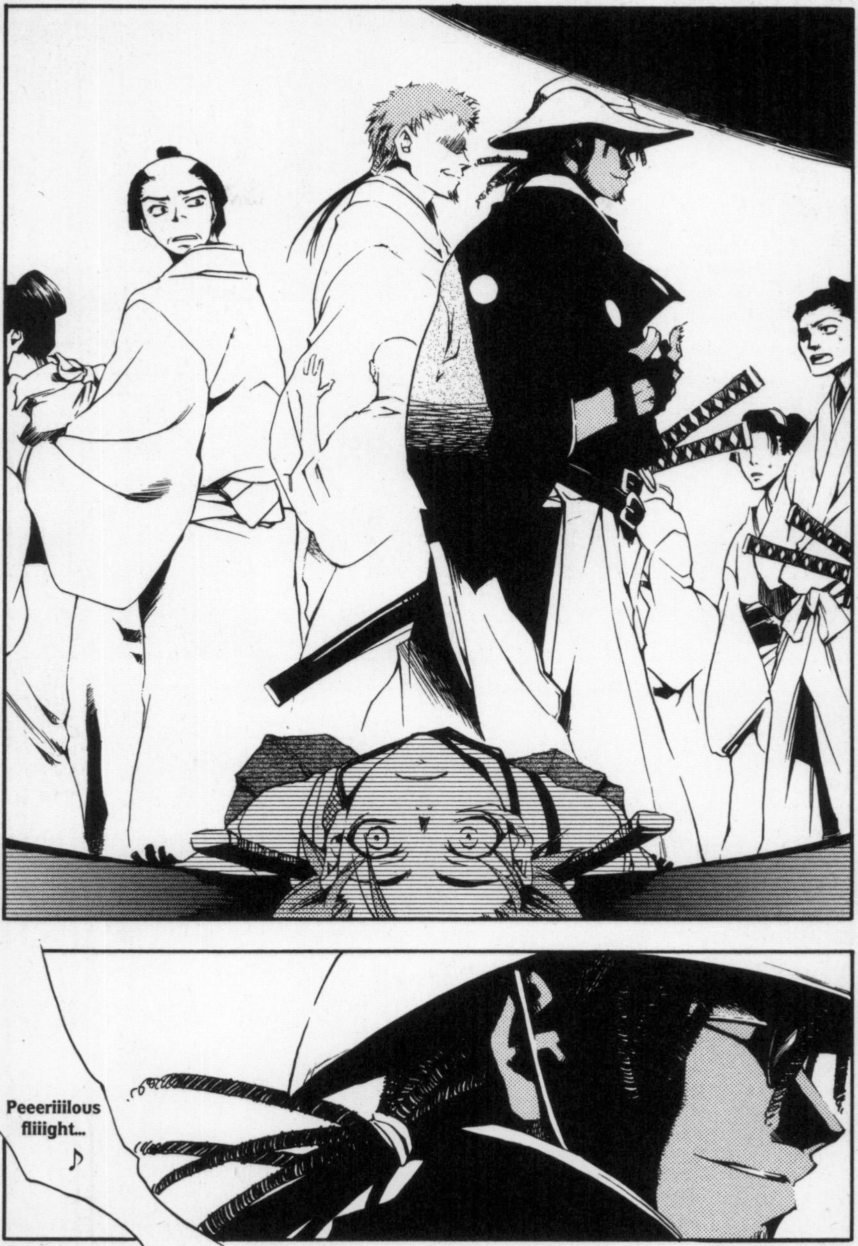
Peeeriiilous fliiight... ♪

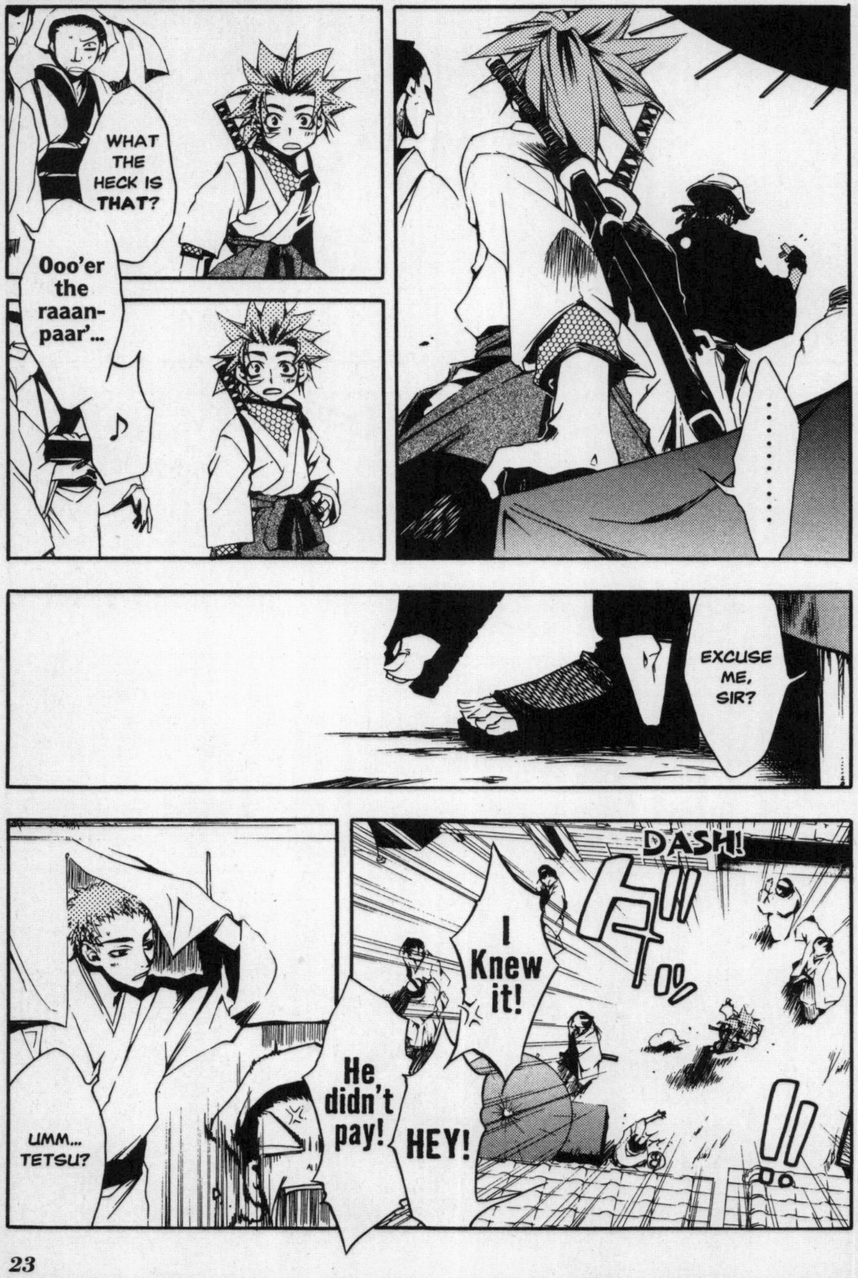
......
WHAT THE HECK IS THAT?
Ooo'er the raaan-paar'... ♪
EXCUSE ME, SIR?
DASH!
I Knew it!
HEY!
He didn't pay!
UMM... TETSU?

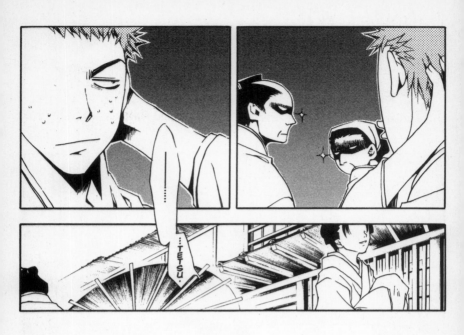

:TETSU.

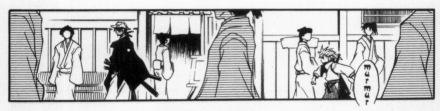

murmur

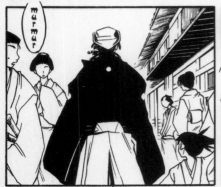

murmur

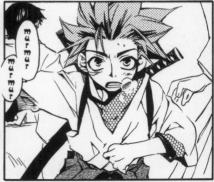

murmur
murmur
murmur

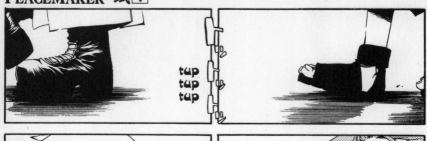

tup
tup
tup

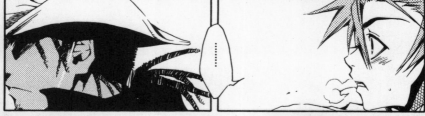

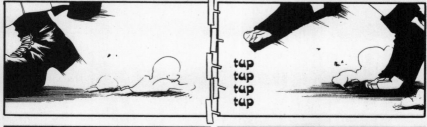

tup
tup
tup
tup

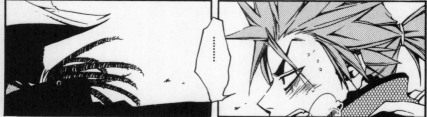

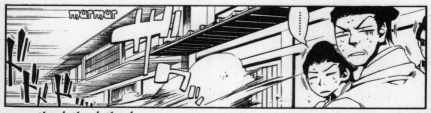

thud thud thud

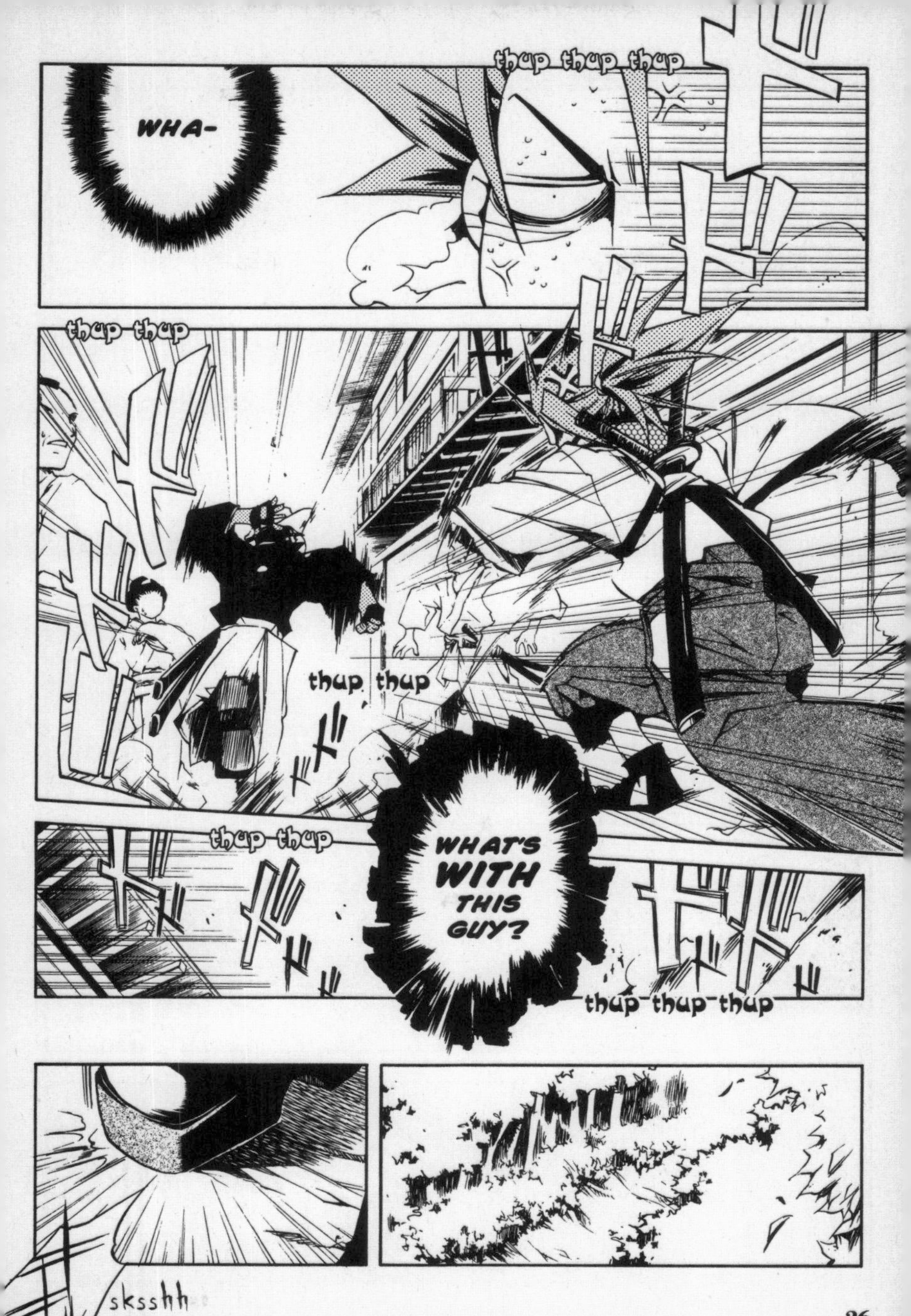
thup thup thup
WHA-
thup thup
thup thup
thup thup
WHAT'S WITH THIS GUY?
thup thup thup
sksshh

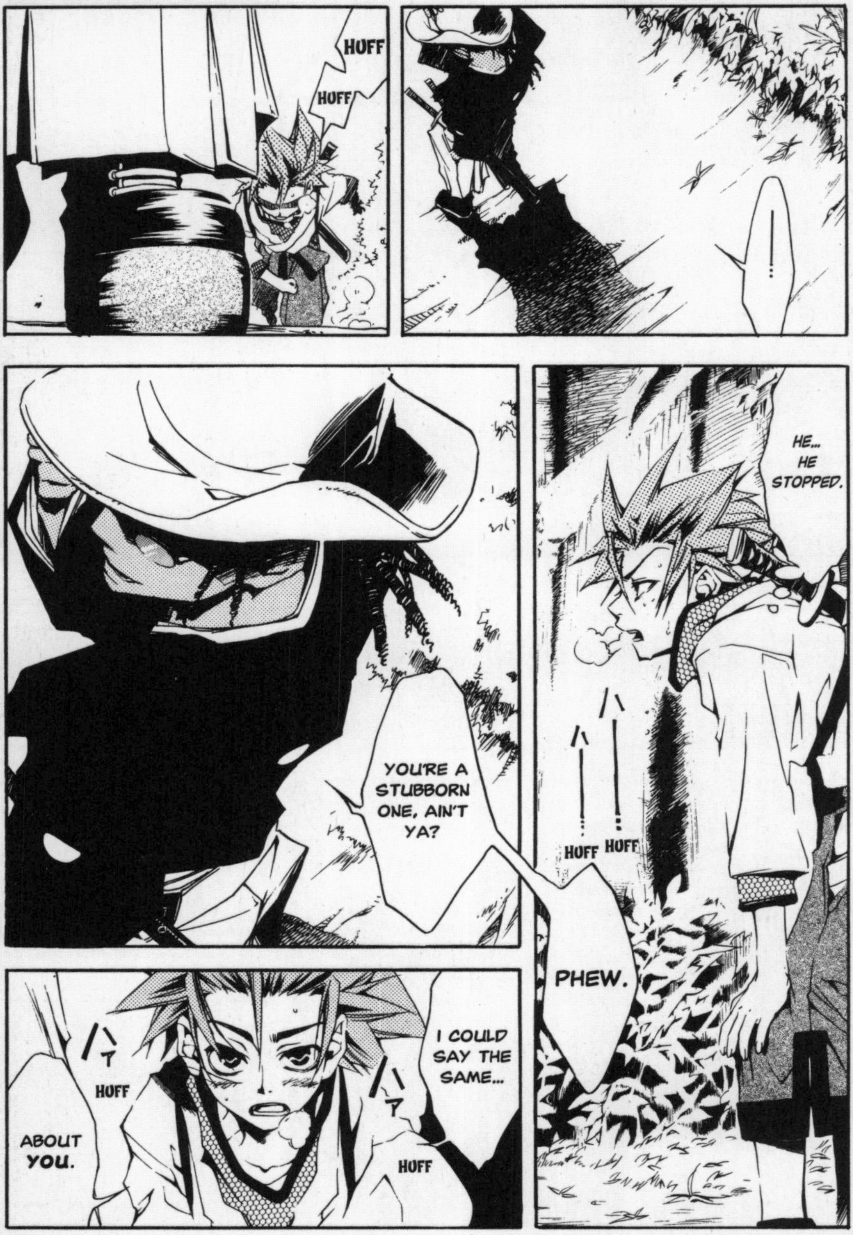
!...
HUFF
HUFF
HE... HE STOPPED.
ハー
ハー
HUFF
HUFF
PHEW.
YOU'RE A STUBBORN ONE, AIN'T YA?
I COULD SAY THE SAME...
ハァ
HUFF
ハァ
HUFF
ABOUT YOU.

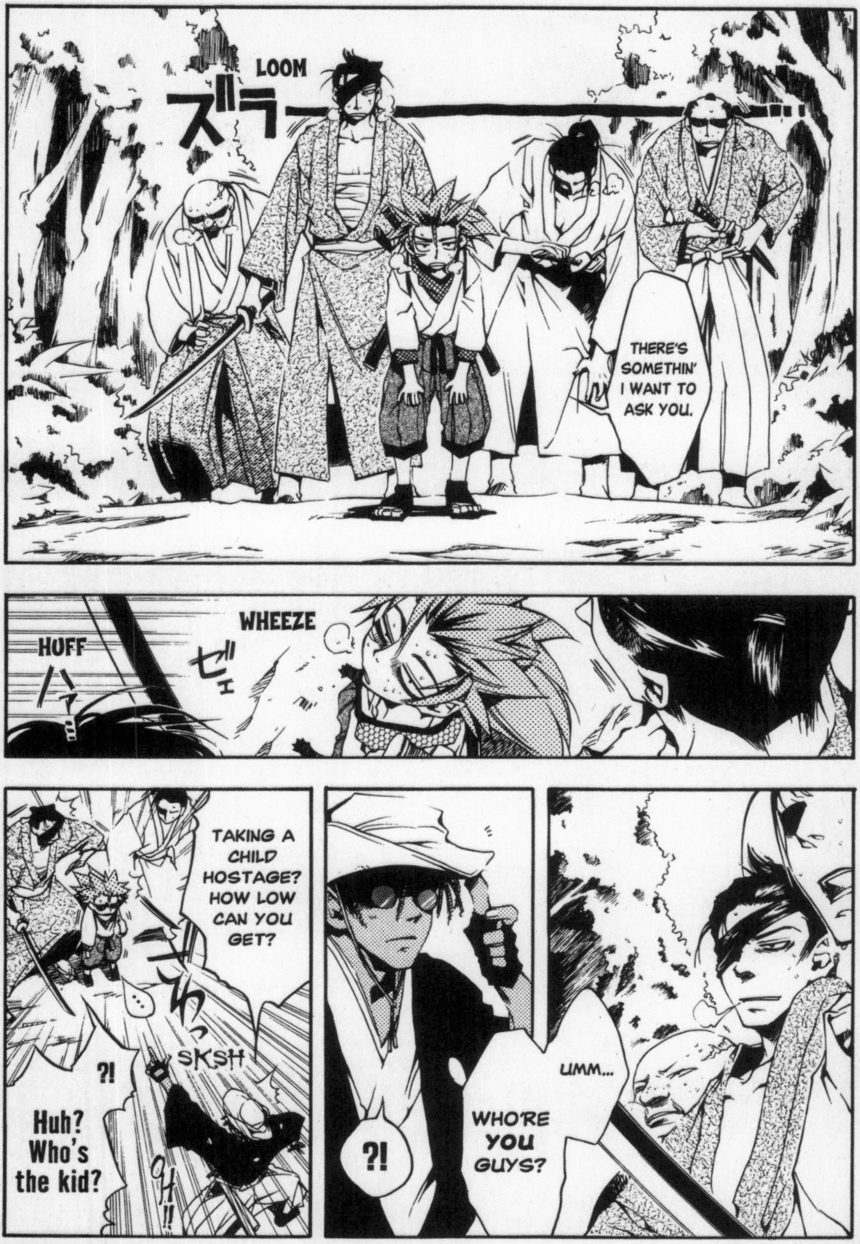
LOOM
ズラー
THERE'S SOMETHIN' I WANT TO ASK YOU.
WHEEZE
ゼェ
HUFF
ハァ
UMM...
WHO'RE YOU GUYS?
?!
TAKING A CHILD HOSTAGE? HOW LOW CAN YOU GET?
SKSH
?!
Huh? Who's the kid?
OH!!

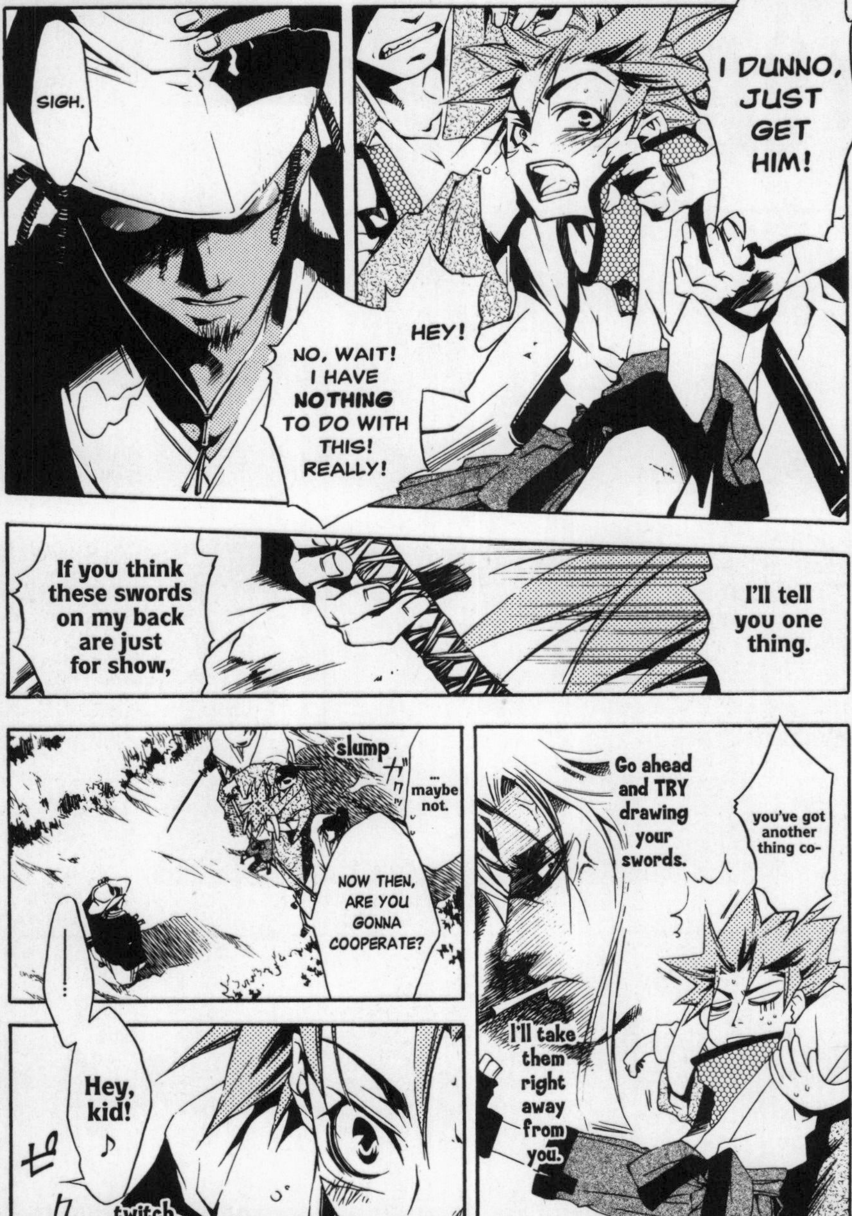
I DUNNO, JUST GET HIM!
HEY!
NO, WAIT! I HAVE **NOTHING** TO DO WITH THIS! REALLY!
SIGH.
I'll tell you one thing.
If you think these swords on my back are just for show,
you've got another thing co-
Go ahead and TRY drawing your swords.
I'll take them right away from you.
slump
ガクッ
... maybe not.
NOW THEN, ARE YOU GONNA COOPERATE?
......
Hey, kid! ♪
ピク,
twitch

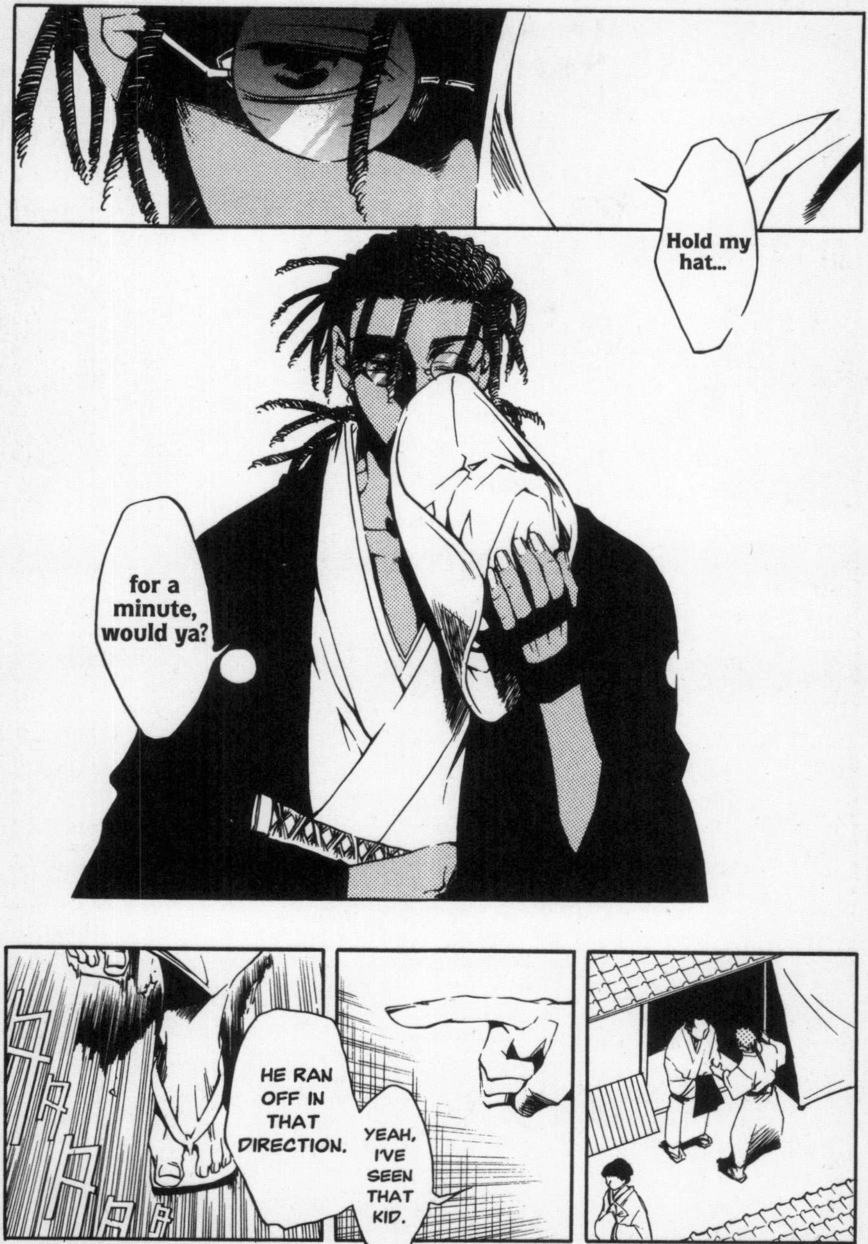
Hold my hat...
for a minute, would ya?
YEAH, I'VE SEEN THAT KID.
HE RAN OFF IN THAT DIRECTION.
tup tup tup tup tup

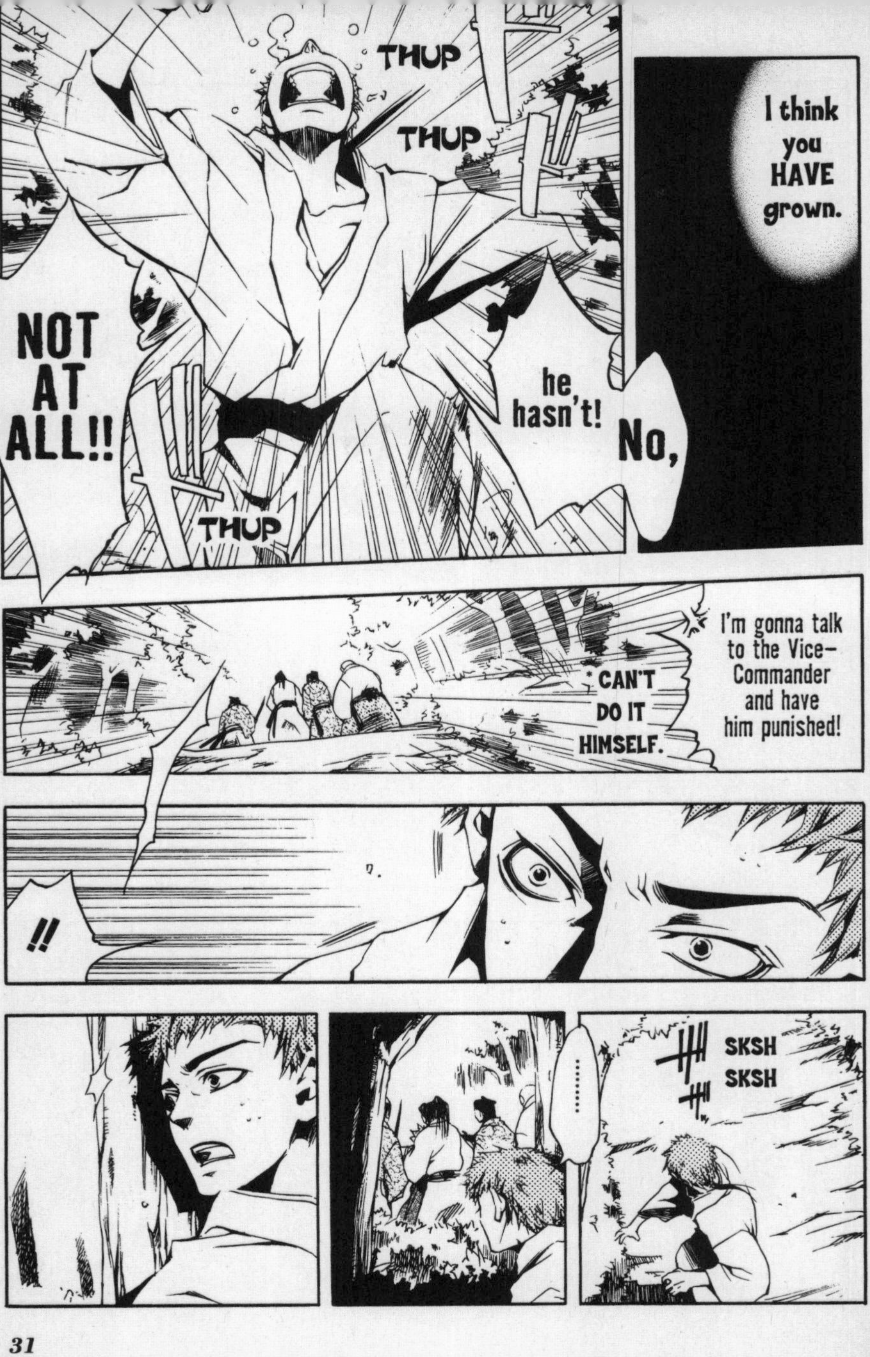
I think you HAVE grown.
No, he hasn't!
NOT AT ALL!!
THUP
THUP
THUP
I'm gonna talk to the Vice-Commander and have him punished!
*CAN'T DO IT HIMSELF.
!!
SKSH SKSH
......

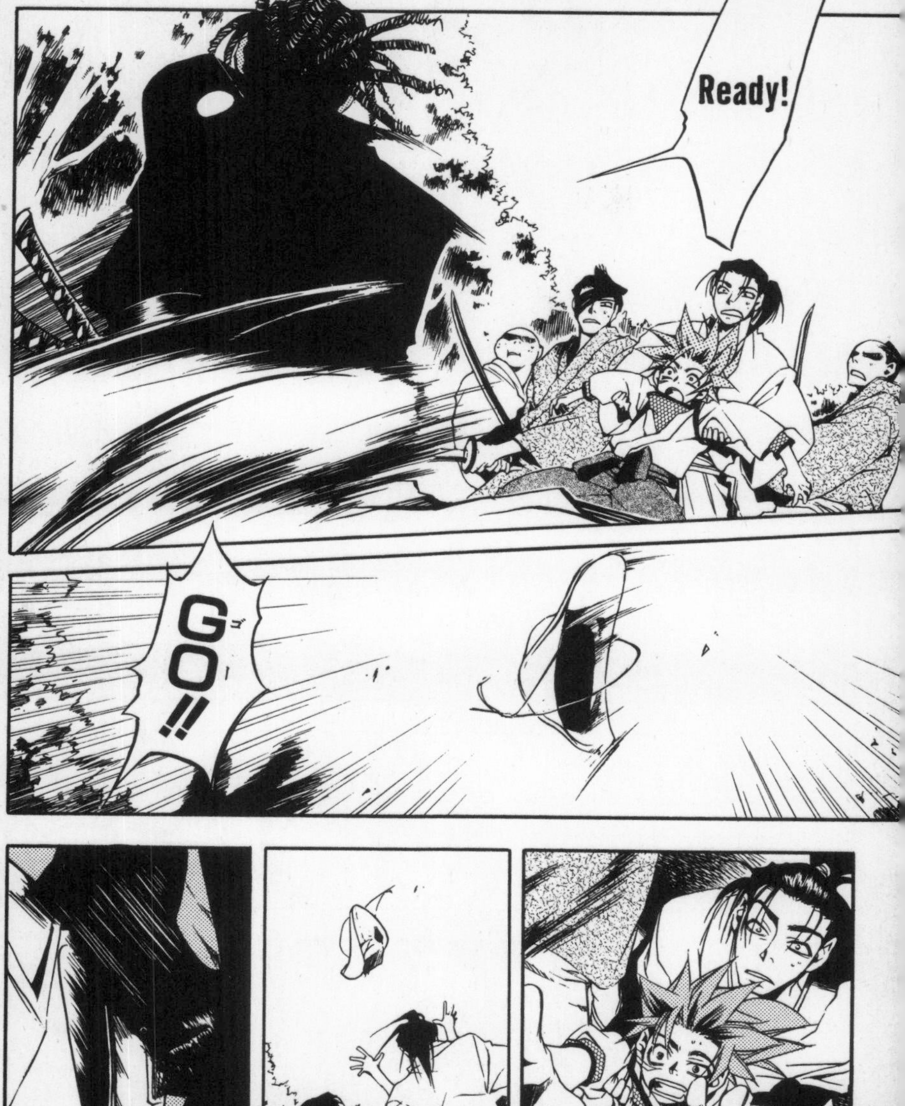
Ready!
GO!!
ゴー

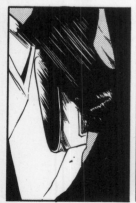

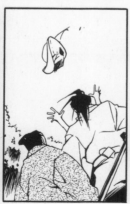

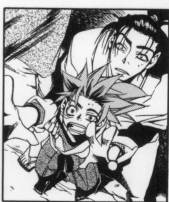

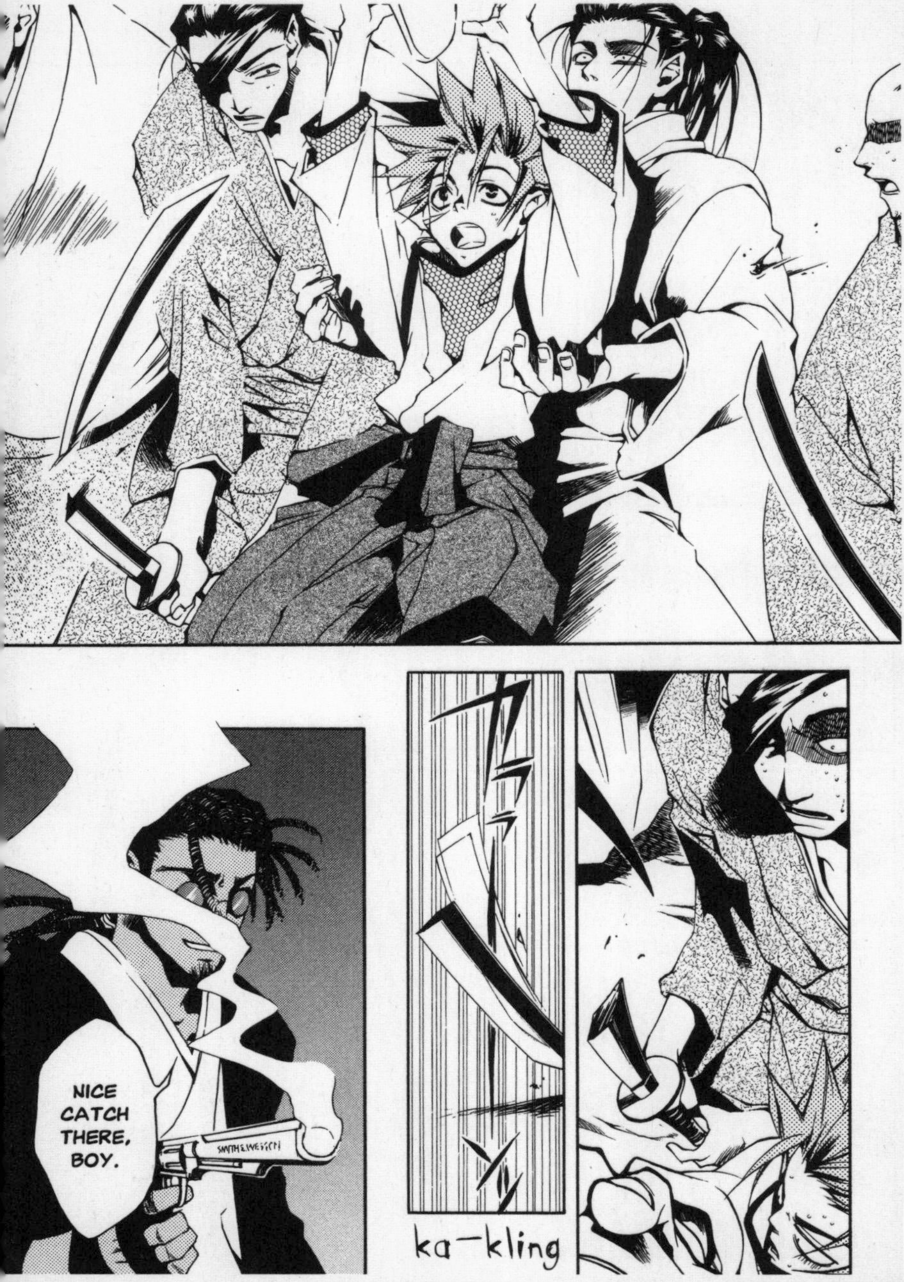
ka-kling
NICE CATCH THERE, BOY.

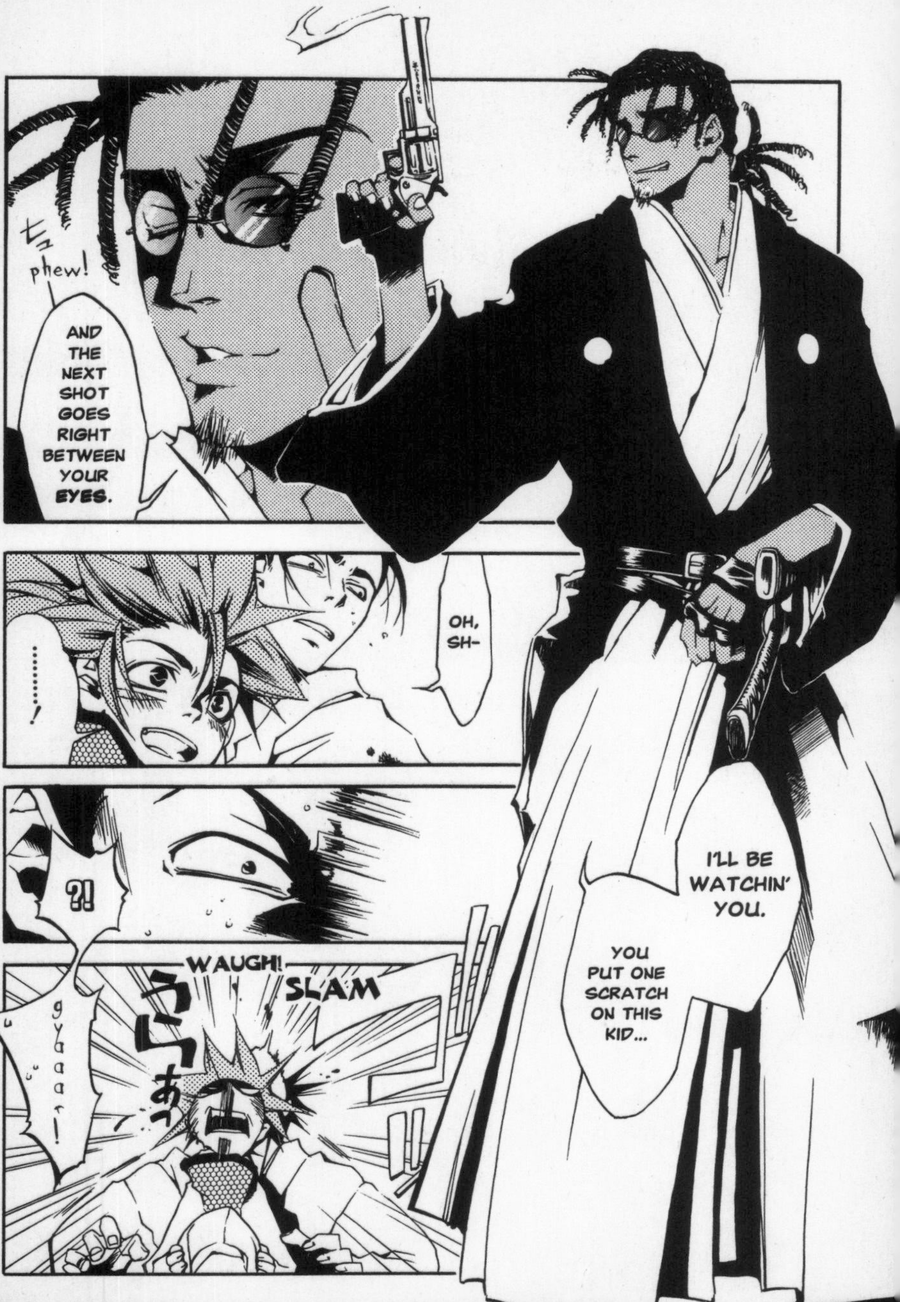
I'LL BE WATCHIN' YOU.
YOU PUT ONE SCRATCH ON THIS KID...
ヒュ
phew!
AND THE NEXT SHOT GOES RIGHT BETWEEN YOUR EYES.
OH, SH-
......!
?!
WAUGH!
SLAM
うらあっ
gyaaar!

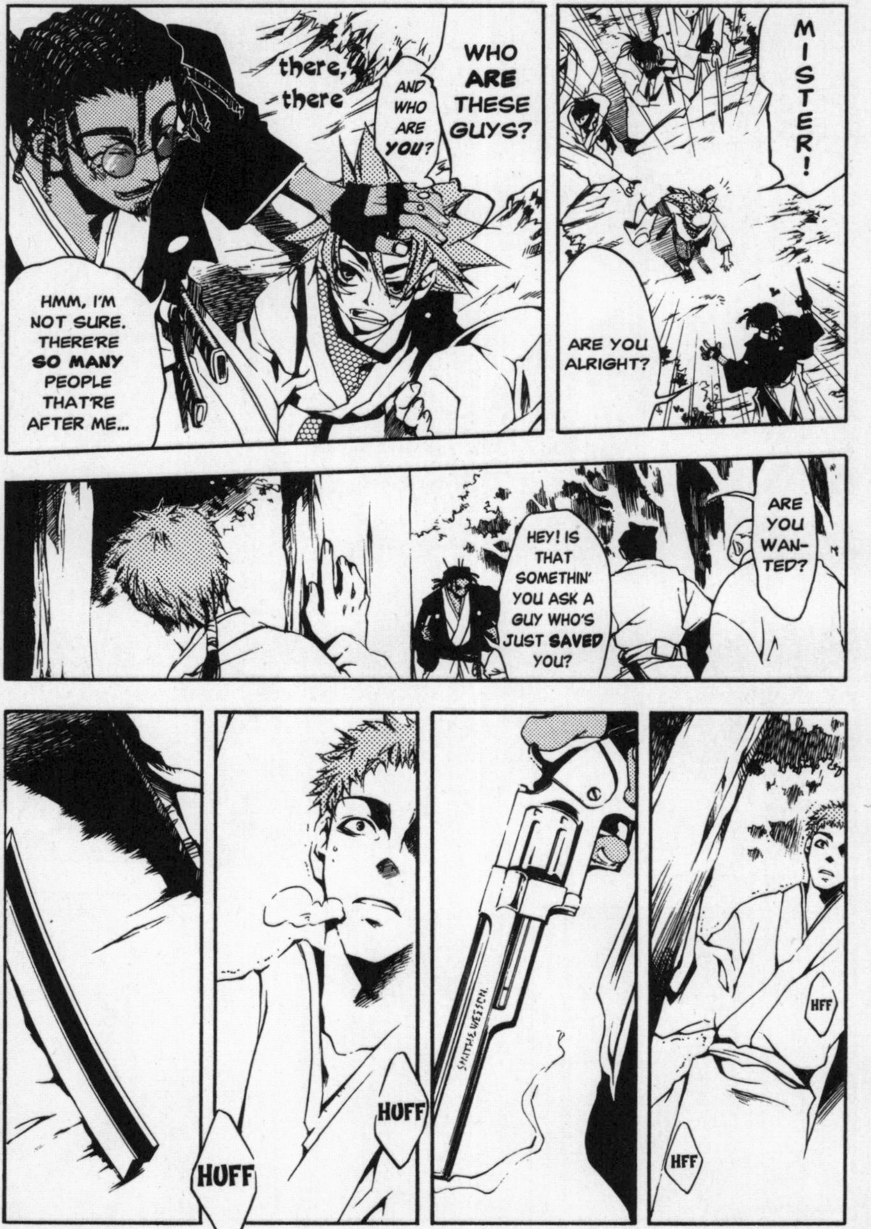
MISTER!
ARE YOU ALRIGHT?
WHO ARE THESE GUYS?
AND WHO ARE YOU?
there, there
HMM, I'M NOT SURE. THERE'RE SO MANY PEOPLE THAT'RE AFTER ME...
ARE YOU WANTED?
HEY! IS THAT SOMETHIN' YOU ASK A GUY WHO'S JUST SAVED YOU?
HFF
HFF
HUFF
HUFF

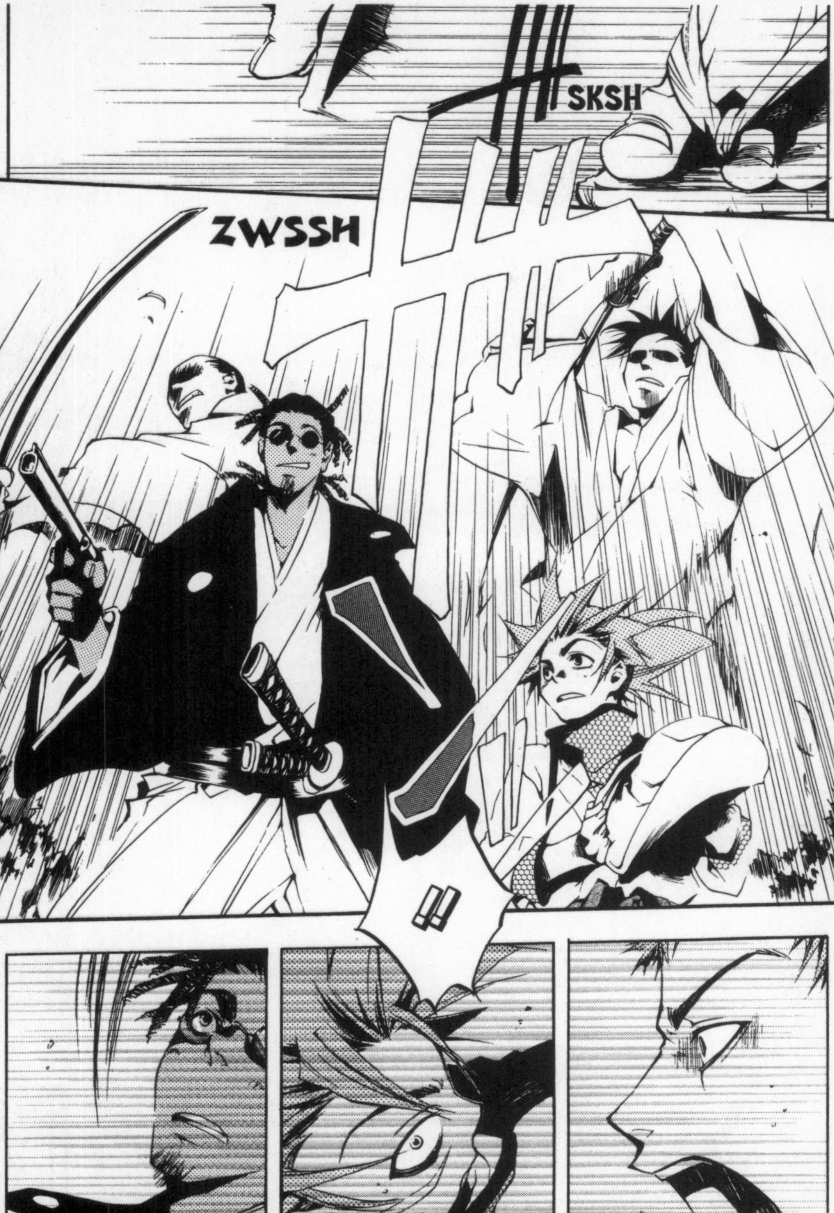
SKSH
ZWSSH
!!

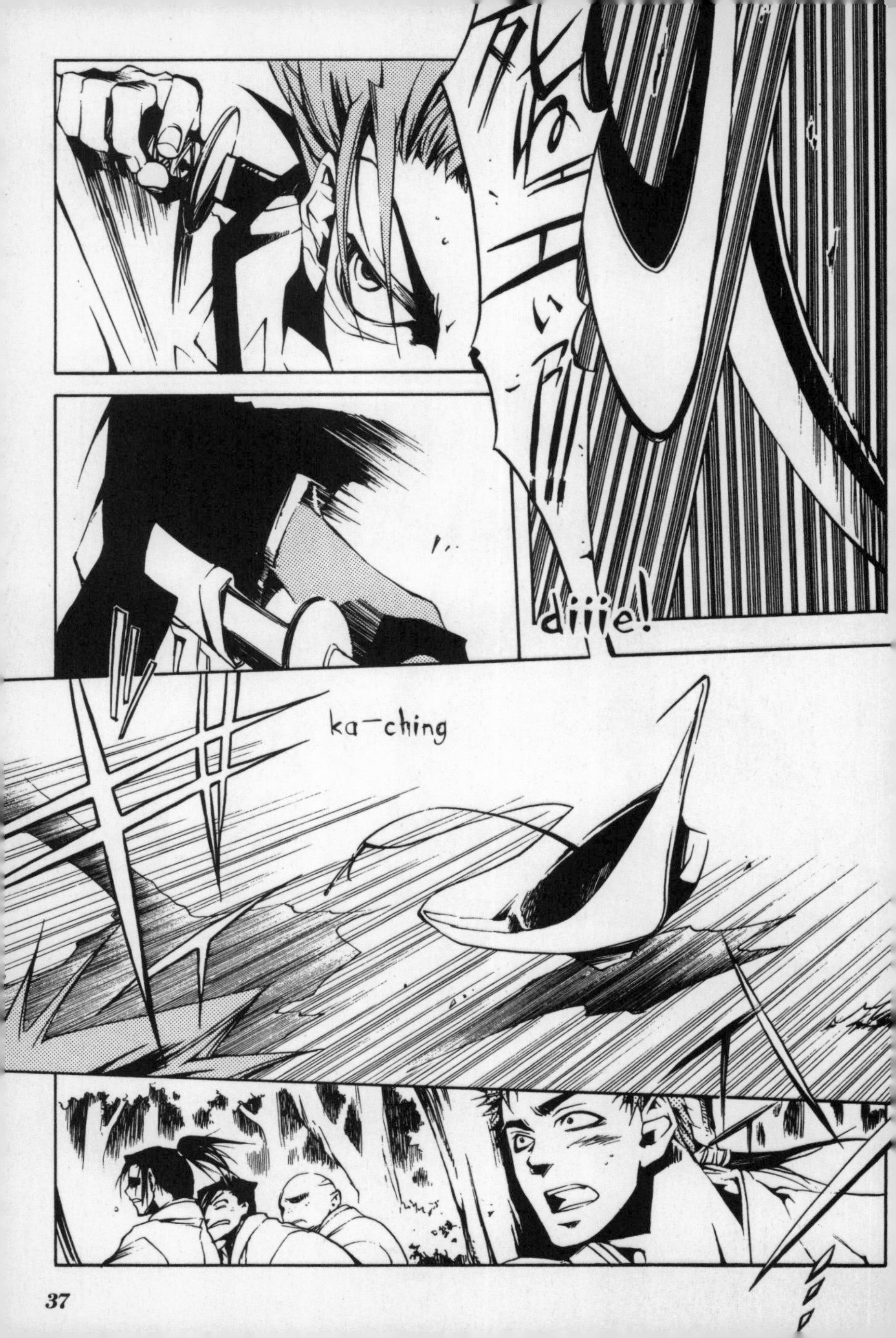
diiie!
ka-ching

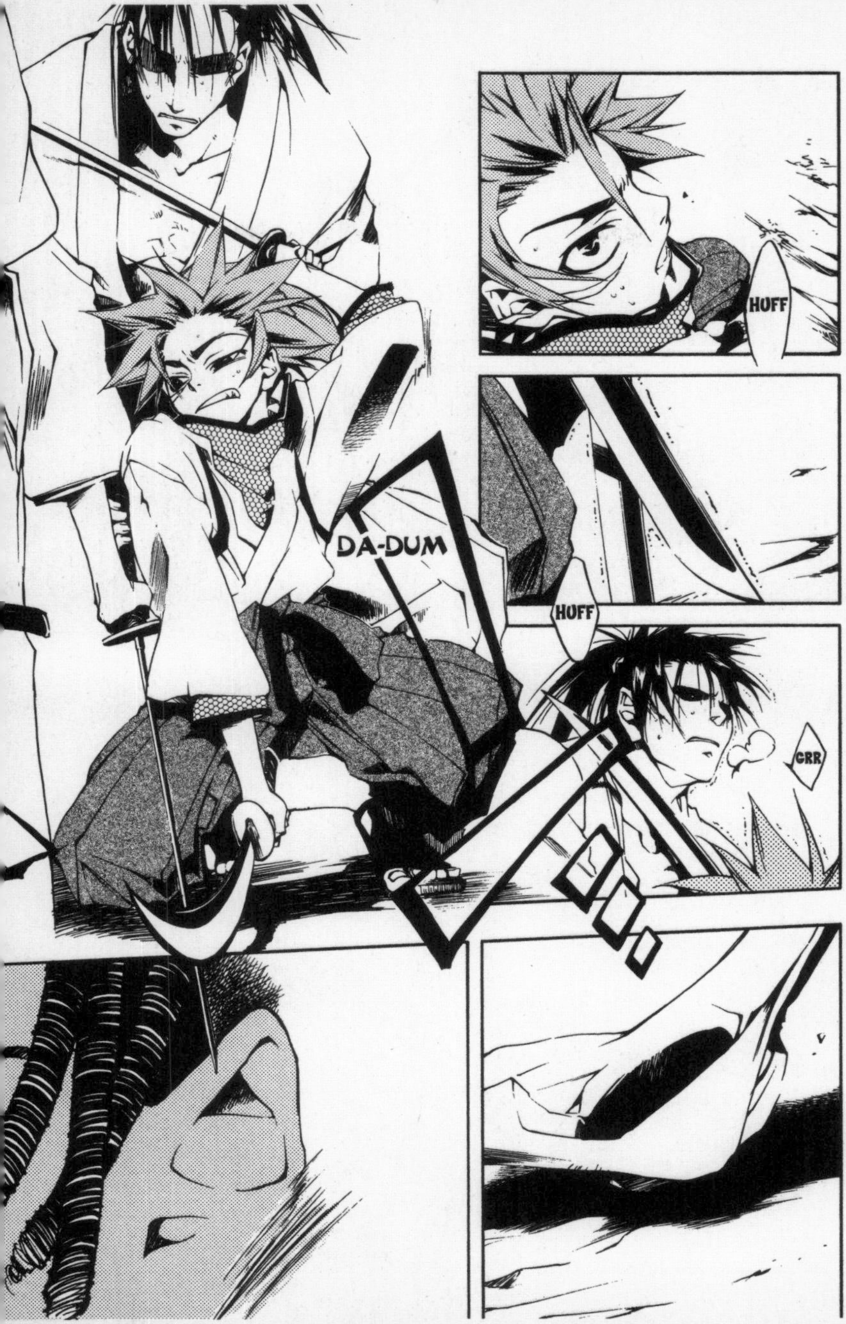
HOFF
HOFF
GRR
DA-DUM

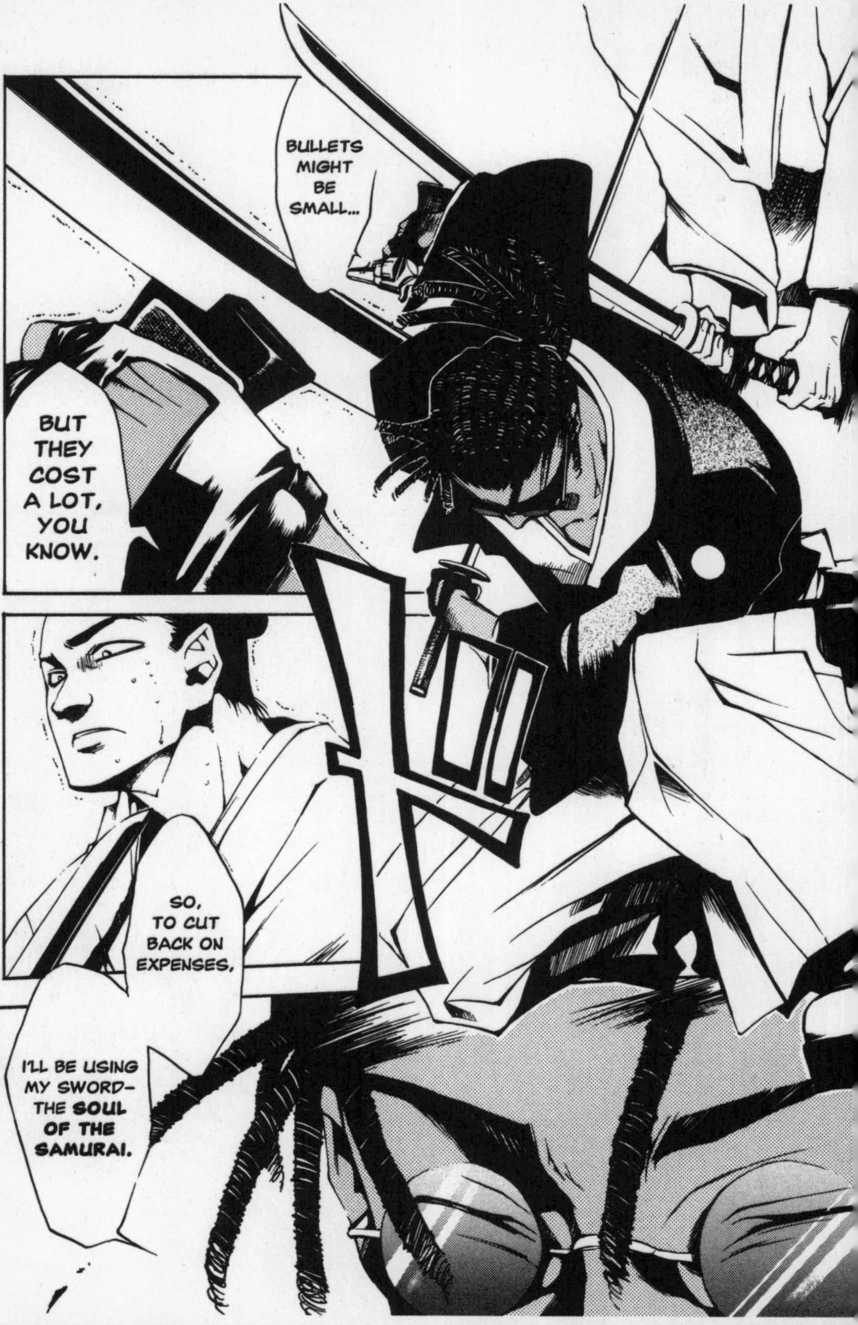
BULLETS MIGHT BE SMALL...
BUT THEY COST A LOT, YOU KNOW.
SO, TO CUT BACK ON EXPENSES,
I'LL BE USING MY SWORD— THE SOUL OF THE SAMURAI.

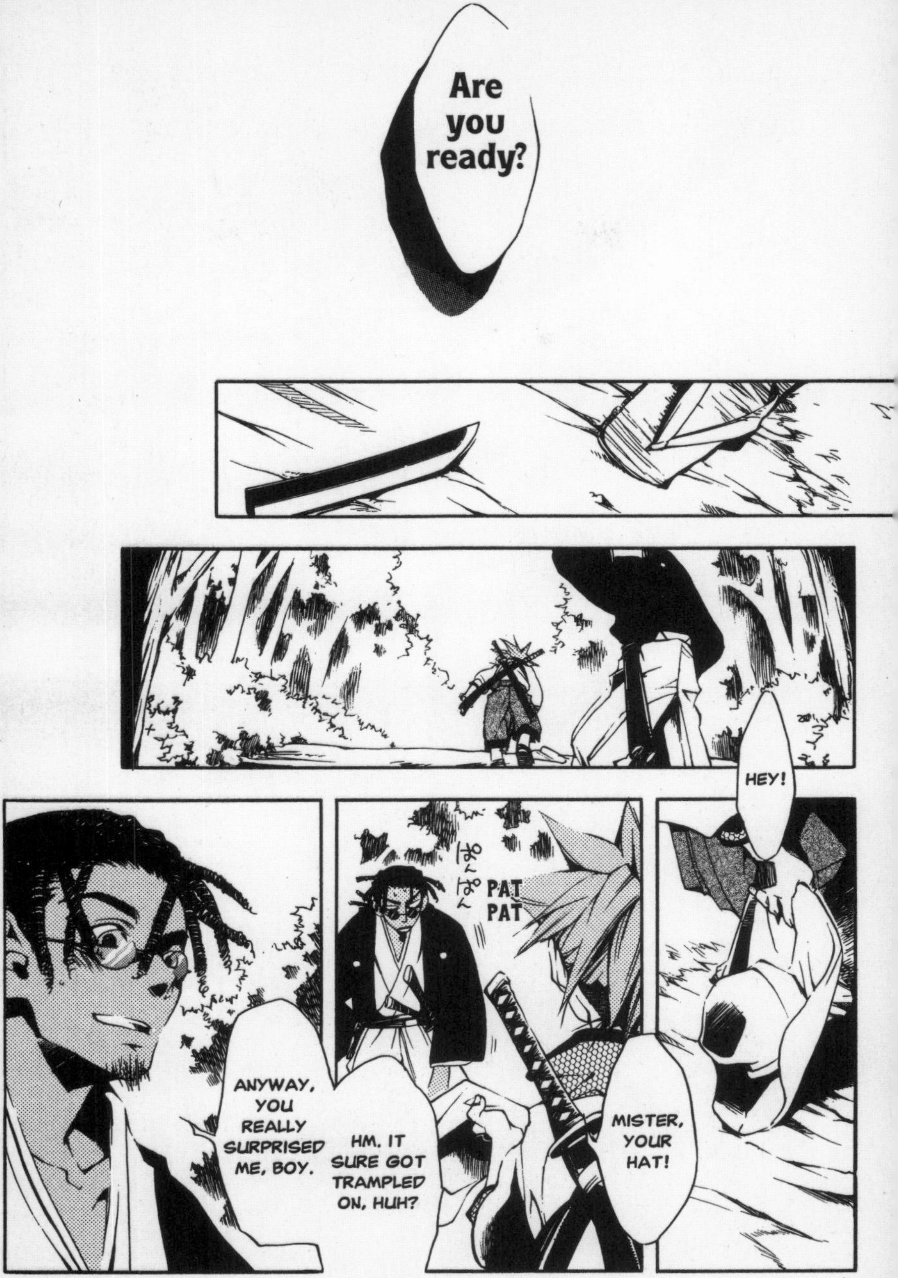
Are you ready?
HEY!
MISTER, YOUR HAT!
ぱんぱん
PAT PAT
HM. IT SURE GOT TRAMPLED ON, HUH?
ANYWAY, YOU REALLY SURPRISED ME, BOY.

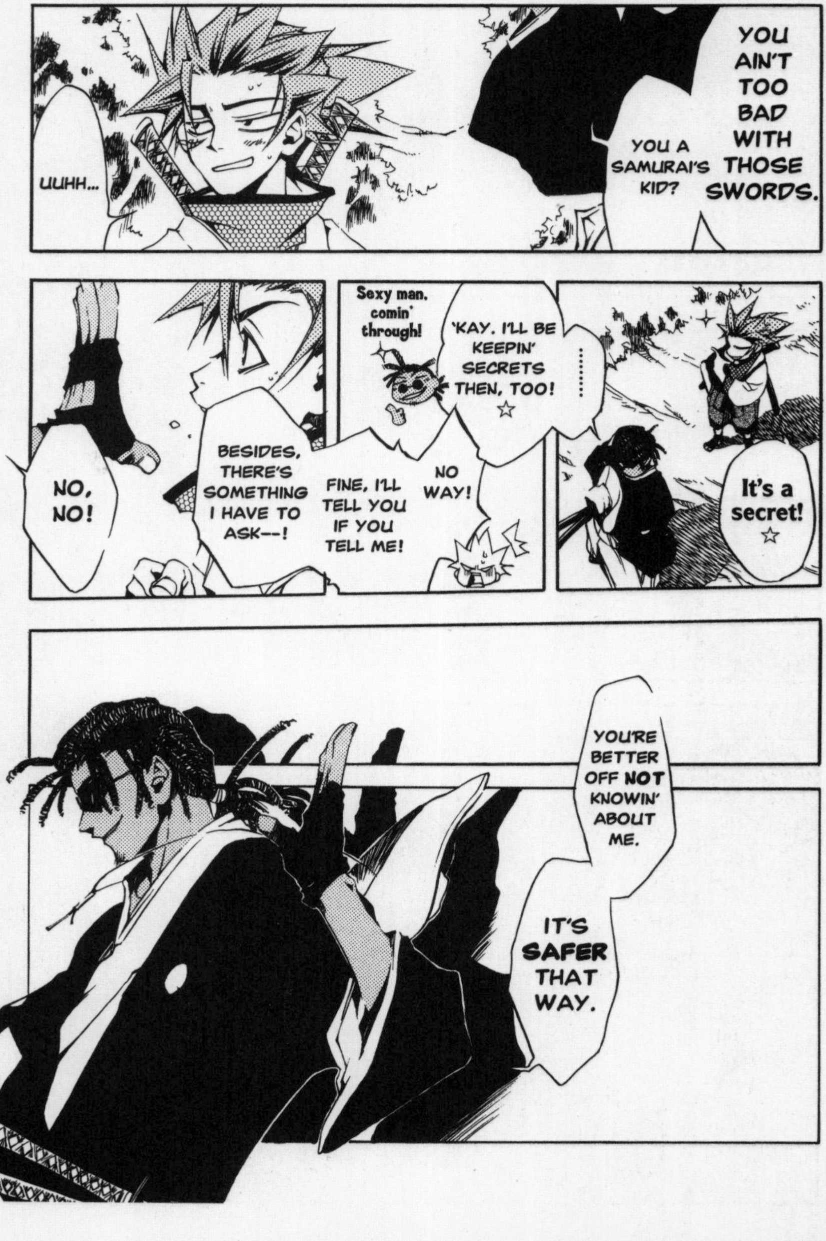
YOU AIN'T TOO BAD WITH THOSE SWORDS.
YOU A SAMURAI'S KID?
UUHH...
It's a secret! ☆
......
'KAY. I'LL BE KEEPIN' SECRETS THEN, TOO! ☆
Sexy man, comin' through!
NO WAY!
FINE, I'LL TELL YOU IF YOU TELL ME!
BESIDES, THERE'S SOMETHING I HAVE TO ASK--!
NO, NO!
YOU'RE BETTER OFF **NOT** KNOWIN' ABOUT ME.
IT'S **SAFER** THAT WAY.

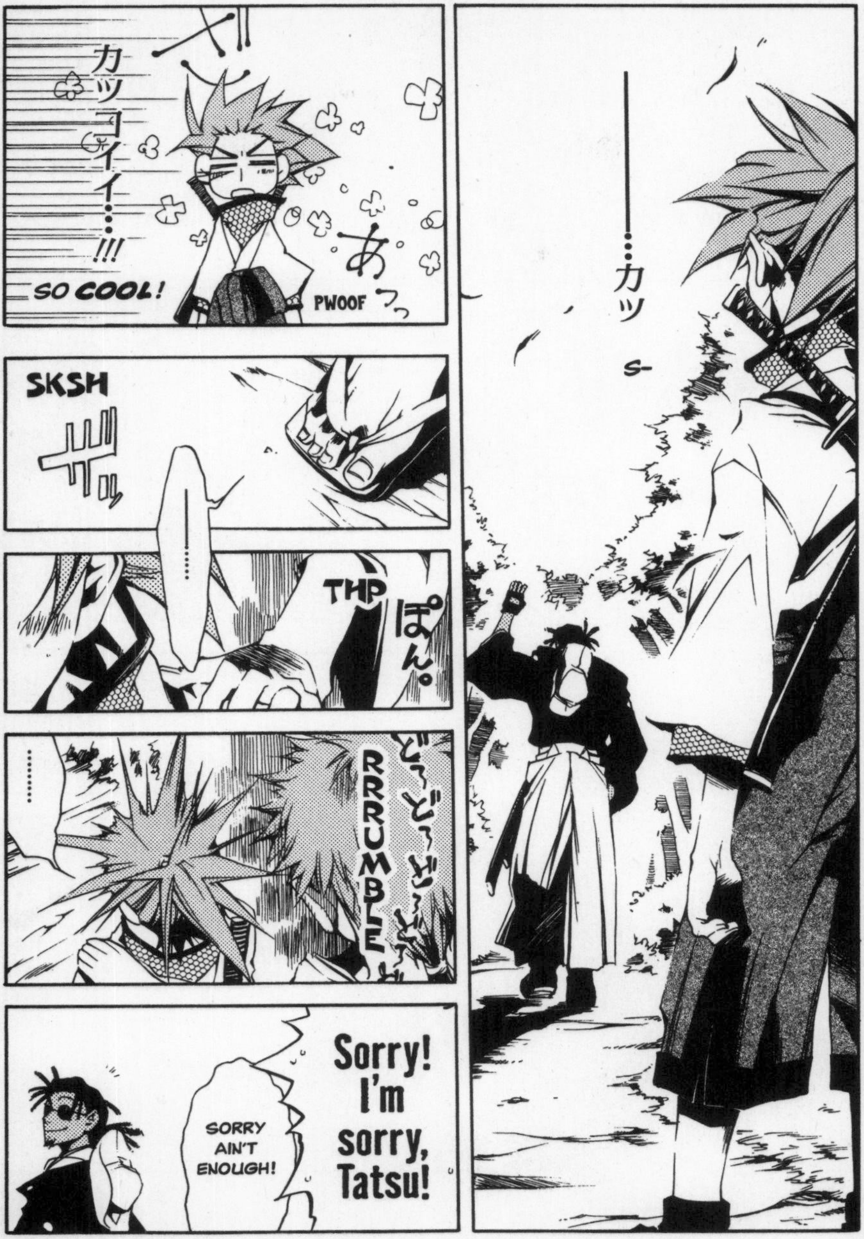
————……カッ
S-
カッコイイー……!!!
SO COOL!
あっ
PWOOF
SKSH
ギュッ
——……
THP
ぽん。
……
どごどごどご
RRRUMBLE
Sorry! I'm sorry, Tatsu!
SORRY AIN'T ENOUGH!

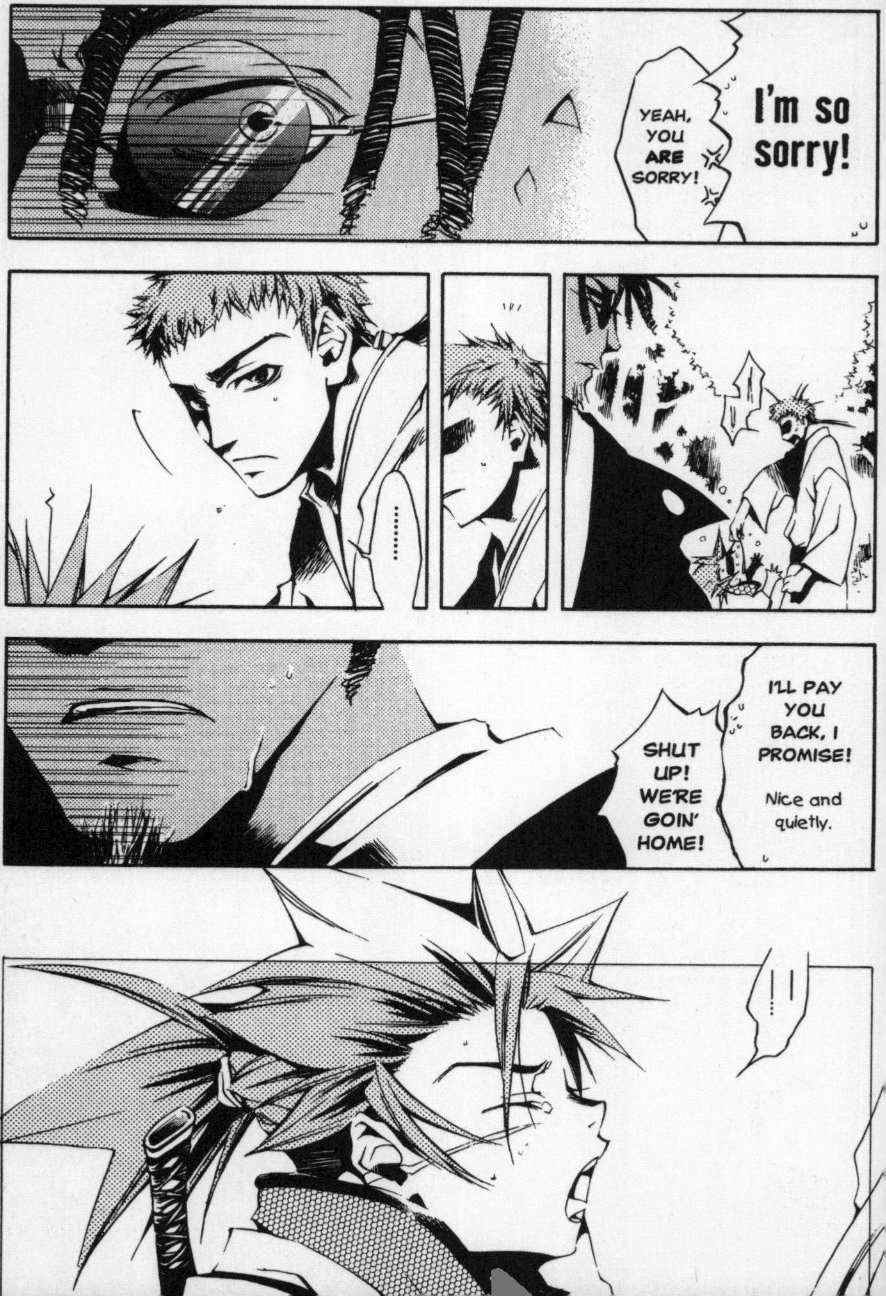
I'm so sorry!
YEAH, YOU ARE SORRY!
I'LL PAY YOU BACK, I PROMISE!
Nice and quietly.
SHUT UP! WE'RE GOIN' HOME!
!!

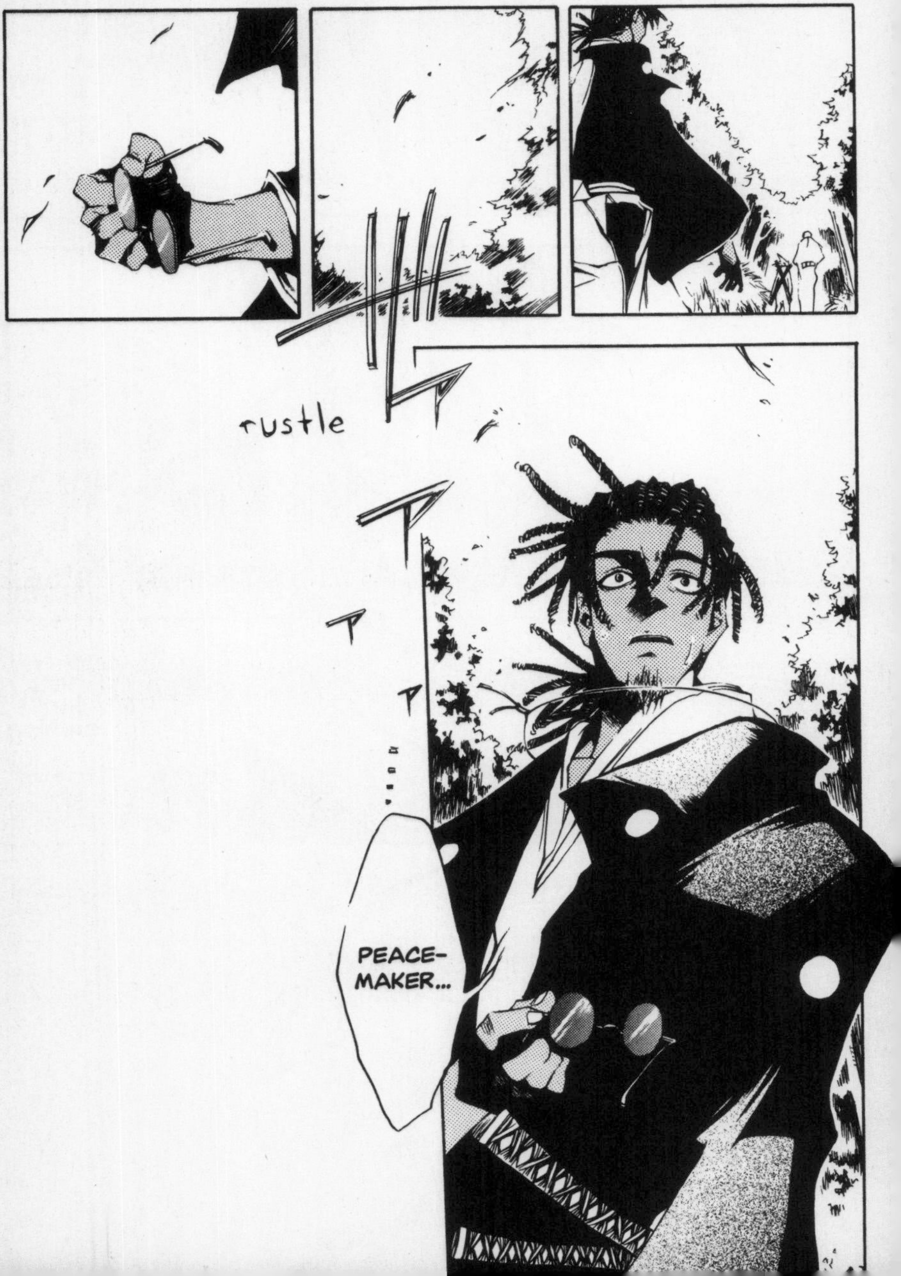
rustle
PEACE-MAKER...

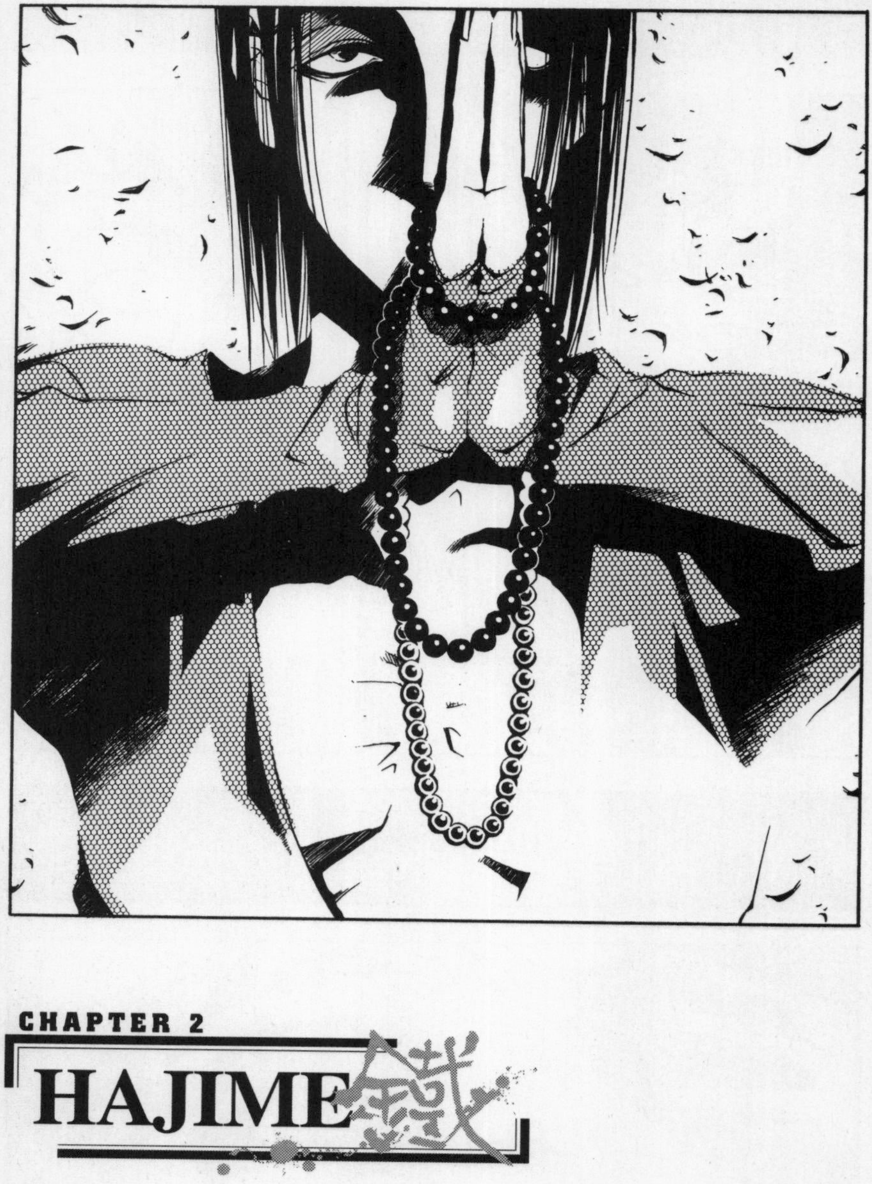

CHAPTER 2

HAJIME 鐵

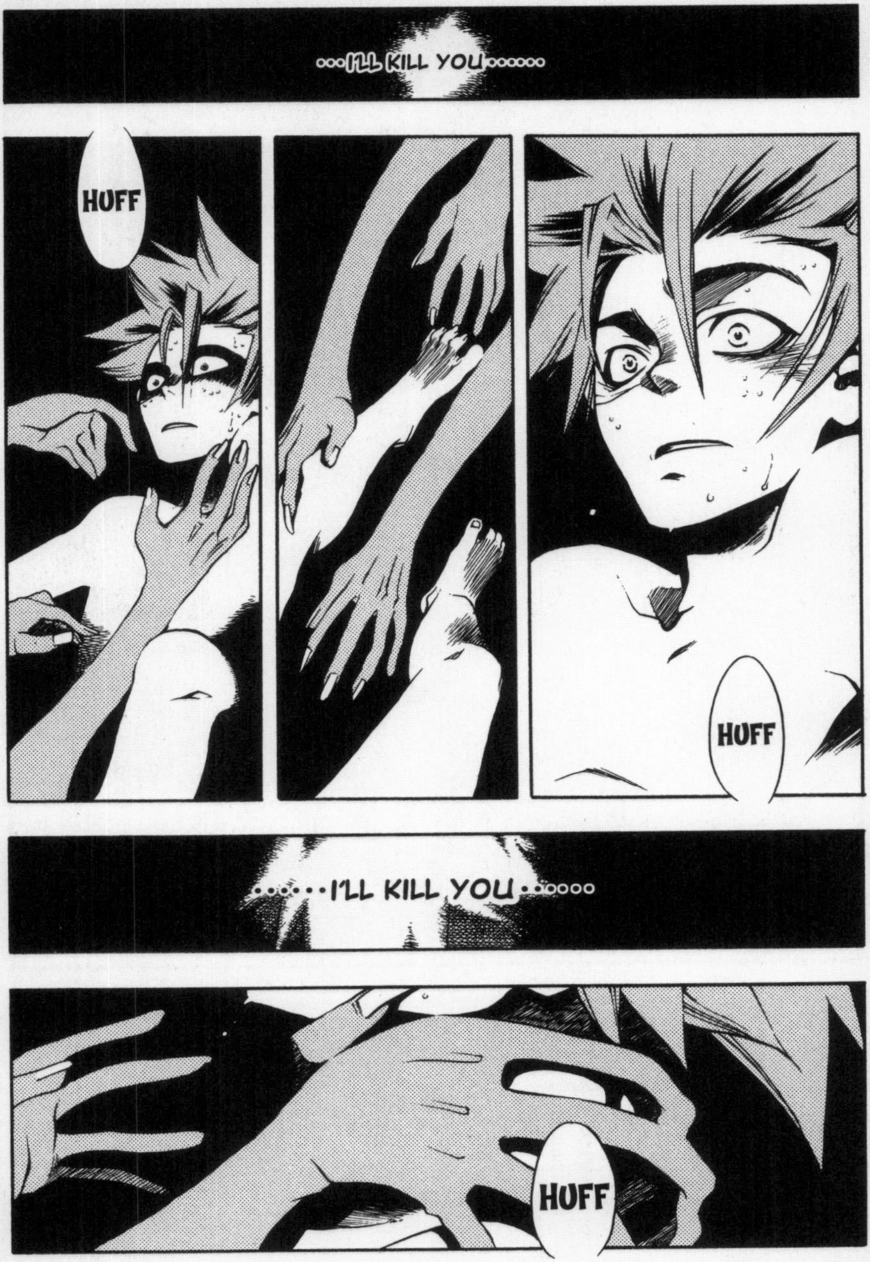
...I'LL KILL YOU......
HUFF
HUFF
.....I'LL KILL YOU......
HUFF

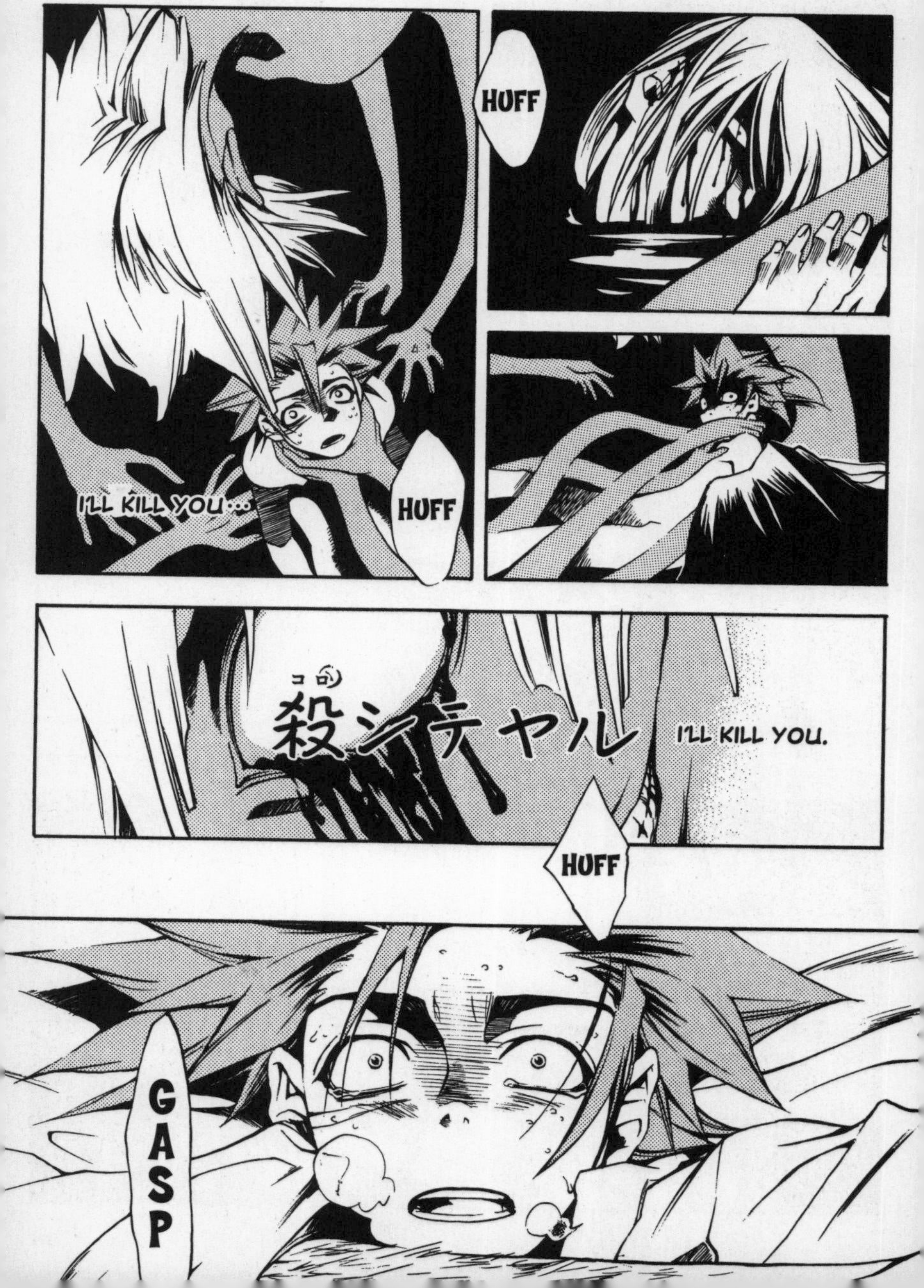
HUFF
HUFF
I'LL KILL YOU...
殺シテヤル
I'LL KILL YOU.
HUFF
GASP

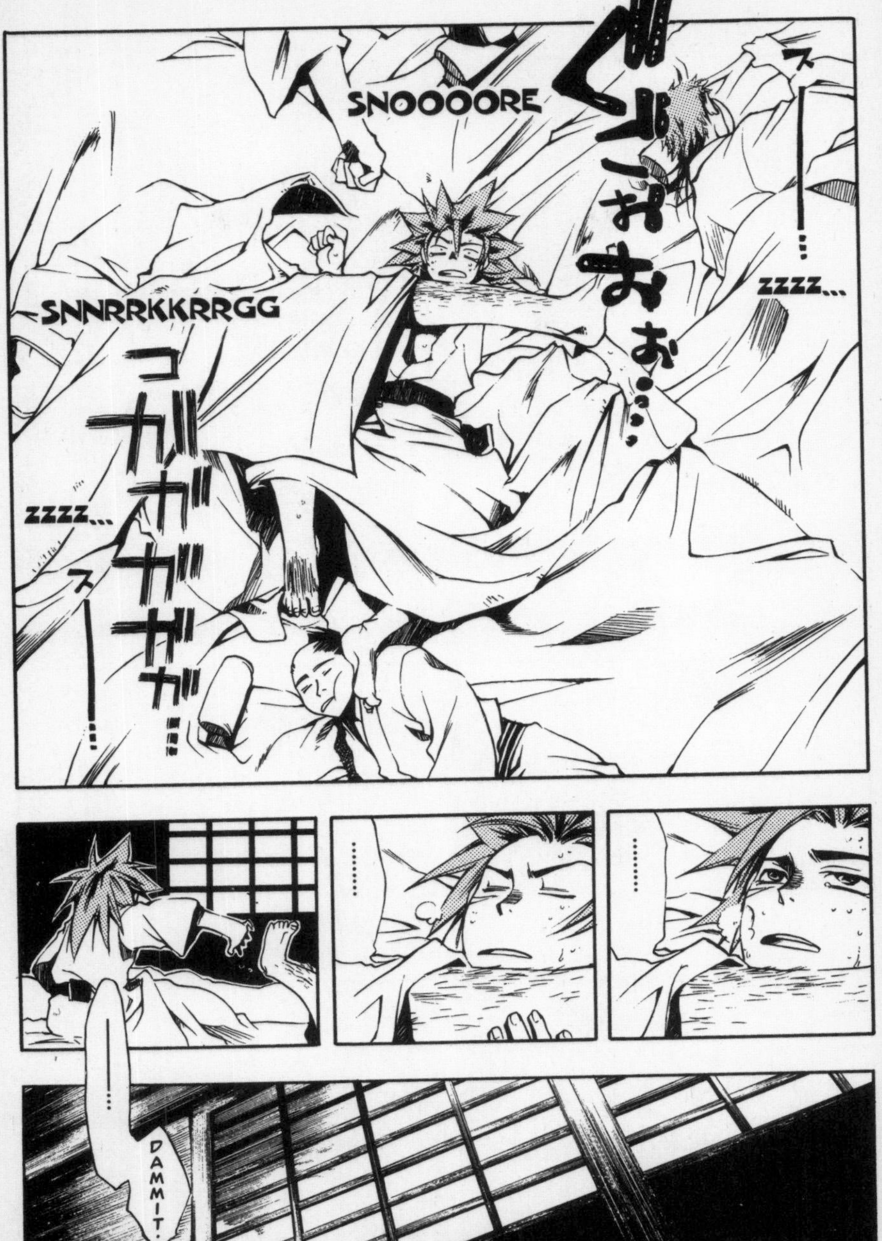

スー…!!
ぐごぉおぉ…
SNOOOORE
ZZZZ...
SNNRRKKRRGG
ゴガガガガ…!!
ZZZZ...
スー…!!
....
....
......
DAMMIT.

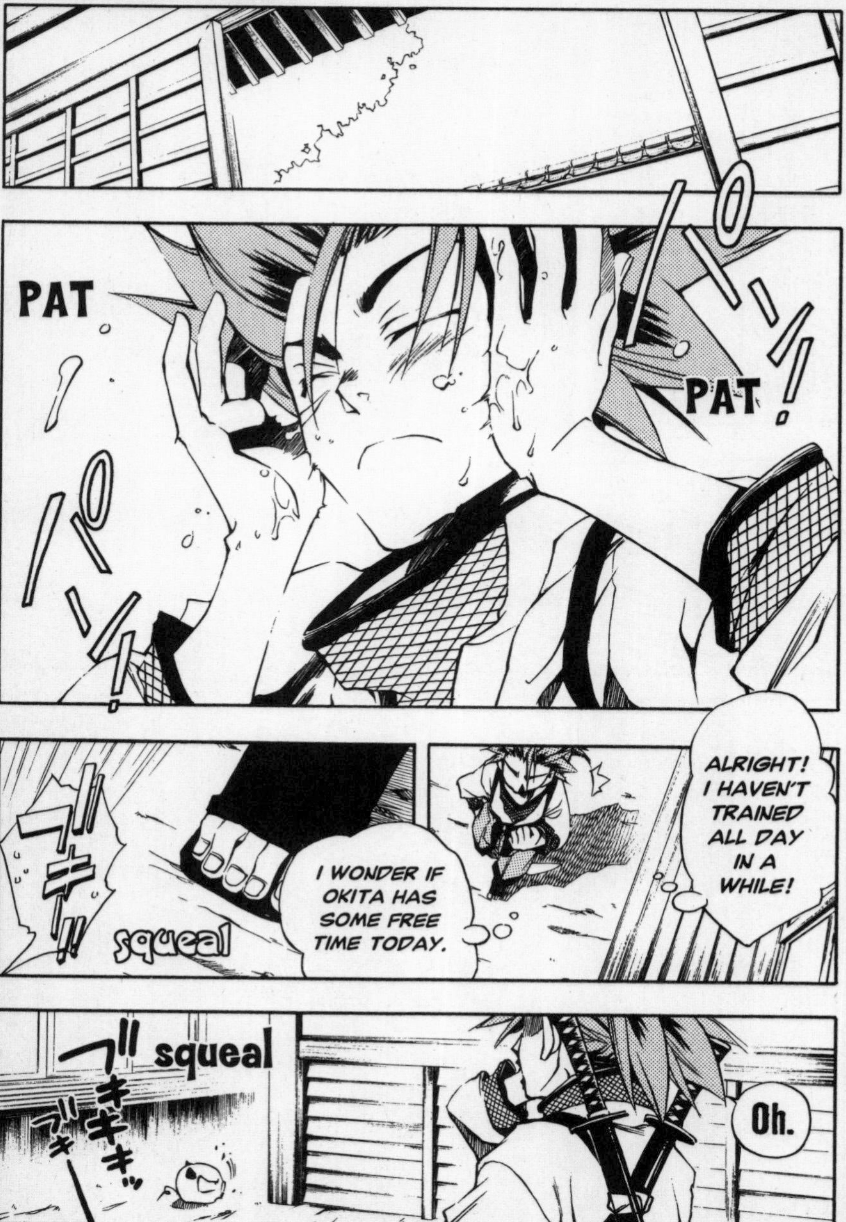
PAT
PAT
ALRIGHT! I HAVEN'T TRAINED ALL DAY IN A WHILE!
I WONDER IF OKITA HAS SOME FREE TIME TODAY.
squeal
Oh.
squeal

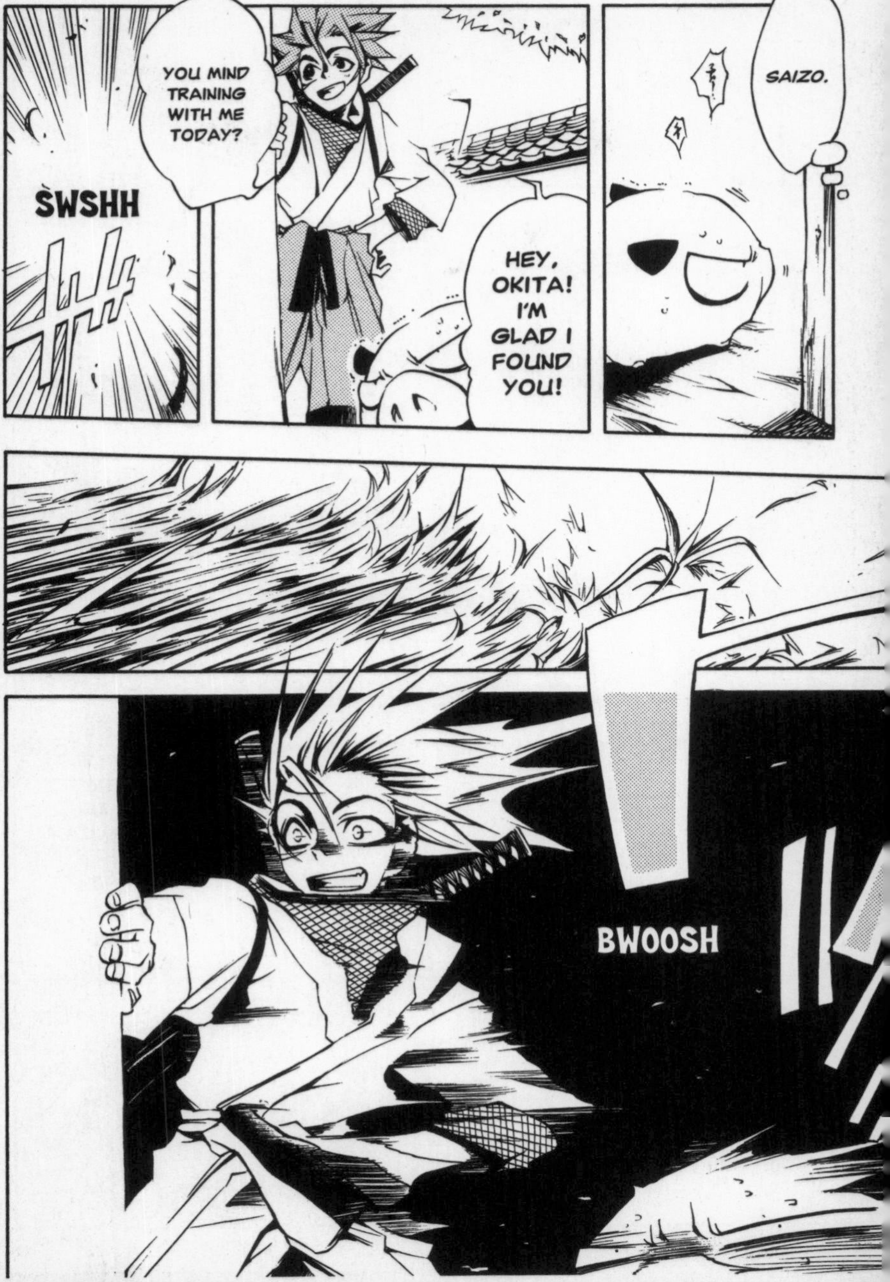
SAIZO.
HEY, OKITA! I'M GLAD I FOUND YOU!
YOU MIND TRAINING WITH ME TODAY?
SWSHH
BWOOSH

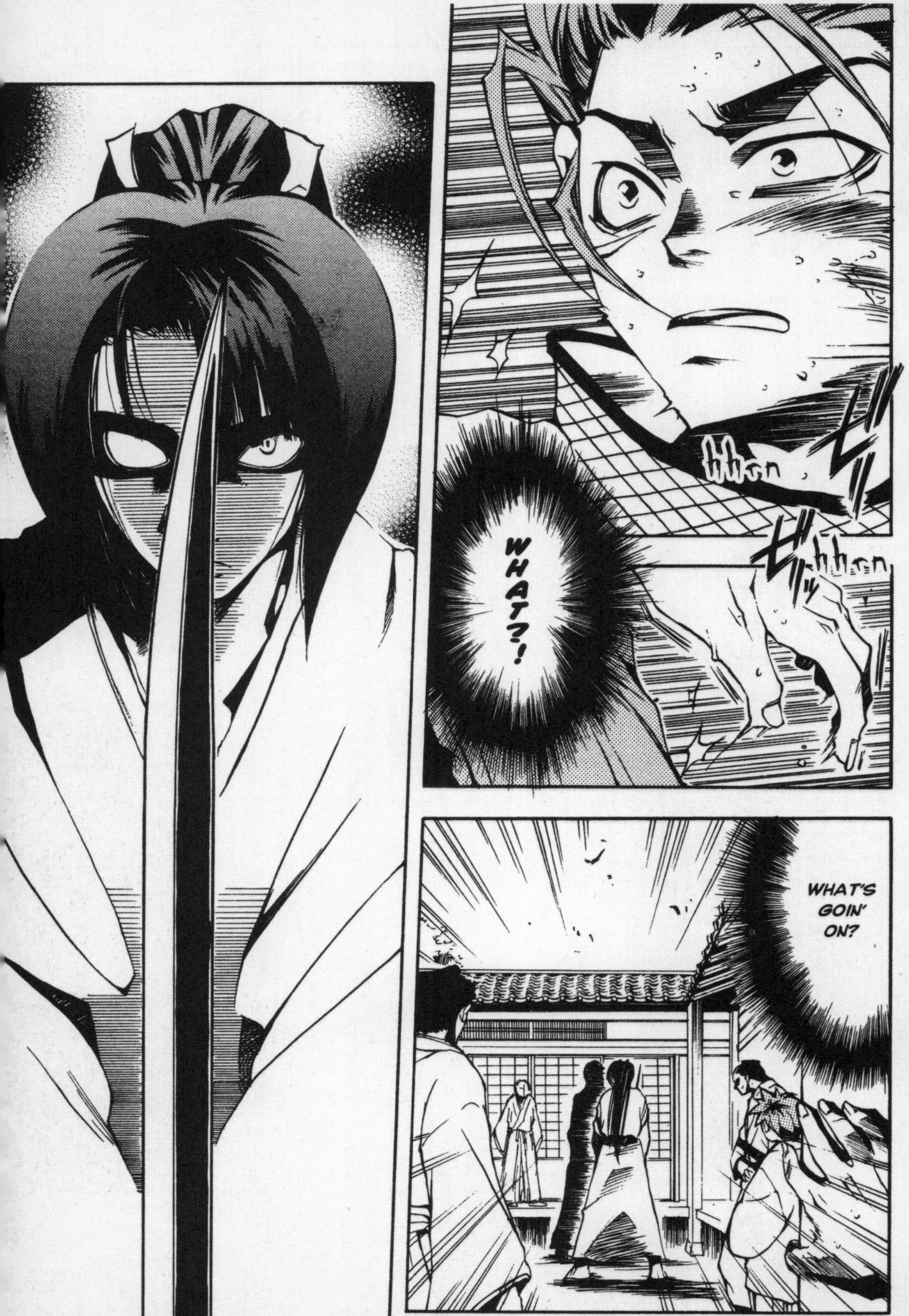
hhhn
hhhn
WHAT?!
WHAT'S GOIN' ON?

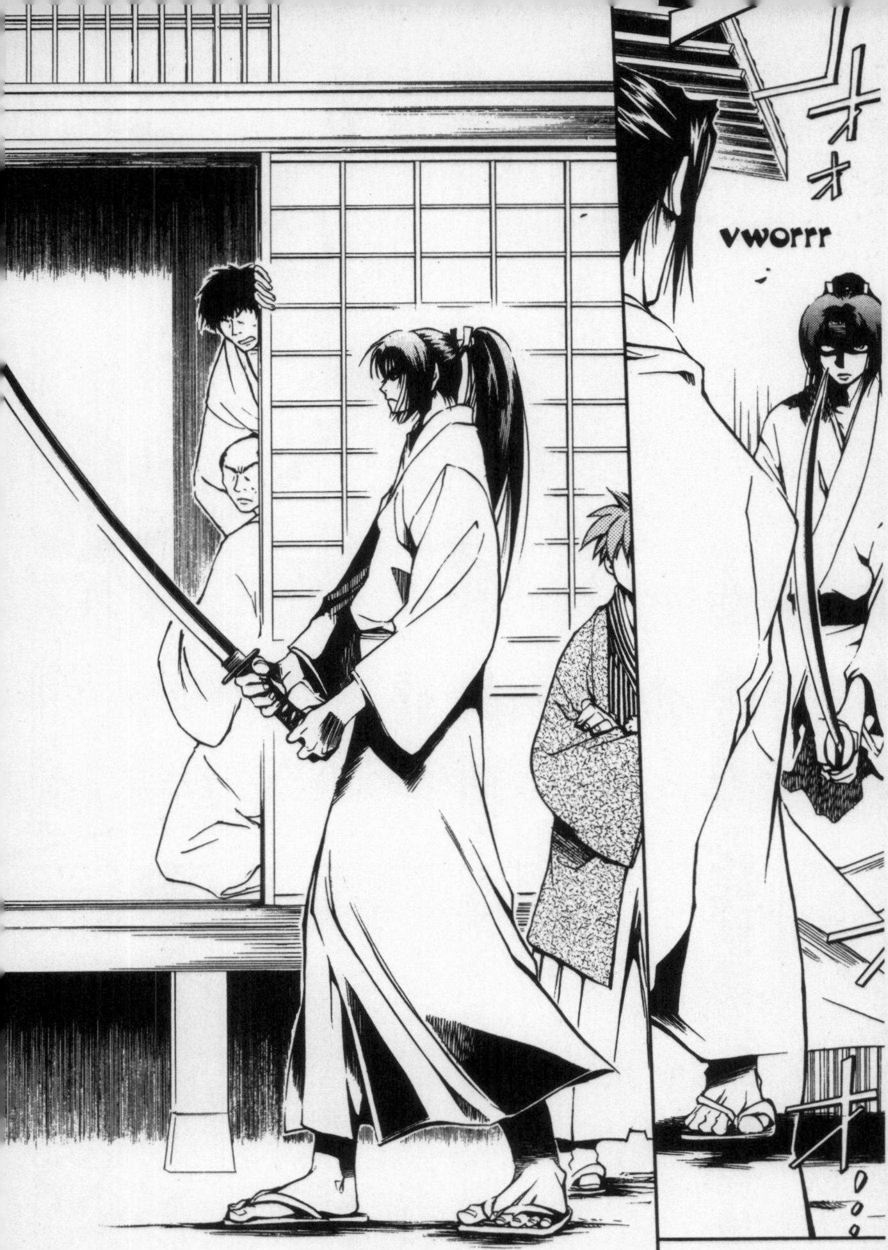
vworrr

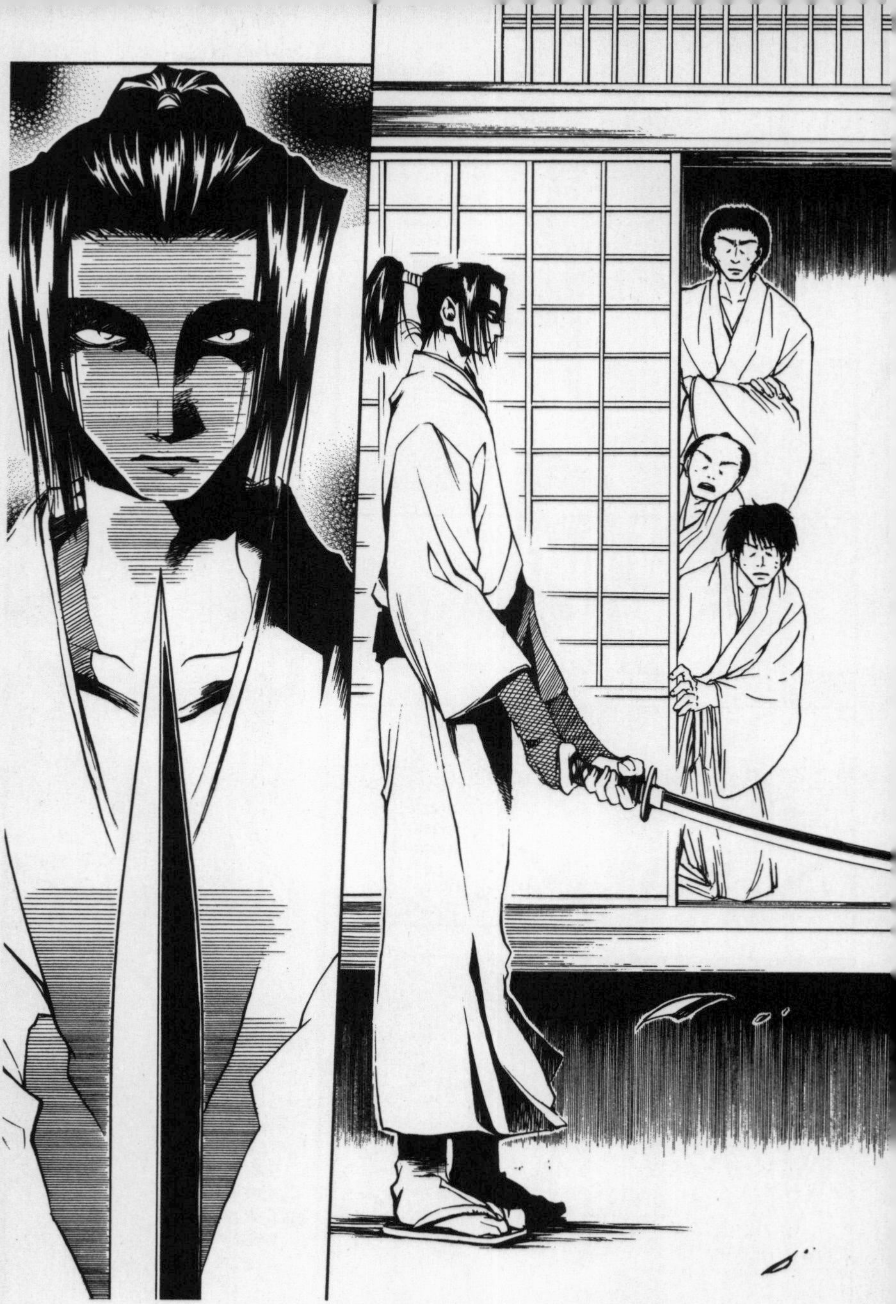

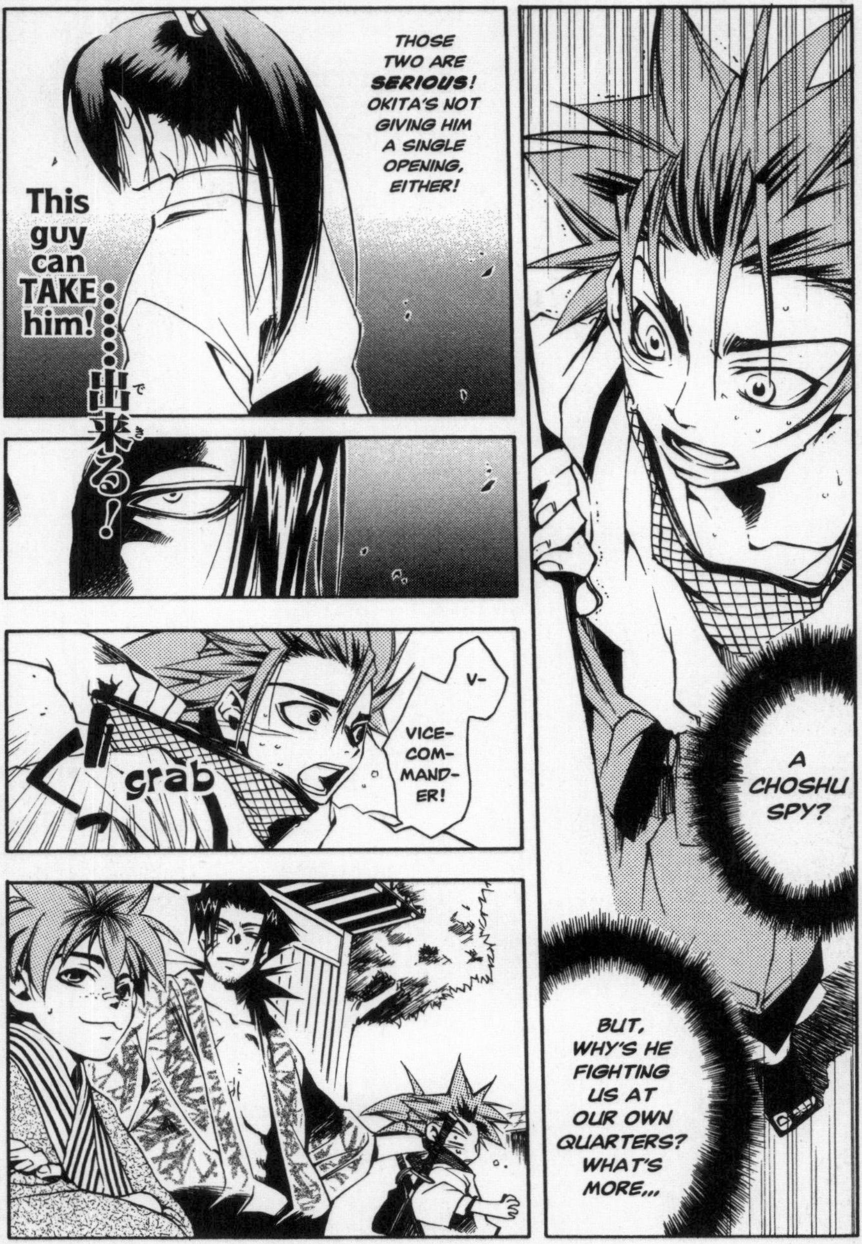
A CHOSHU SPY?
BUT, WHY'S HE FIGHTING US AT OUR OWN QUARTERS? WHAT'S MORE...
THOSE TWO ARE SERIOUS! OKITA'S NOT GIVING HIM A SINGLE OPENING, EITHER!
This guy can TAKE him!
……出来る！
V-
VICE-COM-MAND-ER!
grab

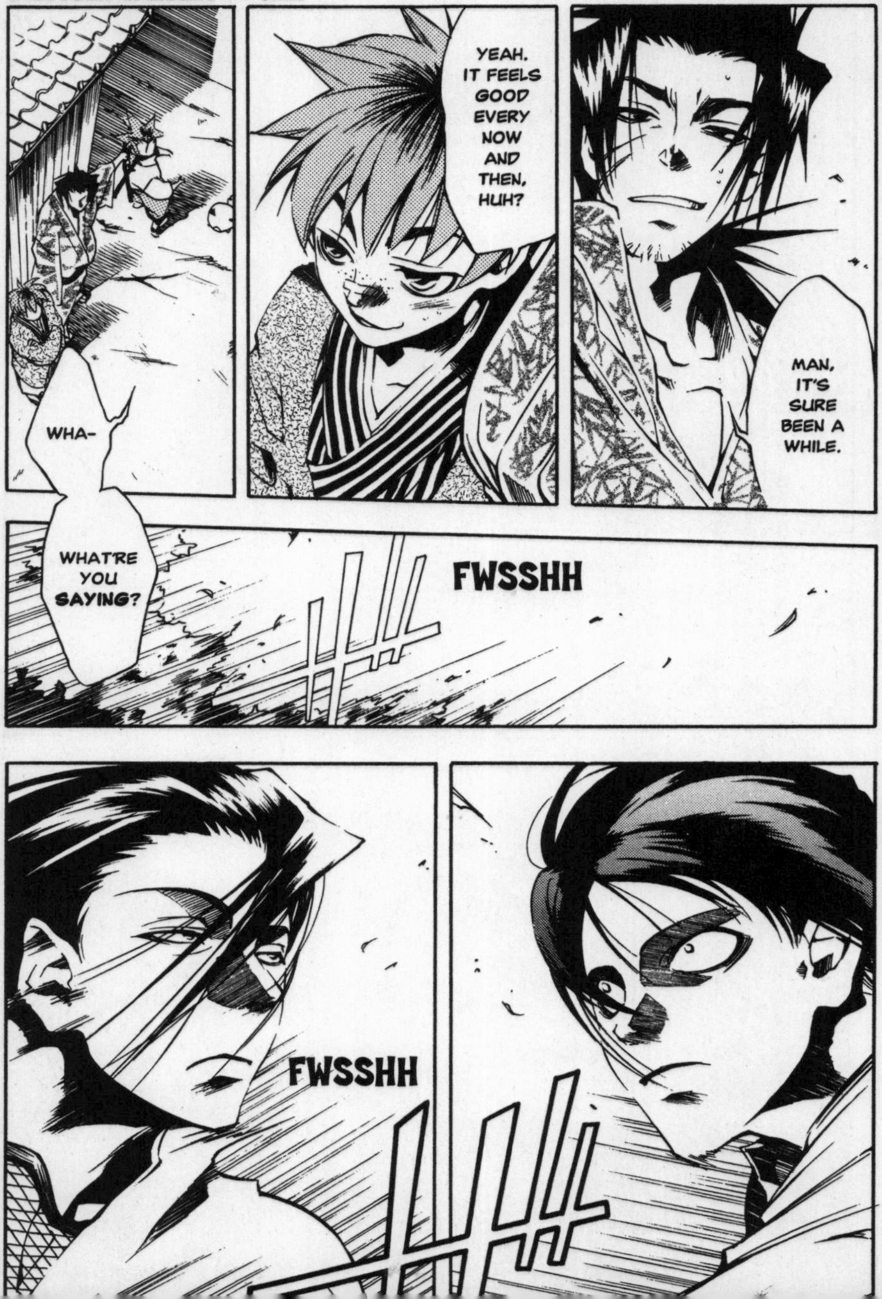
MAN, IT'S SURE BEEN A WHILE.
YEAH. IT FEELS GOOD EVERY NOW AND THEN, HUH?
WHA-
WHAT'RE YOU SAYING?
FWSSHH
FWSSHH

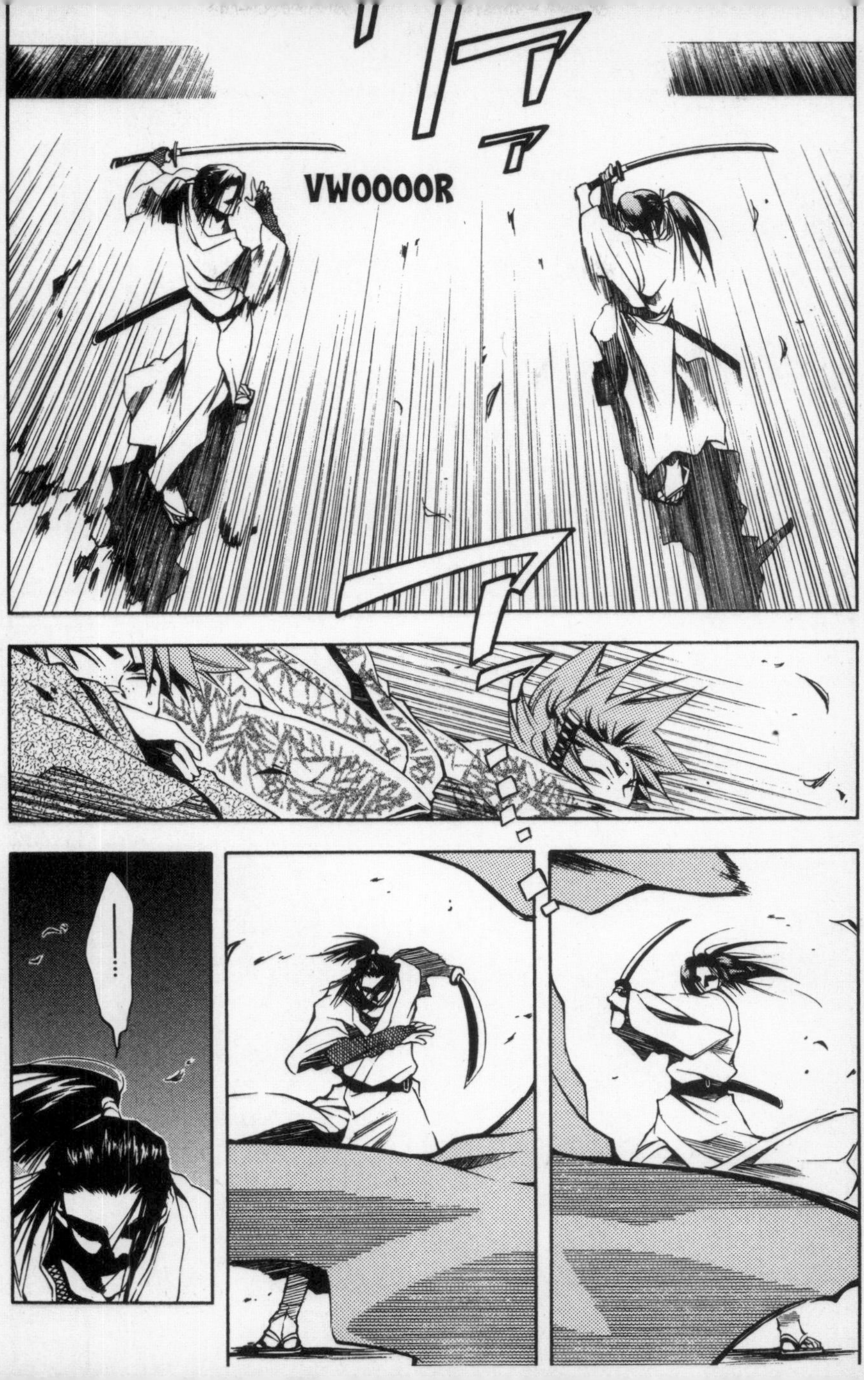
VWOOOOR
ドァァ
…！

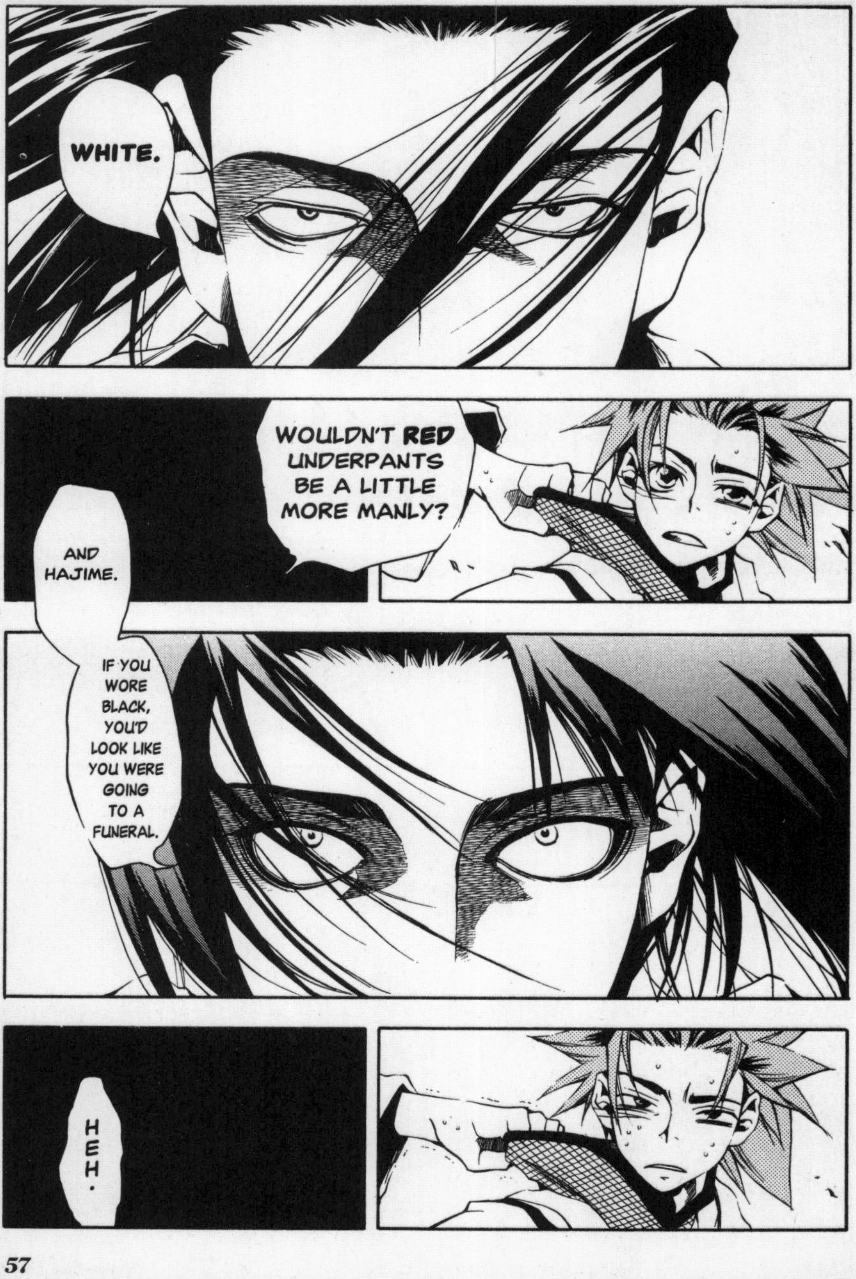
WHITE.
WOULDN'T RED UNDERPANTS BE A LITTLE MORE MANLY?
AND HAJIME.
IF YOU WORE BLACK, YOU'D LOOK LIKE YOU WERE GOING TO A FUNERAL.
HEH.

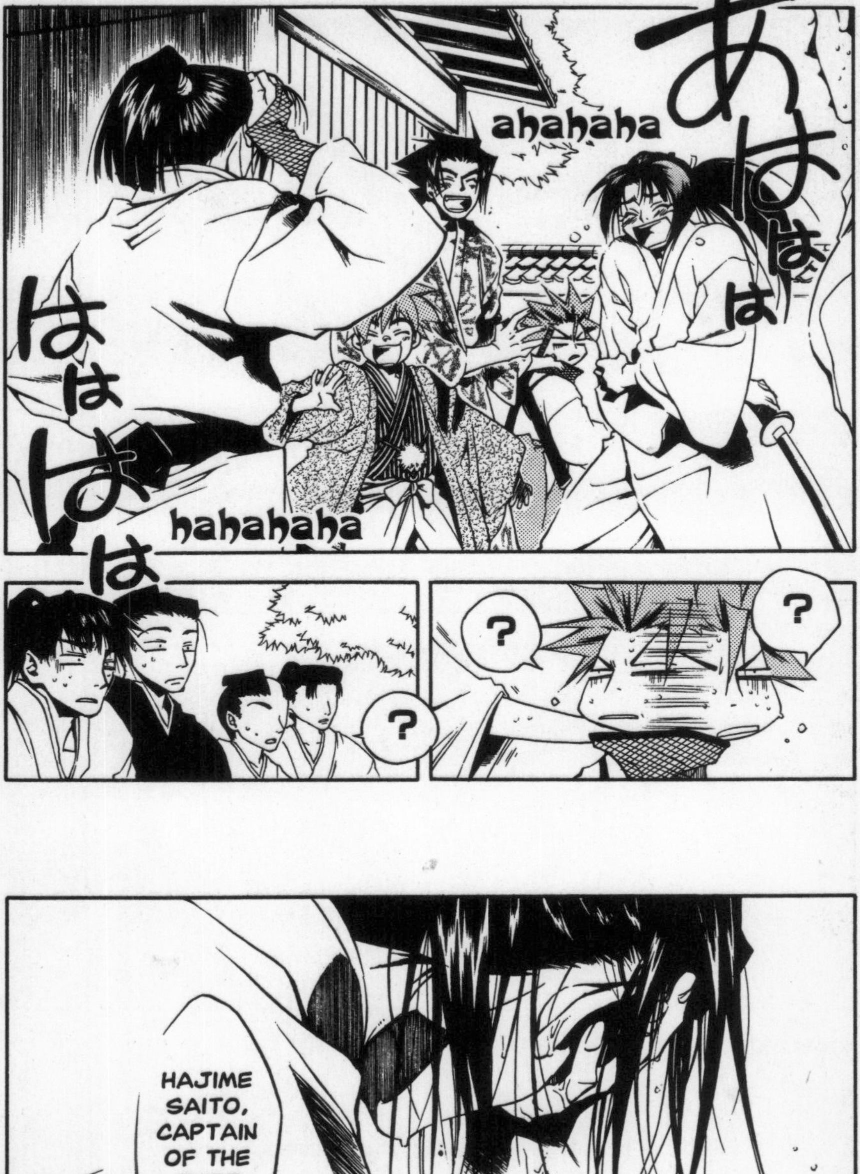

あははは
ahahaha
はははは
hahahaha
?
?
?
HAJIME SAITO, CAPTAIN OF THE THIRD UNIT.

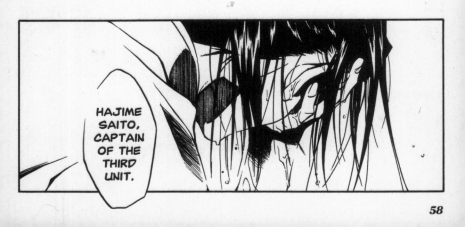

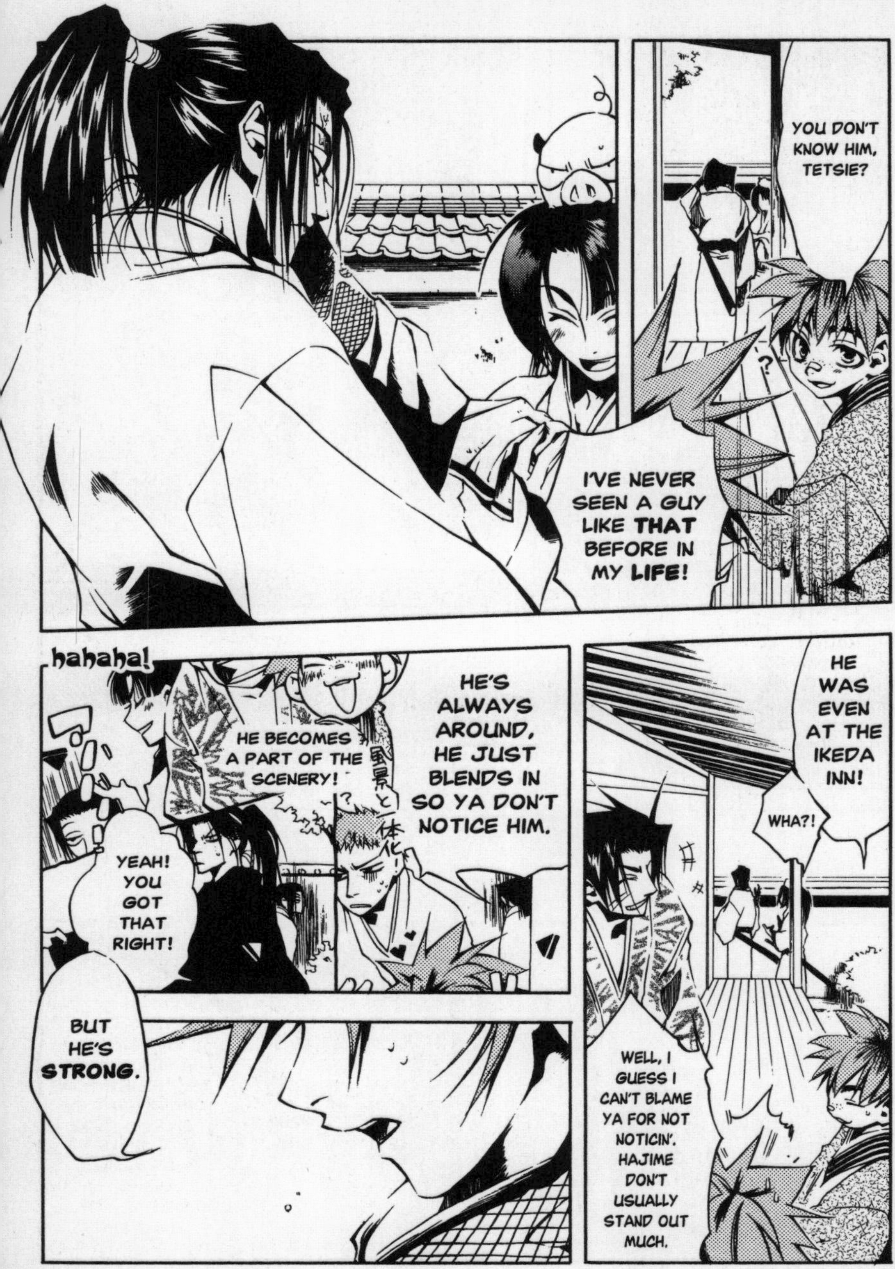
YOU DON'T KNOW HIM, TETSIE?
I'VE NEVER SEEN A GUY LIKE **THAT** BEFORE IN MY **LIFE**!
HE WAS EVEN AT THE IKEDA INN!
WHA?!
WELL, I GUESS I CAN'T BLAME YA FOR NOT NOTICIN'. HAJIME DON'T USUALLY STAND OUT MUCH.
HE'S ALWAYS AROUND, HE JUST BLENDS IN SO YA DON'T NOTICE HIM.
風景と一体化
HE BECOMES A PART OF THE SCENERY!
hahaha!
YEAH! YOU GOT THAT RIGHT!
BUT HE'S **STRONG**.

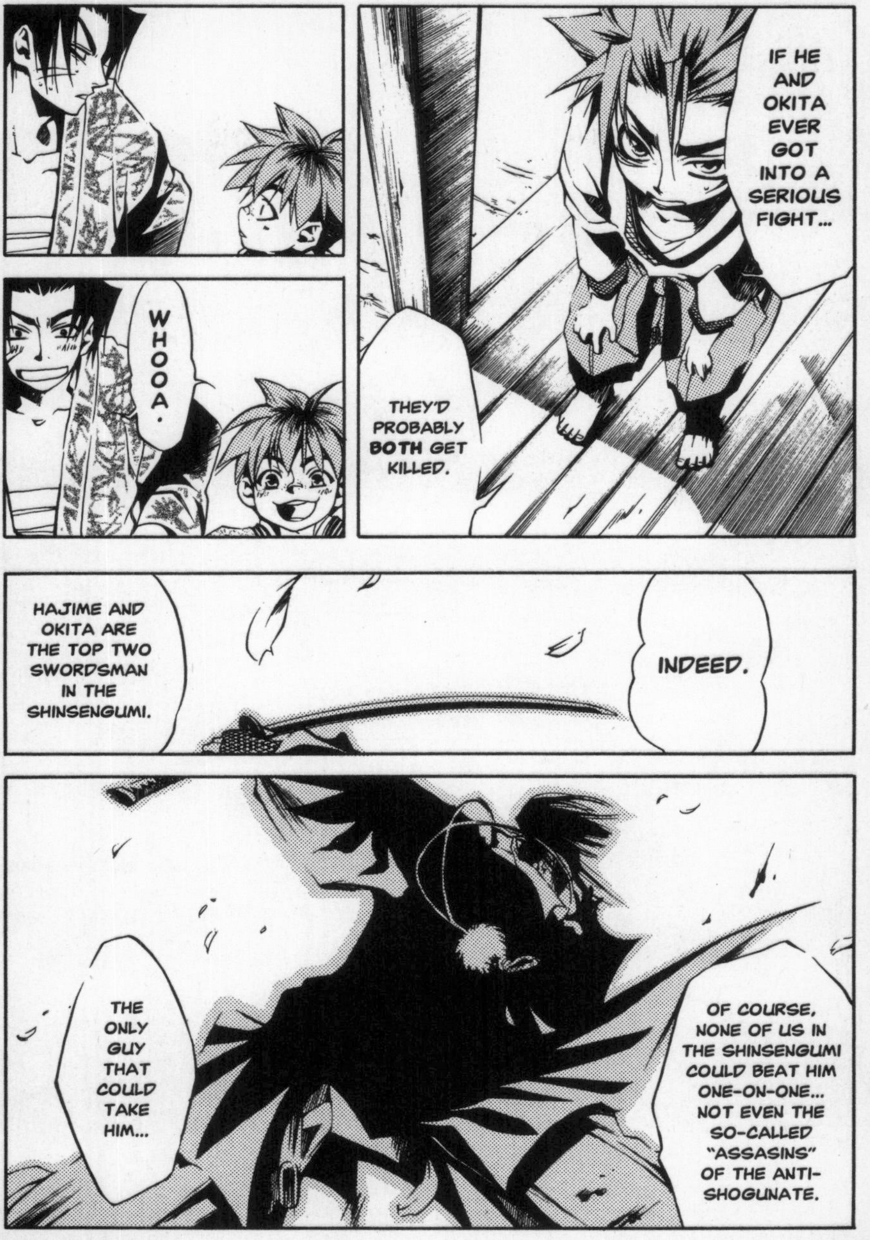
IF HE AND OKITA EVER GOT INTO A SERIOUS FIGHT...
THEY'D PROBABLY **BOTH** GET KILLED.
WHOOA.
INDEED.
HAJIME AND OKITA ARE THE TOP TWO SWORDSMAN IN THE SHINSENGUMI.
OF COURSE, NONE OF US IN THE SHINSENGUMI COULD BEAT HIM ONE-ON-ONE... NOT EVEN THE SO-CALLED "ASSASINS" OF THE ANTI-SHOGUNATE.
THE ONLY GUY THAT COULD TAKE HIM...

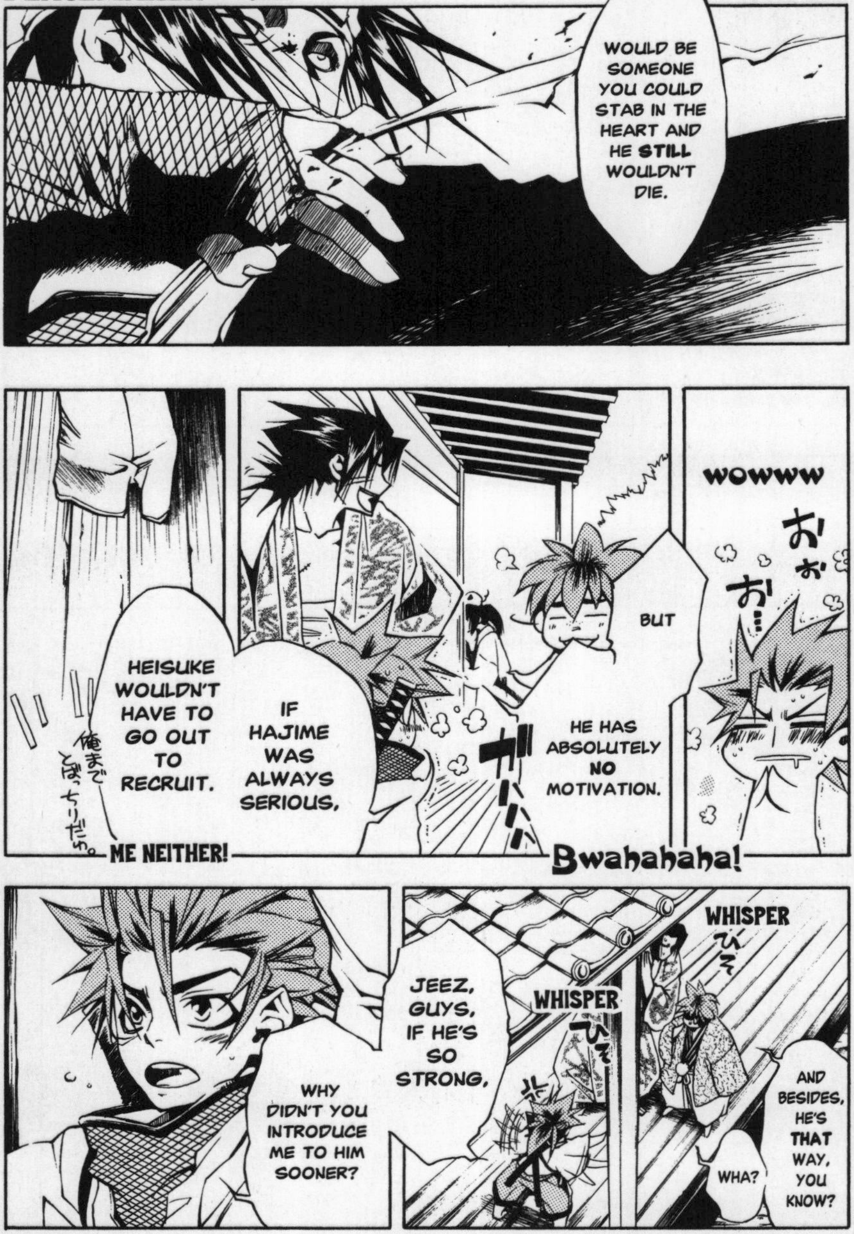
WOULD BE SOMEONE YOU COULD STAB IN THE HEART AND HE STILL WOULDN'T DIE.
WOWWW
おぉお…
BUT
HE HAS ABSOLUTELY NO MOTIVATION.
Bwahahaha!
IF HAJIME WAS ALWAYS SERIOUS,
HEISUKE WOULDN'T HAVE TO GO OUT TO RECRUIT.
俺までとばっちりだっ。
ME NEITHER!
WHISPER
ひそ
WHISPER
ひそ
AND BESIDES, HE'S THAT WAY, YOU KNOW?
WHA?
JEEZ, GUYS, IF HE'S SO STRONG,
WHY DIDN'T YOU INTRODUCE ME TO HIM SOONER?

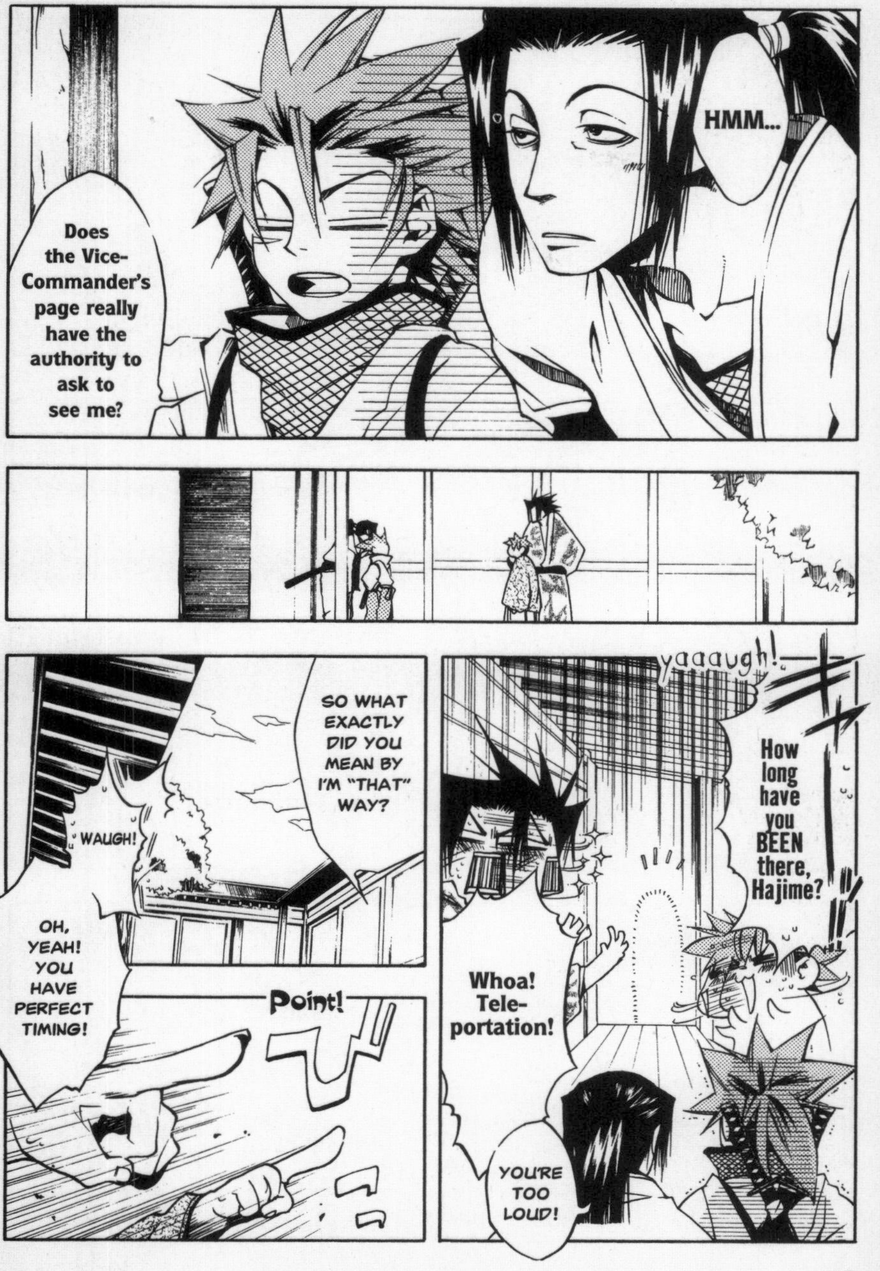
HMM...
Does the Vice-Commander's page really have the authority to ask to see me?
yaaaugh!
How long have you BEEN there, Hajime?
Whoa! Tele-portation!
YOU'RE TOO LOUD!
SO WHAT EXACTLY DID YOU MEAN BY I'M "THAT" WAY?
WAUGH!
OH, YEAH! YOU HAVE PERFECT TIMING!
Point!

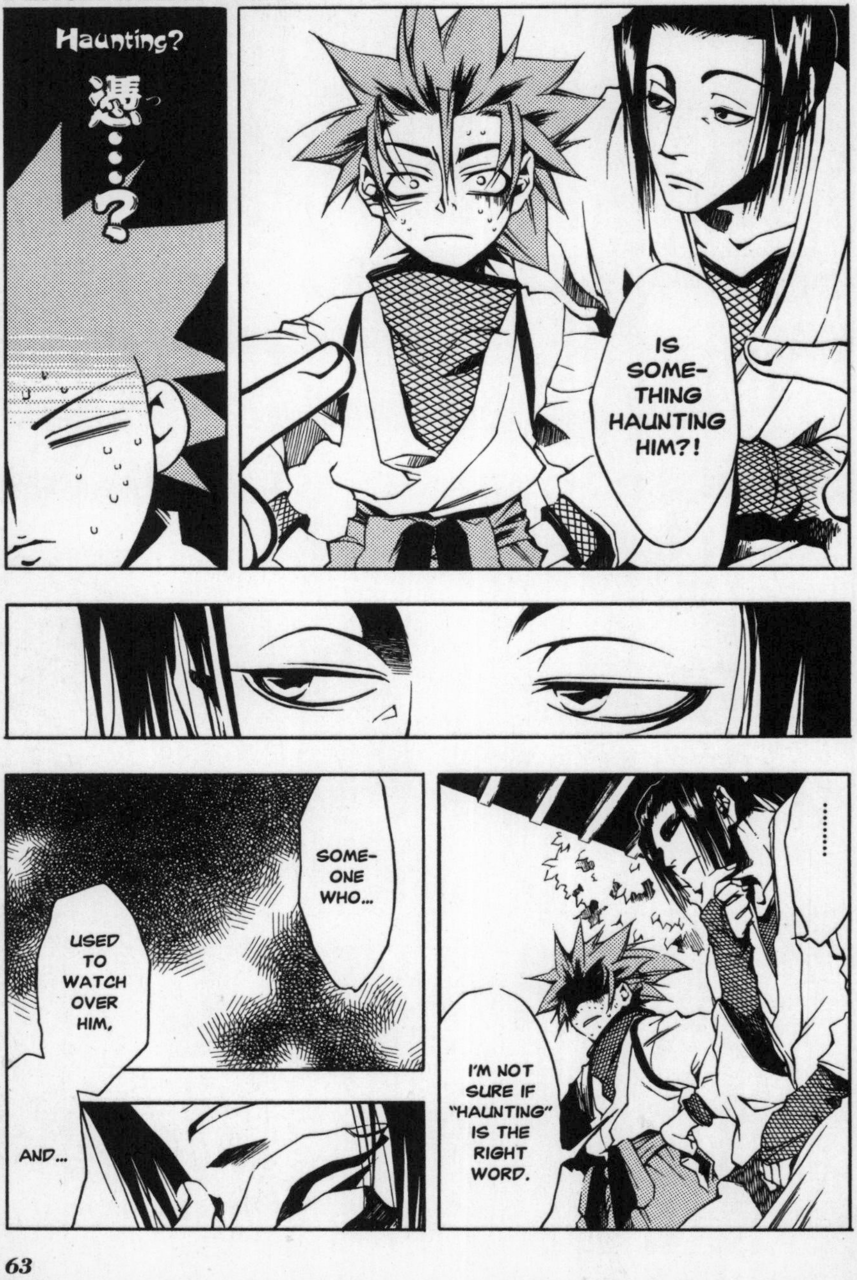
IS SOME-THING HAUNTING HIM?!
Haunting?
憑…?
......
I'M NOT SURE IF "HAUNTING" IS THE RIGHT WORD.
SOME-ONE WHO...
USED TO WATCH OVER HIM,
AND...

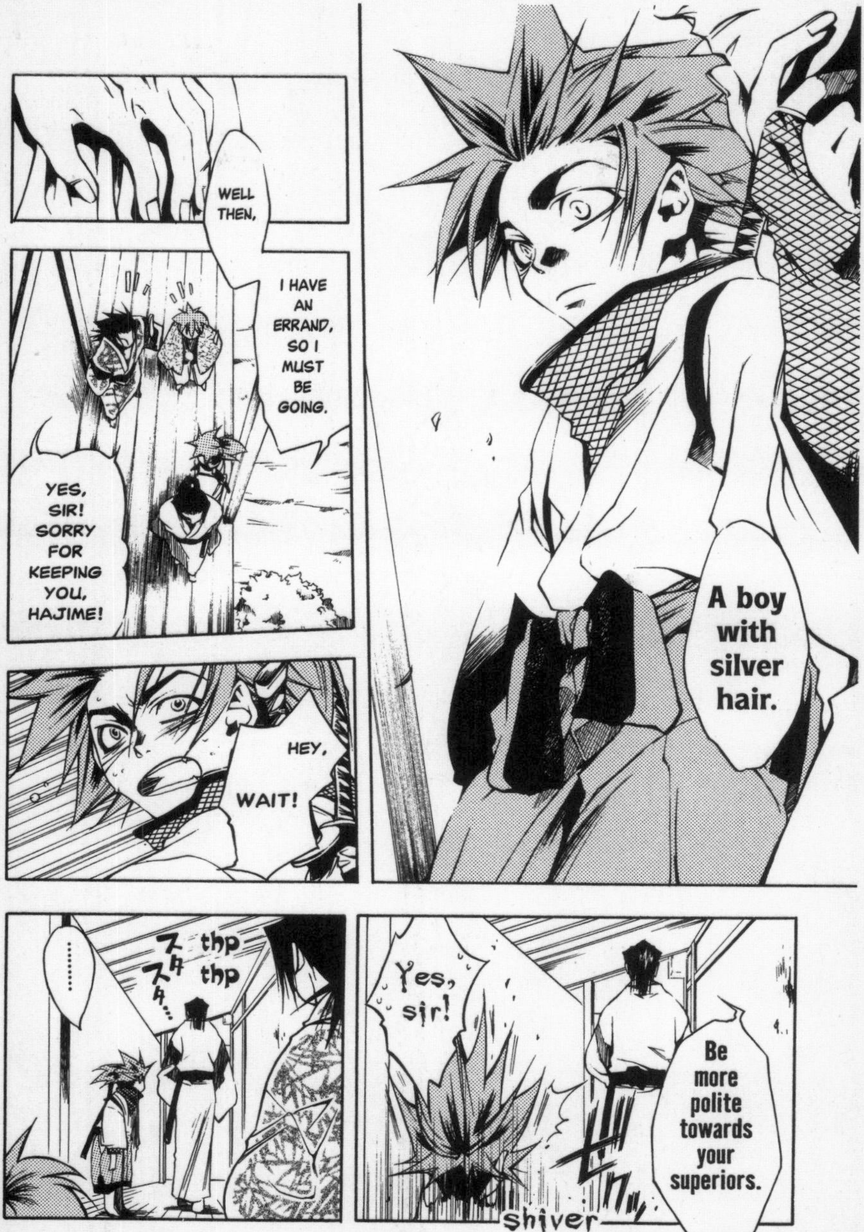
A boy with silver hair.
WELL THEN,
I HAVE AN ERRAND, SO I MUST BE GOING.
YES, SIR! SORRY FOR KEEPING YOU, HAJIME!
HEY, WAIT!
Be more polite towards your superiors.
Yes, sir!
shiver
スタスタ… thp thp
……

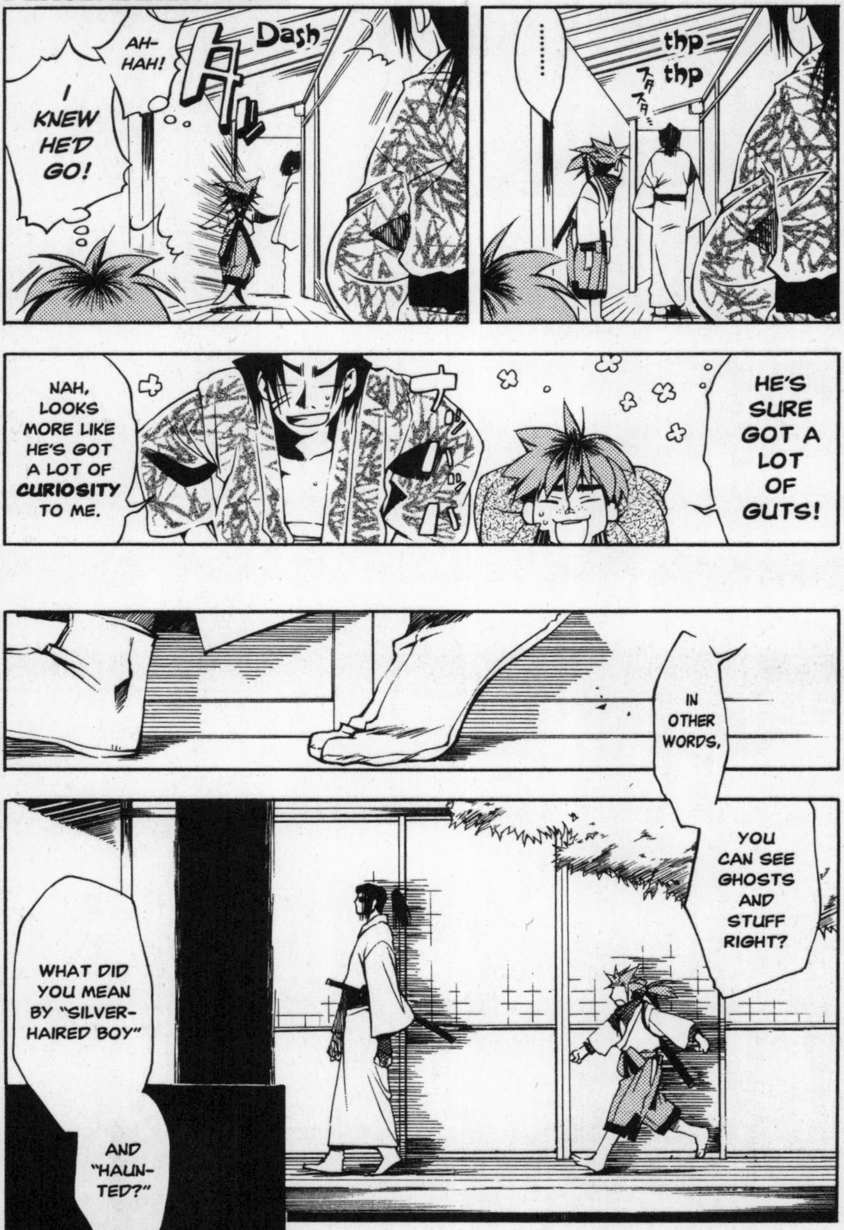
......
thp thp
AH-HAH!
I KNEW HE'D GO!
Dash
HE'S SURE GOT A LOT OF GUTS!
NAH, LOOKS MORE LIKE HE'S GOT A LOT OF CURIOSITY TO ME.
IN OTHER WORDS,
YOU CAN SEE GHOSTS AND STUFF RIGHT?
WHAT DID YOU MEAN BY "SILVER-HAIRED BOY"
AND "HAUNTED?"

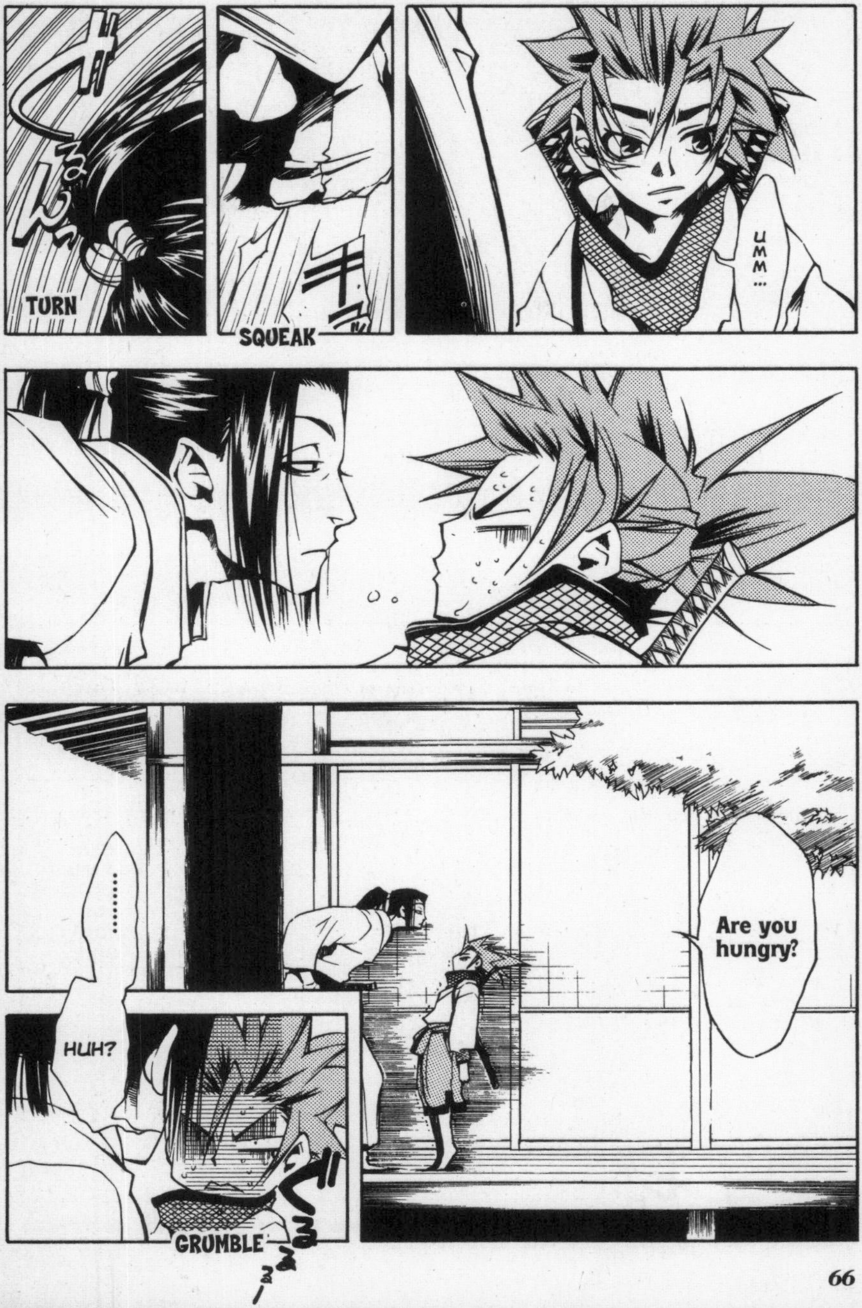
UMM...
SQUEAK
TURN
Are you hungry?
....
HUH?
GRUMBLE

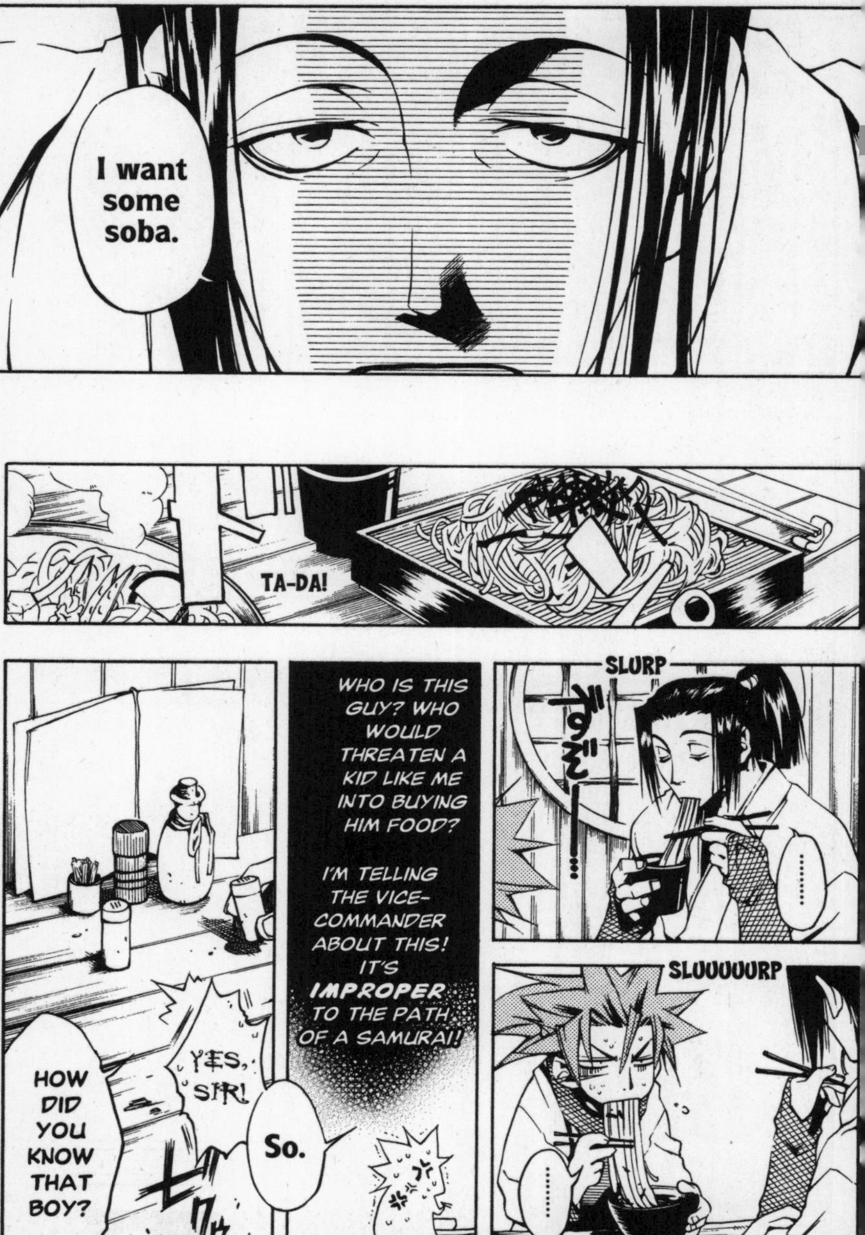

I want some soba.
TA-DA!
SLURP
....
SLUUUUURP
....
WHO IS THIS GUY? WHO WOULD THREATEN A KID LIKE ME INTO BUYING HIM FOOD?
I'M TELLING THE VICE-COMMANDER ABOUT THIS! IT'S *IMPROPER* TO THE PATH OF A SAMURAI!
So.
YES, SIR!
jump
HOW DID YOU KNOW THAT BOY?

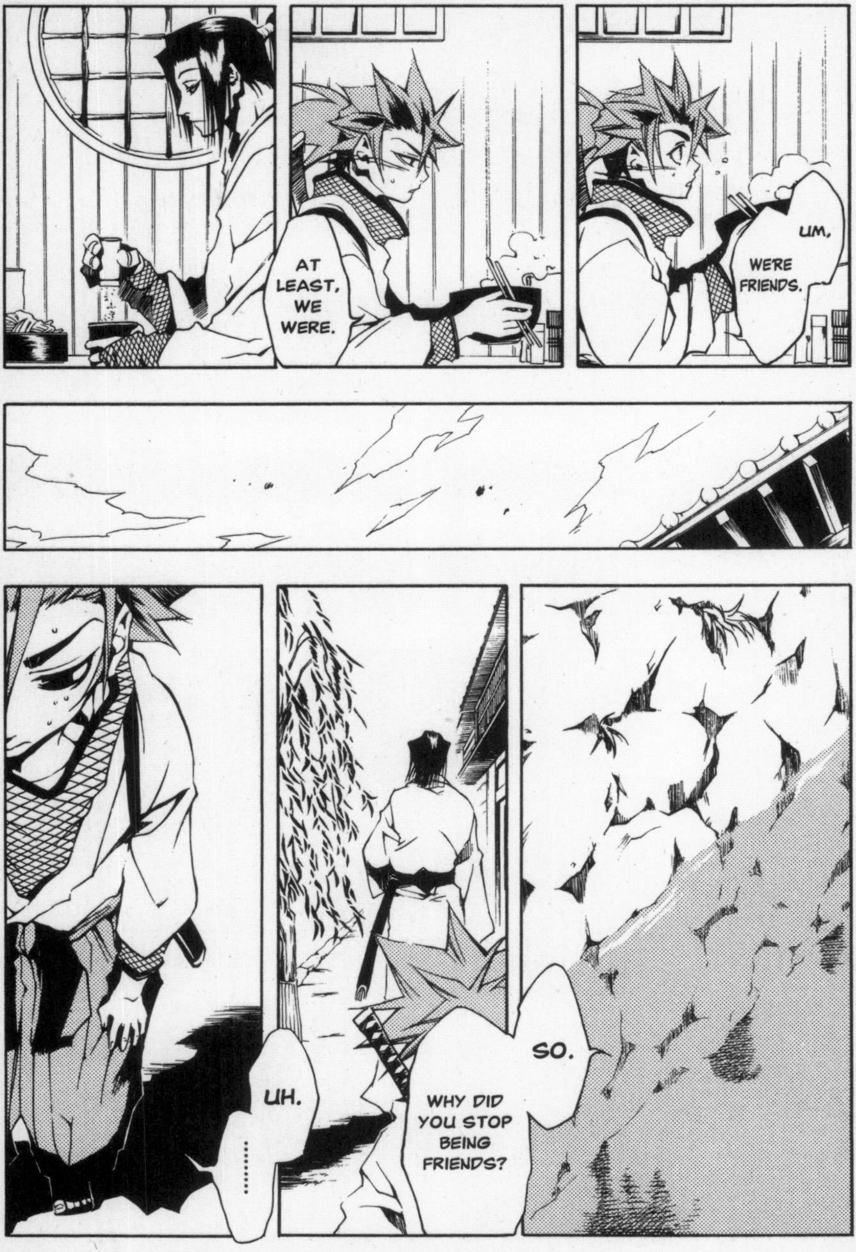
UM, WE'RE FRIENDS.
AT LEAST, WE WERE.
SO.
WHY DID YOU STOP BEING FRIENDS?
UH.
......

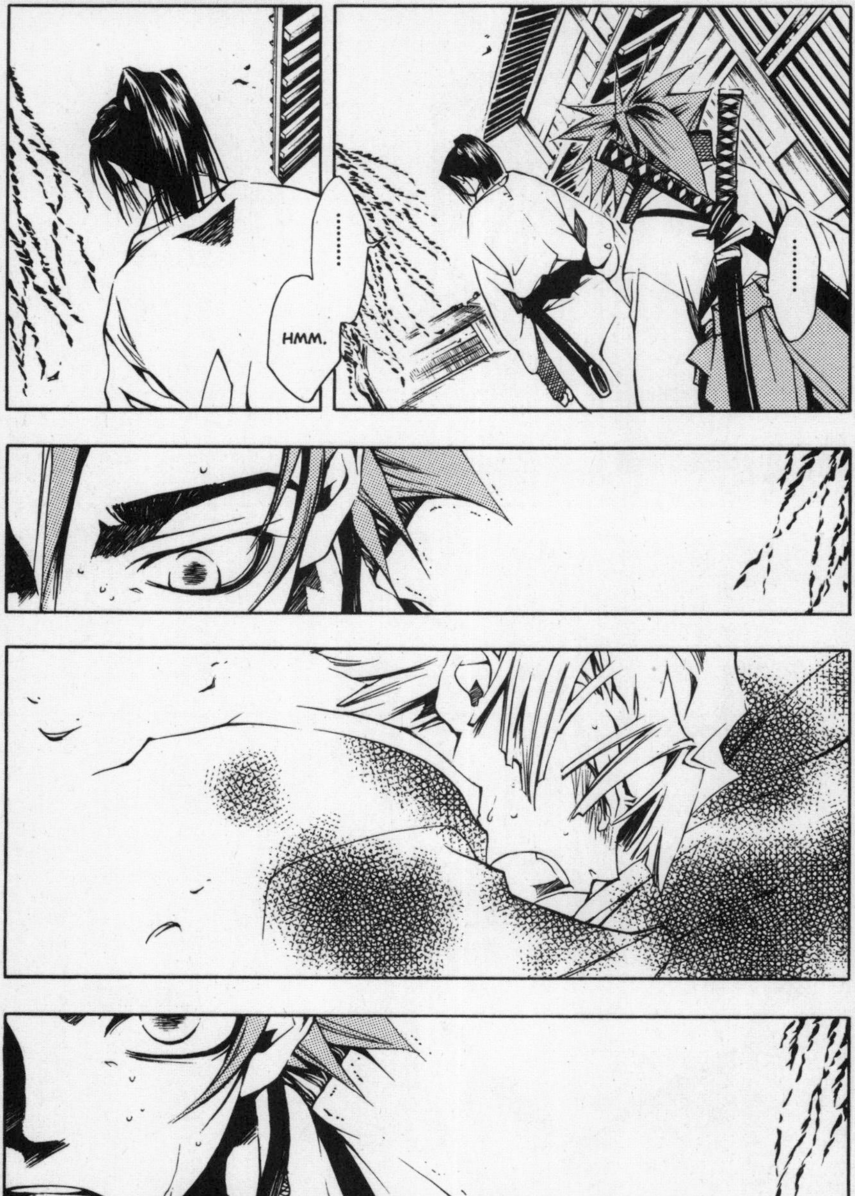
......
......
HMM.

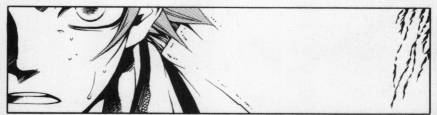

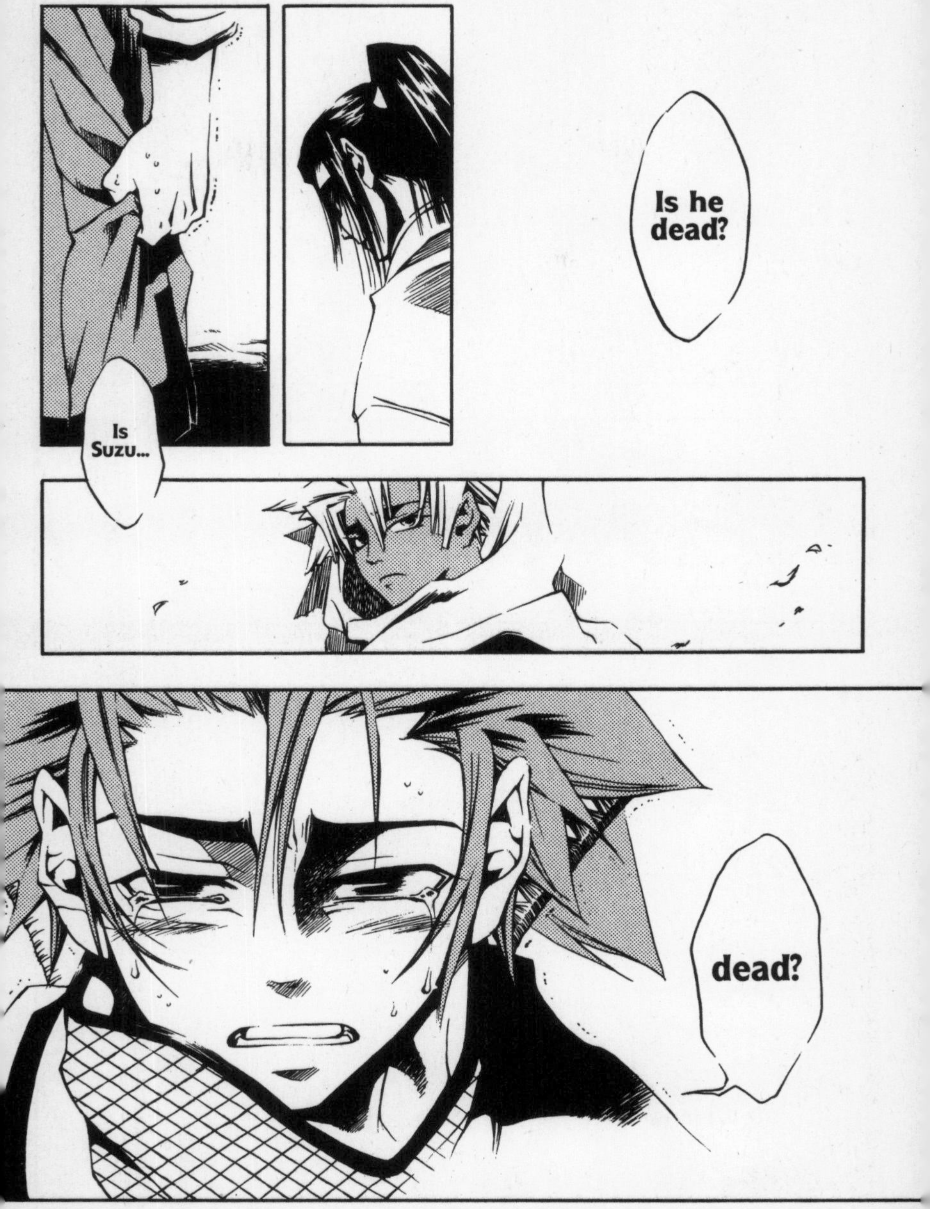
Is he dead?
Is Suzu...
dead?

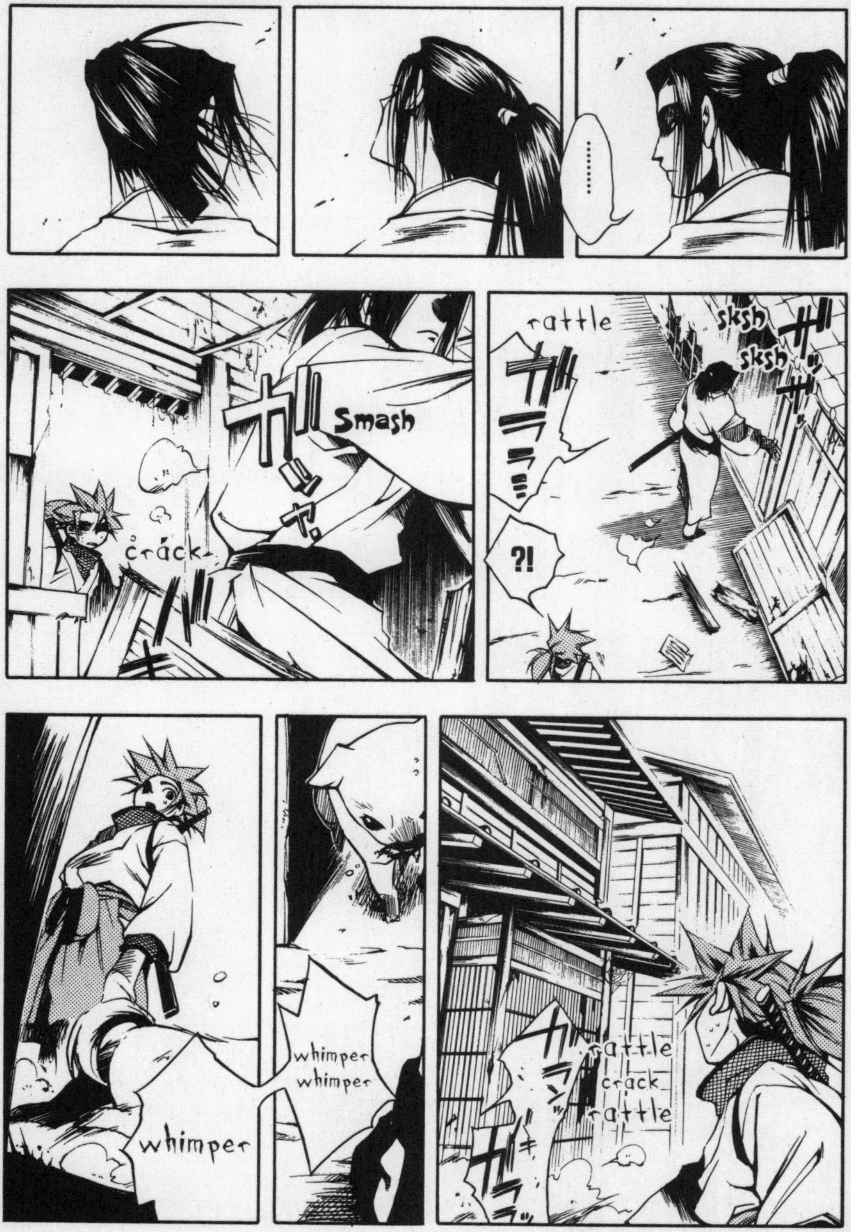
....
rattle
sksh
sksh
?!
Smash
crack
rattle
crack
rattle
whimper
whimper
whimper

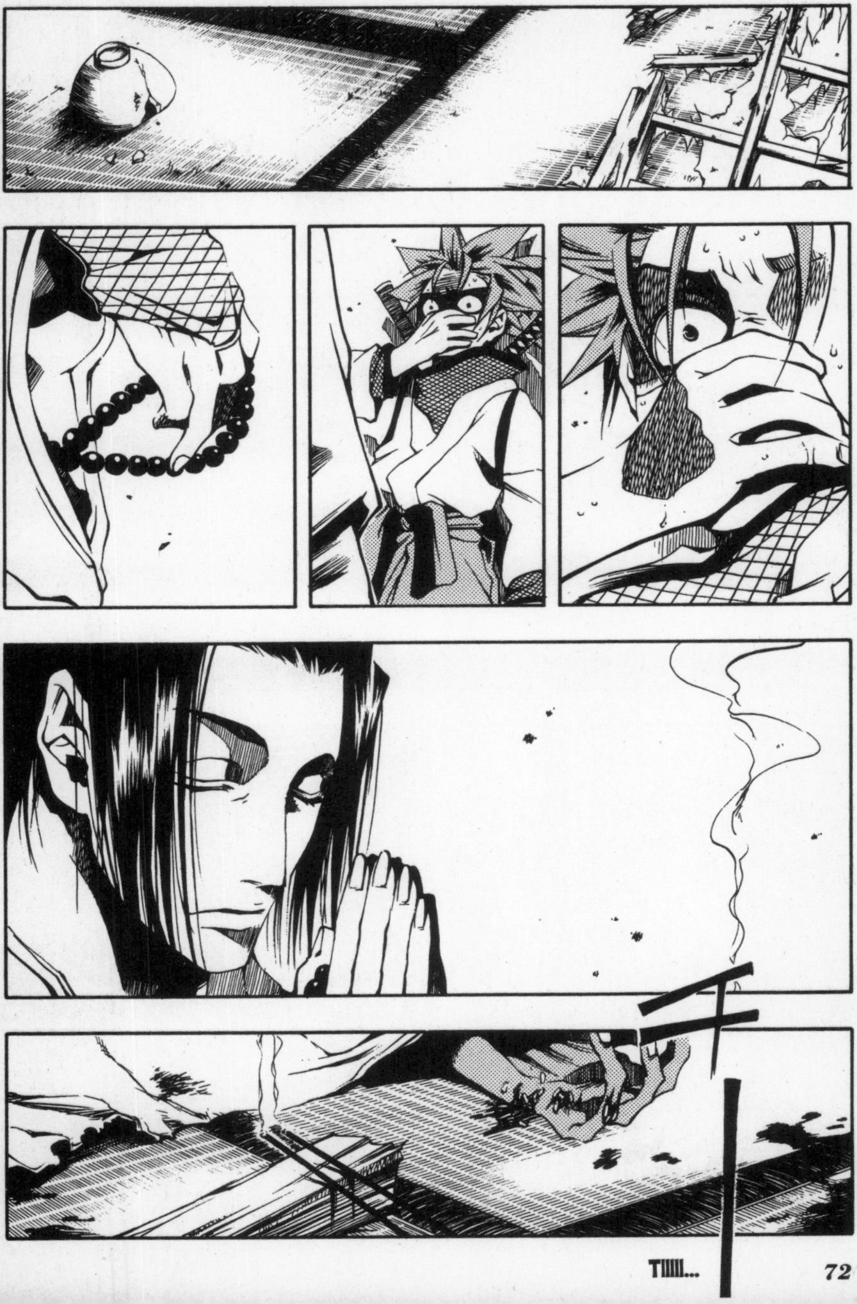
チー
TIIIII...

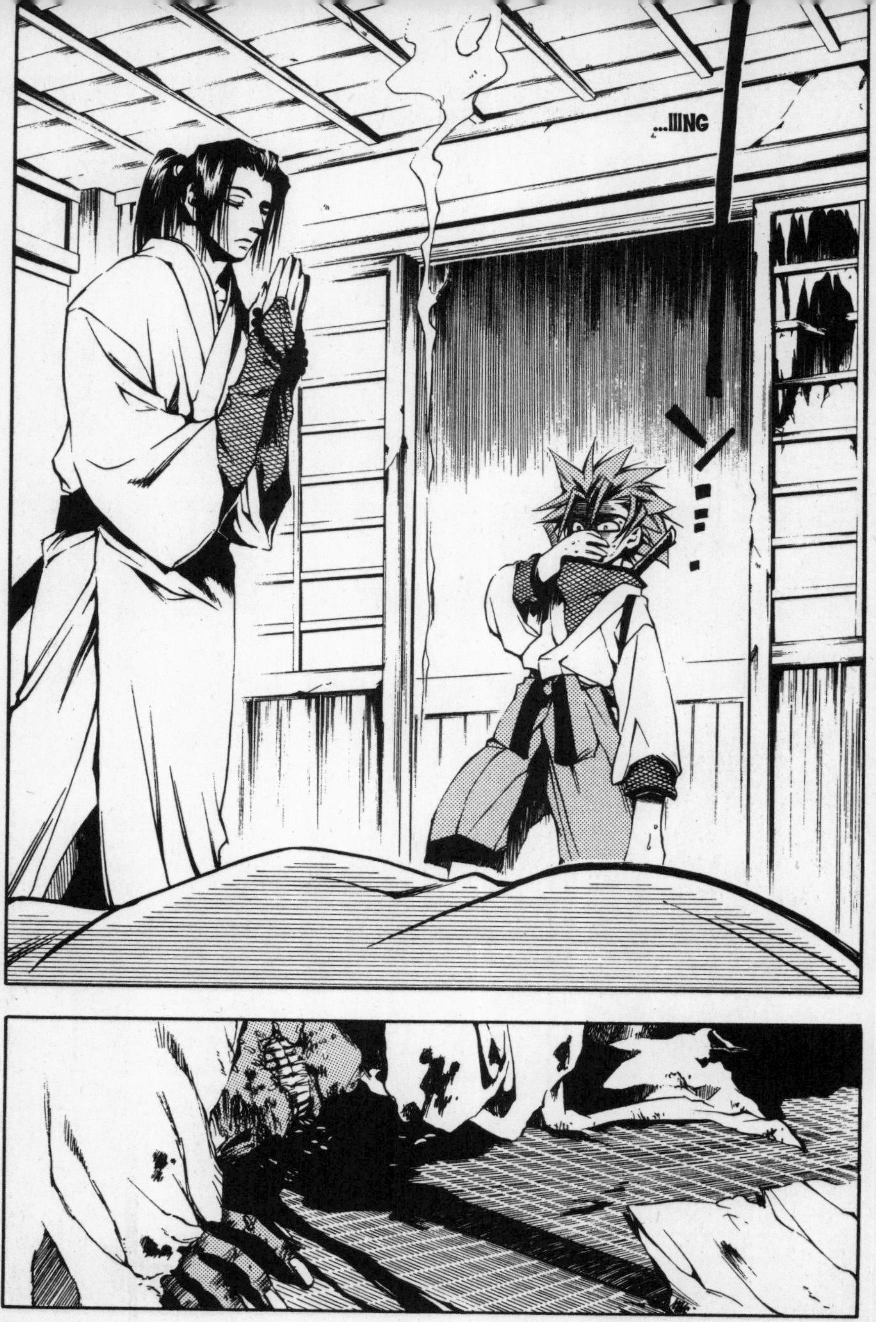
...IIING
!...

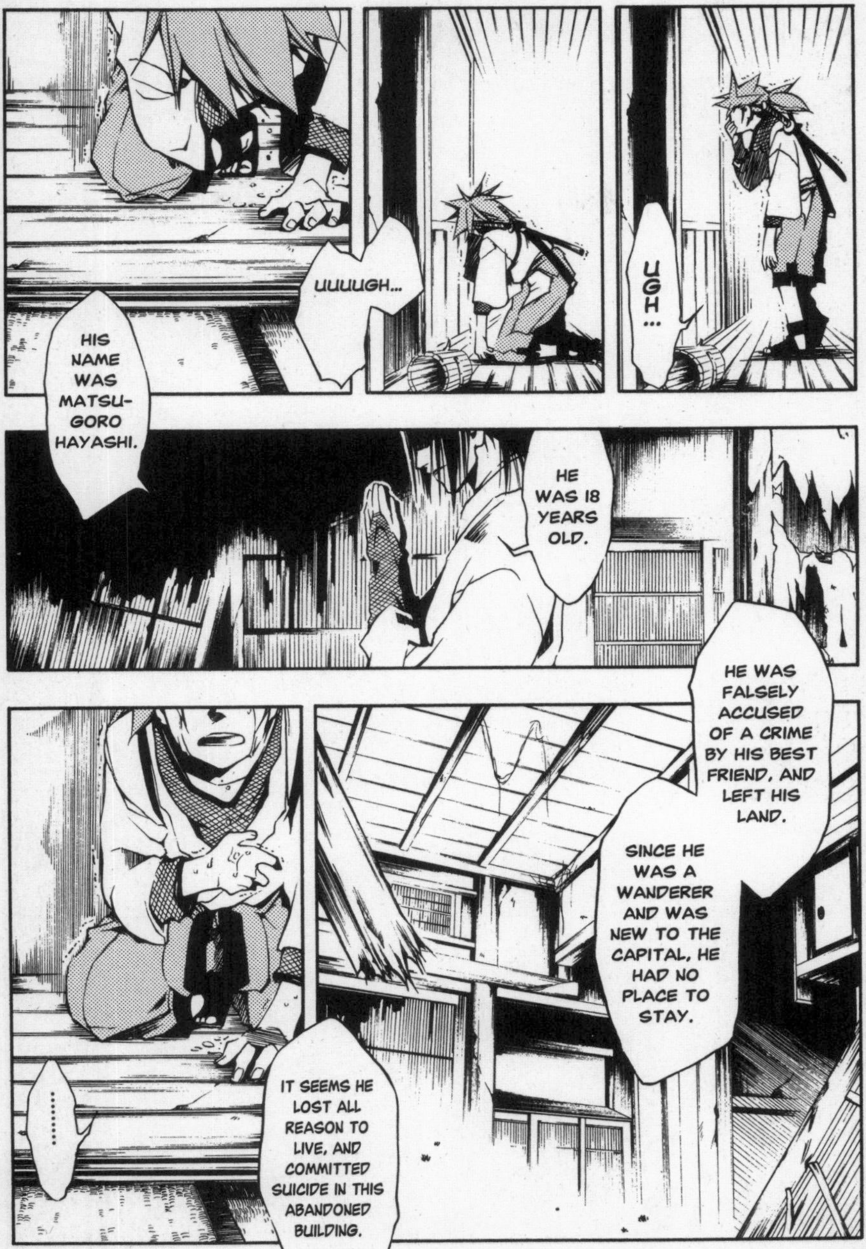
UGH...
UUUUGH...
HIS NAME WAS MATSU-GORO HAYASHI.
HE WAS 18 YEARS OLD.
HE WAS FALSELY ACCUSED OF A CRIME BY HIS BEST FRIEND, AND LEFT HIS LAND.
SINCE HE WAS A WANDERER AND WAS NEW TO THE CAPITAL, HE HAD NO PLACE TO STAY.
IT SEEMS HE LOST ALL REASON TO LIVE, AND COMMITTED SUICIDE IN THIS ABANDONED BUILDING.
....

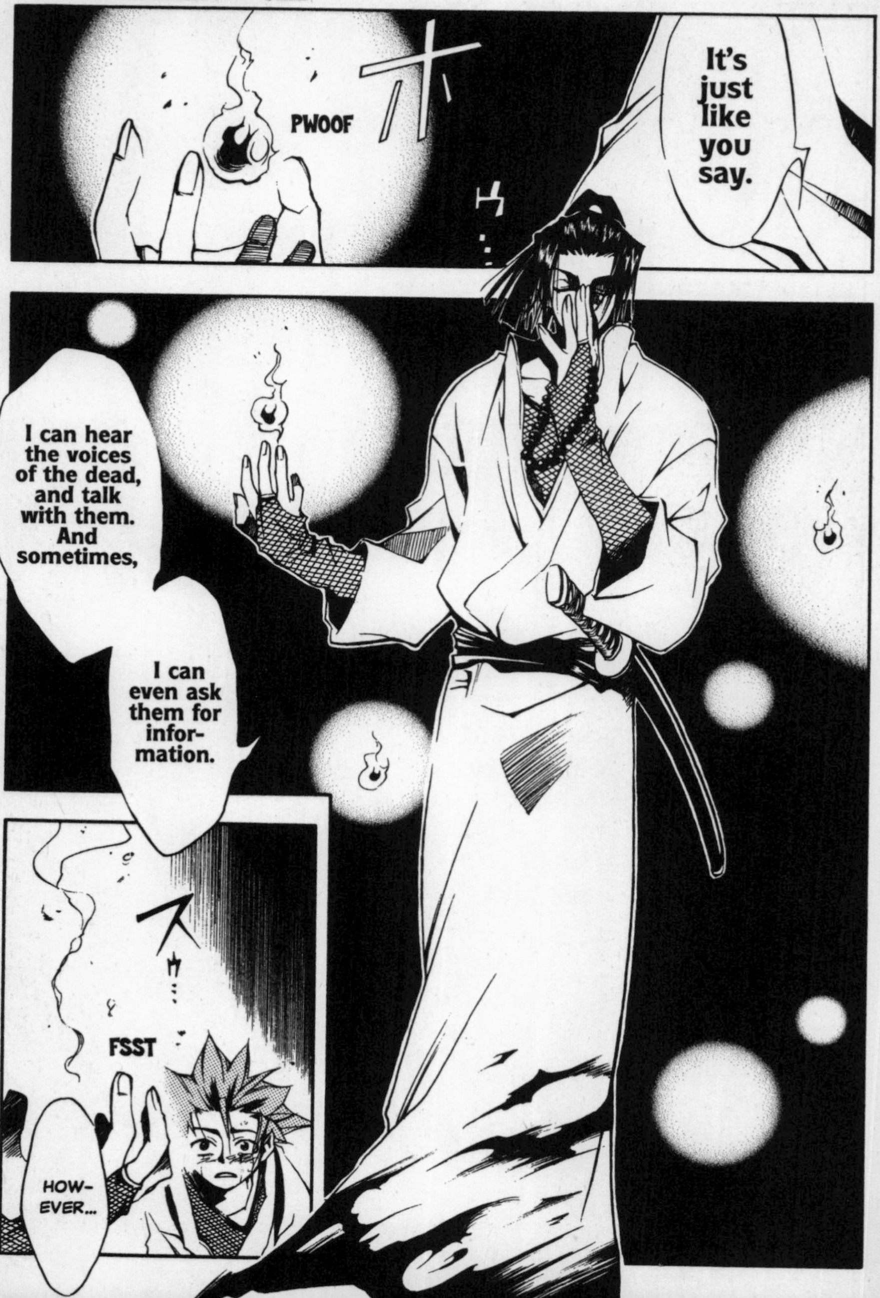
It's just like you say.
PWOOF
I can hear the voices of the dead, and talk with them. And sometimes,
I can even ask them for information.
FSST
HOW-EVER...

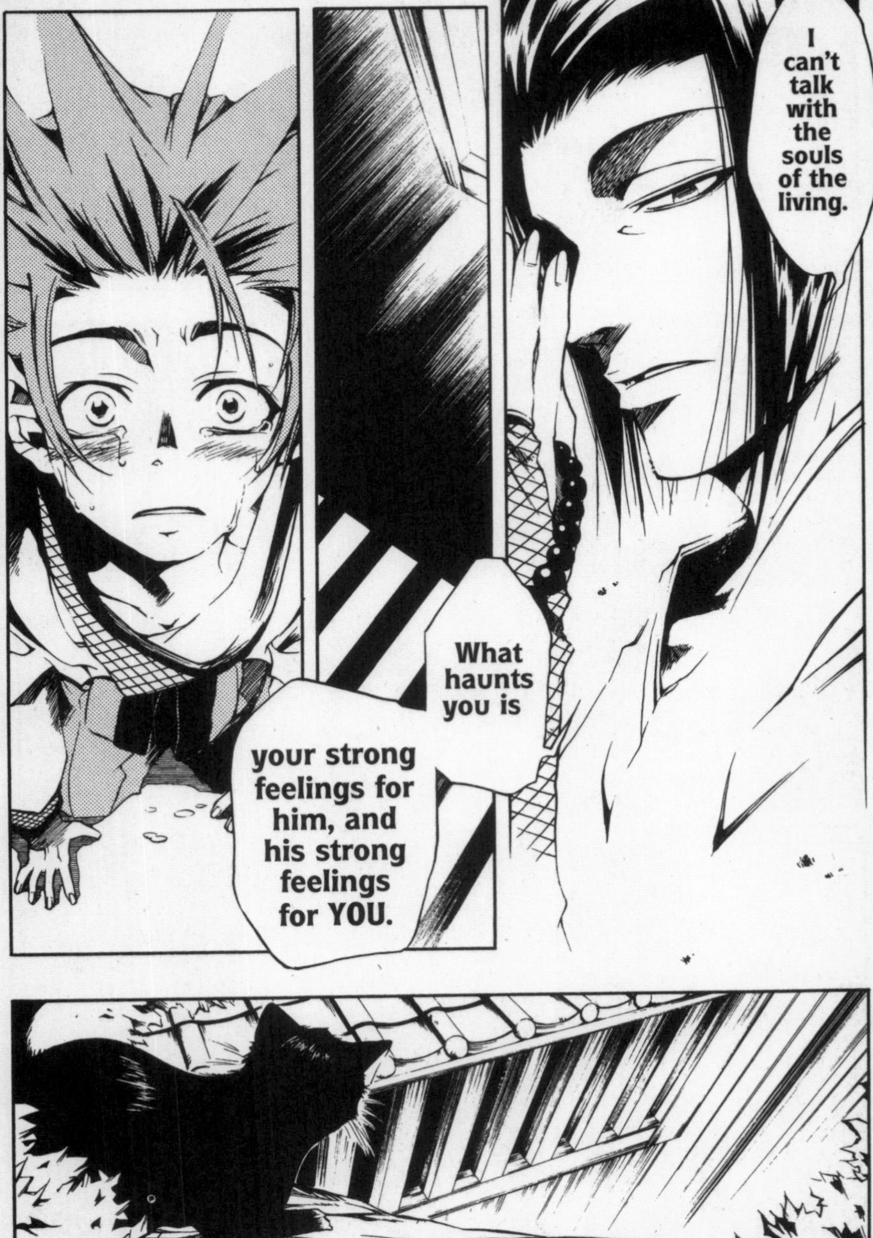
I can't talk with the souls of the living.
What haunts you is
your strong feelings for him, and his strong feelings for YOU.

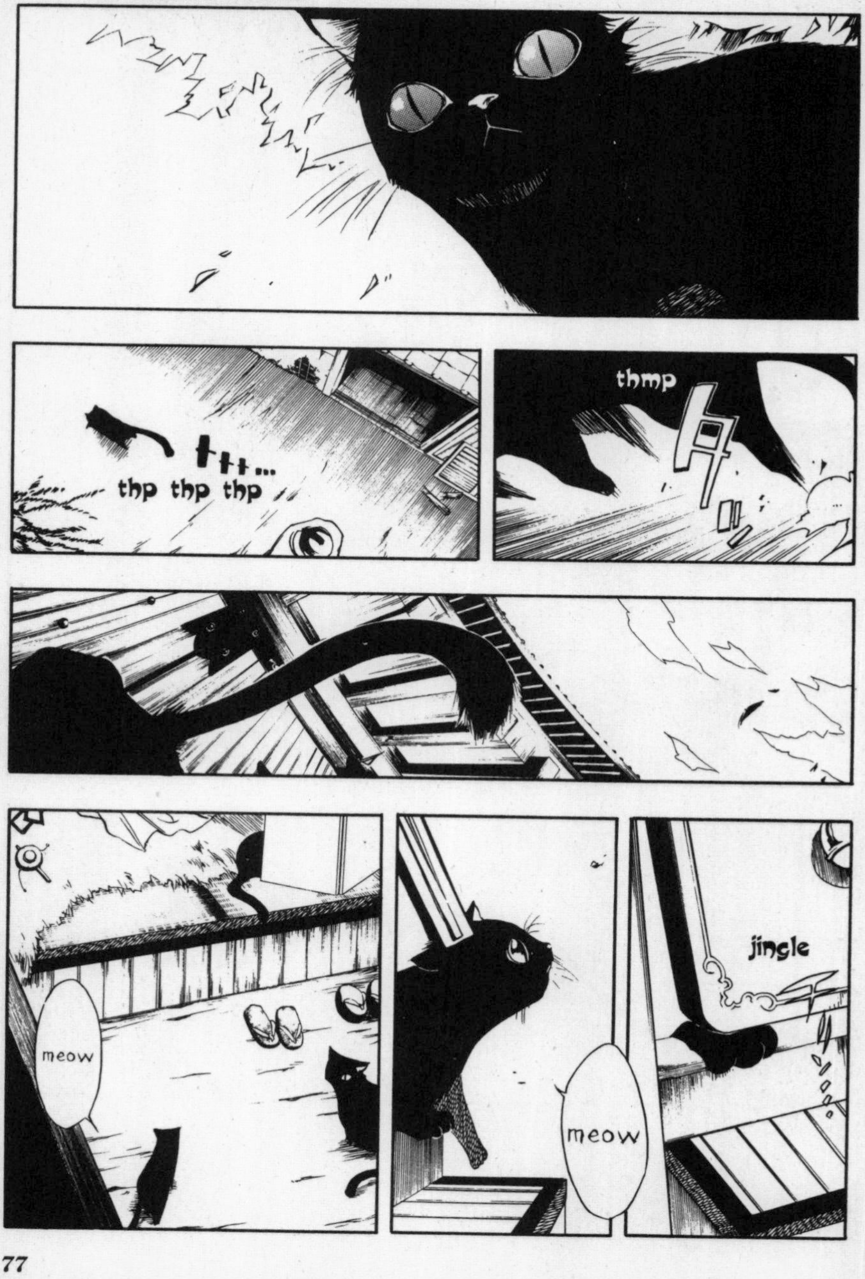
thmp
ttt...
thp thp thp
jingle
meow
meow

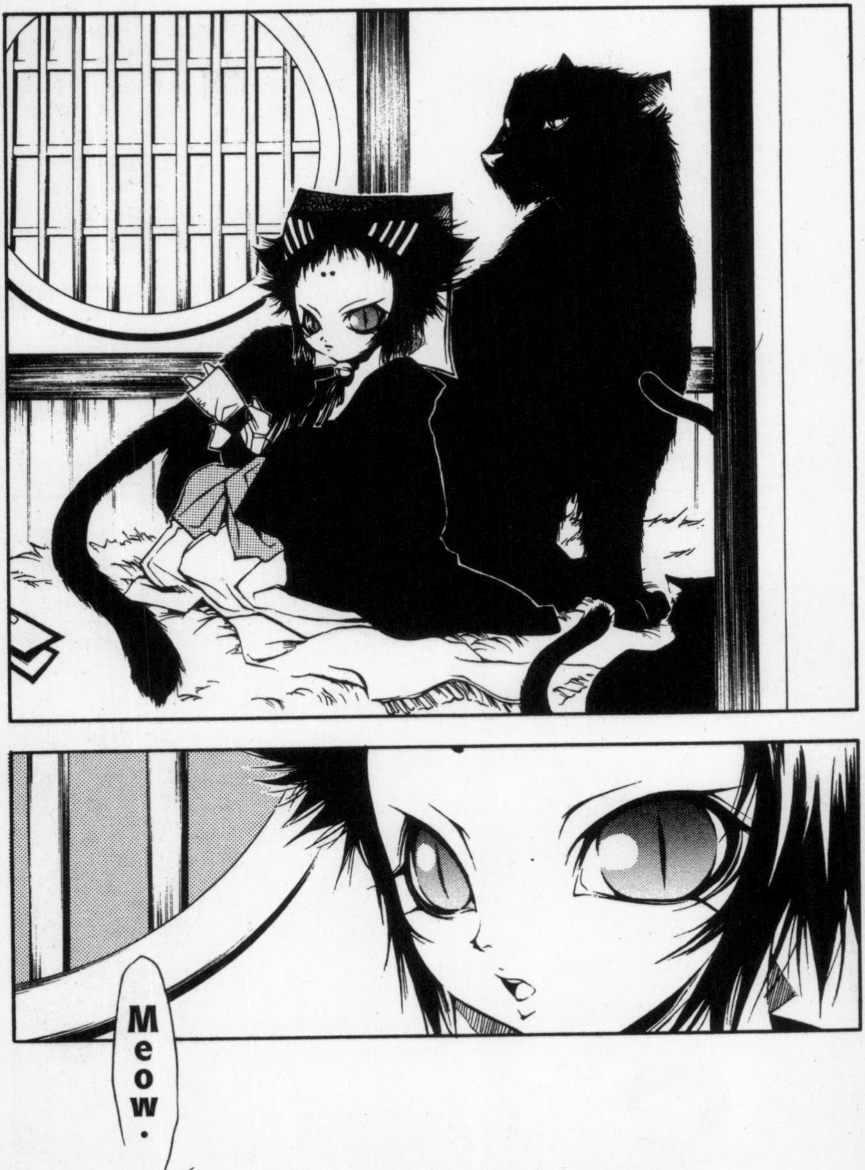
Meow.

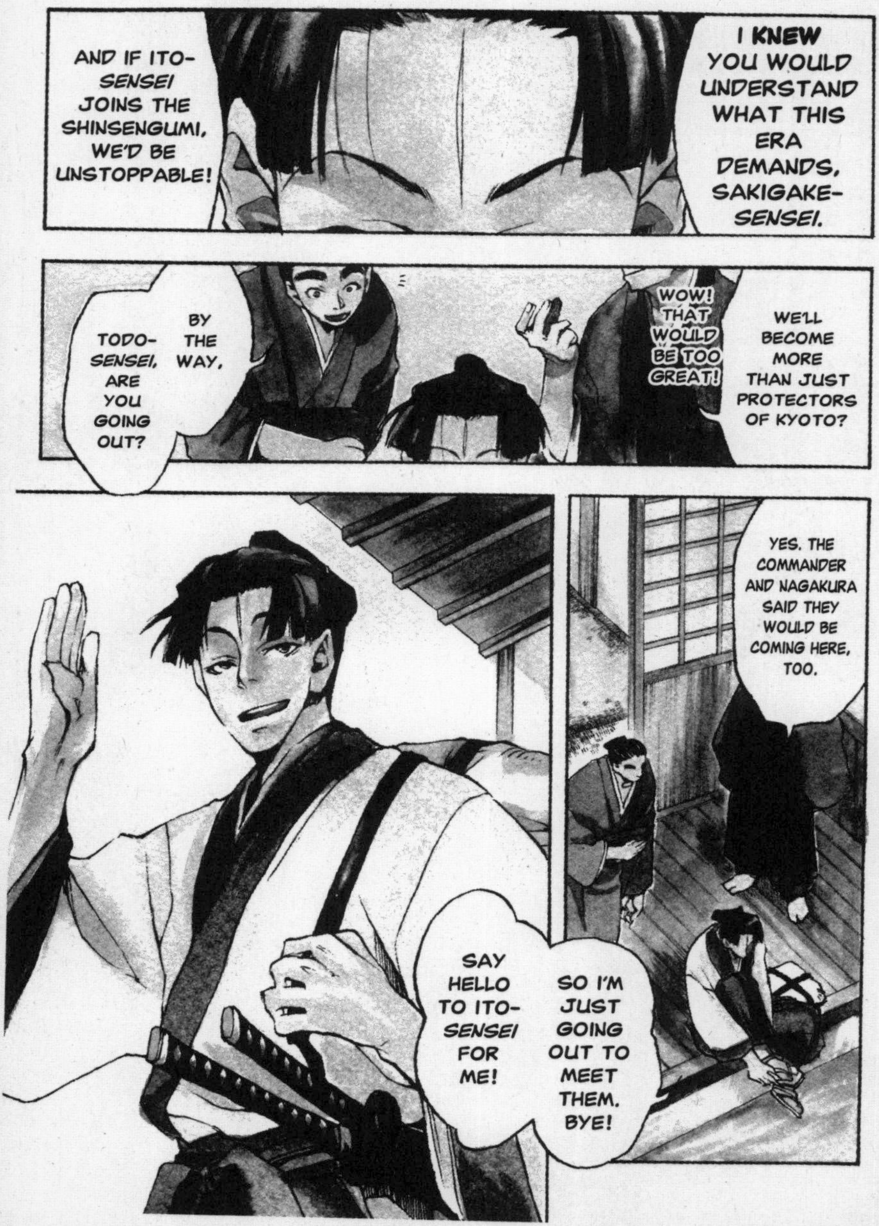
I KNEW YOU WOULD UNDERSTAND WHAT THIS ERA DEMANDS, SAKIGAKE-SENSEI.
AND IF ITO-SENSEI JOINS THE SHINSENGUMI, WE'D BE UNSTOPPABLE!
WE'LL BECOME MORE THAN JUST PROTECTORS OF KYOTO?
WOW! THAT WOULD BE TOO GREAT!
BY THE WAY,
TODO-SENSEI, ARE YOU GOING OUT?
YES. THE COMMANDER AND NAGAKURA SAID THEY WOULD BE COMING HERE, TOO.
SO I'M JUST GOING OUT TO MEET THEM. BYE!
SAY HELLO TO ITO-SENSEI FOR ME!

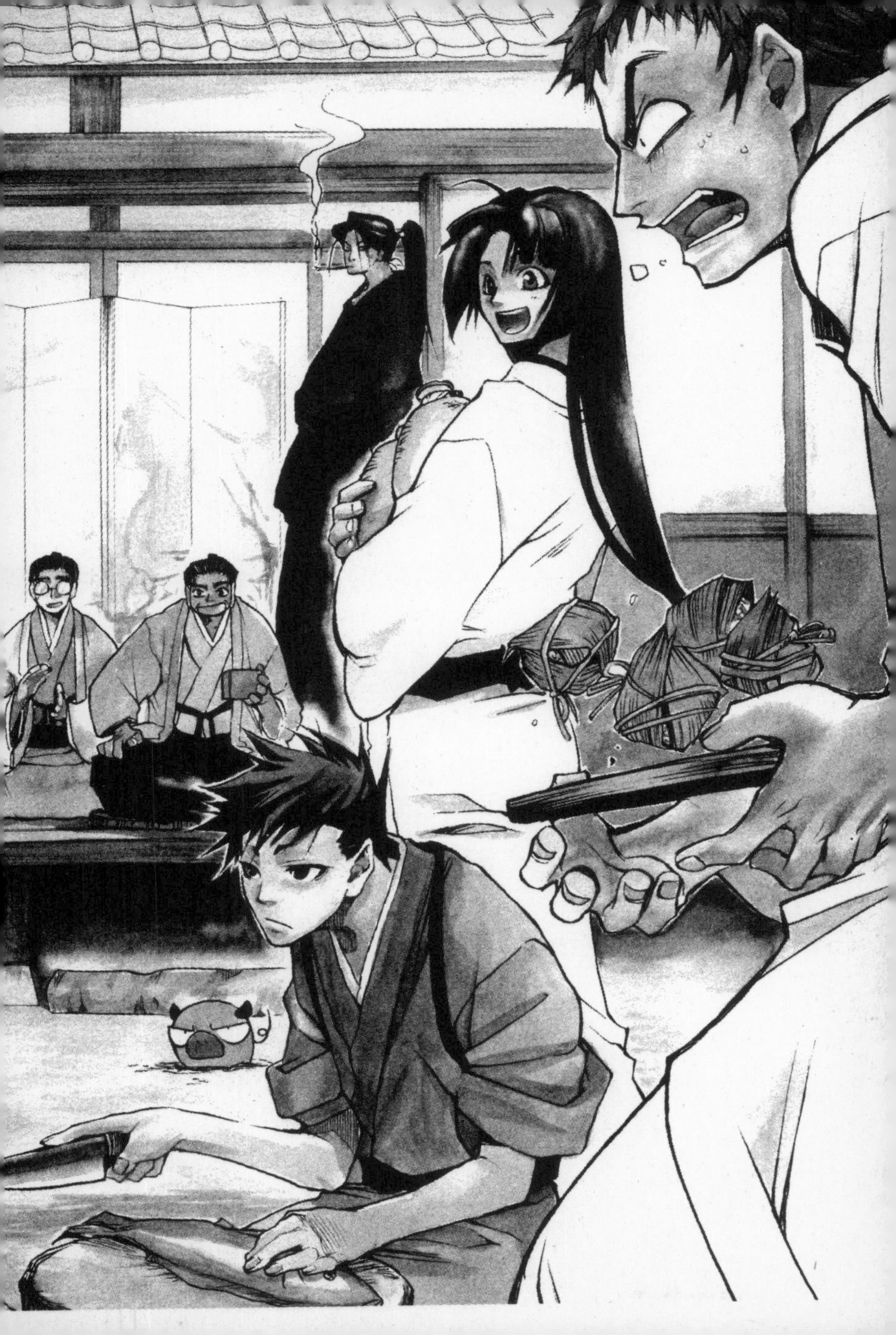

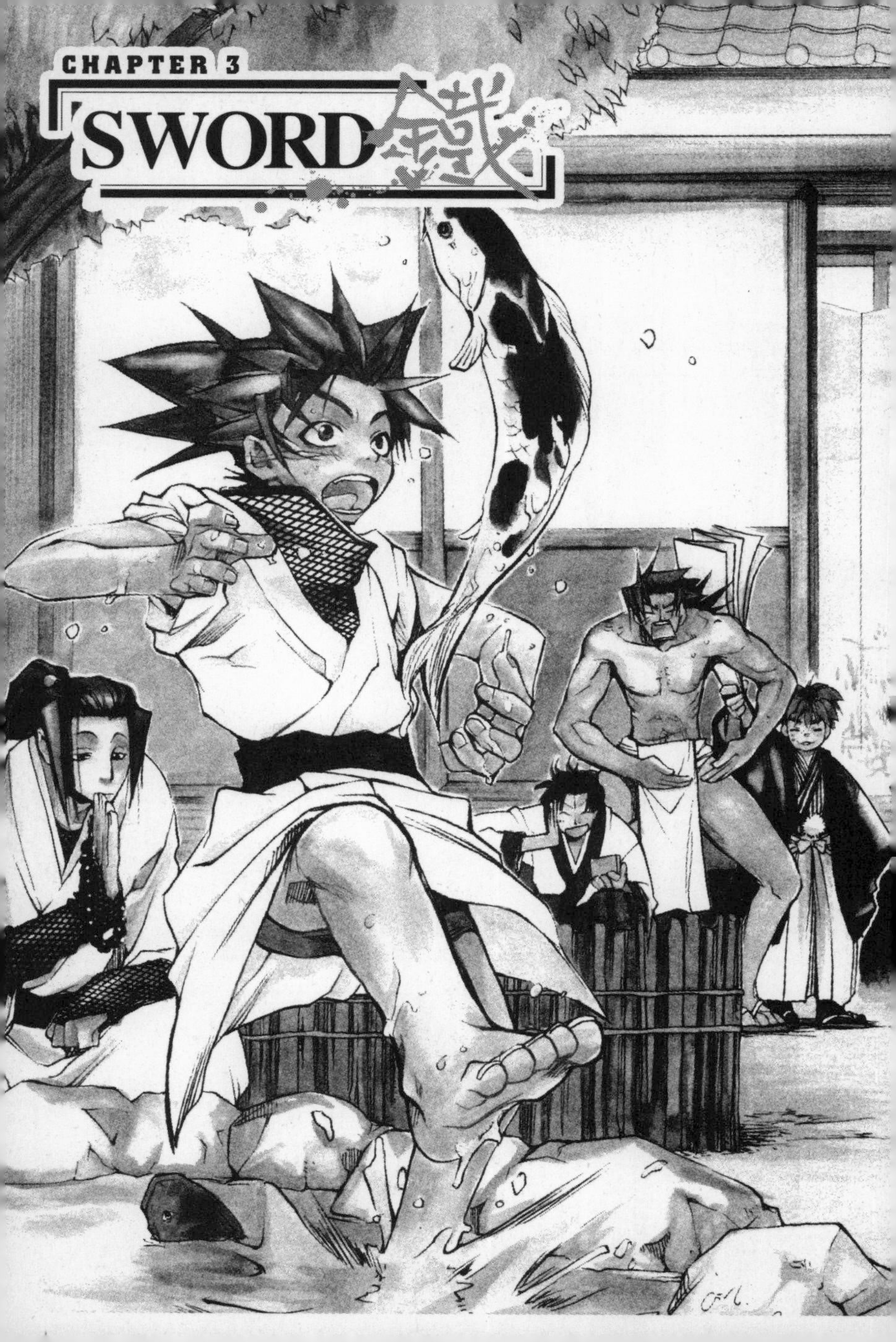
CHAPTER 3
SWORD

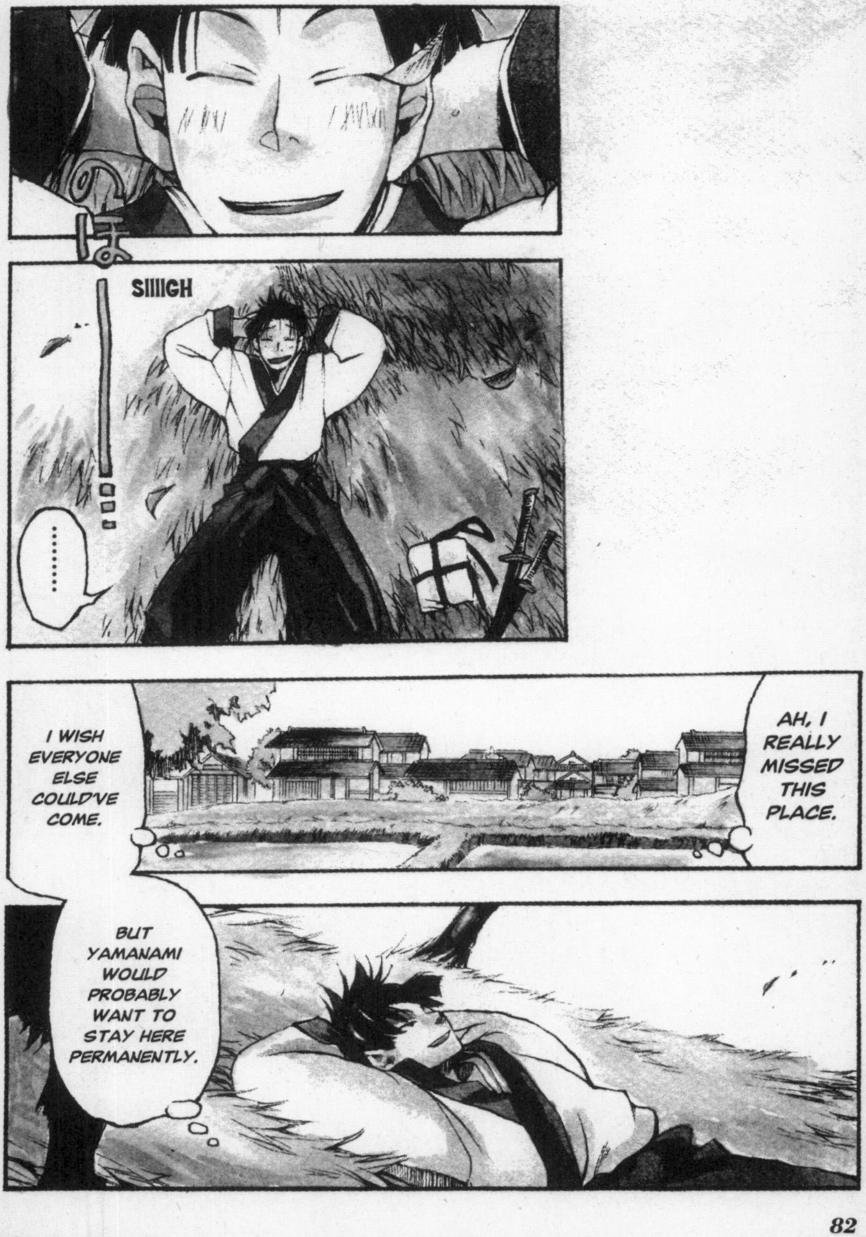
SIIIIGH
......
AH, I REALLY MISSED THIS PLACE.
I WISH EVERYONE ELSE COULD'VE COME.
BUT YAMANAMI WOULD PROBABLY WANT TO STAY HERE PERMANENTLY.

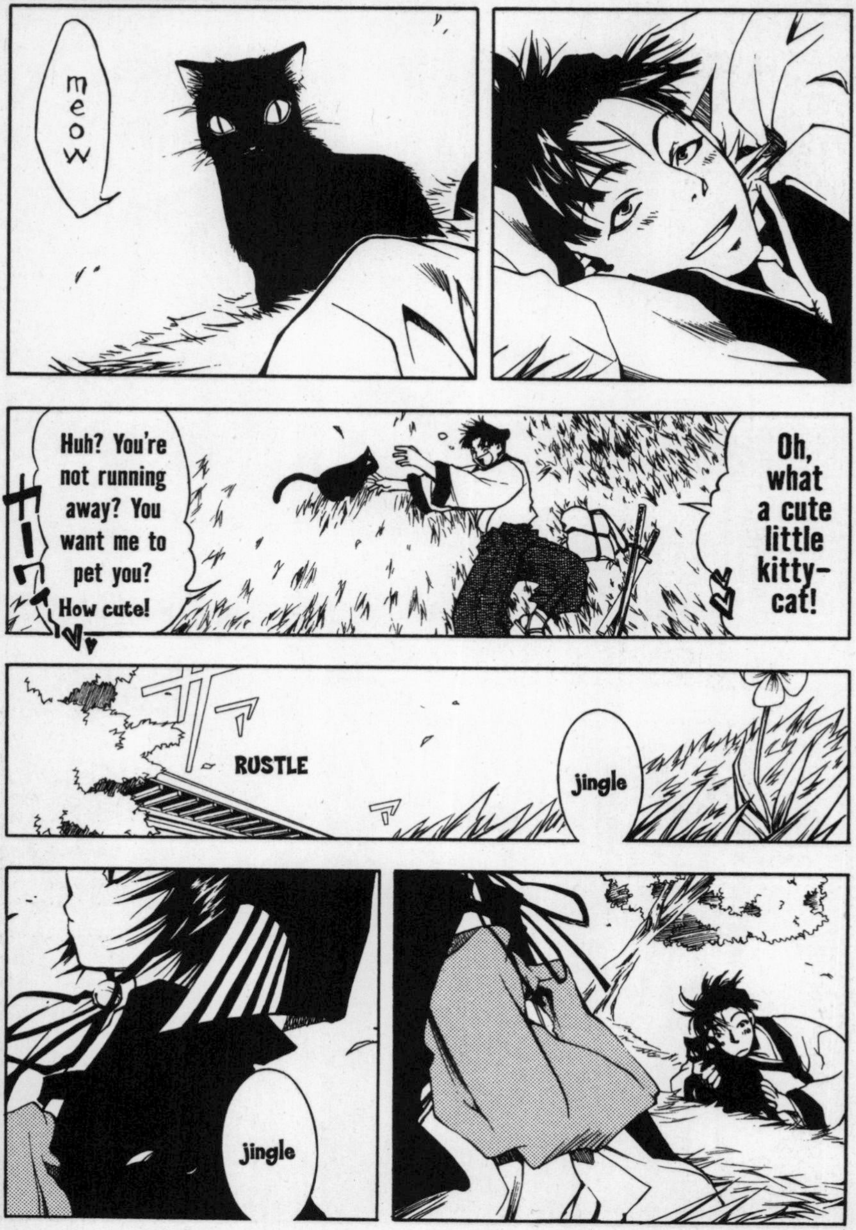
meow
Oh, what a cute little kitty-cat!
Huh? You're not running away? You want me to pet you? How cute!
jingle
RUSTLE
jingle

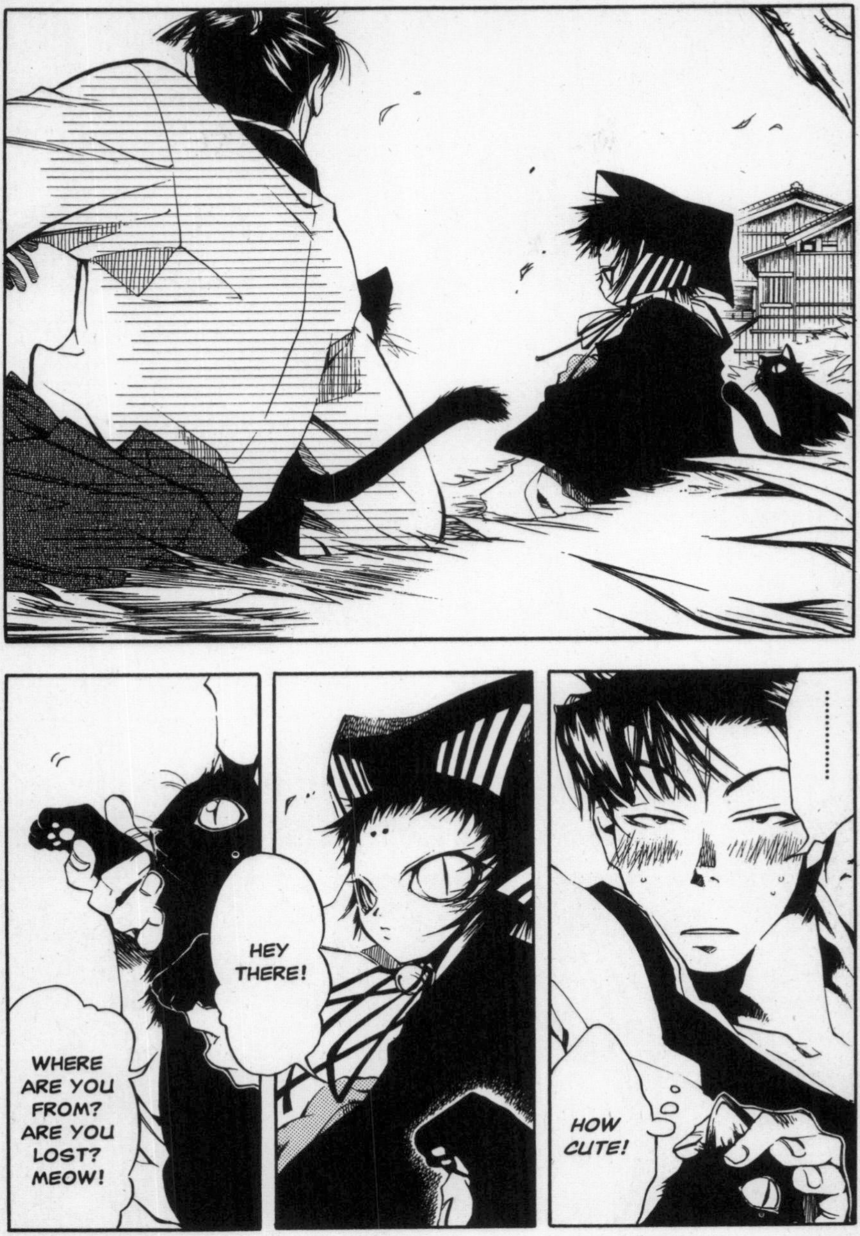

......
HOW CUTE!
HEY THERE!
WHERE ARE YOU FROM? ARE YOU LOST? MEOW!

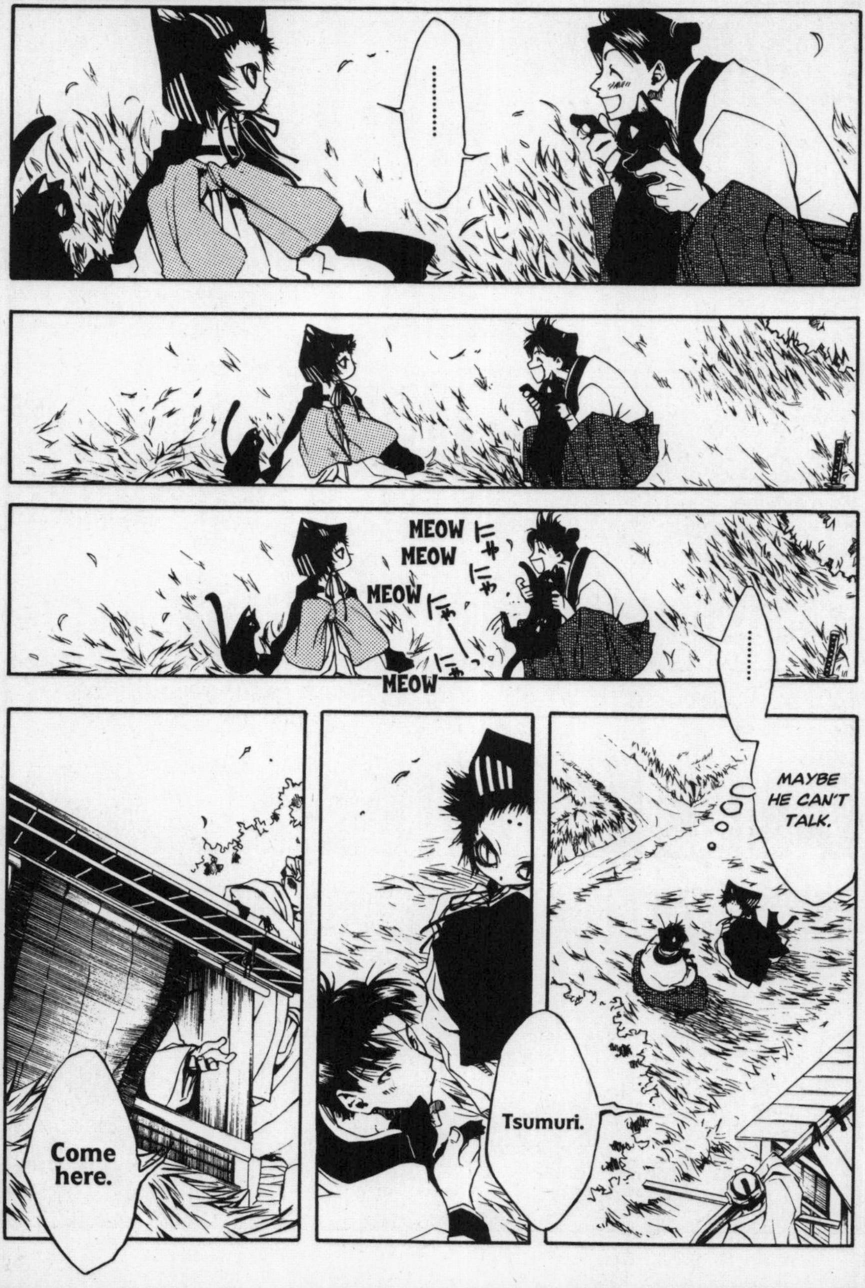
......
MEOW
MEOW
MEOW
MEOW
......
MAYBE HE CAN'T TALK.
Tsumuri.
Come here.

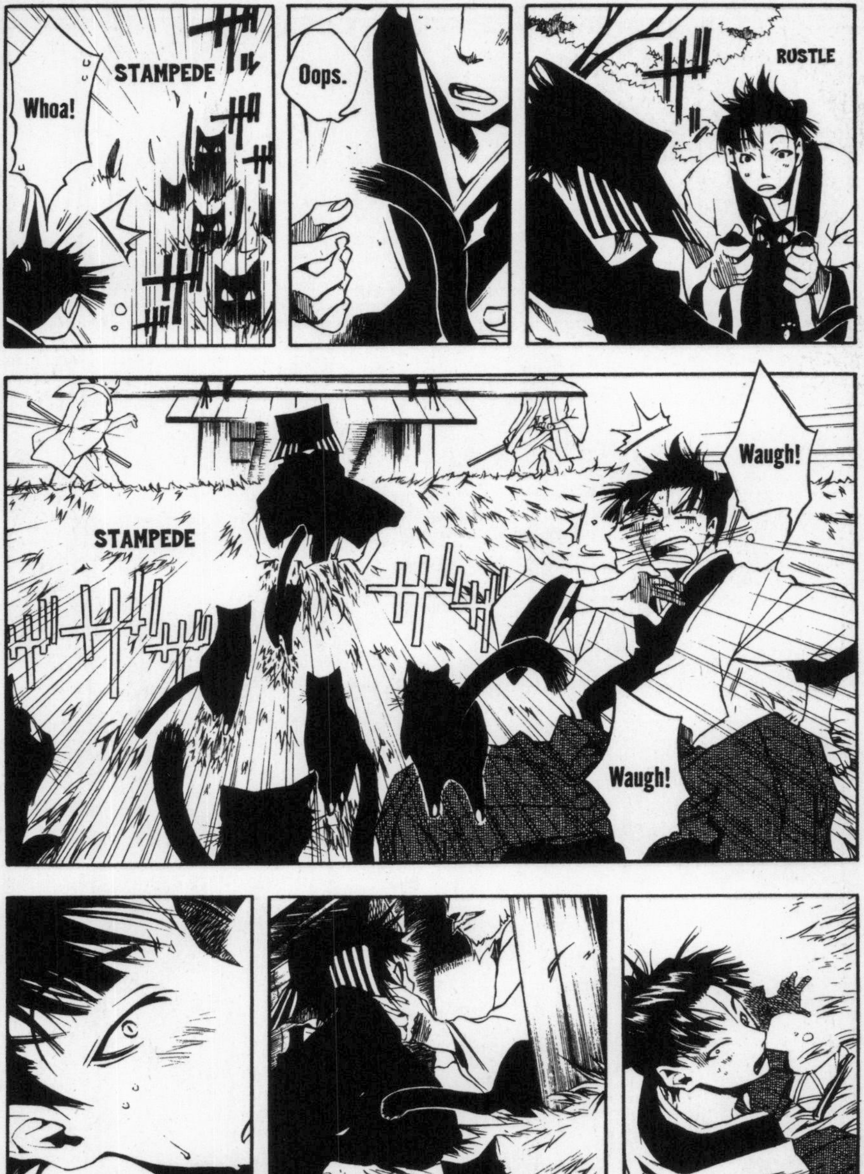
RUSTLE
Oops.
Whoa!
STAMPEDE
Waugh!
Waugh!
STAMPEDE

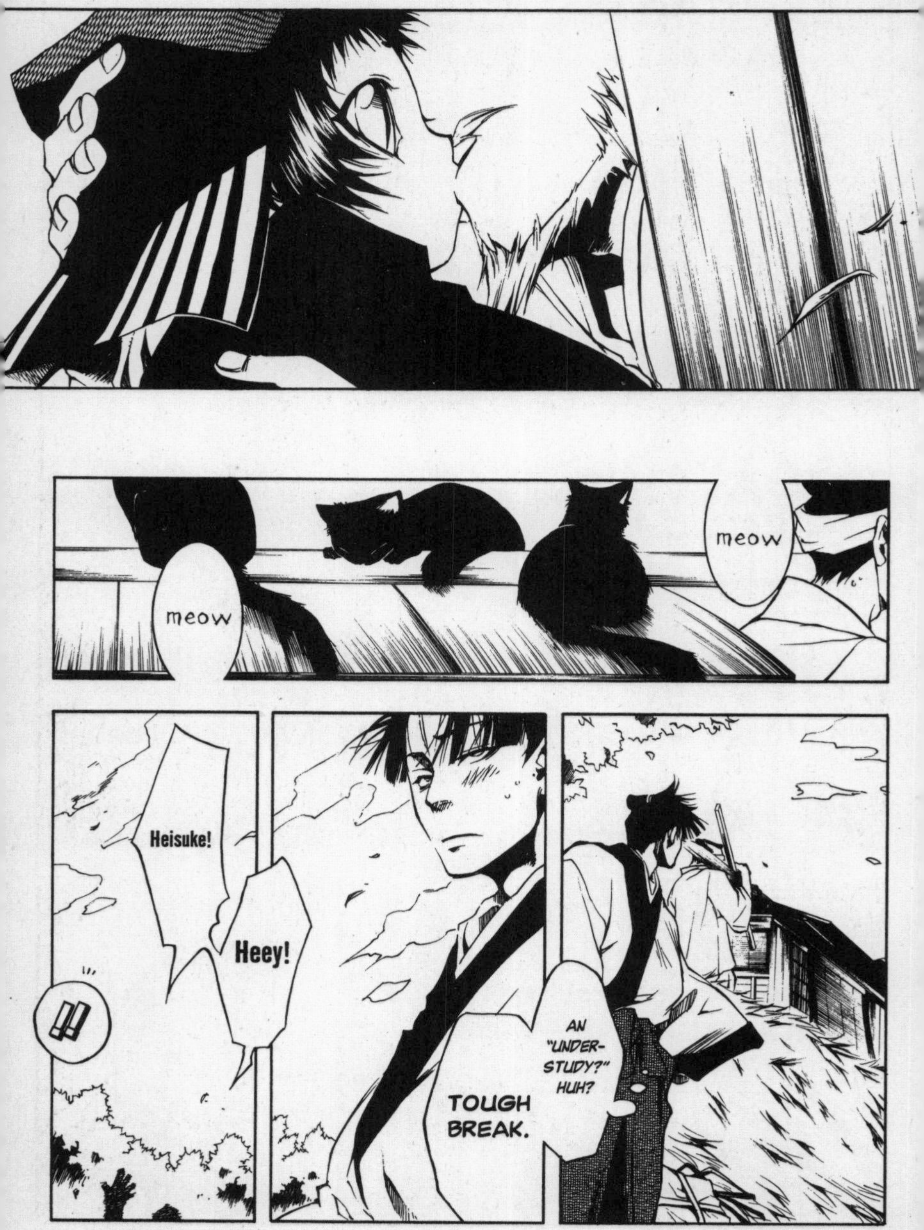
meow
meow
AN "UNDER-STUDY?" HUH?
TOUGH BREAK.
Heisuke!
Heey!
!!

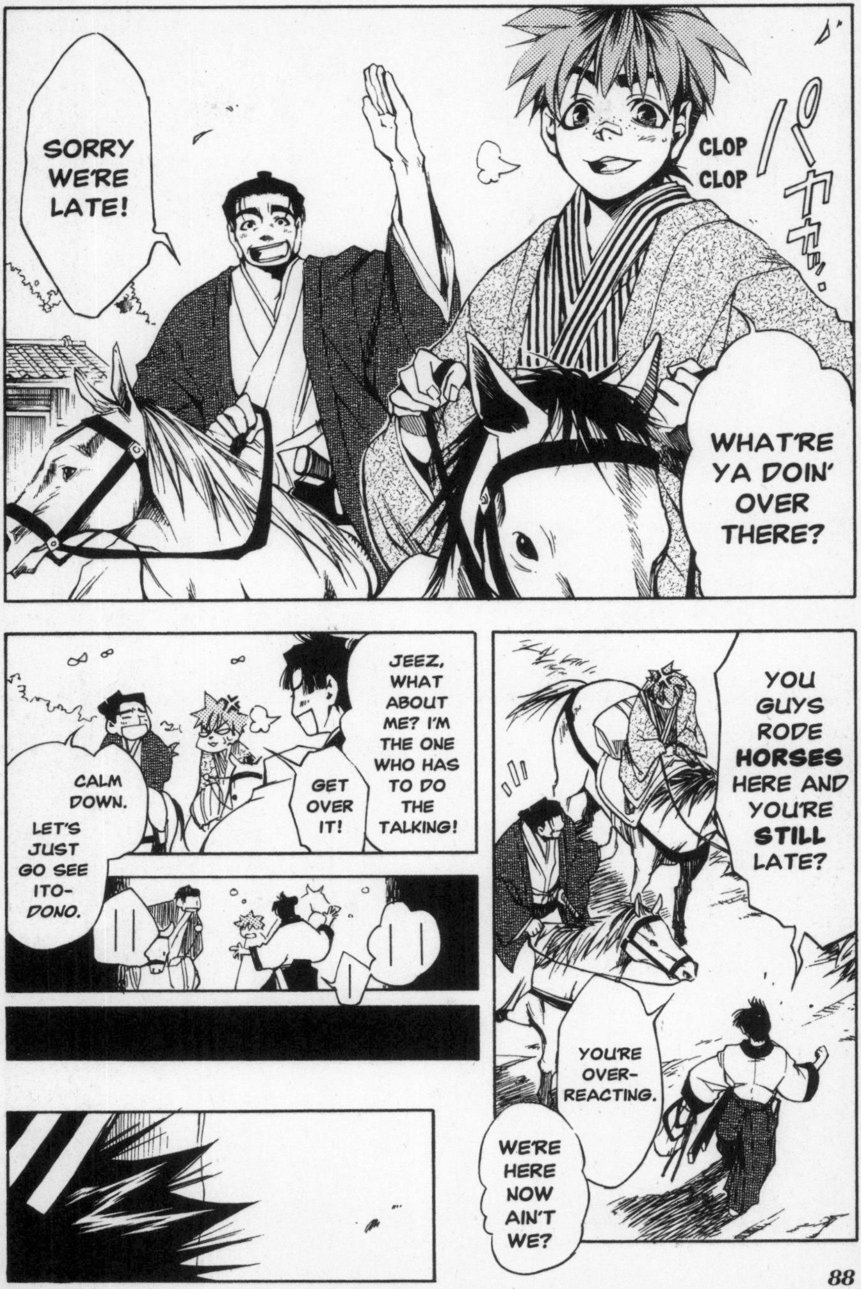

CLOP CLOP
SORRY WE'RE LATE!
WHAT'RE YA DOIN' OVER THERE?
YOU GUYS RODE **HORSES** HERE AND YOU'RE **STILL** LATE?
YOU'RE OVER-REACTING.
WE'RE HERE NOW AIN'T WE?
JEEZ, WHAT ABOUT ME? I'M THE ONE WHO HAS TO DO THE TALKING!
GET OVER IT!
CALM DOWN.
LET'S JUST GO SEE ITO-DONO.

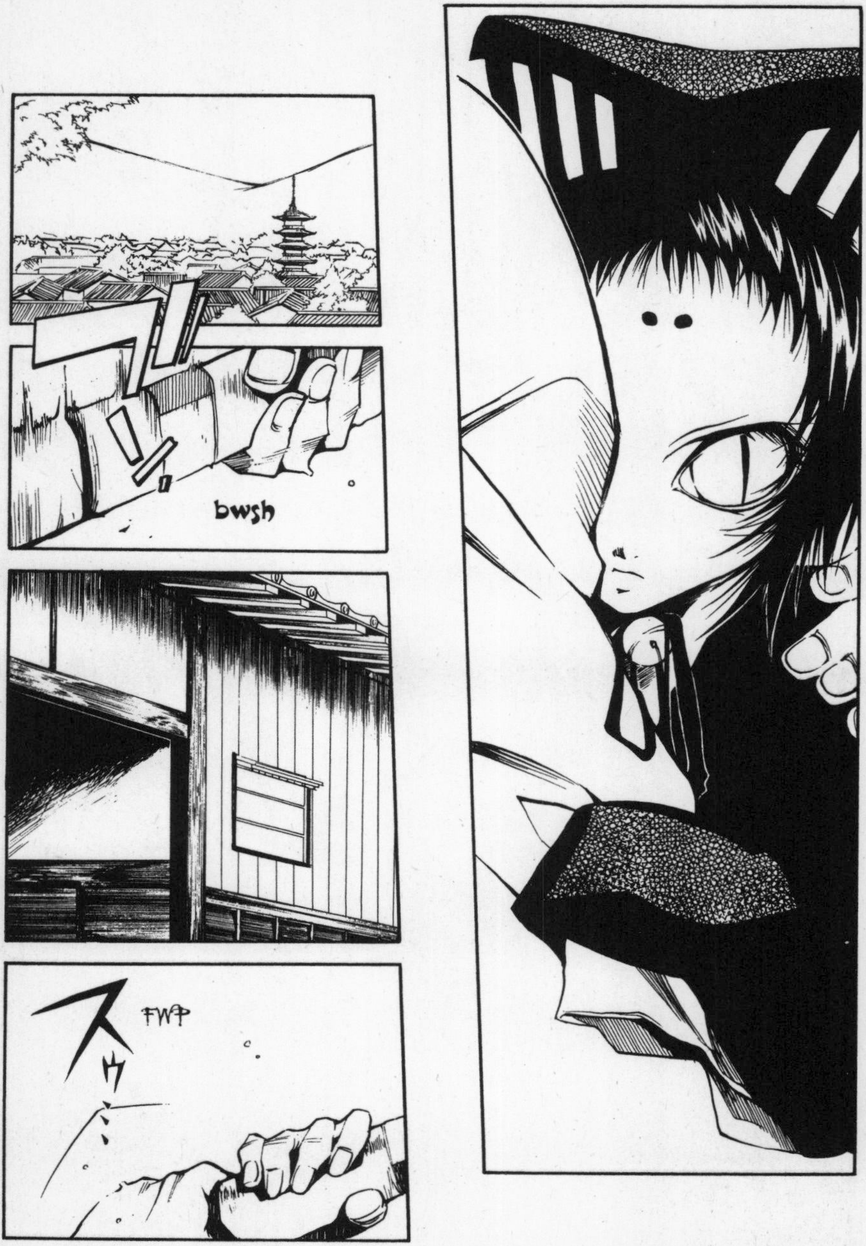
bwsh
スゥ…
FWP

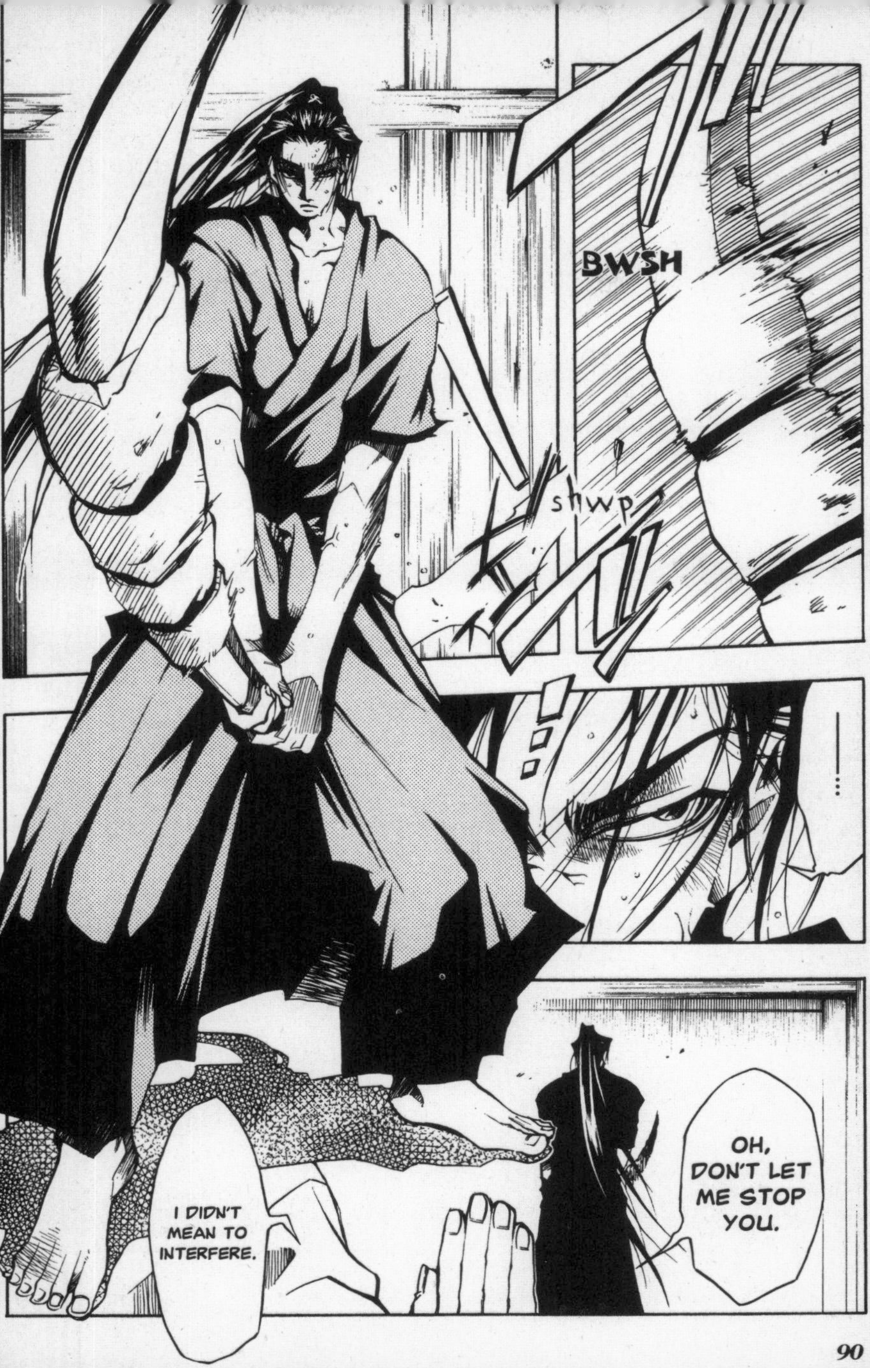
BWSH
shwp
!
...
OH, DON'T LET ME STOP YOU.
I DIDN'T MEAN TO INTERFERE.

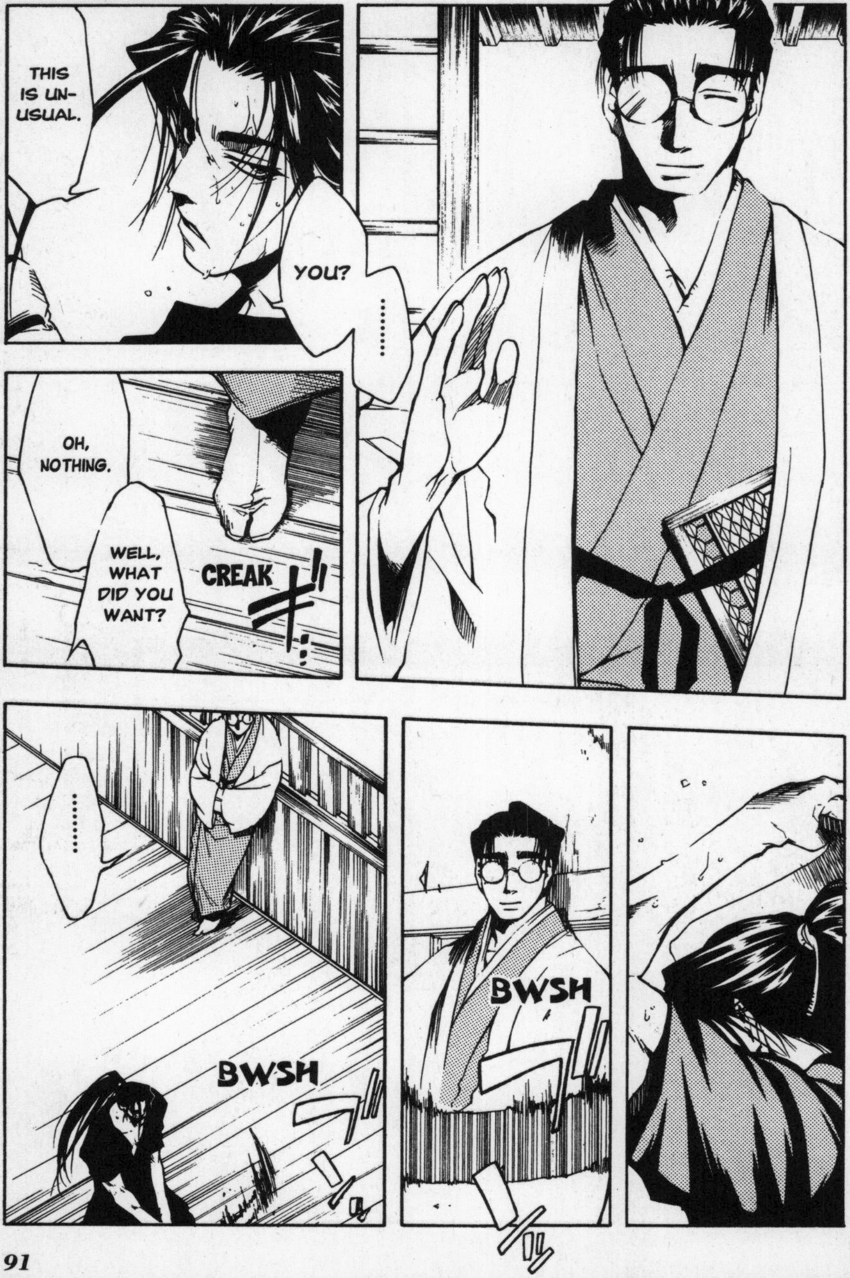
YOU?
......
THIS IS UN-USUAL.
OH, NOTHING.
WELL, WHAT DID YOU WANT?
CREAK
BWSH
......
BWSH

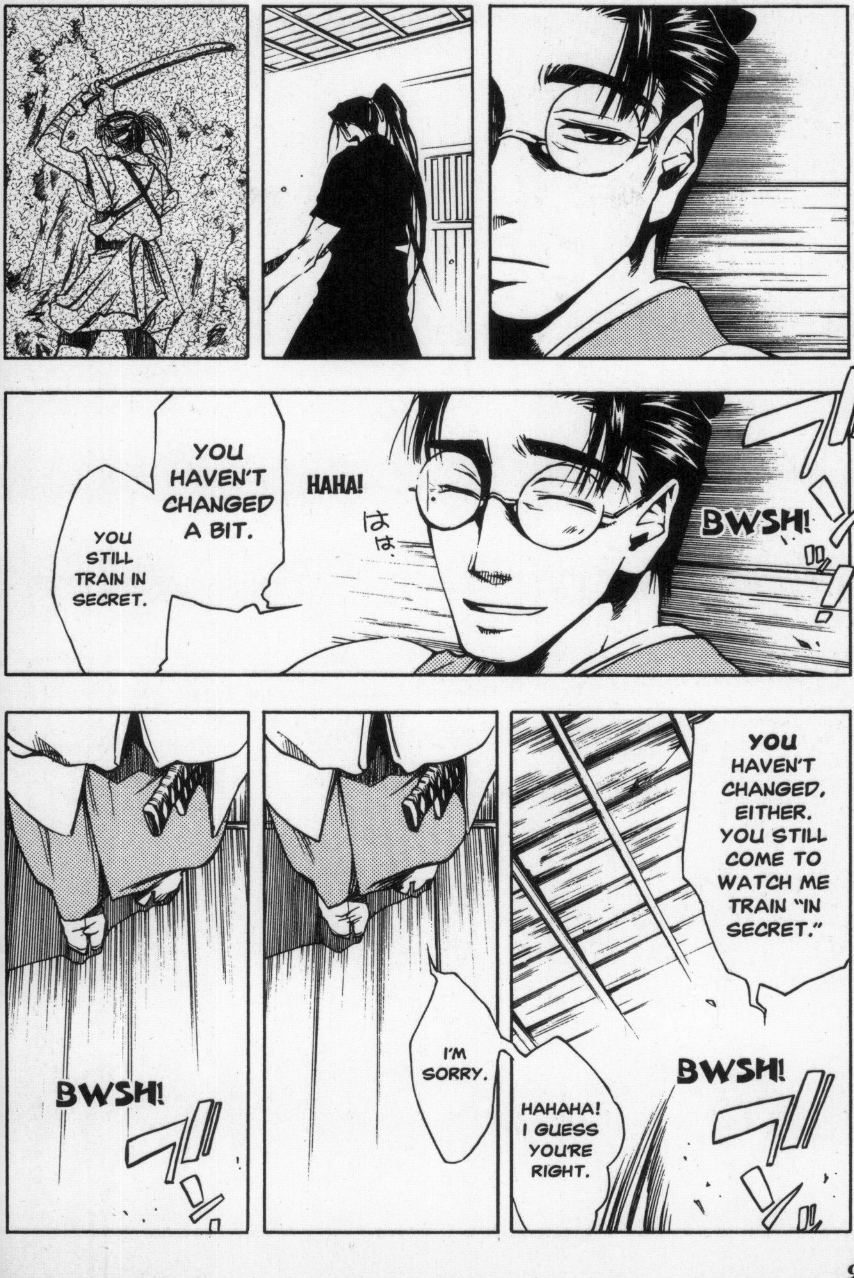
BWSH!
HAHA!
はは
YOU HAVEN'T CHANGED A BIT.
YOU STILL TRAIN IN SECRET.
YOU HAVEN'T CHANGED, EITHER. YOU STILL COME TO WATCH ME TRAIN "IN SECRET."
BWSH!
HAHAHA! I GUESS YOU'RE RIGHT.
I'M SORRY.
BWSH!

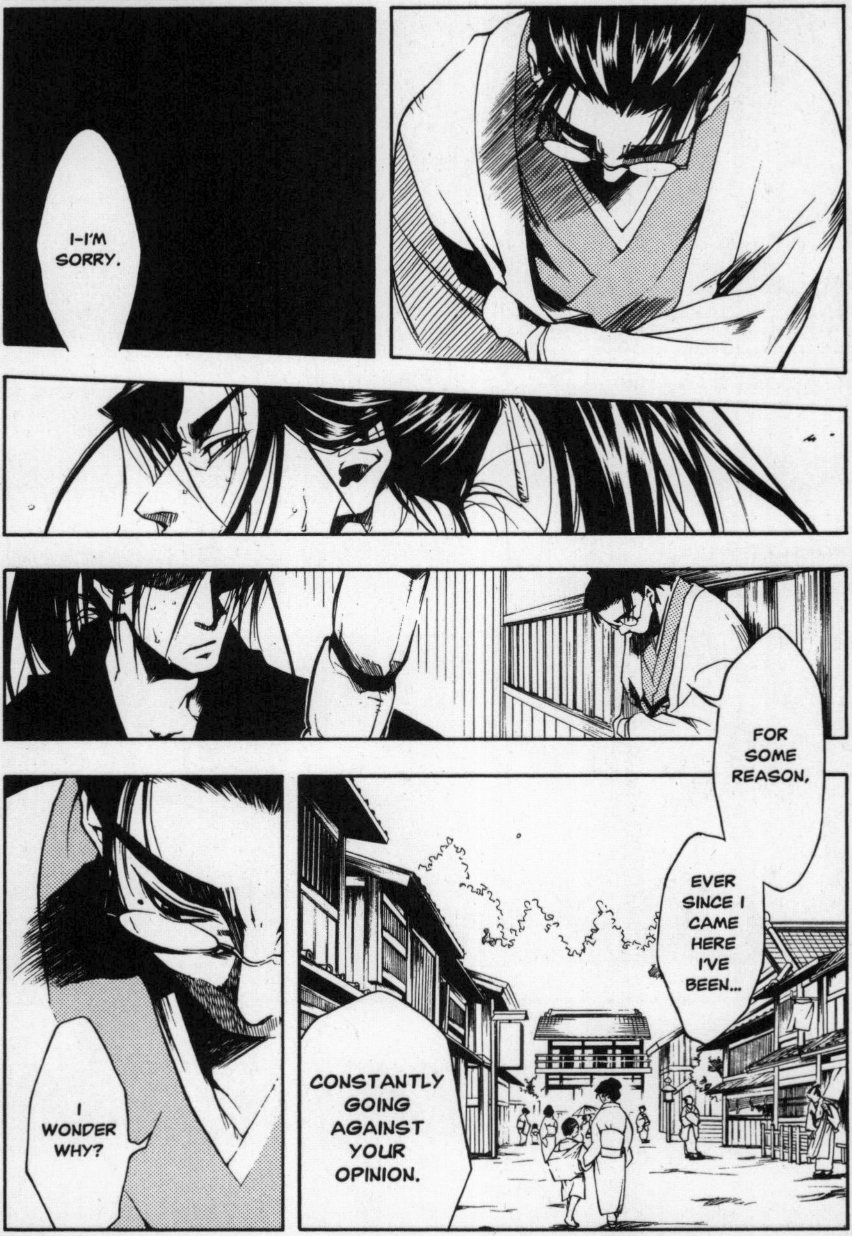
I-I'M SORRY.
FOR SOME REASON,
EVER SINCE I CAME HERE I'VE BEEN...
CONSTANTLY GOING AGAINST YOUR OPINION.
I WONDER WHY?

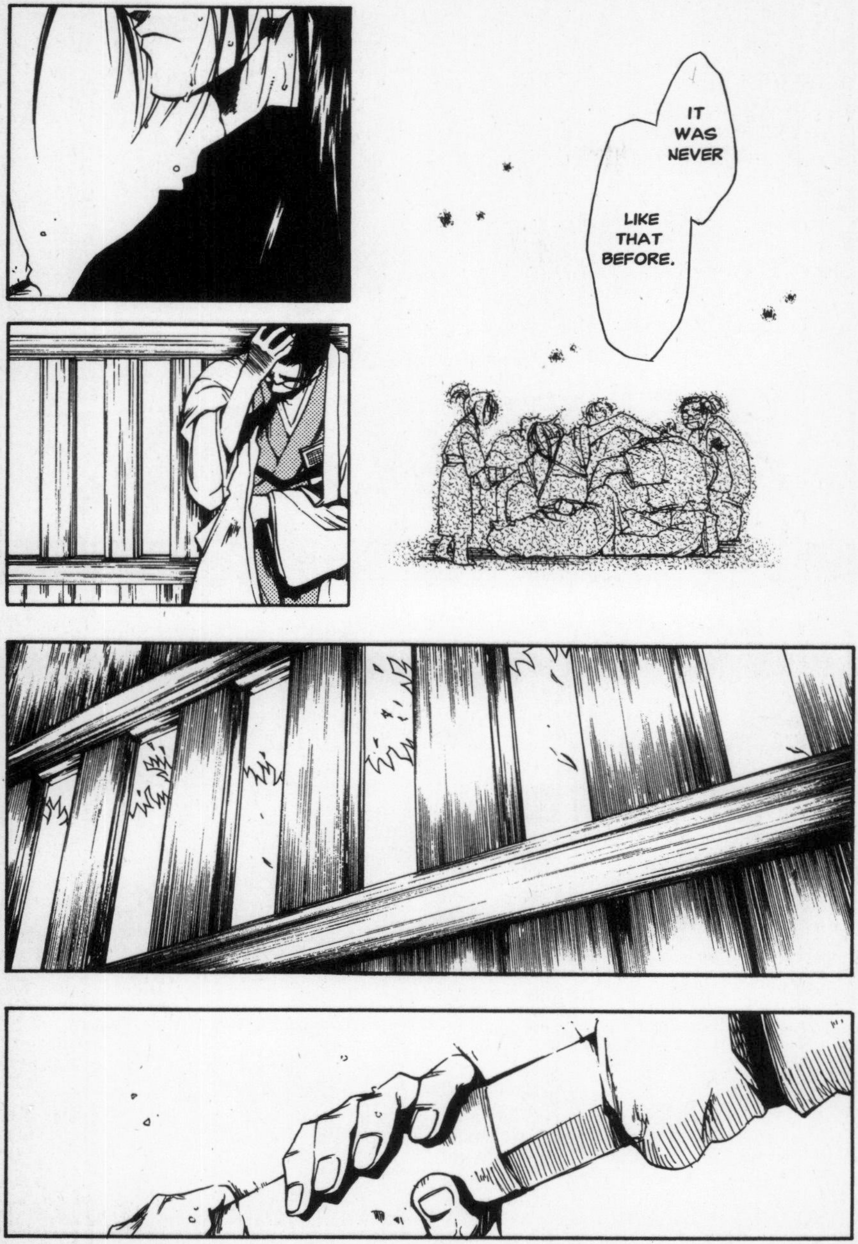
IT WAS NEVER LIKE THAT BEFORE.

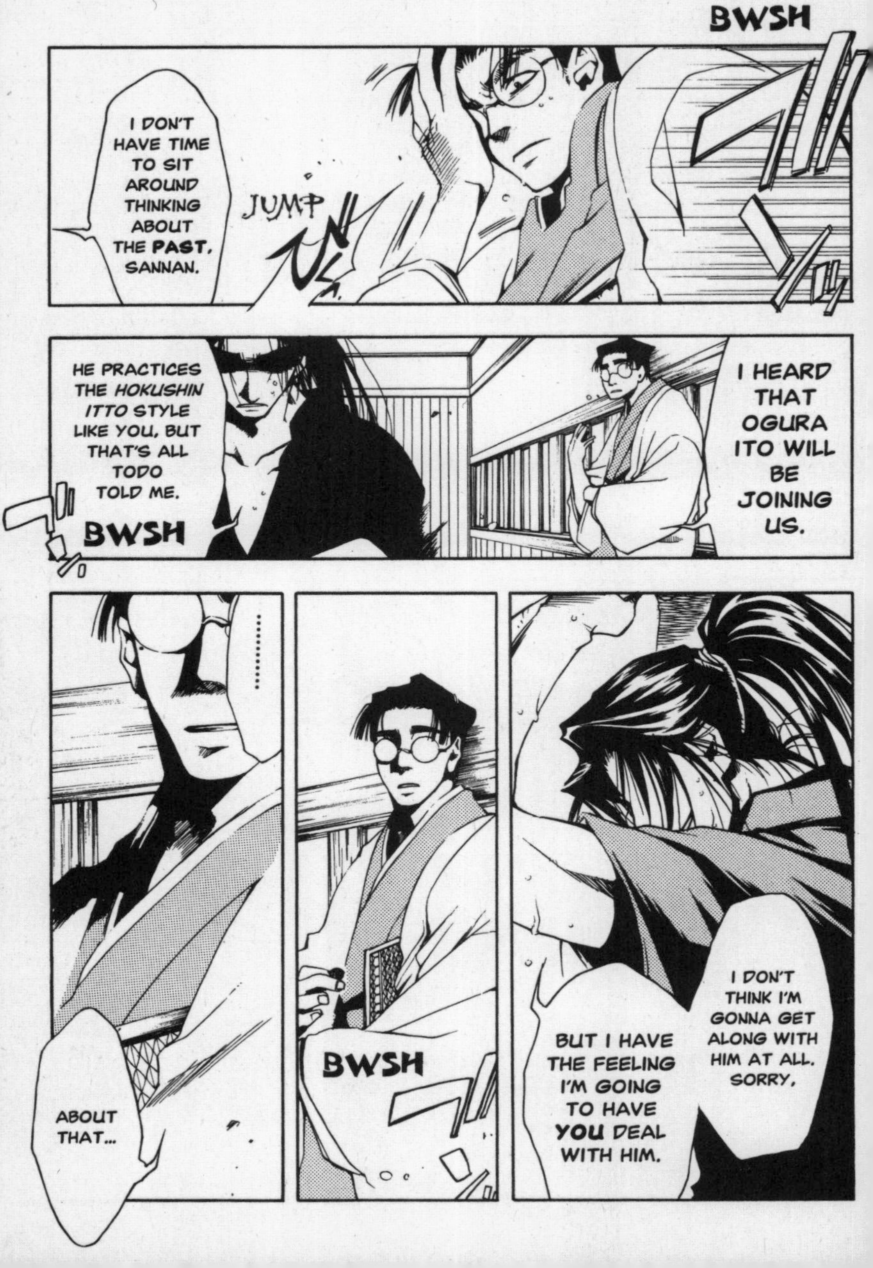
BWSH
I DON'T HAVE TIME TO SIT AROUND THINKING ABOUT THE **PAST**, SANNAN.
JUMP
I HEARD THAT OGURA ITO WILL BE JOINING US.
HE PRACTICES THE *HOKUSHIN ITTO* STYLE LIKE YOU, BUT THAT'S ALL TODO TOLD ME.
BWSH
I DON'T THINK I'M GONNA GET ALONG WITH HIM AT ALL. SORRY,
BUT I HAVE THE FEELING I'M GOING TO HAVE **YOU** DEAL WITH HIM.
BWSH
......
ABOUT THAT...

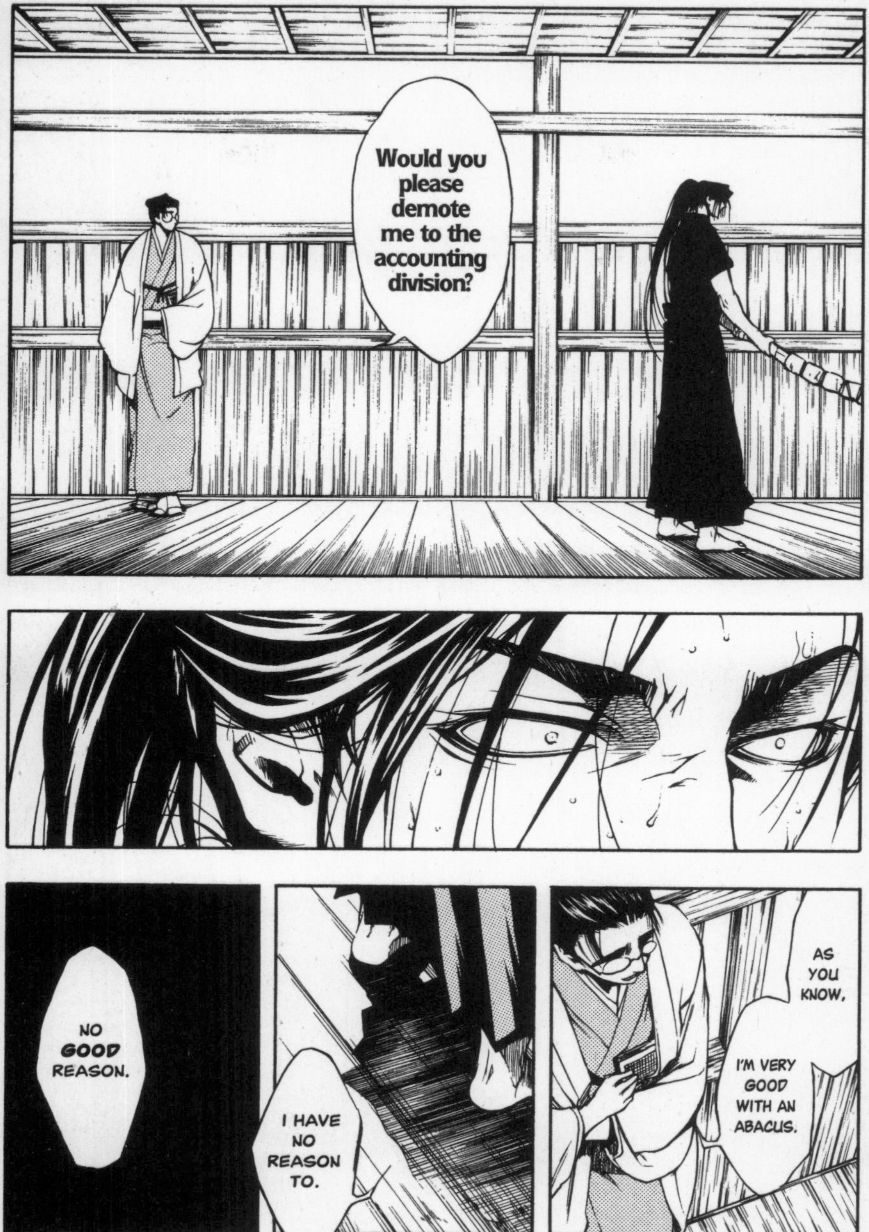
Would you please demote me to the accounting division?
AS YOU KNOW,
I'M VERY GOOD WITH AN ABACUS.
I HAVE NO REASON TO.
NO GOOD REASON.

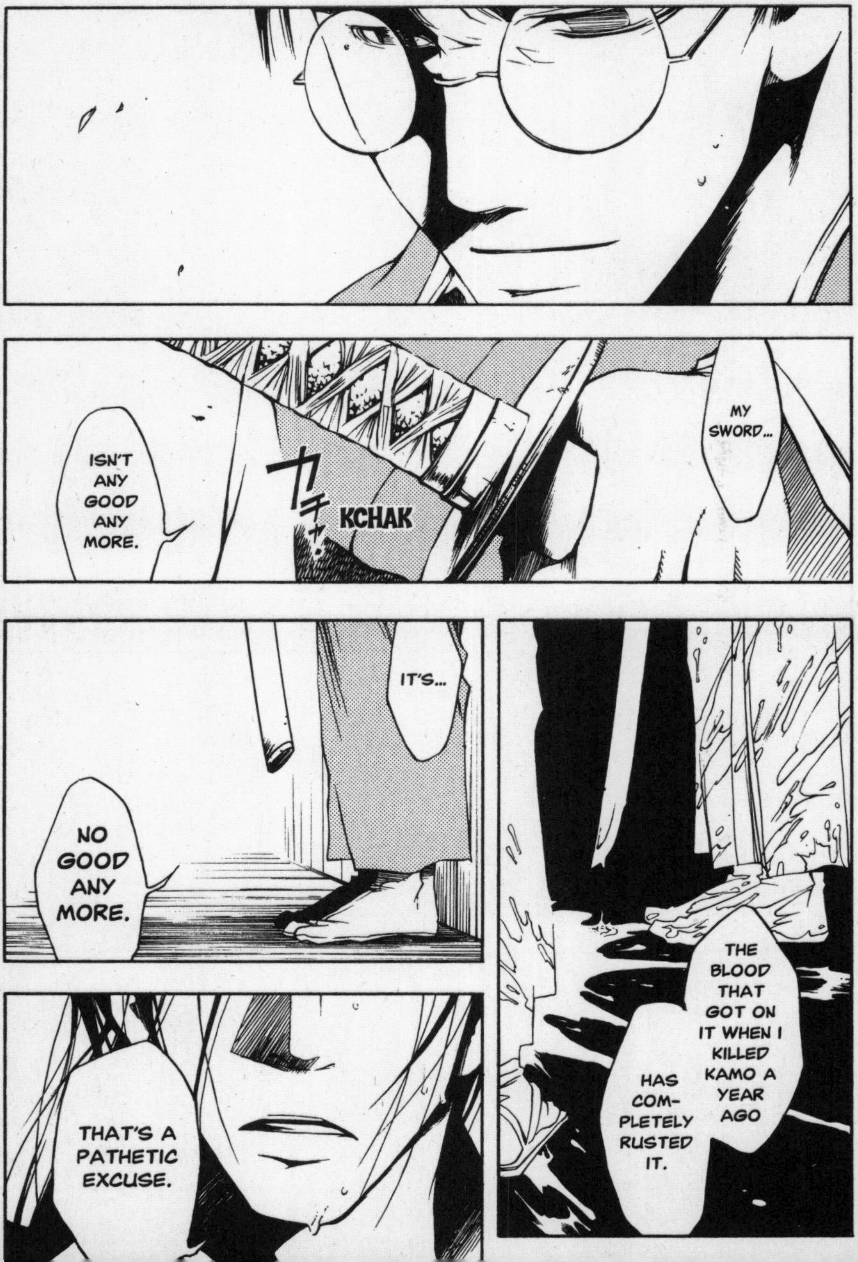
MY SWORD...
KCHAK
ISN'T ANY GOOD ANY MORE.
THE BLOOD THAT GOT ON IT WHEN I KILLED KAMO A YEAR AGO
HAS COM-PLETELY RUSTED IT.
IT'S...
NO GOOD ANY MORE.
THAT'S A PATHETIC EXCUSE.

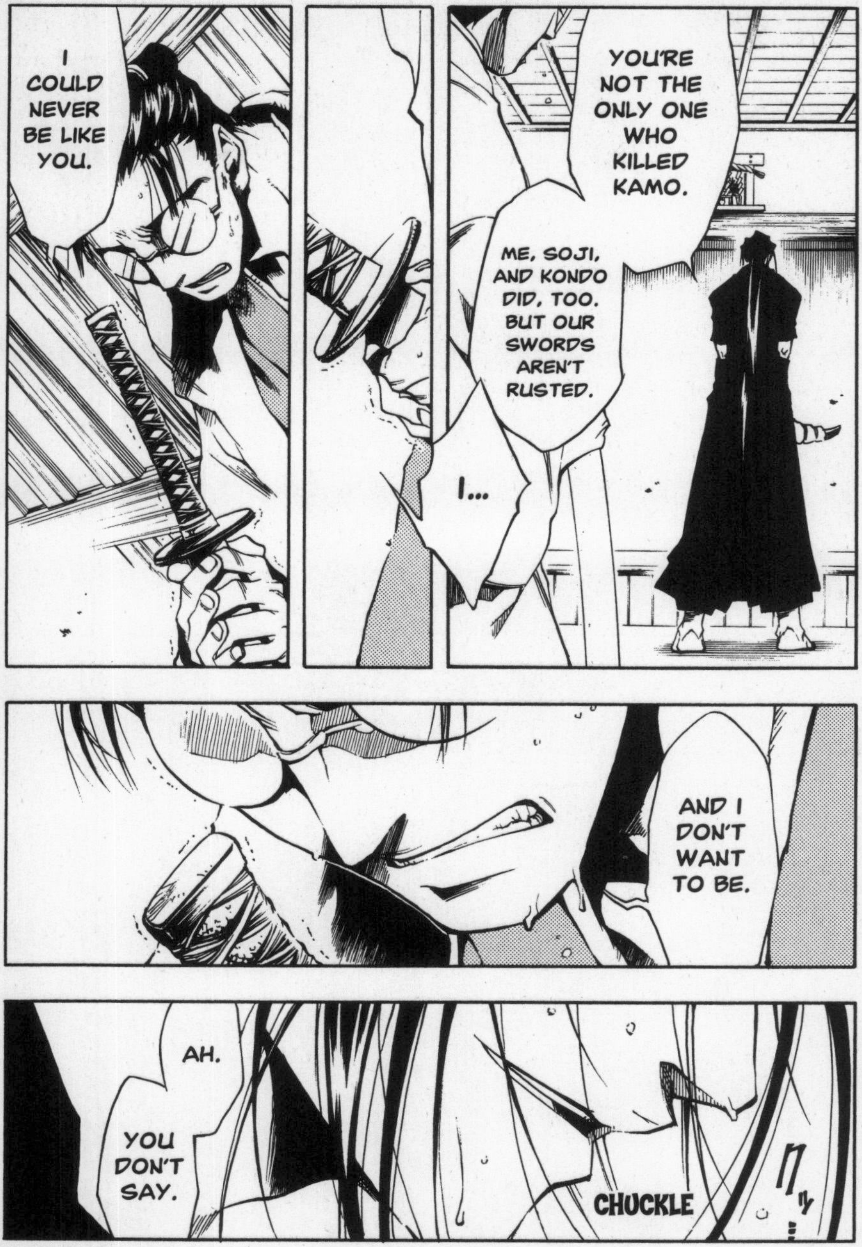
YOU'RE NOT THE ONLY ONE WHO KILLED KAMO.
ME, SOJI, AND KONDO DID, TOO. BUT OUR SWORDS AREN'T RUSTED.
I...
I COULD NEVER BE LIKE YOU.
AND I DON'T WANT TO BE.
CHUCKLE
AH.
YOU DON'T SAY.

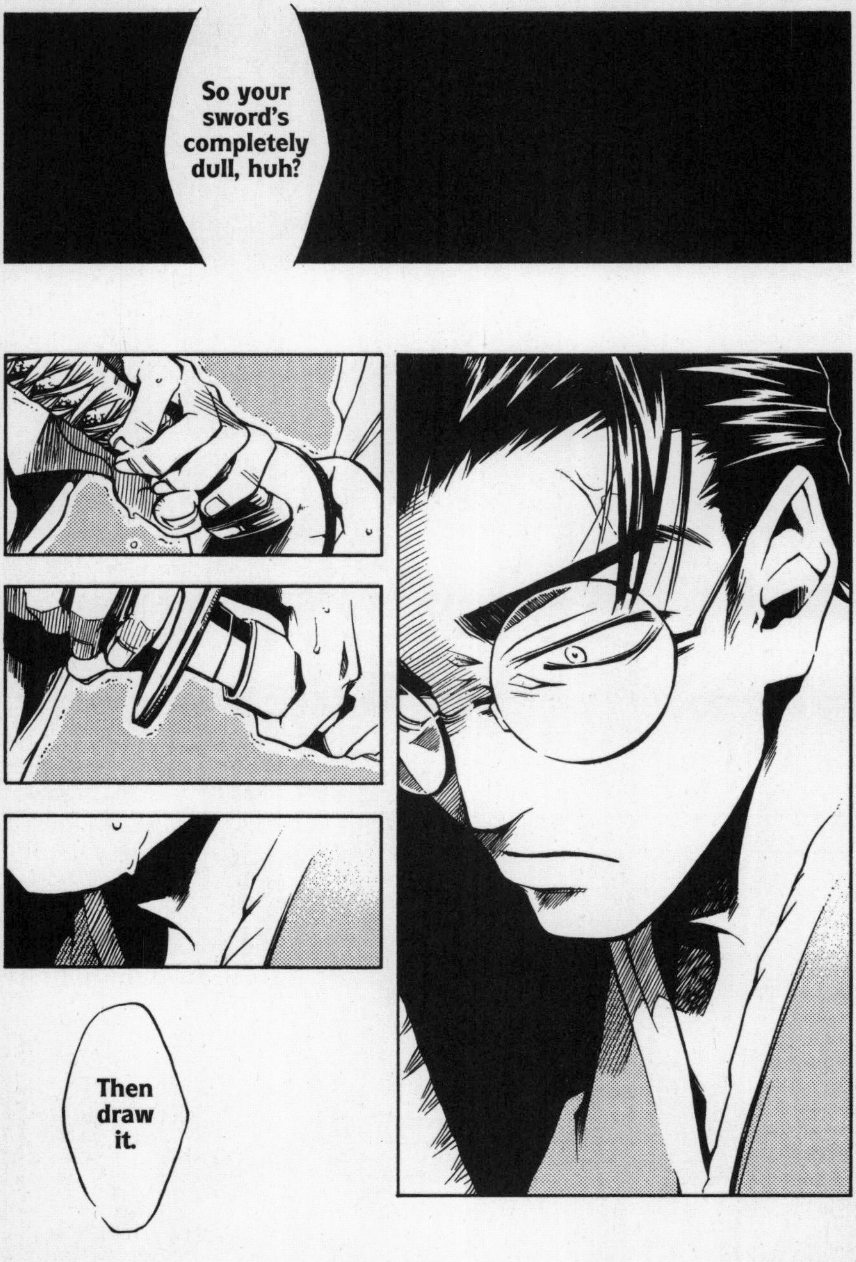
So your sword's completely dull, huh?
Then draw it.

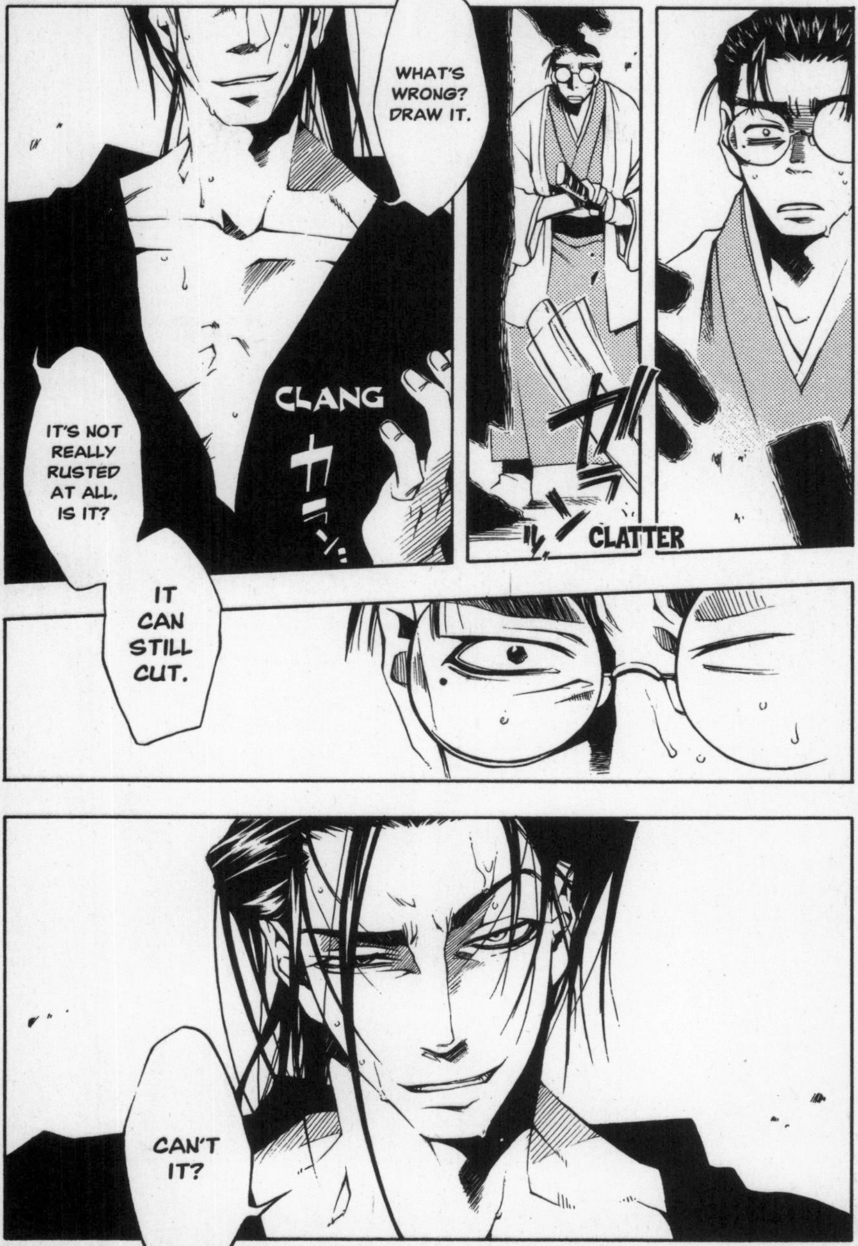
CLATTER
WHAT'S WRONG? DRAW IT.
CLANG
IT'S NOT REALLY RUSTED AT ALL, IS IT?
IT CAN STILL CUT.
CAN'T IT?

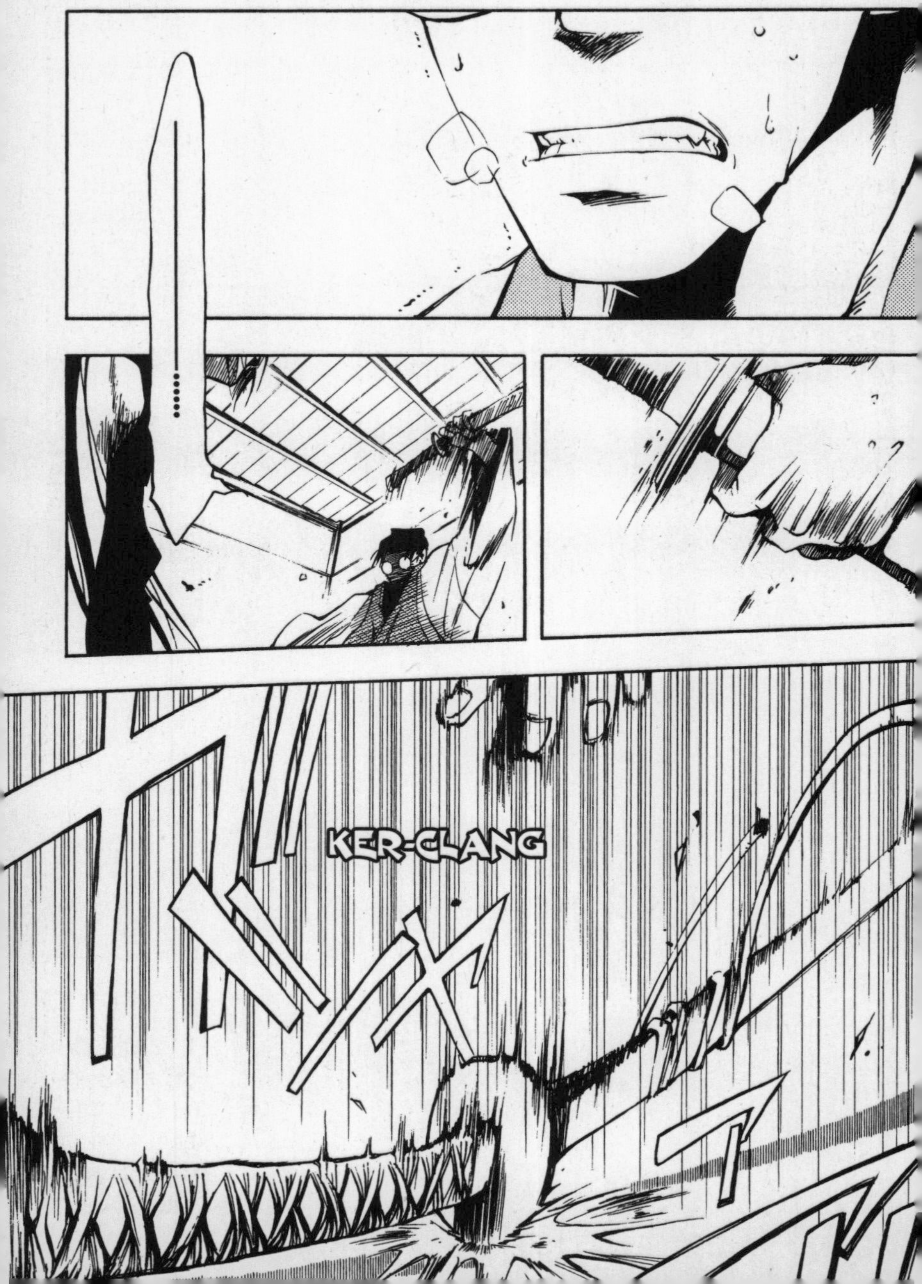

KER-CLANG

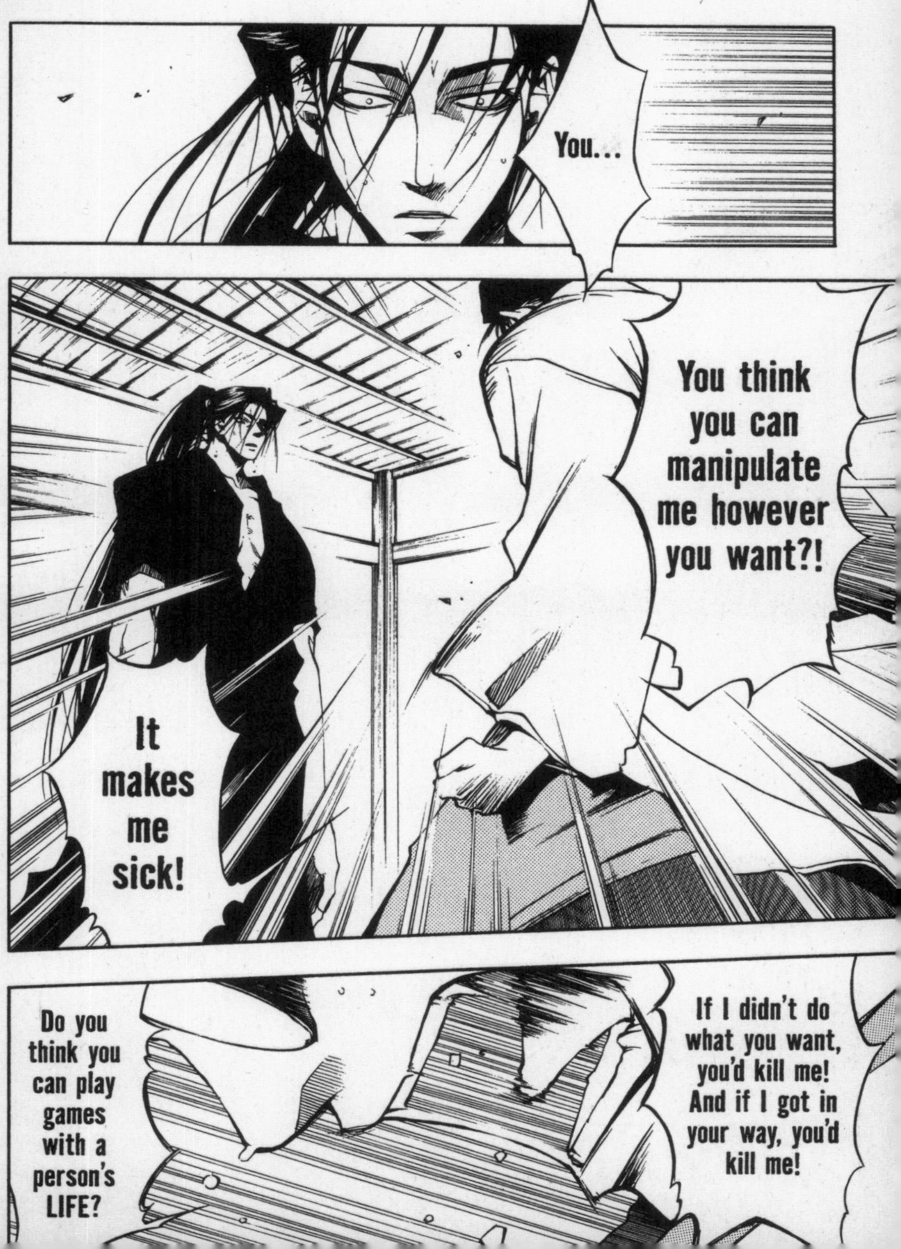
You...
You think you can manipulate me however you want?!
It makes me sick!
If I didn't do what you want, you'd kill me! And if I got in your way, you'd kill me!
Do you think you can play games with a person's LIFE?

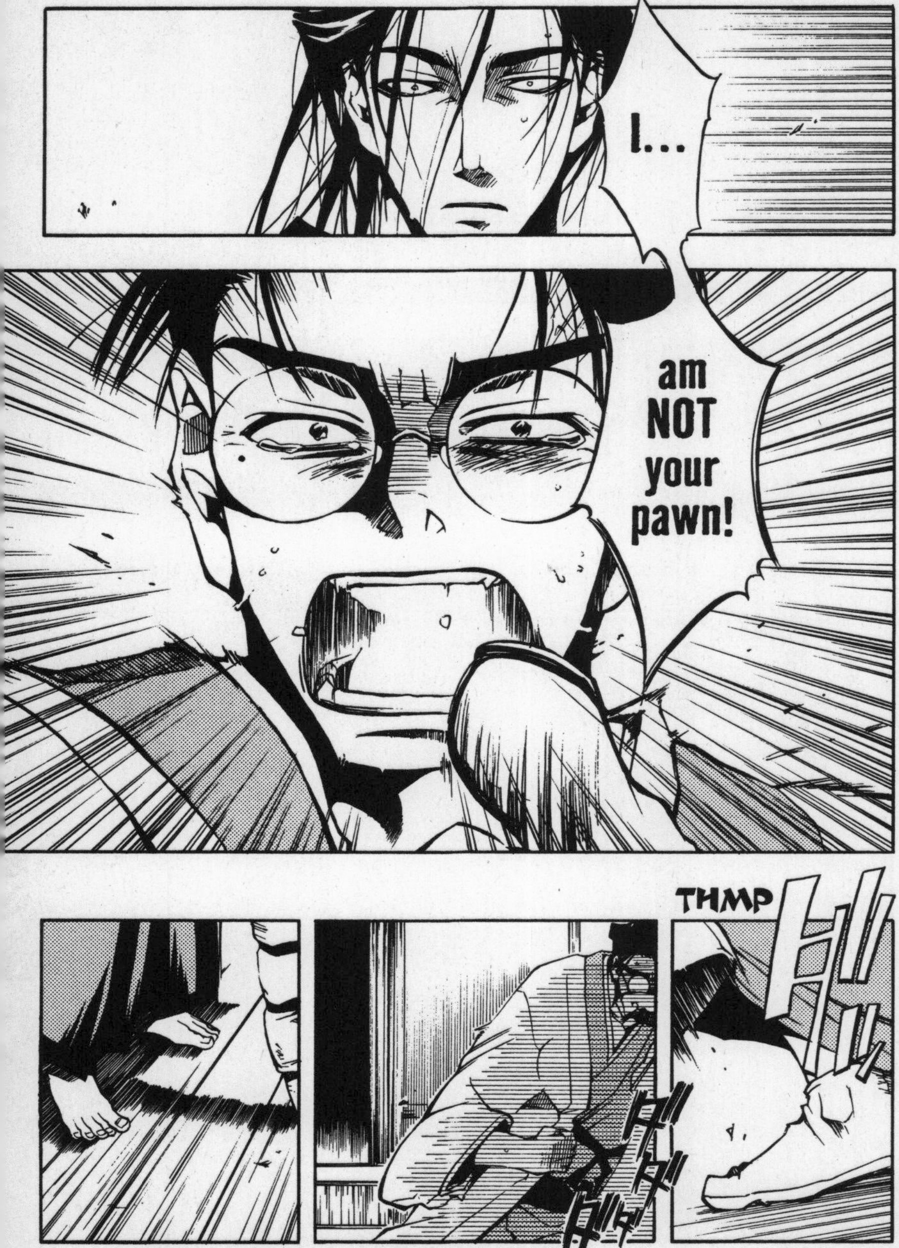
I...
am NOT your pawn!
THMP
THUMP THUMP THUMP THUMP

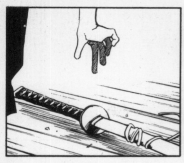
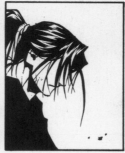
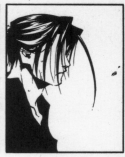
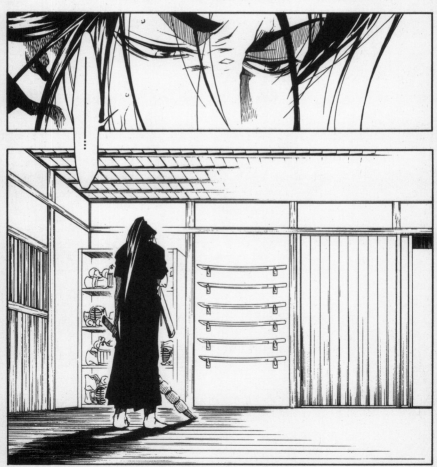

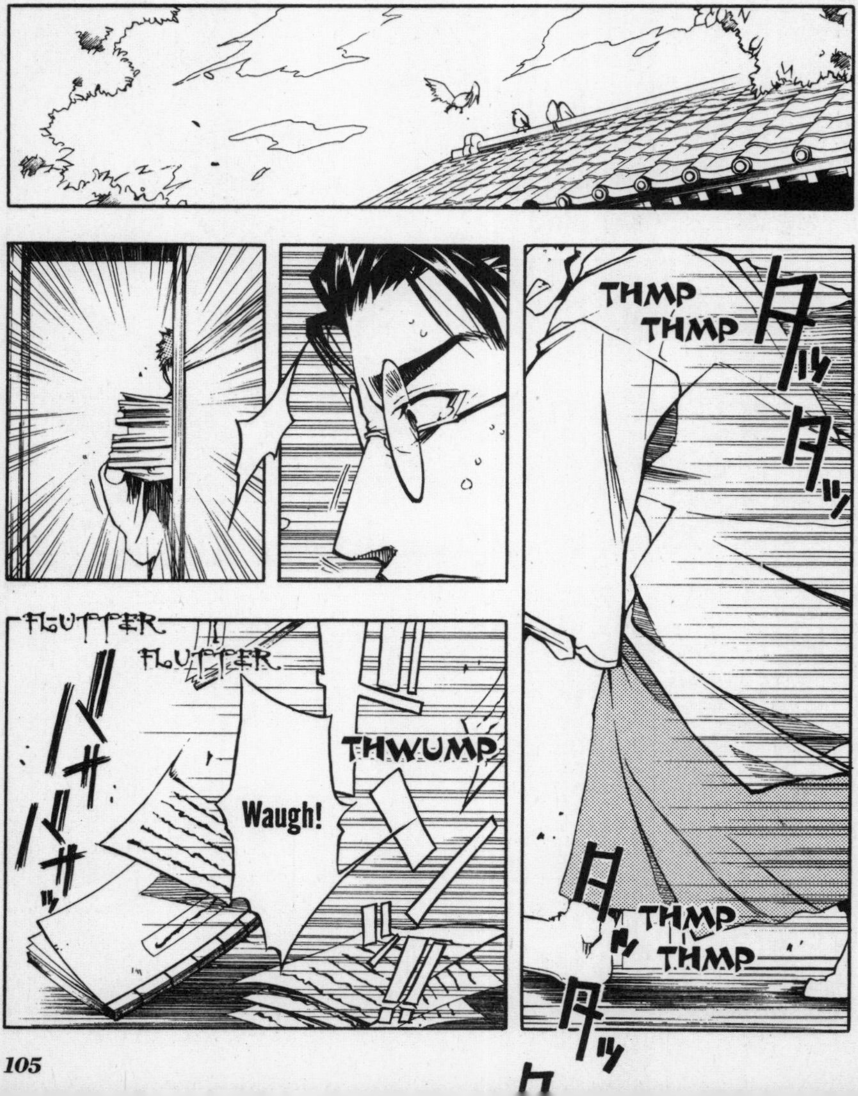
THMP
THMP
THMP
THMP
FLUTTER
FLUTTER
THWUMP
Waugh!

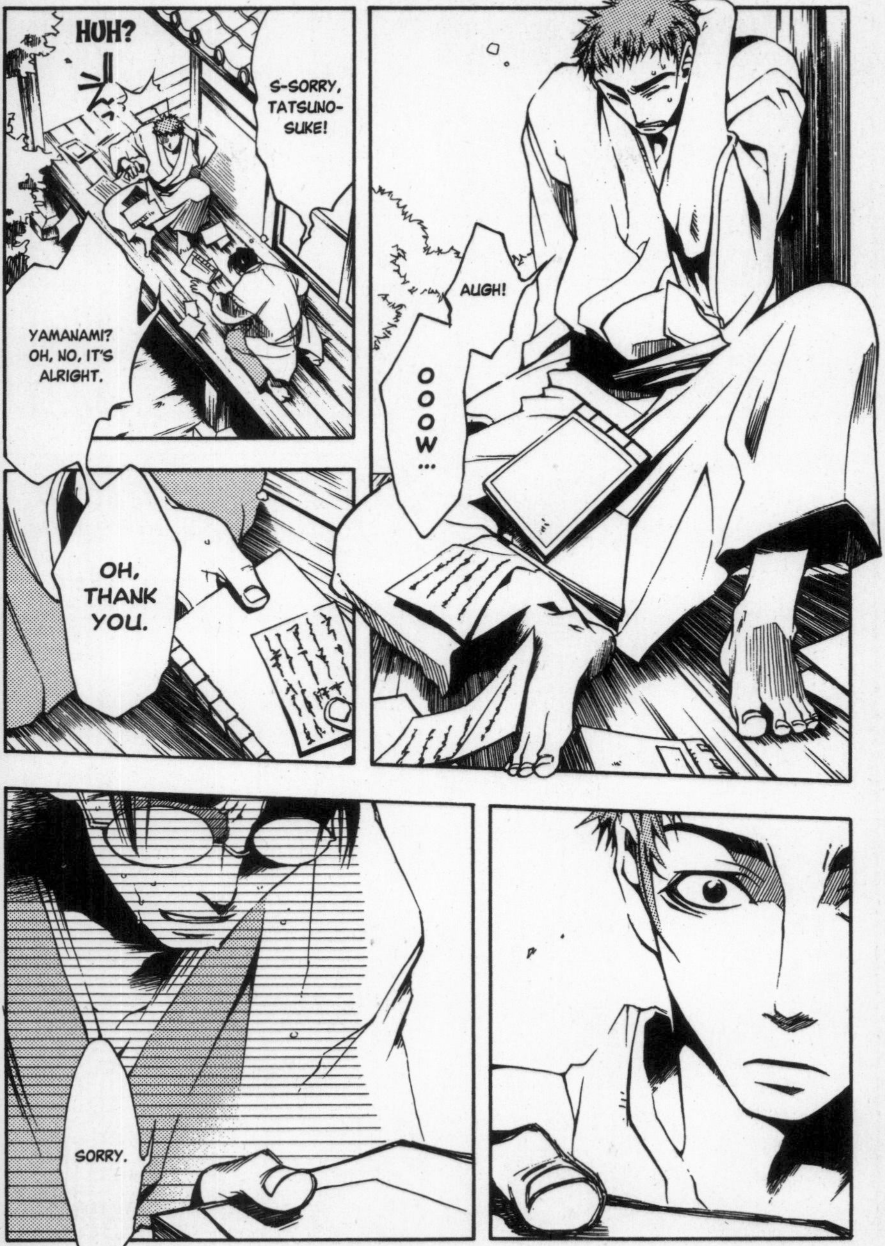
AUGH!
OOOW...
S-SORRY, TATSUNOSUKE!
HUH?
YAMANAMI? OH, NO, IT'S ALRIGHT.
OH, THANK YOU.
SORRY.

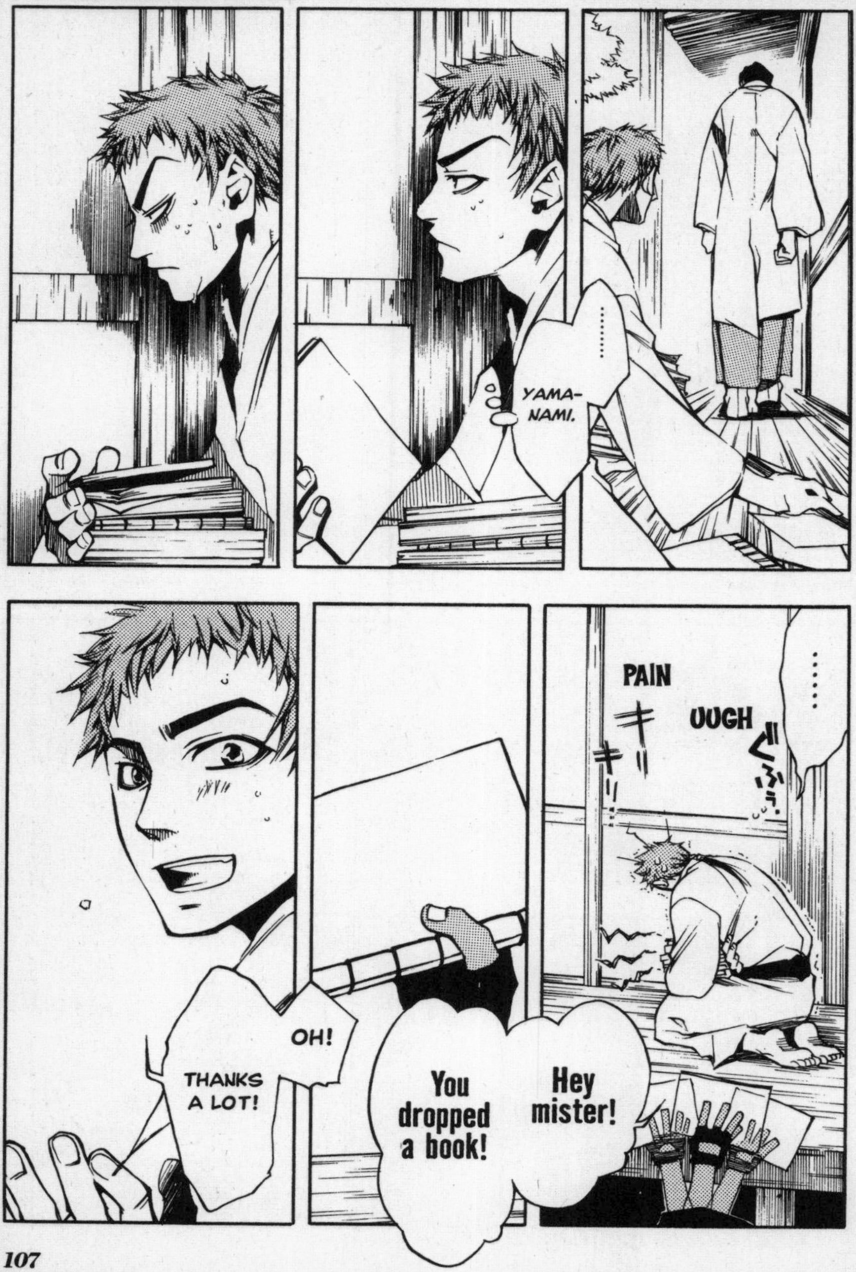
......
YAMA-NAMI.
PAIN
UUGH
......
Hey mister!
You dropped a book!
OH!
THANKS A LOT!

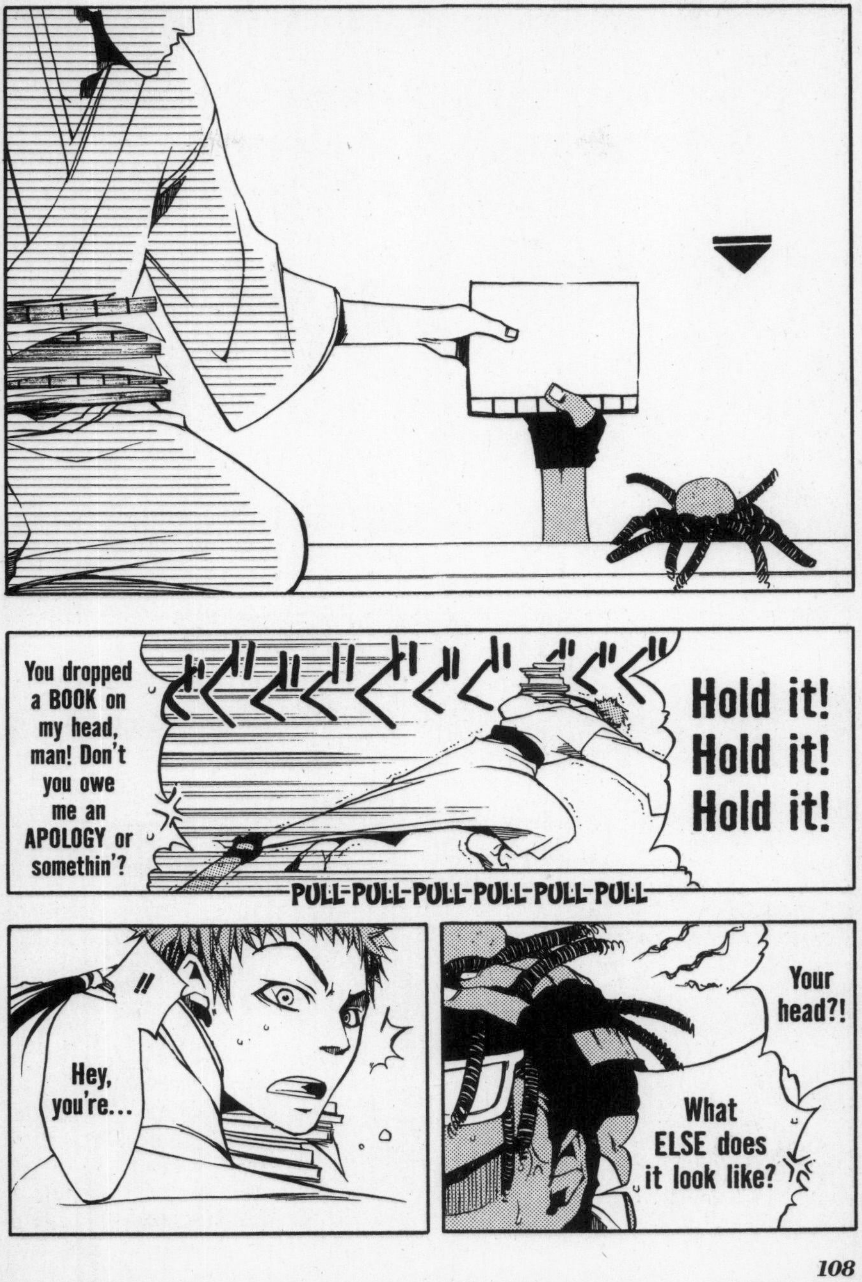
Hold it! Hold it! Hold it!
You dropped a BOOK on my head, man! Don't you owe me an APOLOGY or somethin'?
PULL-PULL-PULL-PULL-PULL-PULL
Your head?!
What ELSE does it look like?
!!
Hey, you're...

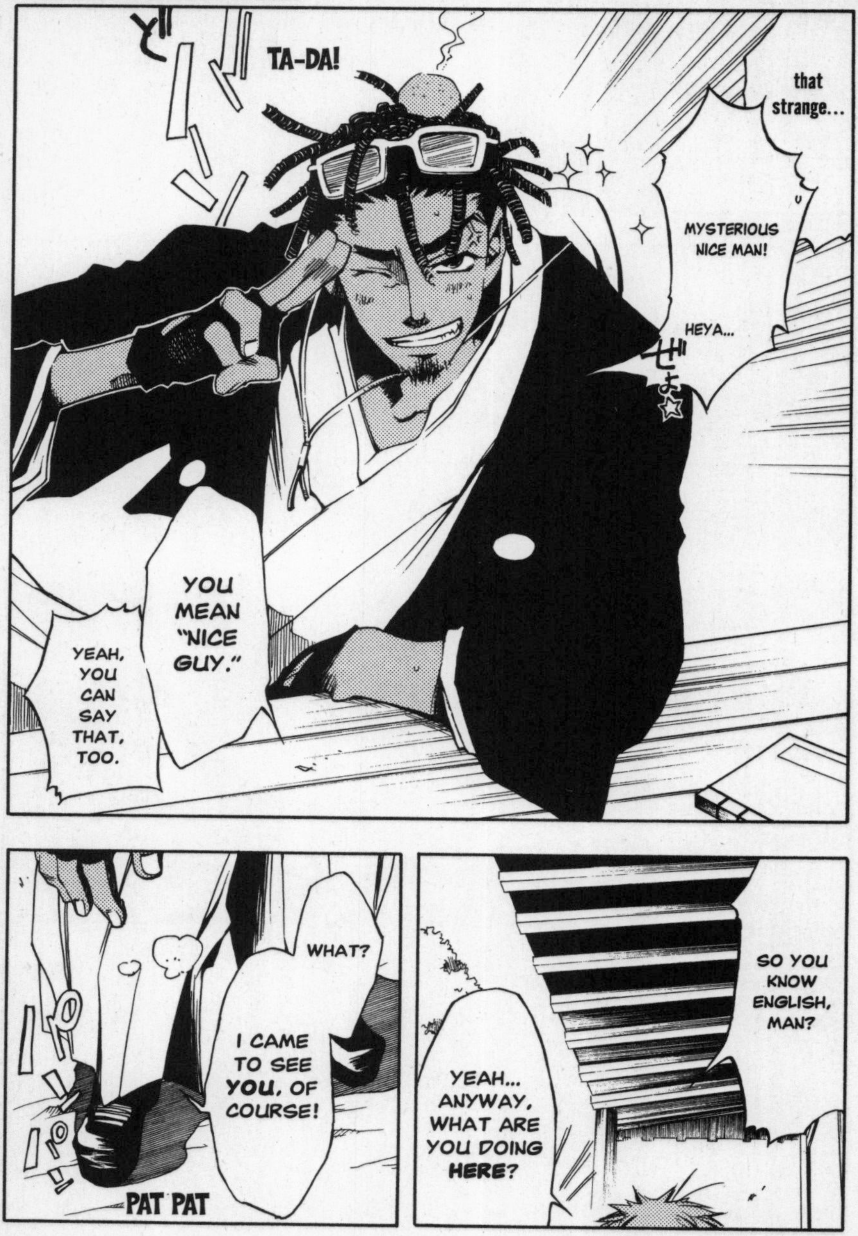
that strange... MYSTERIOUS NICE MAN!
HEYA...
ぜよ☆
TA-DA!
YOU MEAN "NICE GUY."
YEAH, YOU CAN SAY THAT, TOO.
SO YOU KNOW ENGLISH, MAN?
YEAH... ANYWAY, WHAT ARE YOU DOING HERE?
WHAT?
I CAME TO SEE YOU, OF COURSE!
PAT PAT

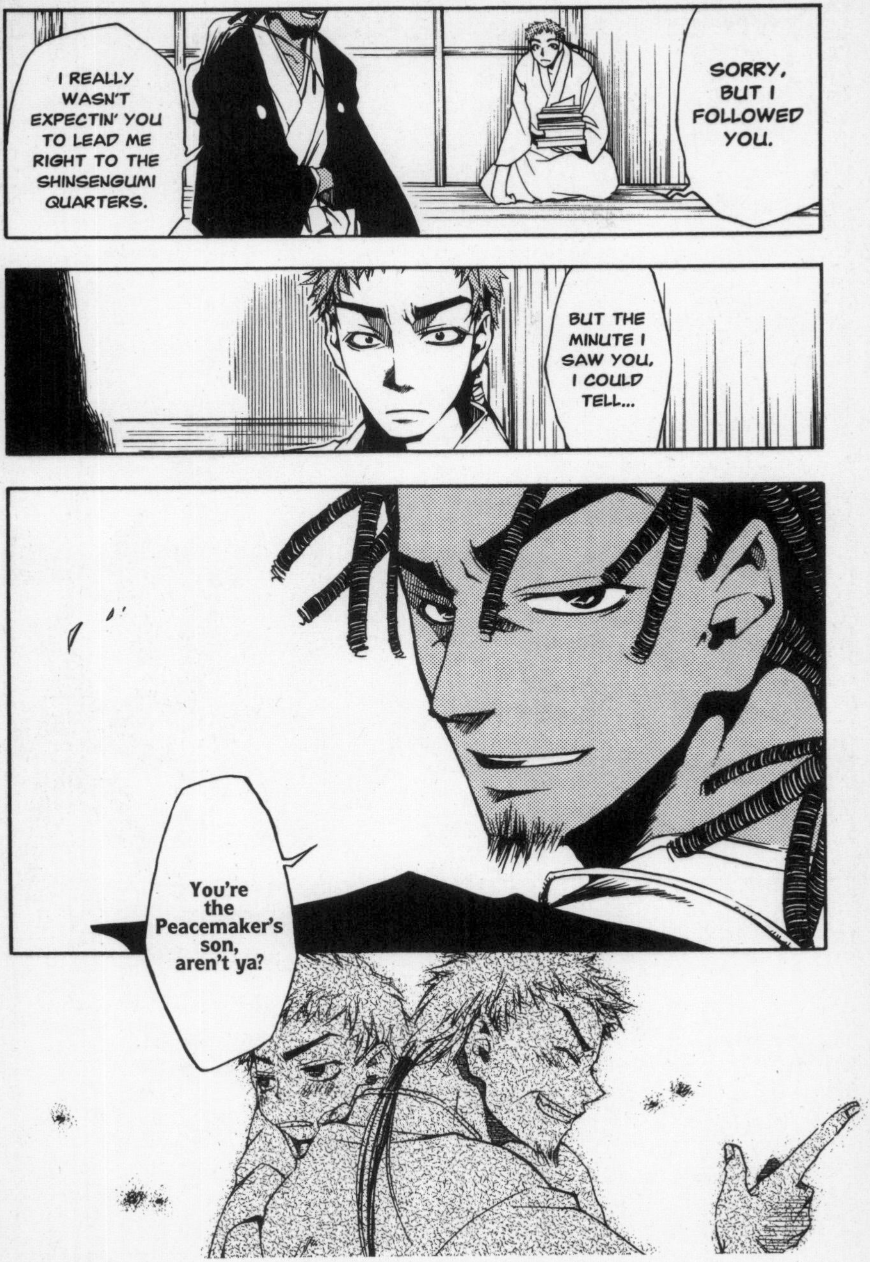
SORRY, BUT I FOLLOWED YOU.
I REALLY WASN'T EXPECTIN' YOU TO LEAD ME RIGHT TO THE SHINSENGUMI QUARTERS.
BUT THE MINUTE I SAW YOU, I COULD TELL...
You're the Peacemaker's son, aren't ya?

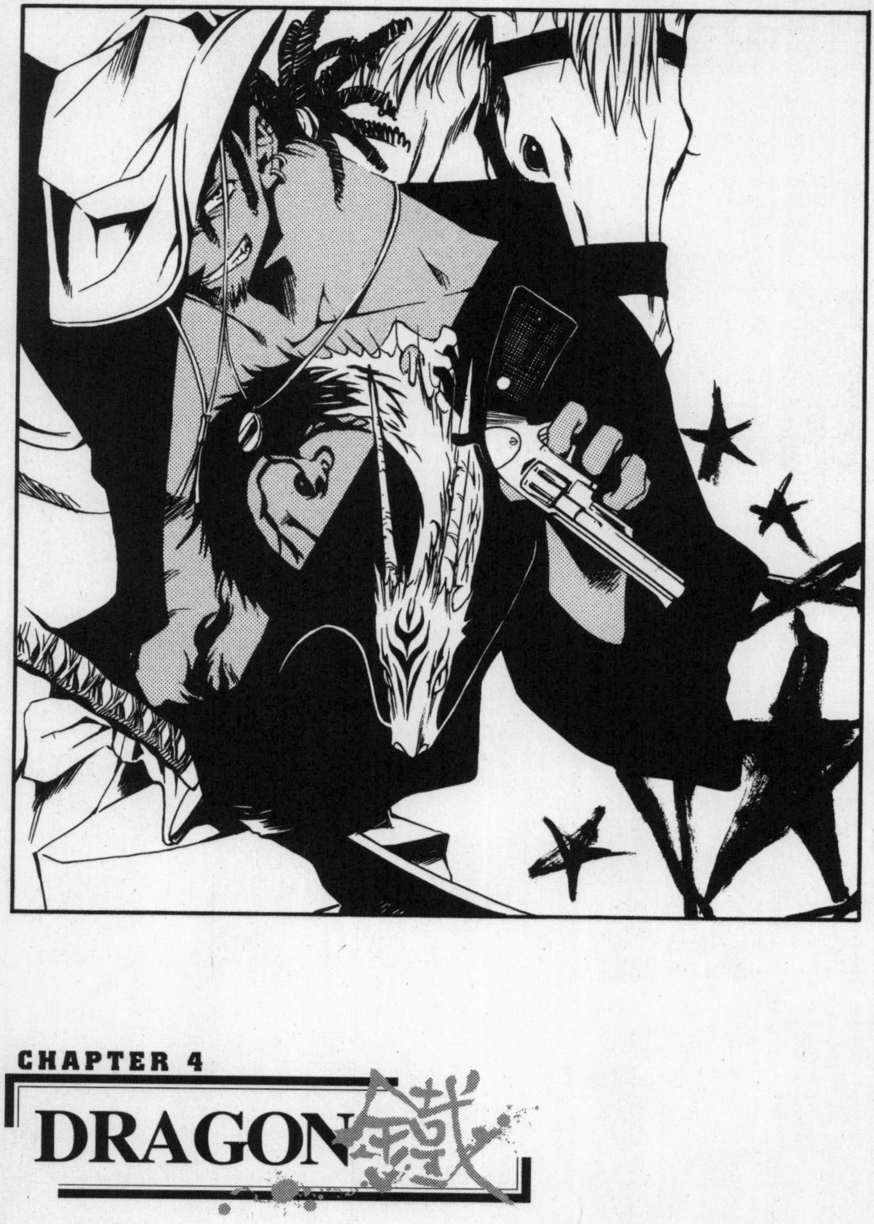

CHAPTER 4

DRAGON 鐵

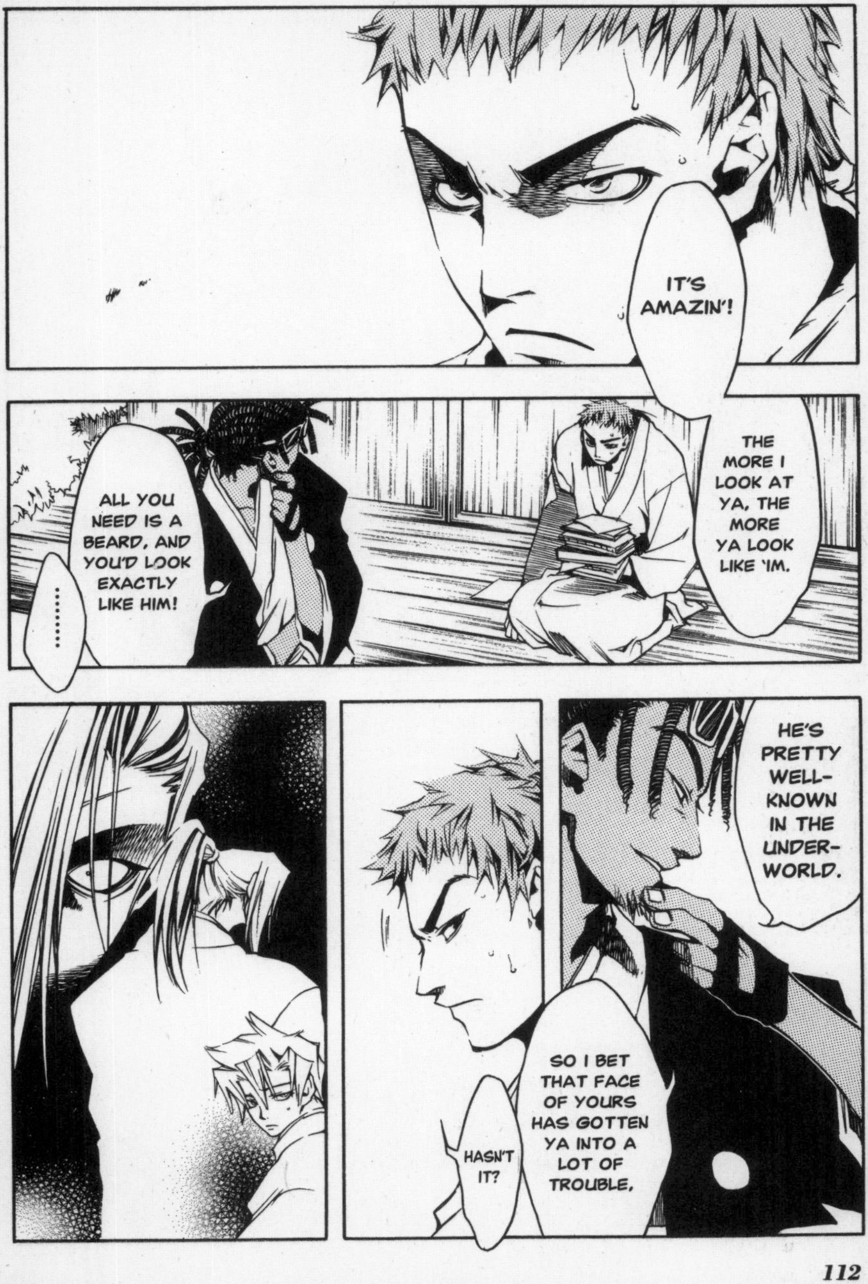
IT'S AMAZIN'!
THE MORE I LOOK AT YA, THE MORE YA LOOK LIKE 'IM.
ALL YOU NEED IS A BEARD, AND YOU'D LOOK EXACTLY LIKE HIM!
......
HE'S PRETTY WELL-KNOWN IN THE UNDER-WORLD.
SO I BET THAT FACE OF YOURS HAS GOTTEN YA INTO A LOT OF TROUBLE,
HASN'T IT?

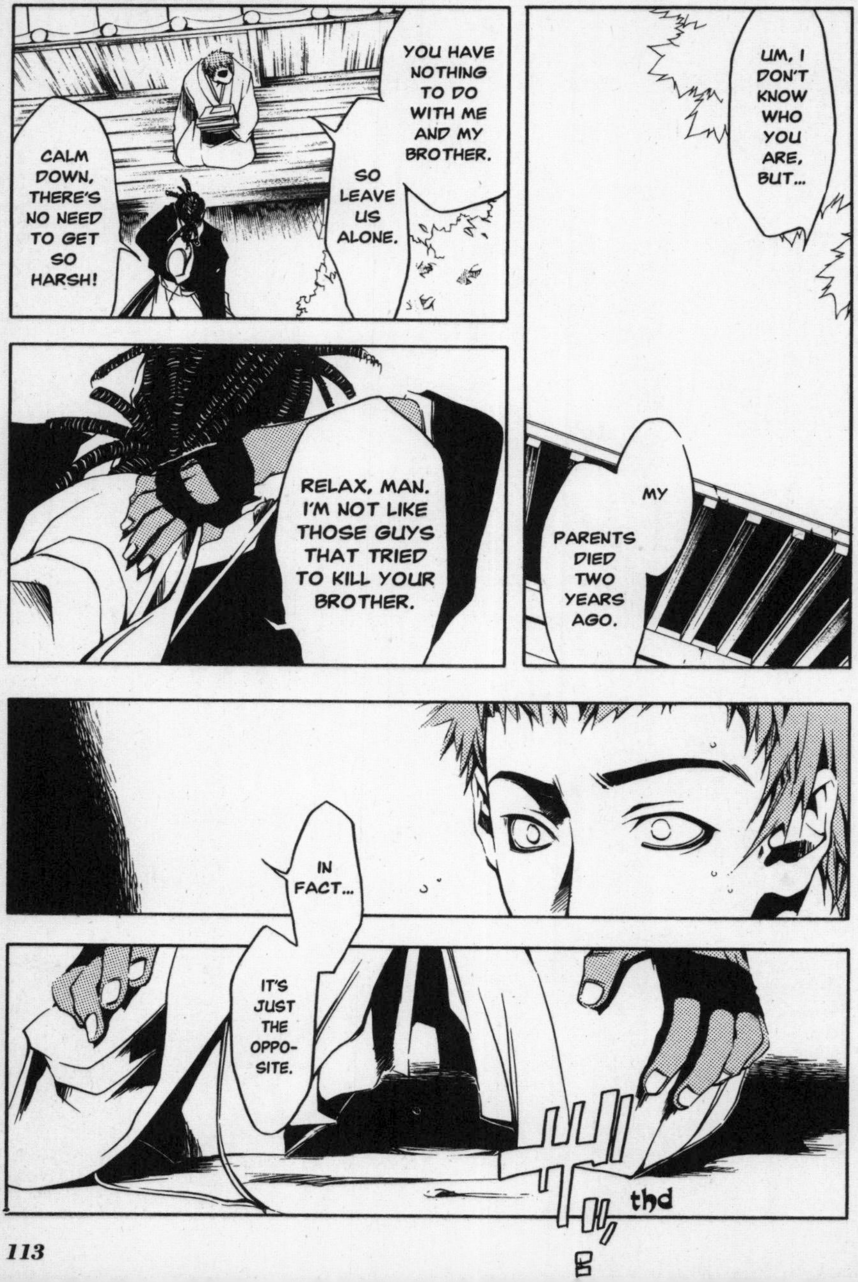
UM, I DON'T KNOW WHO YOU ARE, BUT...
MY PARENTS DIED TWO YEARS AGO.
YOU HAVE NOTHING TO DO WITH ME AND MY BROTHER.
SO LEAVE US ALONE.
CALM DOWN, THERE'S NO NEED TO GET SO HARSH!
RELAX, MAN. I'M NOT LIKE THOSE GUYS THAT TRIED TO KILL YOUR BROTHER.
IN FACT...
IT'S JUST THE OPPOSITE.
thd

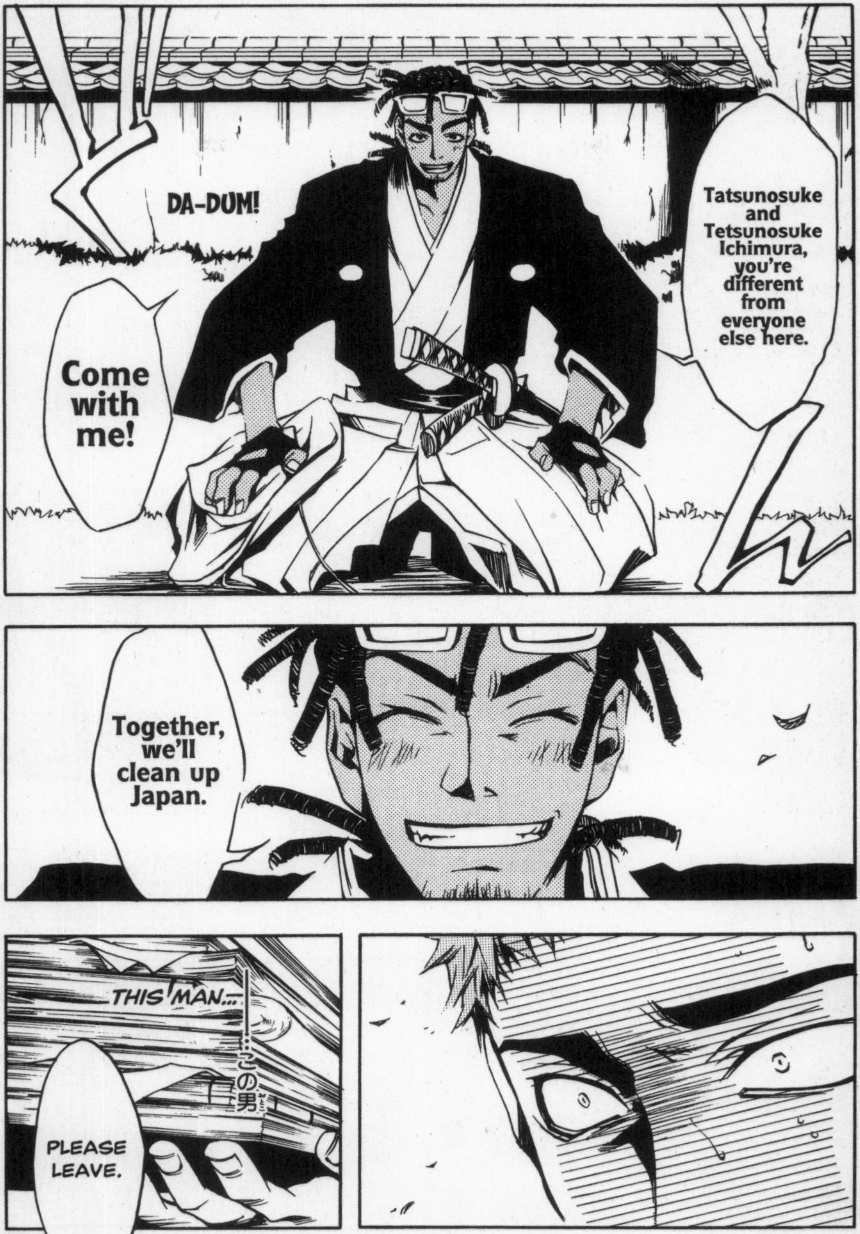
Tatsunosuke and Tetsunosuke Ichimura, you're different from everyone else here.
DA-DUM!
Come with me!
Together, we'll clean up Japan.
――……この男
THIS MAN...
PLEASE LEAVE.

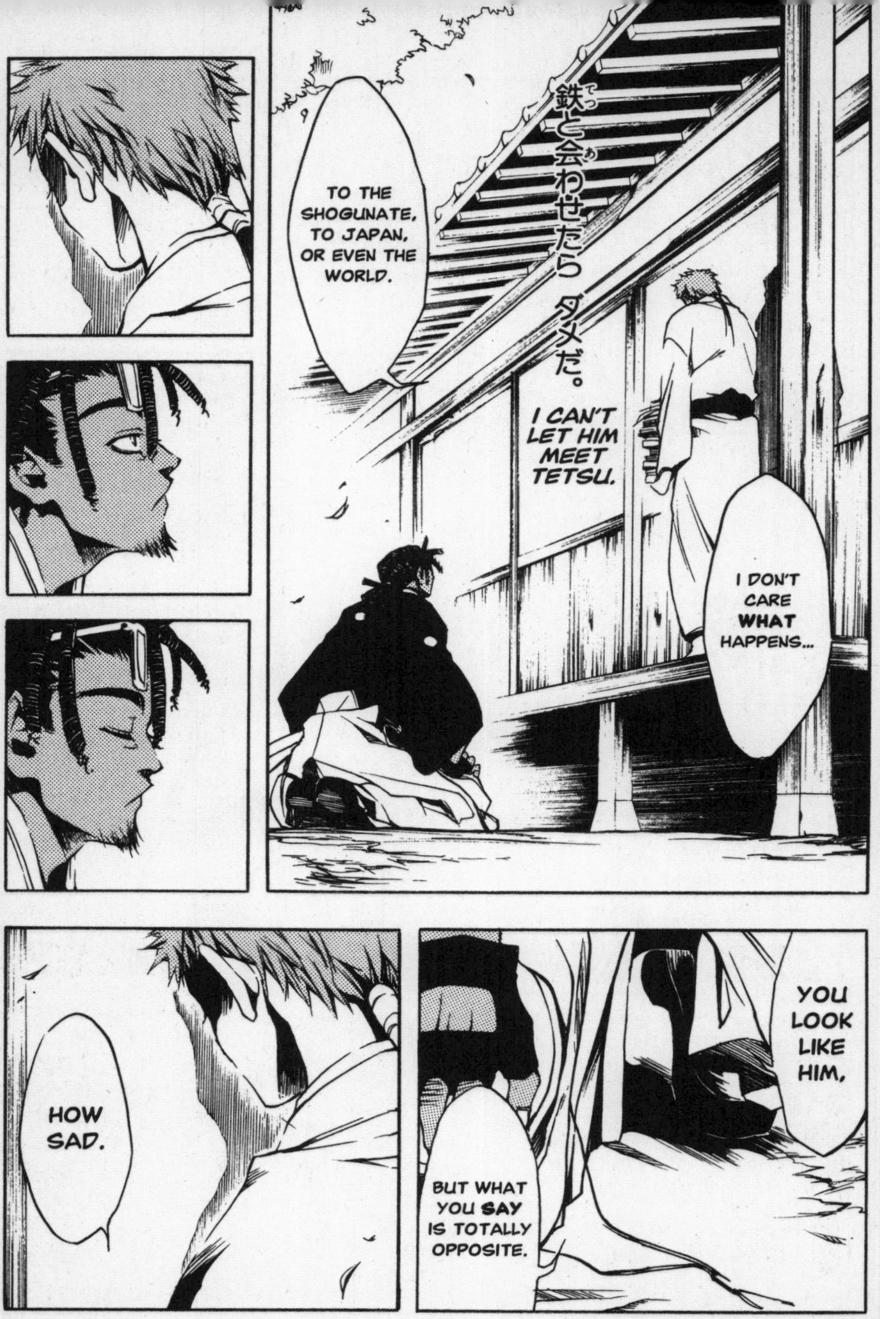
I DON'T CARE WHAT HAPPENS...
TO THE SHOGUNATE, TO JAPAN, OR EVEN THE WORLD.
鉄と会わせたら ダメだ。
I CAN'T LET HIM MEET TETSU.
YOU LOOK LIKE HIM,
BUT WHAT YOU SAY IS TOTALLY OPPOSITE.
HOW SAD.

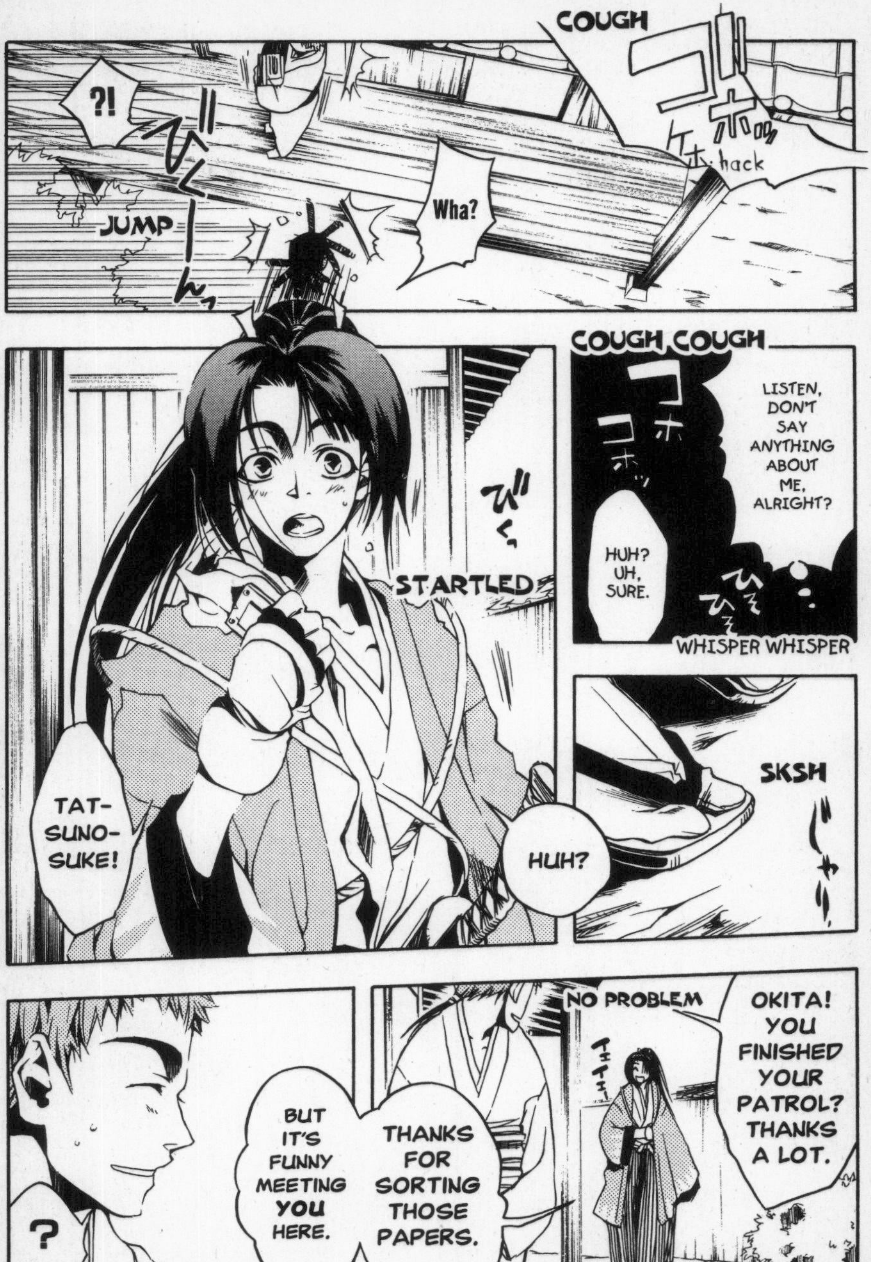
COUGH
hack
Wha?
?!
JUMP
COUGH COUGH
LISTEN, DON'T SAY ANYTHING ABOUT ME, ALRIGHT?
HUH? UH, SURE.
WHISPER WHISPER
SKSH
STARTLED
HUH?
TAT-SUNO-SUKE!
OKITA! YOU FINISHED YOUR PATROL? THANKS A LOT.
NO PROBLEM
THANKS FOR SORTING THOSE PAPERS.
BUT IT'S FUNNY MEETING YOU HERE.
?

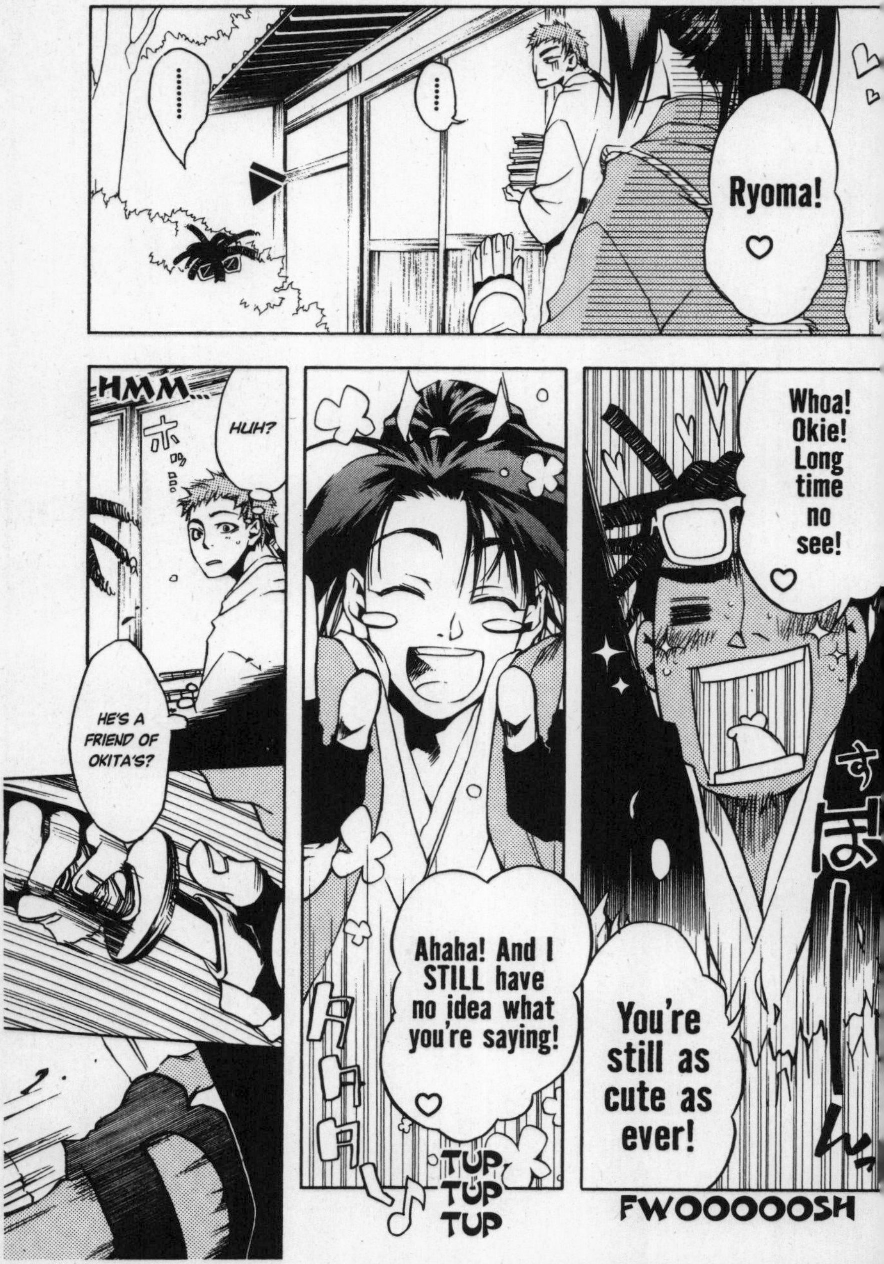
Ryoma! ♥
......
......
Whoa! Okie! Long time no see! ♥
You're still as cute as ever!
FWOOOOOSH
Ahaha! And I STILL have no idea what you're saying! ♥
TUP TUP TUP
HMM...
HUH?
HE'S A FRIEND OF OKITA'S?

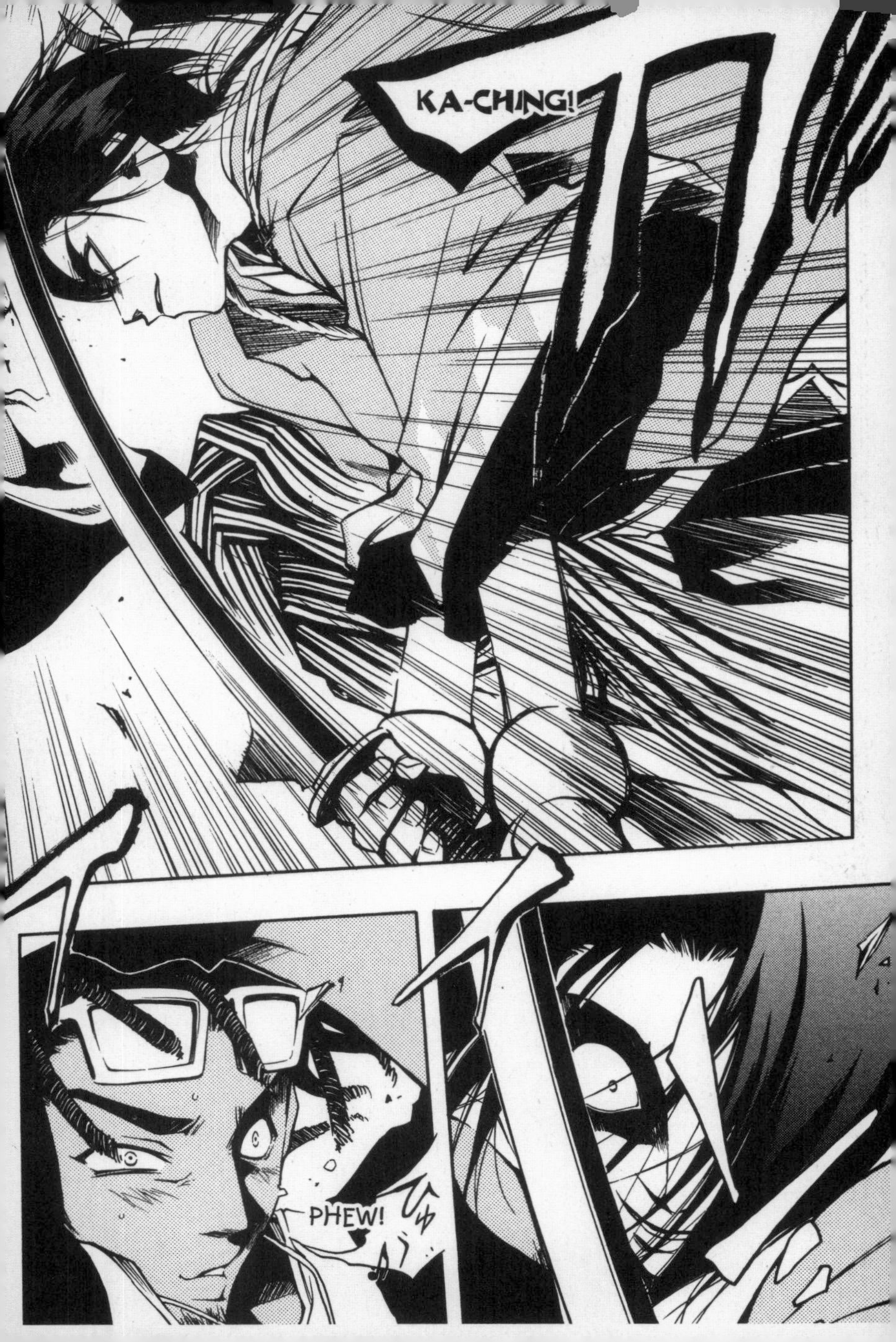
KA-CHING!
PHEW!

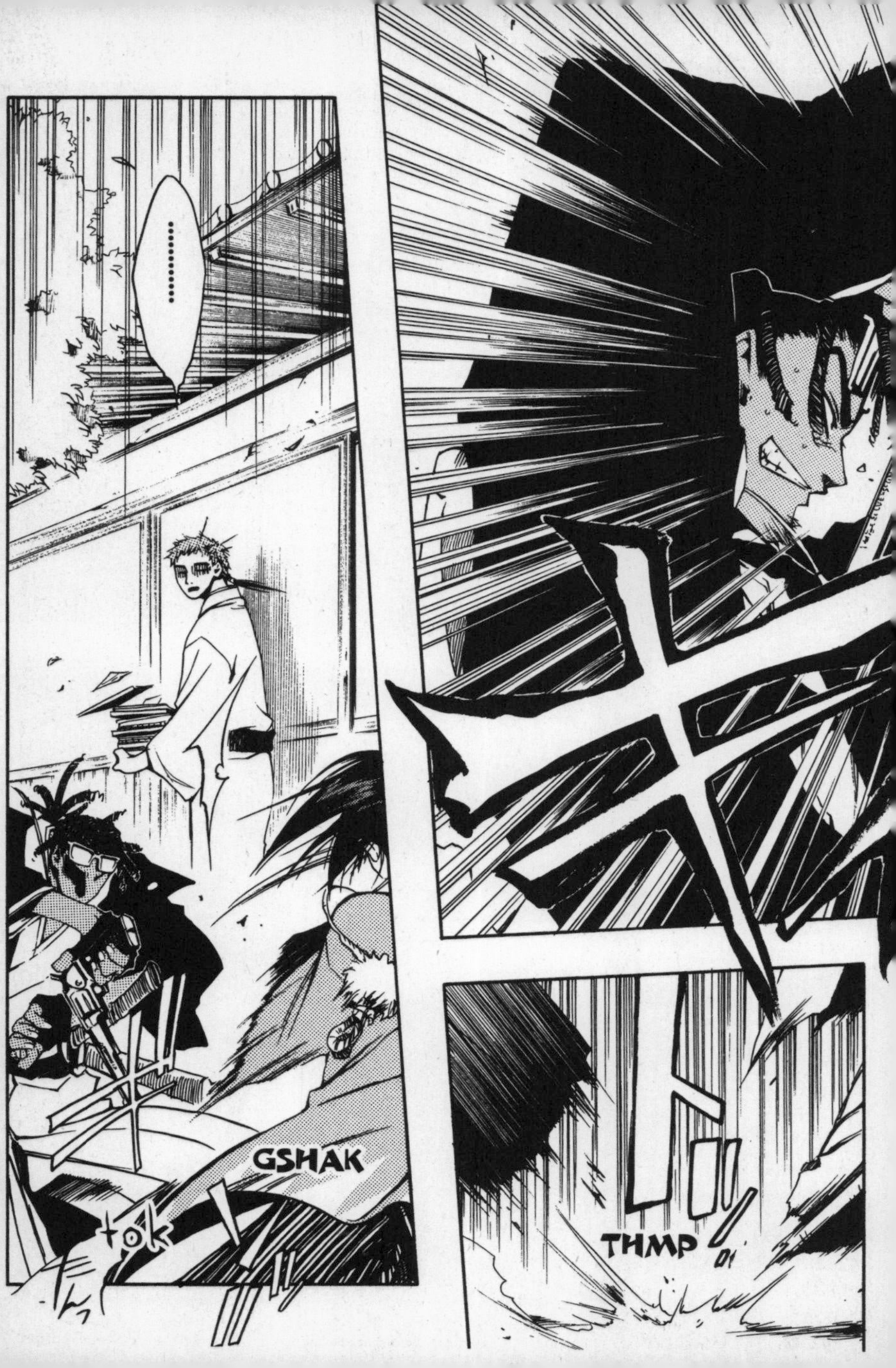
THMP
......
GSHAK
tok

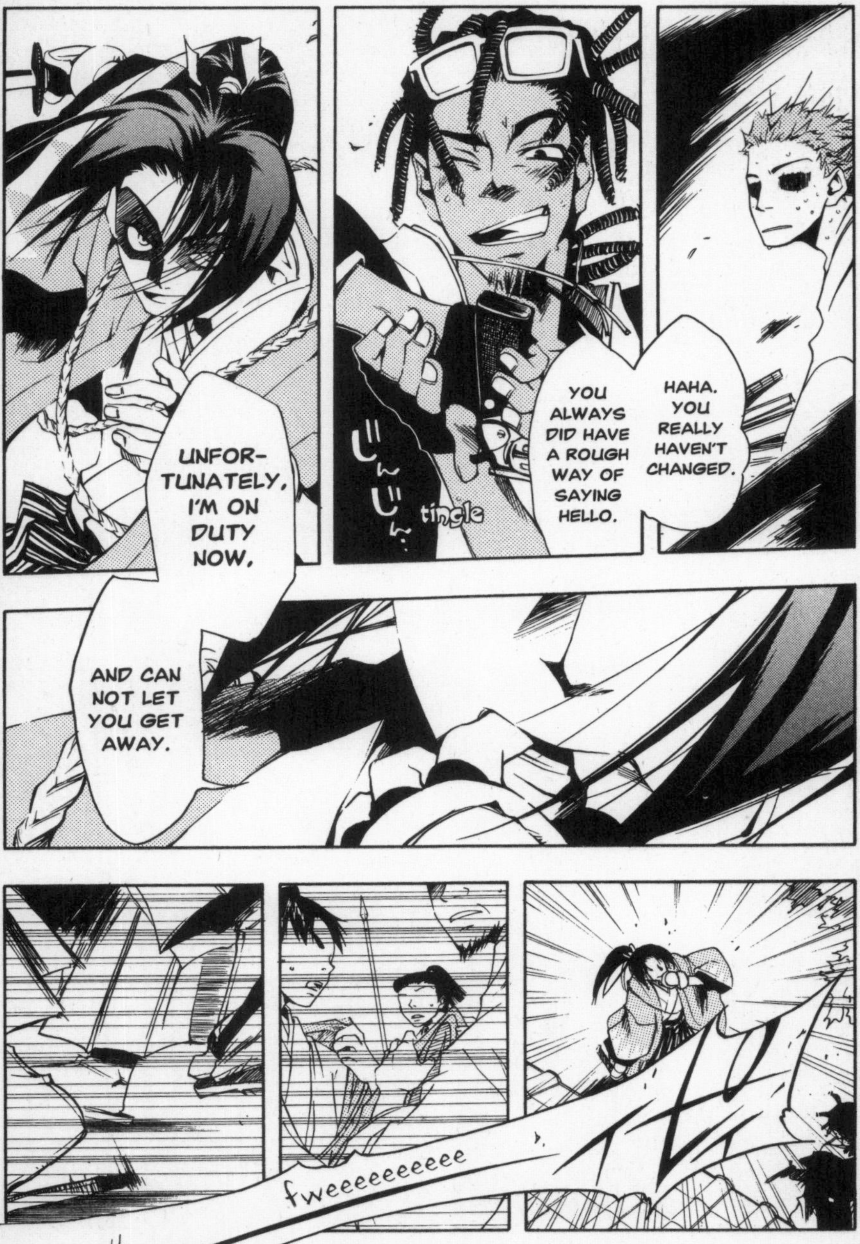
HAHA. YOU REALLY HAVEN'T CHANGED.
YOU ALWAYS DID HAVE A ROUGH WAY OF SAYING HELLO.
じんじん…
tingle
UNFOR-TUNATELY, I'M ON DUTY NOW,
AND CAN NOT LET YOU GET AWAY.
fweeeeeeeeee

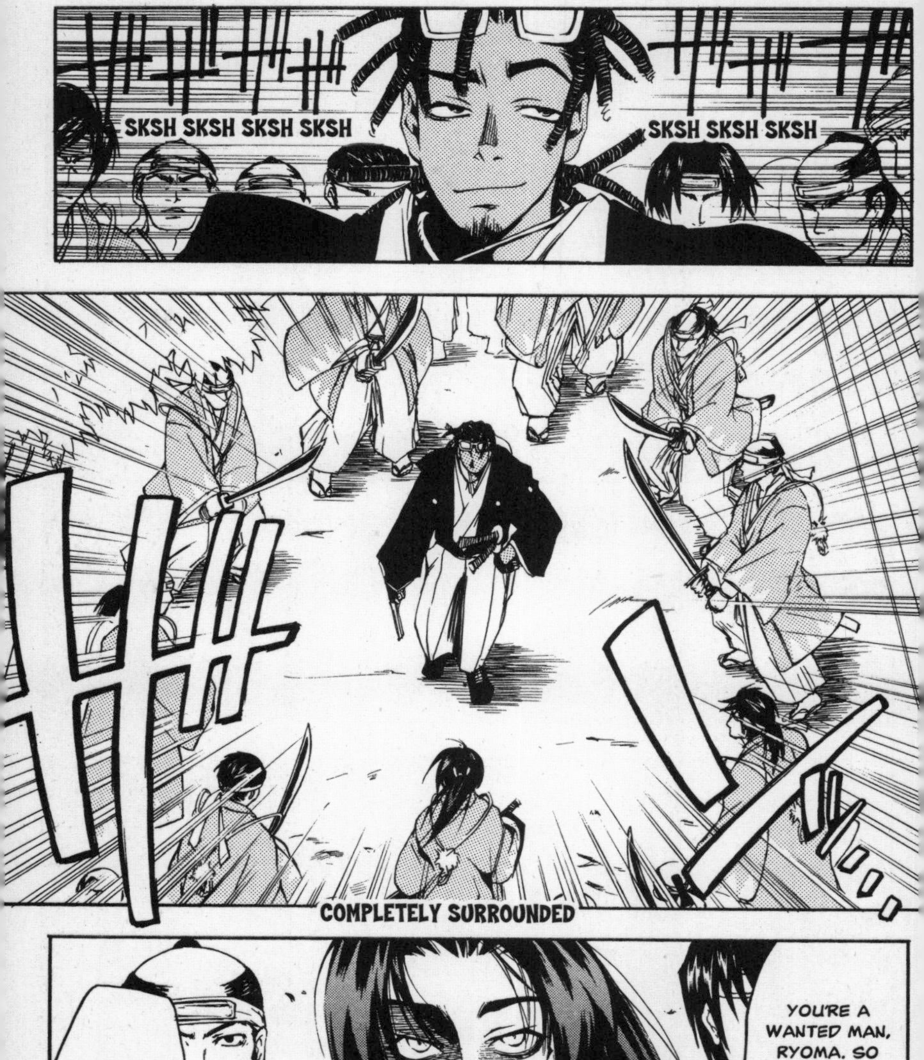
SKSH SKSH SKSH
SKSH SKSH SKSH SKSH
COMPLETELY SURROUNDED
YOU'RE A WANTED MAN, RYOMA. SO WHY'D YOU COME TO THE SHINSENGUMI QUARTERS?
DID YOU FIND ANOTHER PERSON YOU WANT TO SCOUT?

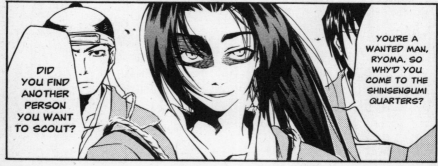

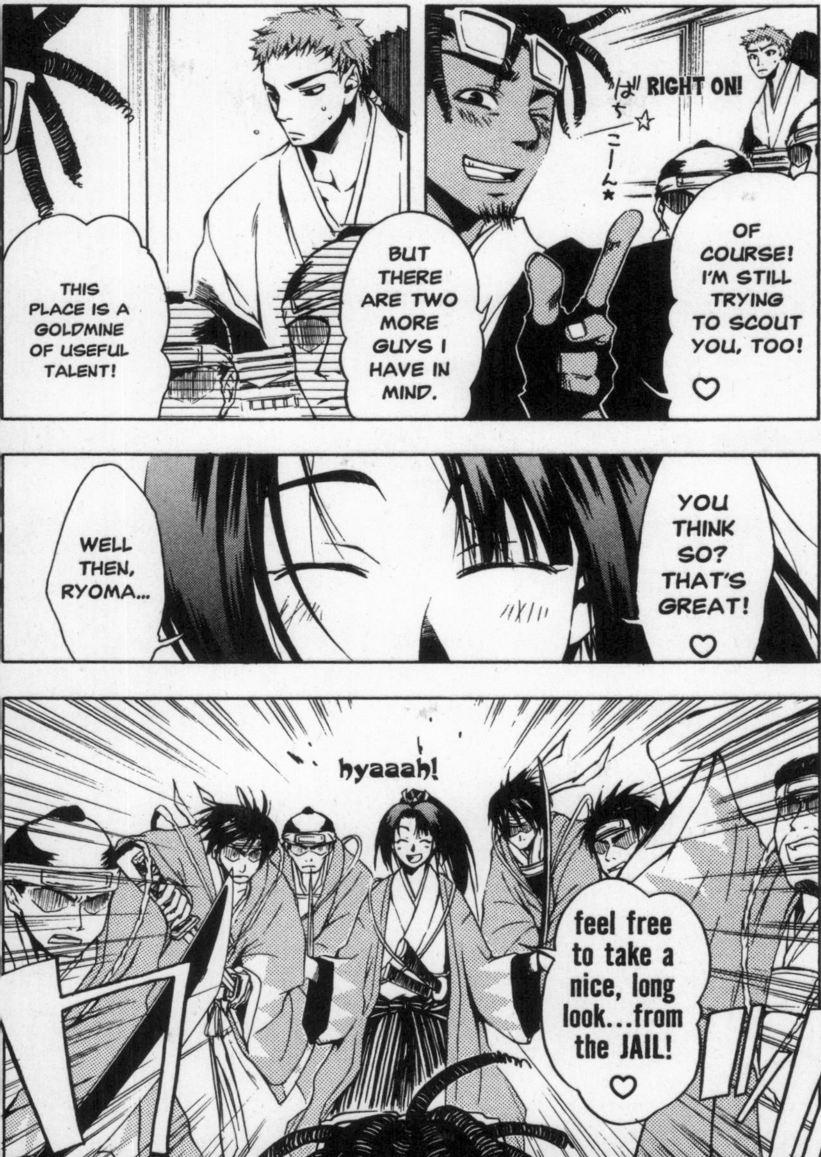
RIGHT ON!
ぱち☆
こーん★
OF COURSE! I'M STILL TRYING TO SCOUT YOU, TOO! ♡
BUT THERE ARE TWO MORE GUYS I HAVE IN MIND.
THIS PLACE IS A GOLDMINE OF USEFUL TALENT!
YOU THINK SO? THAT'S GREAT! ♡
WELL THEN, RYOMA...
hyaaah!
feel free to take a nice, long look...from the JAIL! ♡

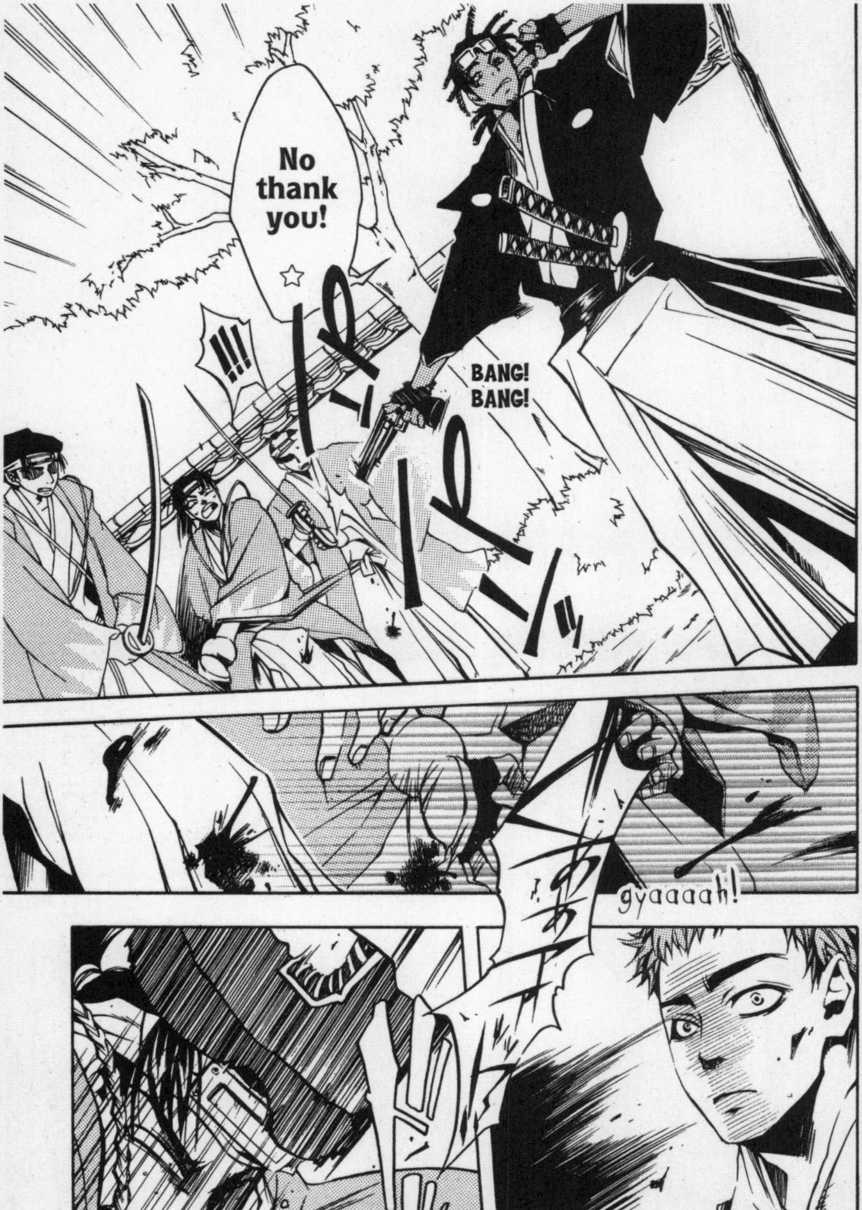
No thank you! ☆
BANG! BANG!
!!!
gyaaaah!
THWUMP!

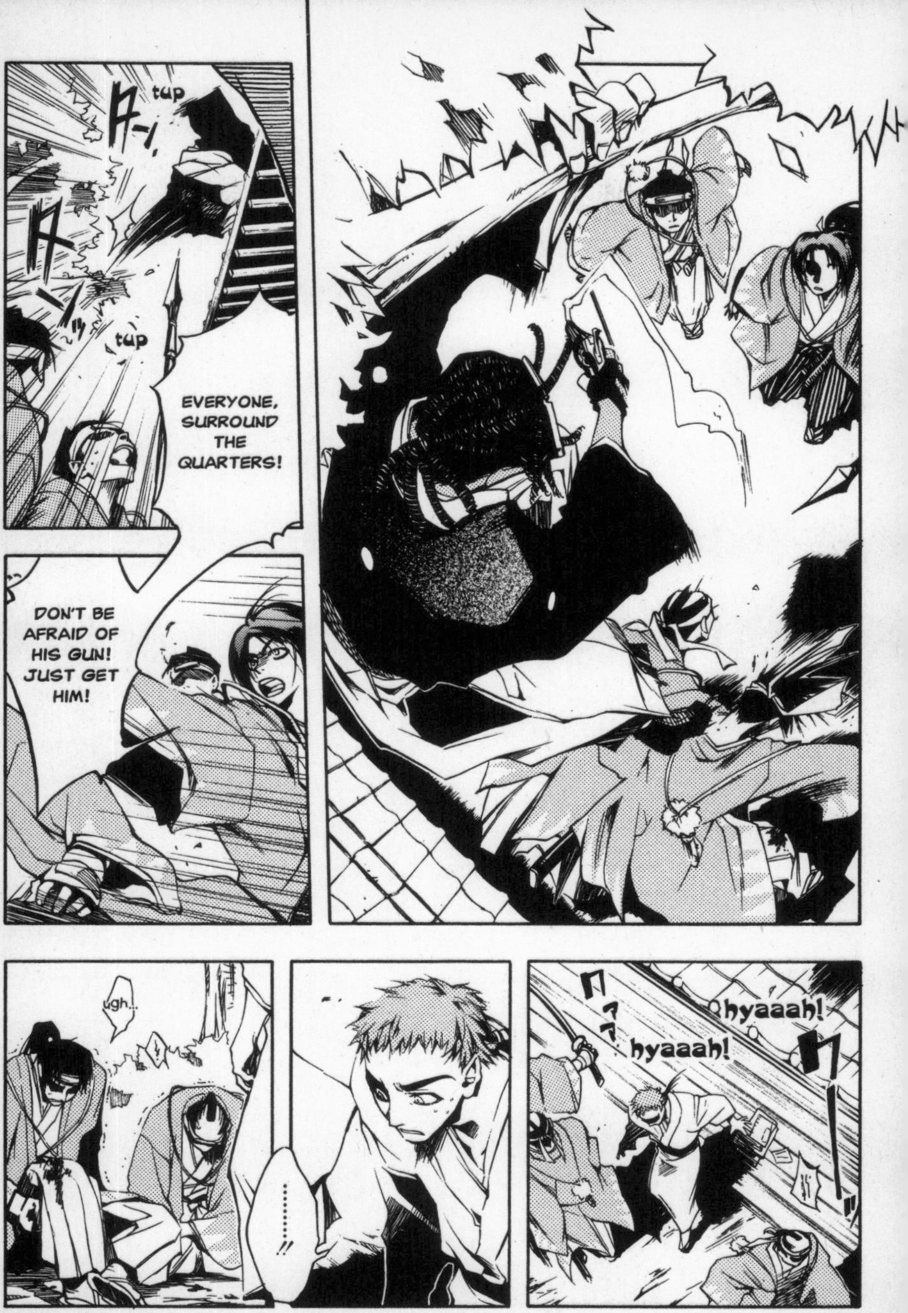
tup
tup
EVERYONE, SURROUND THE QUARTERS!
DON'T BE AFRAID OF HIS GUN! JUST GET HIM!
hyaaah!
hyaaah!
......!!
ugh...

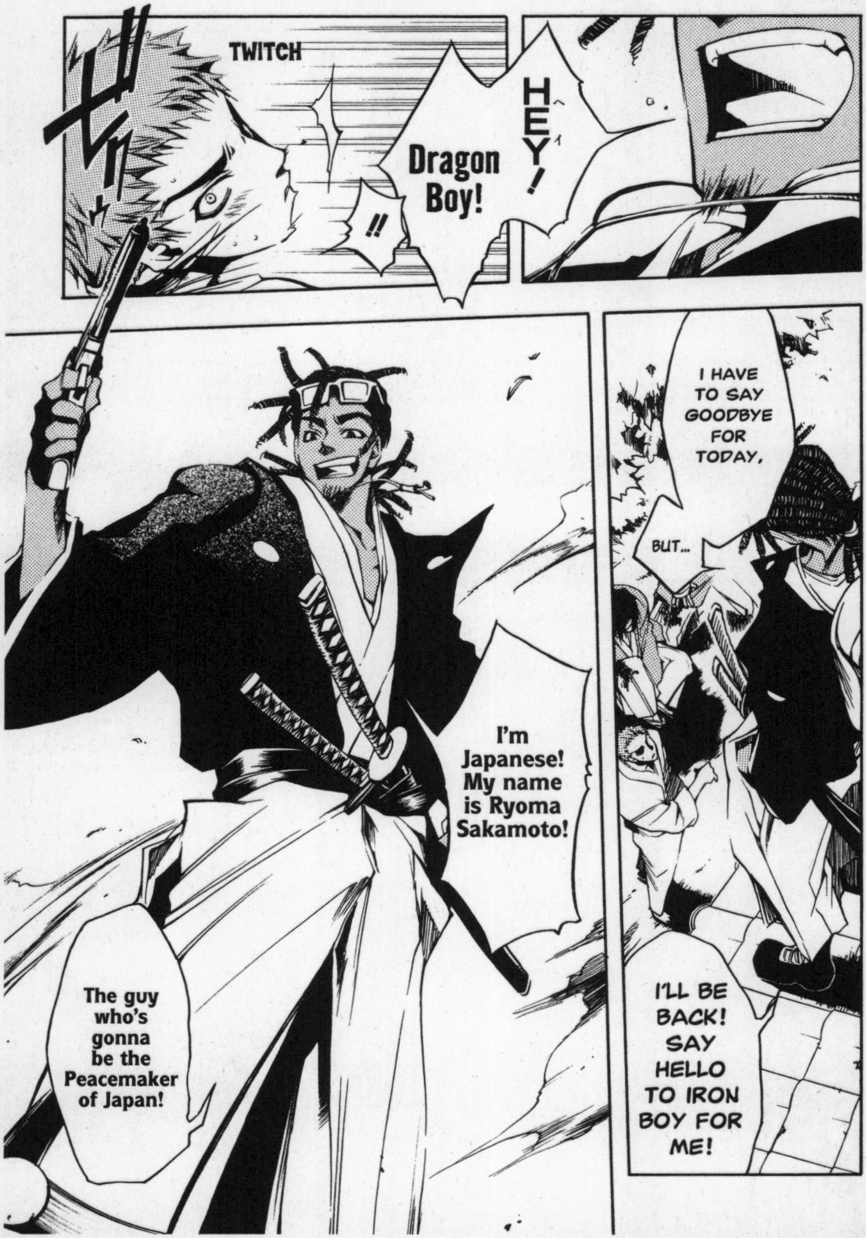
HEY! Dragon Boy!
TWITCH
!!
I HAVE TO SAY GOODBYE FOR TODAY,
BUT...
I'LL BE BACK! SAY HELLO TO IRON BOY FOR ME!
I'm Japanese! My name is Ryoma Sakamoto!
The guy who's gonna be the Peacemaker of Japan!

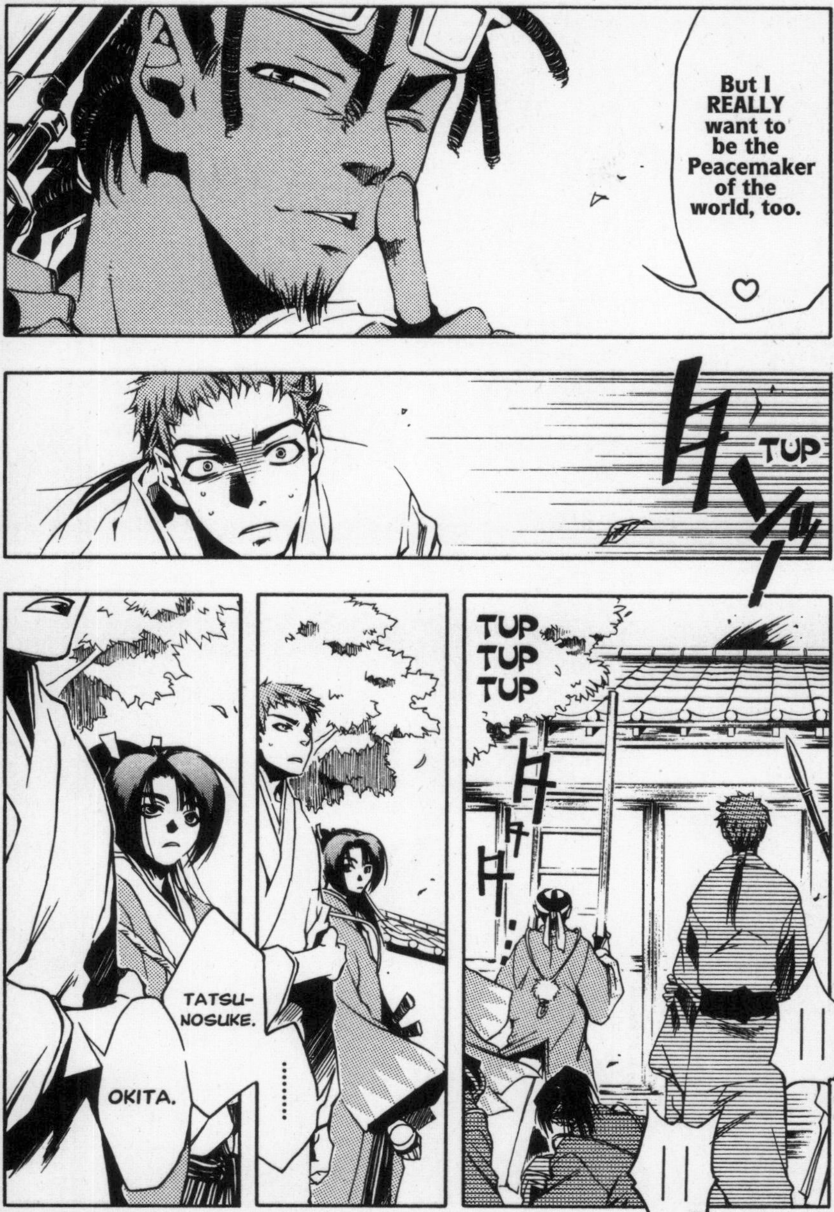
But I REALLY want to be the Peacemaker of the world, too. ♡
TUP
TUP TUP TUP
......
TATSU-NOSUKE.
OKITA.

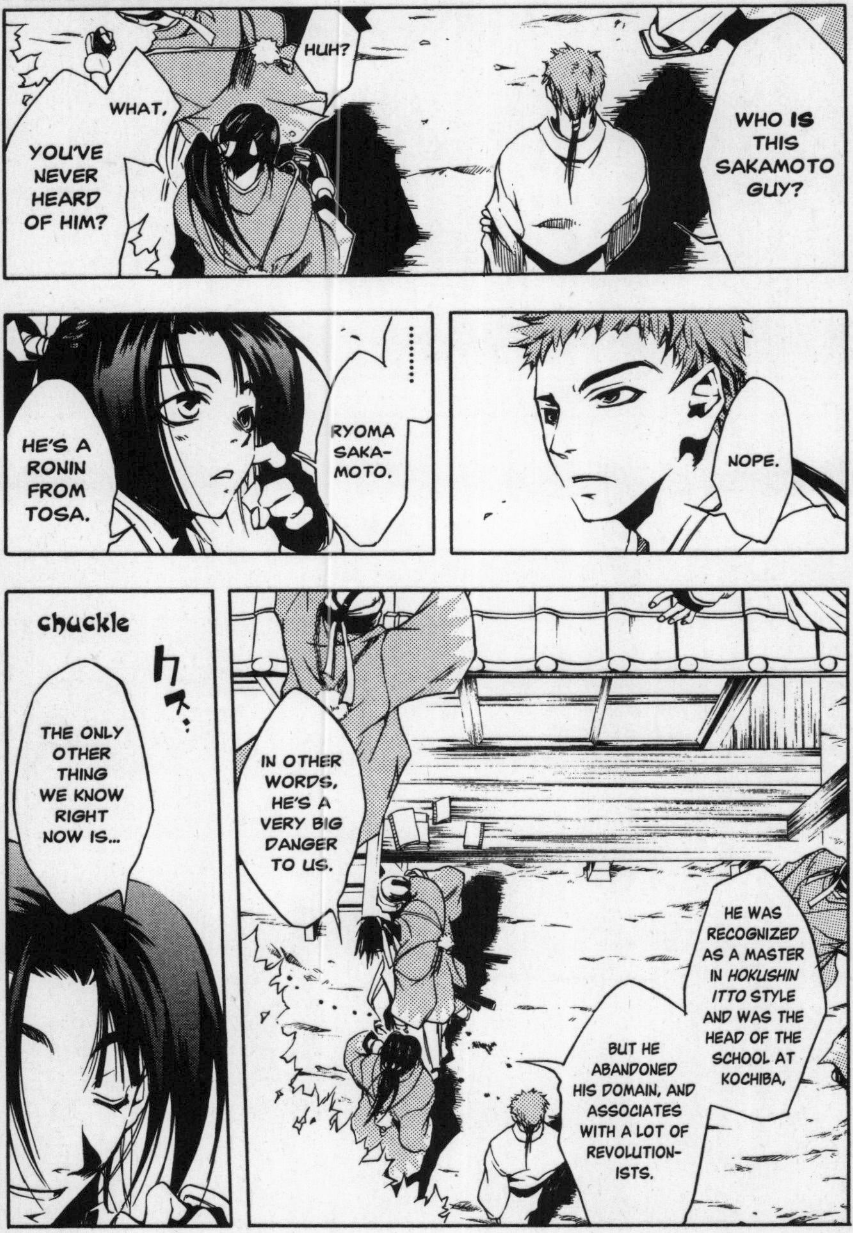
WHO IS THIS SAKAMOTO GUY?
HUH?
WHAT,
YOU'VE NEVER HEARD OF HIM?
NOPE.
......
RYOMA SAKA-MOTO.
HE'S A RONIN FROM TOSA.
HE WAS RECOGNIZED AS A MASTER IN *HOKUSHIN ITTO* STYLE AND WAS THE HEAD OF THE SCHOOL AT KOCHIBA,
BUT HE ABANDONED HIS DOMAIN, AND ASSOCIATES WITH A LOT OF REVOLUTION-ISTS.
IN OTHER WORDS, HE'S A VERY BIG DANGER TO US.
chuckle
クス
THE ONLY OTHER THING WE KNOW RIGHT NOW IS...

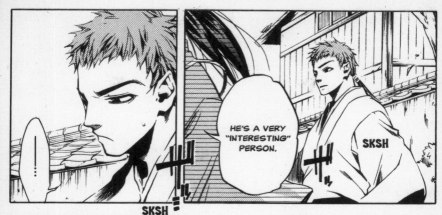

HE'S A VERY "INTERESTING" PERSON.

SKSH

SKSH

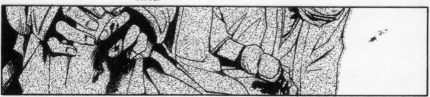

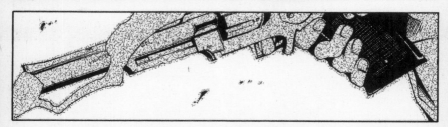

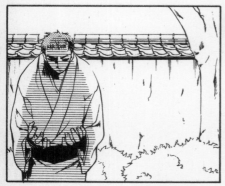

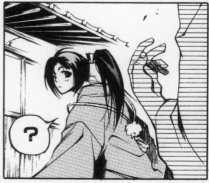

?

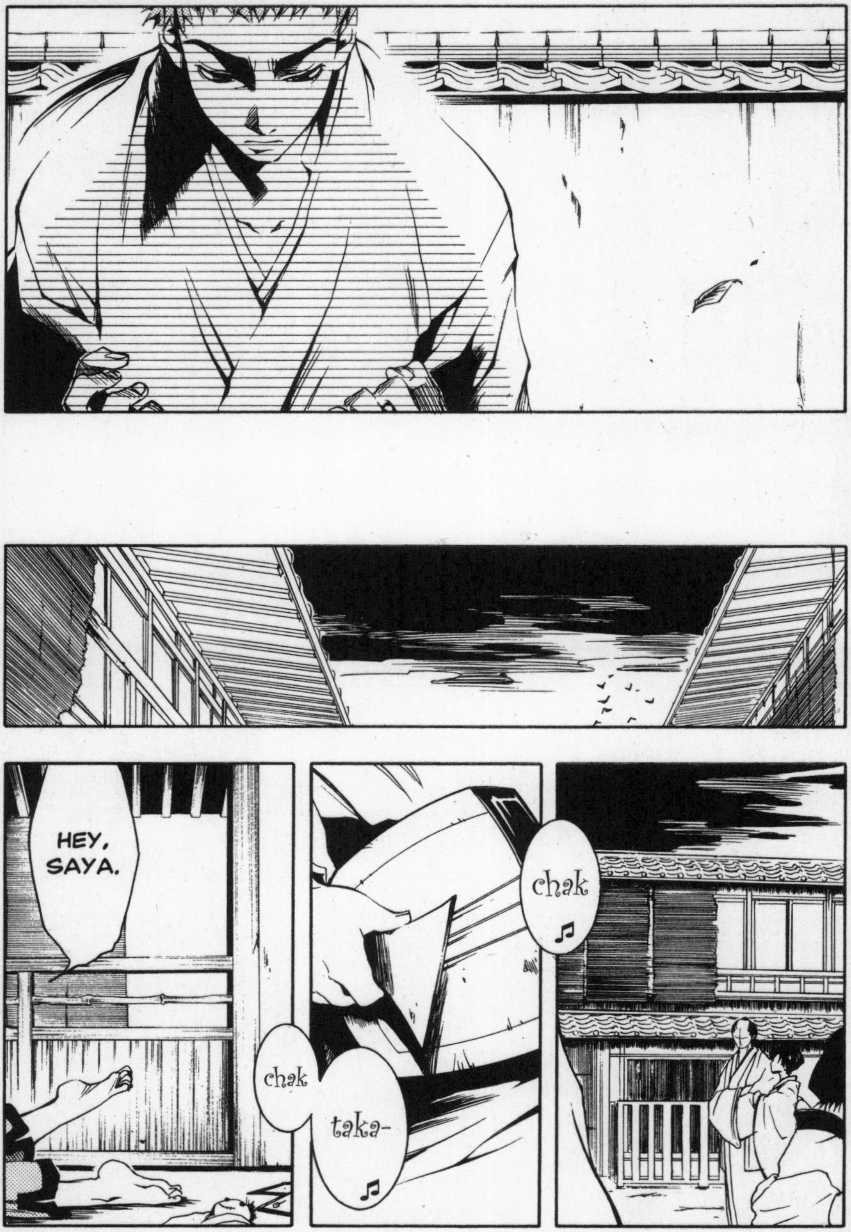
chak ♫
chak
taka- ♫
HEY, SAYA.

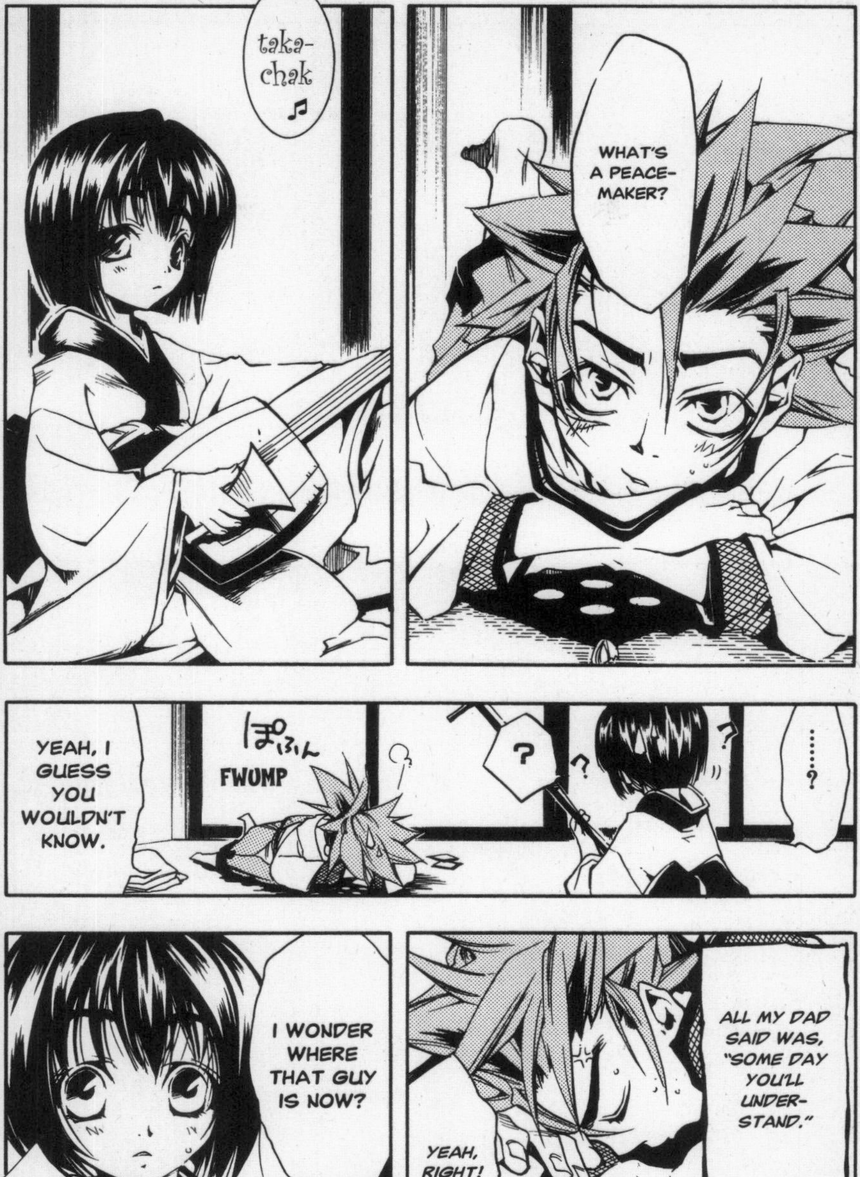
WHAT'S A PEACE-MAKER?
taka-chak ♫
......?
?
?
?
ぽふん
FWUMP
YEAH, I GUESS YOU WOULDN'T KNOW.
ALL MY DAD SAID WAS, "SOME DAY YOU'LL UNDER-STAND."
YEAH, RIGHT!
I WONDER WHERE THAT GUY IS NOW?
!!

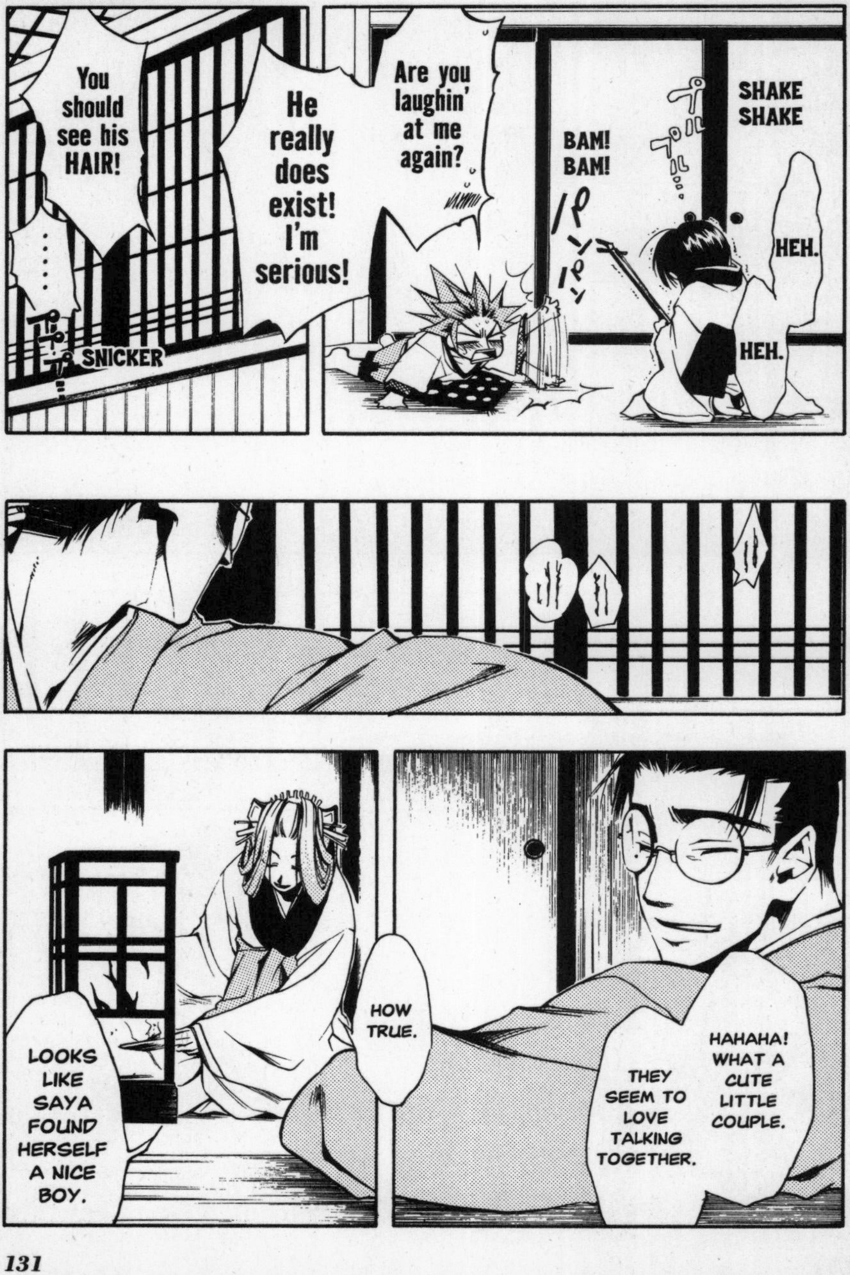
SHAKE SHAKE
HEH.
HEH.
BAM! BAM!
Are you laughin' at me again?
He really does exist! I'm serious!
You should see his HAIR!
......
SNICKER
HAHAHA! WHAT A CUTE LITTLE COUPLE.
THEY SEEM TO LOVE TALKING TOGETHER.
HOW TRUE.
LOOKS LIKE SAYA FOUND HERSELF A NICE BOY.

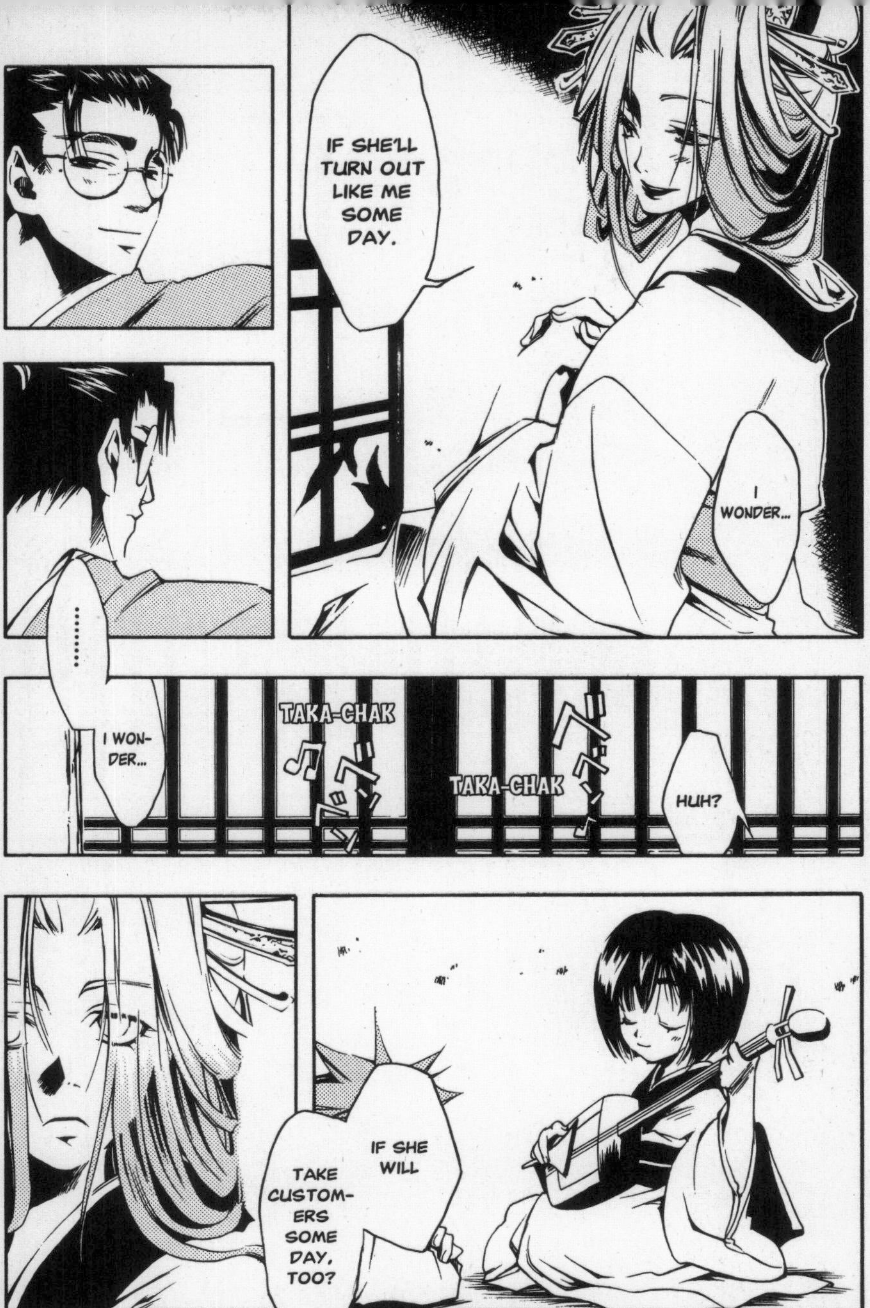
IF SHE'LL TURN OUT LIKE ME SOME DAY.
I WONDER...
......
HUH?
TAKA-CHAK
TAKA-CHAK
I WONDER...
IF SHE WILL TAKE CUSTOMERS SOME DAY, TOO?

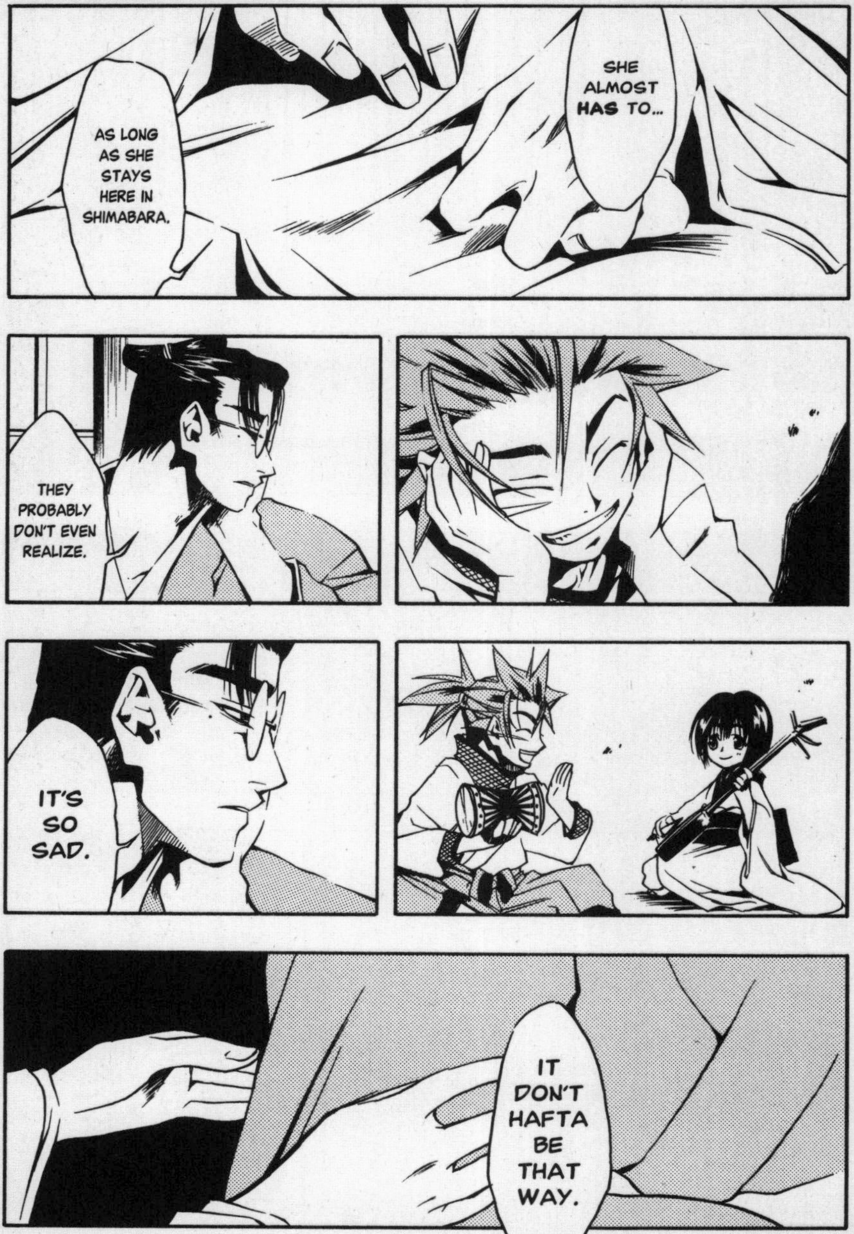
SHE ALMOST HAS TO...
AS LONG AS SHE STAYS HERE IN SHIMABARA.
THEY PROBABLY DON'T EVEN REALIZE.
IT'S SO SAD.
IT DON'T HAFTA BE THAT WAY.

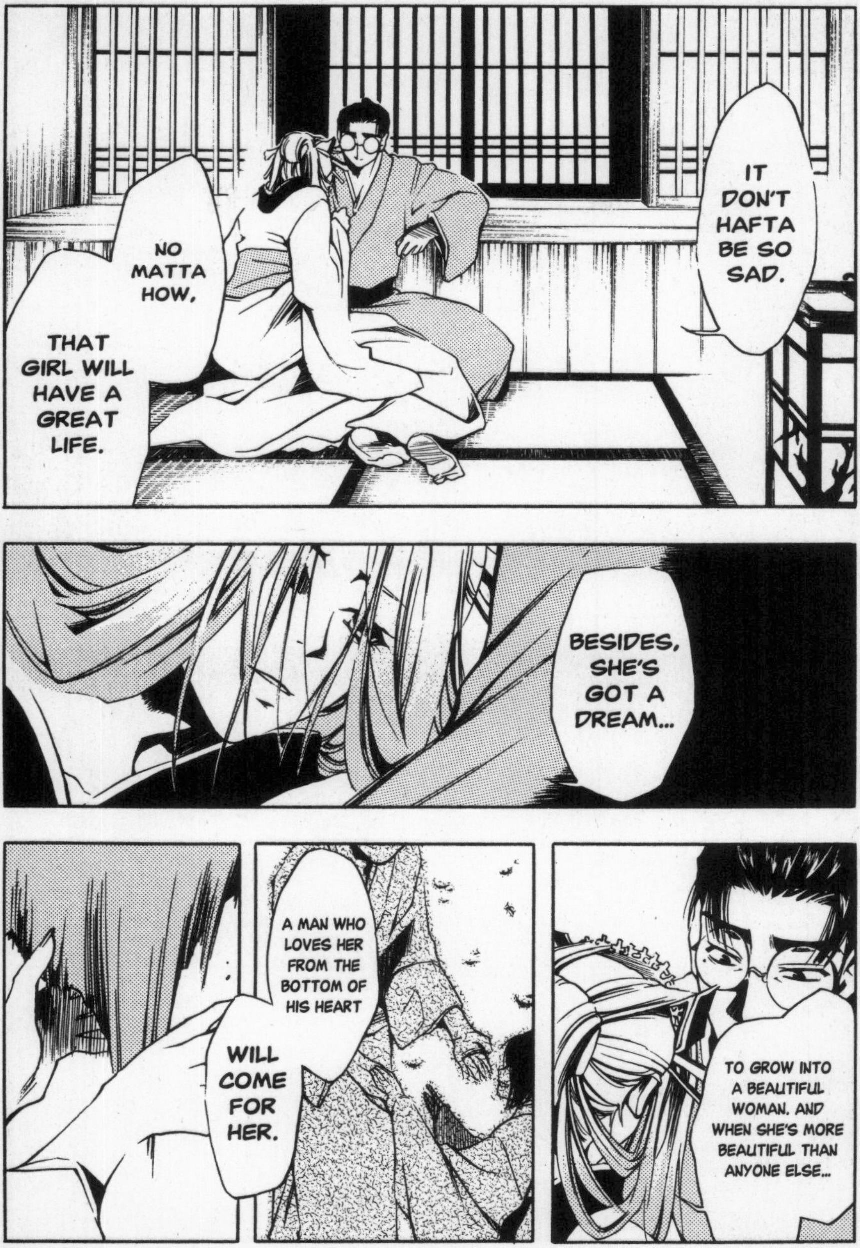
IT DON'T HAFTA BE SO SAD.
NO MATTA HOW,
THAT GIRL WILL HAVE A GREAT LIFE.
BESIDES, SHE'S GOT A DREAM...
TO GROW INTO A BEAUTIFUL WOMAN. AND WHEN SHE'S MORE BEAUTIFUL THAN ANYONE ELSE...
A MAN WHO LOVES HER FROM THE BOTTOM OF HIS HEART
WILL COME FOR HER.

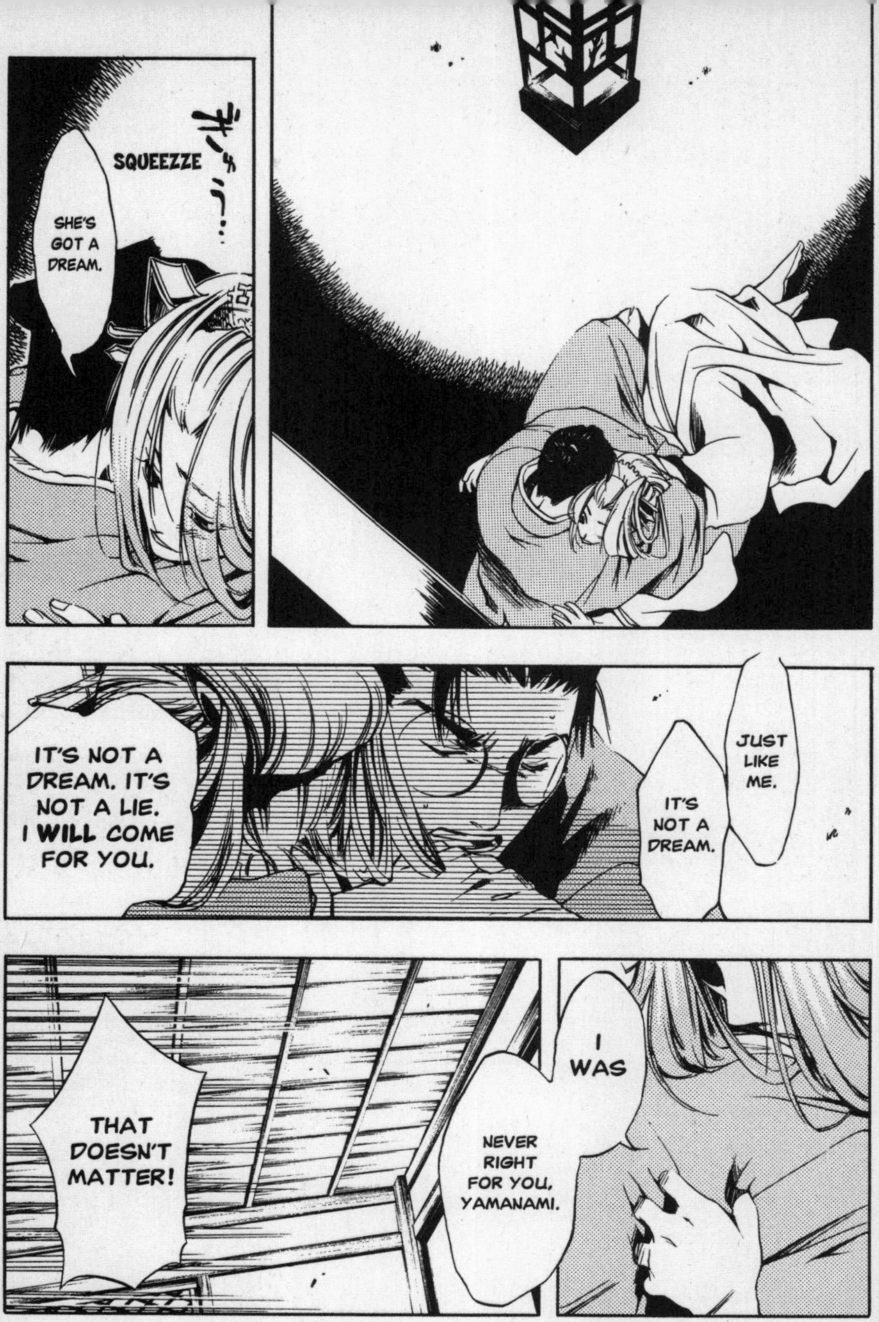
SQUEEZZE
SHE'S GOT A DREAM.
JUST LIKE ME.
IT'S NOT A DREAM.
IT'S NOT A DREAM. IT'S NOT A LIE. I **WILL** COME FOR YOU.
I WAS
NEVER RIGHT FOR YOU, YAMANAMI.
THAT DOESN'T MATTER!

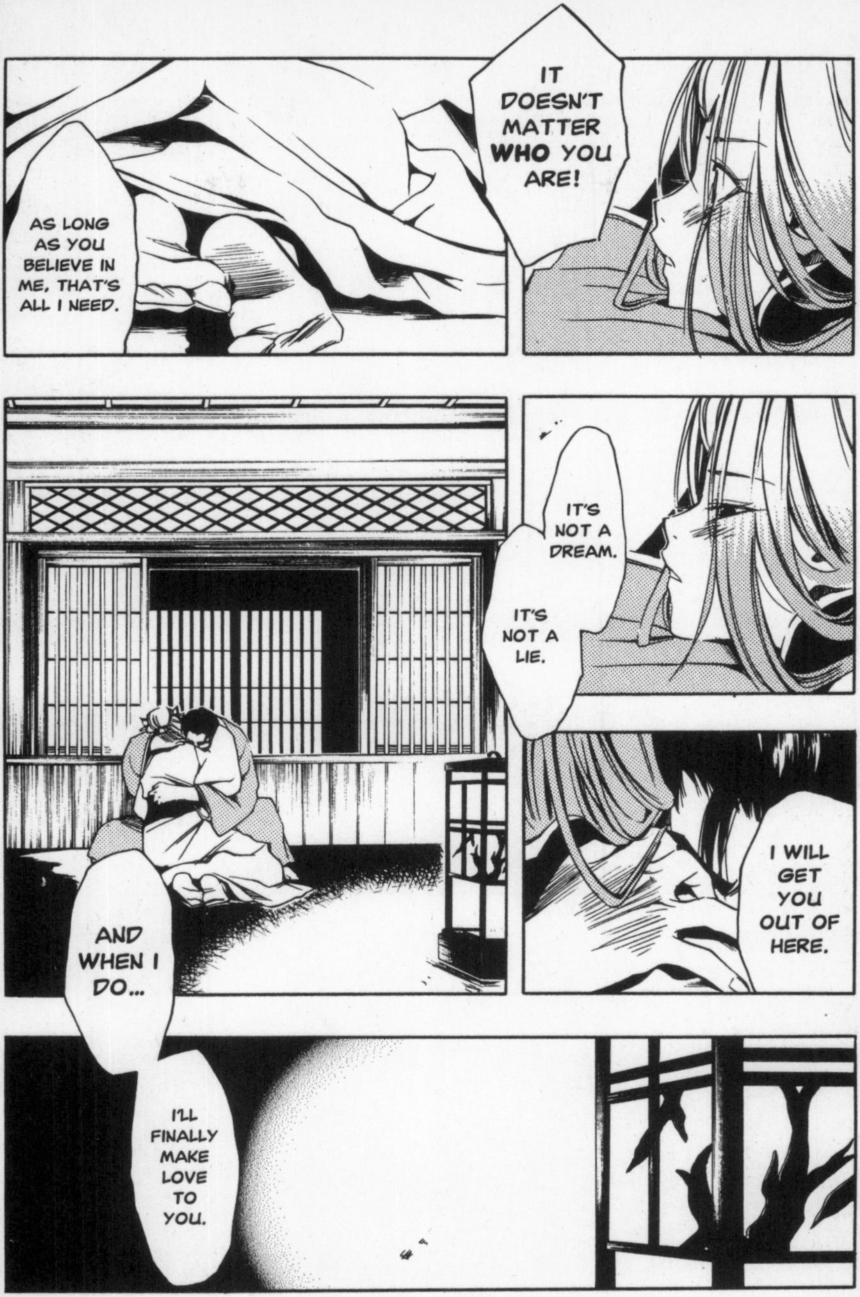
IT DOESN'T MATTER **WHO** YOU ARE!
AS LONG AS YOU BELIEVE IN ME, THAT'S ALL I NEED.
IT'S NOT A DREAM.
IT'S NOT A LIE.
I WILL GET YOU OUT OF HERE.
AND WHEN I DO...
I'LL FINALLY MAKE LOVE TO YOU.

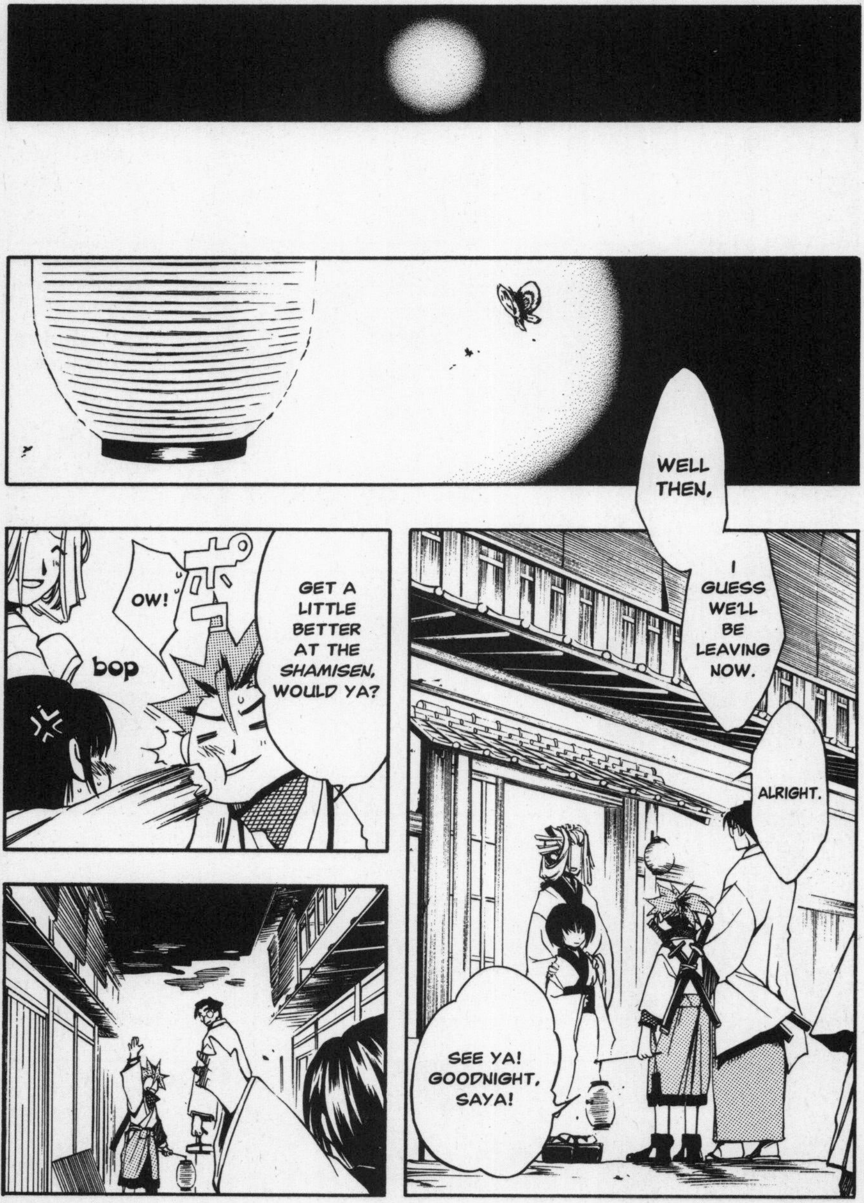
WELL THEN,
I GUESS WE'LL BE LEAVING NOW.
ALRIGHT.
SEE YA! GOODNIGHT, SAYA!
GET A LITTLE BETTER AT THE *SHAMISEN*, WOULD YA?
OW!
bop

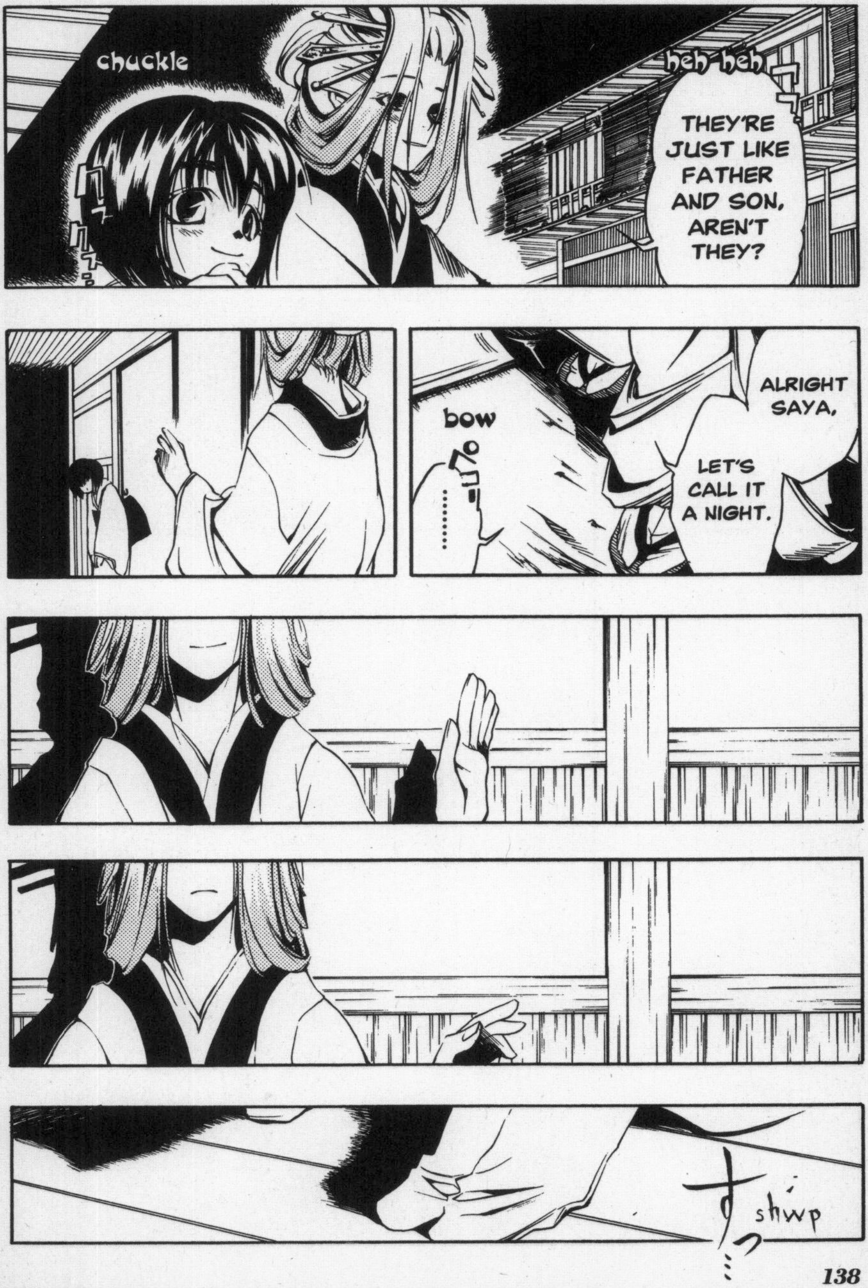
heh heh
THEY'RE JUST LIKE FATHER AND SON, AREN'T THEY?
chuckle
ALRIGHT SAYA,
LET'S CALL IT A NIGHT.
bow
......
shwp

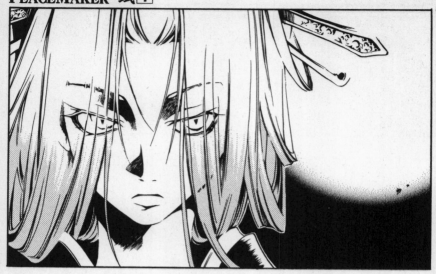

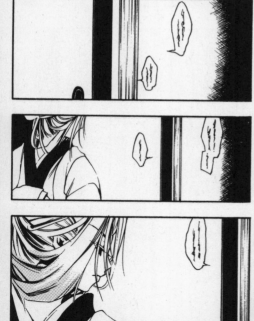

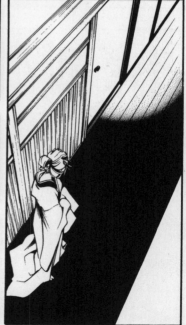

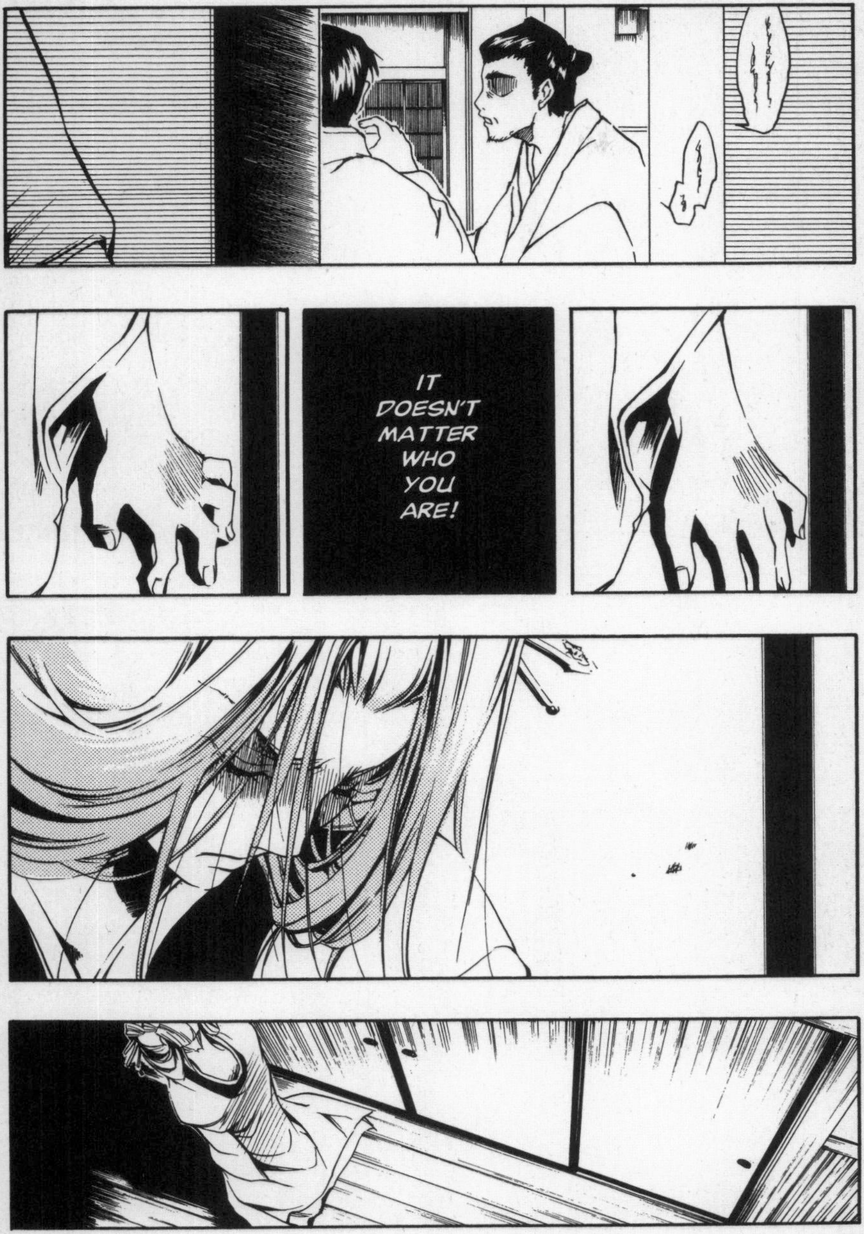
IT DOESN'T MATTER WHO YOU ARE!

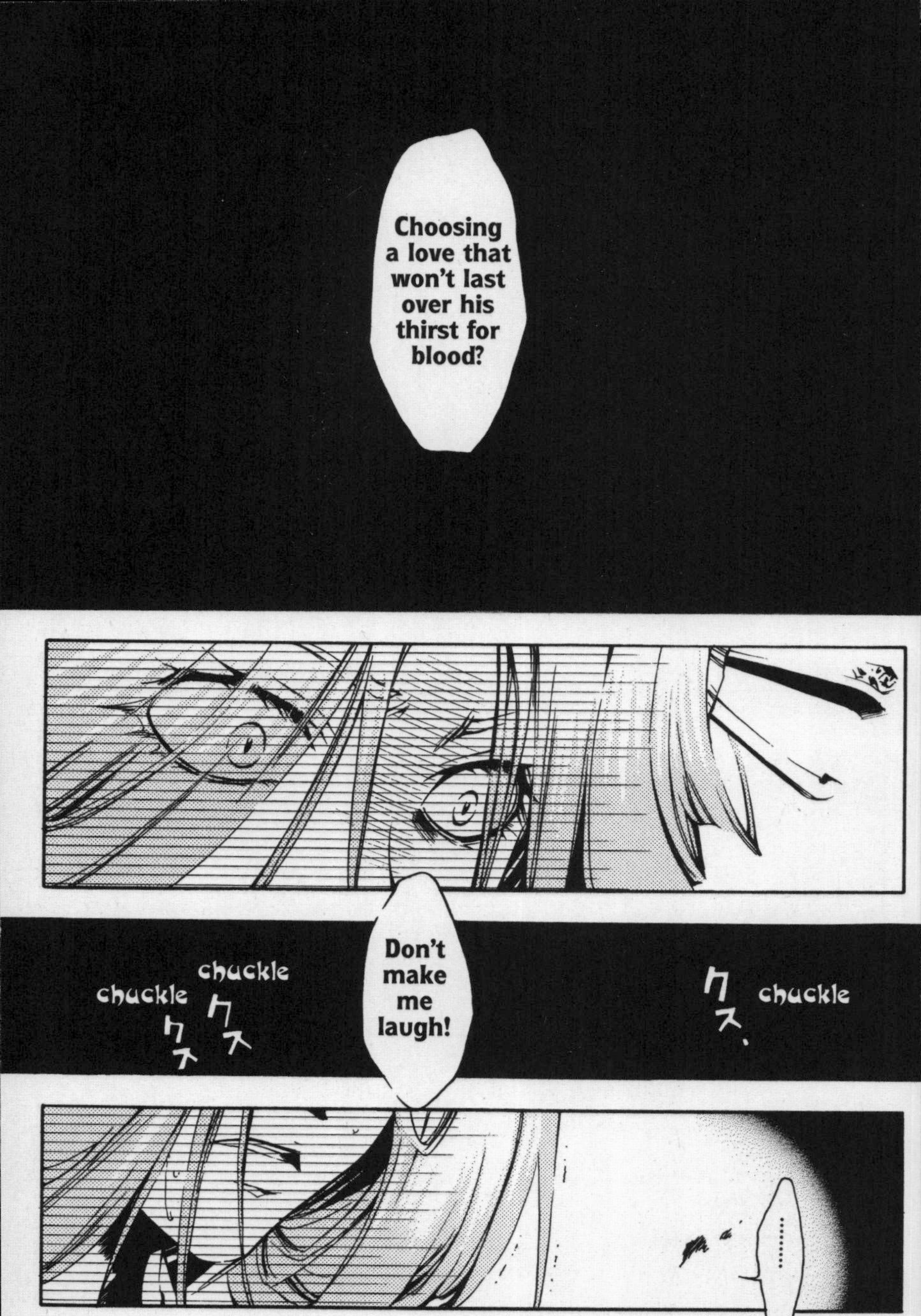

Choosing a love that won't last over his thirst for blood?
クス.
chuckle
Don't make me laugh!
chuckle
クス
chuckle
クス
....

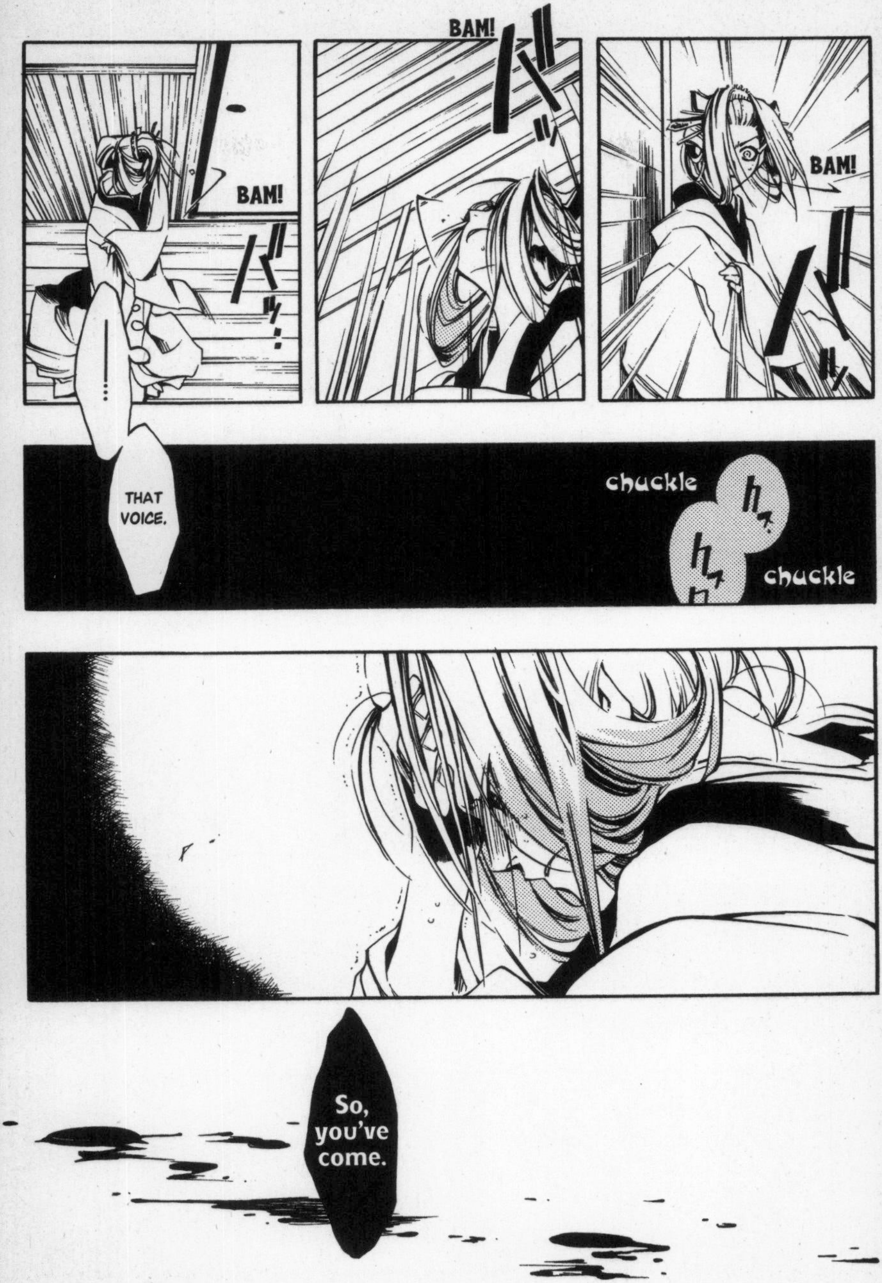
BAM!
BAM!
BAM!
......
THAT VOICE.
chuckle
chuckle
So, you've come.

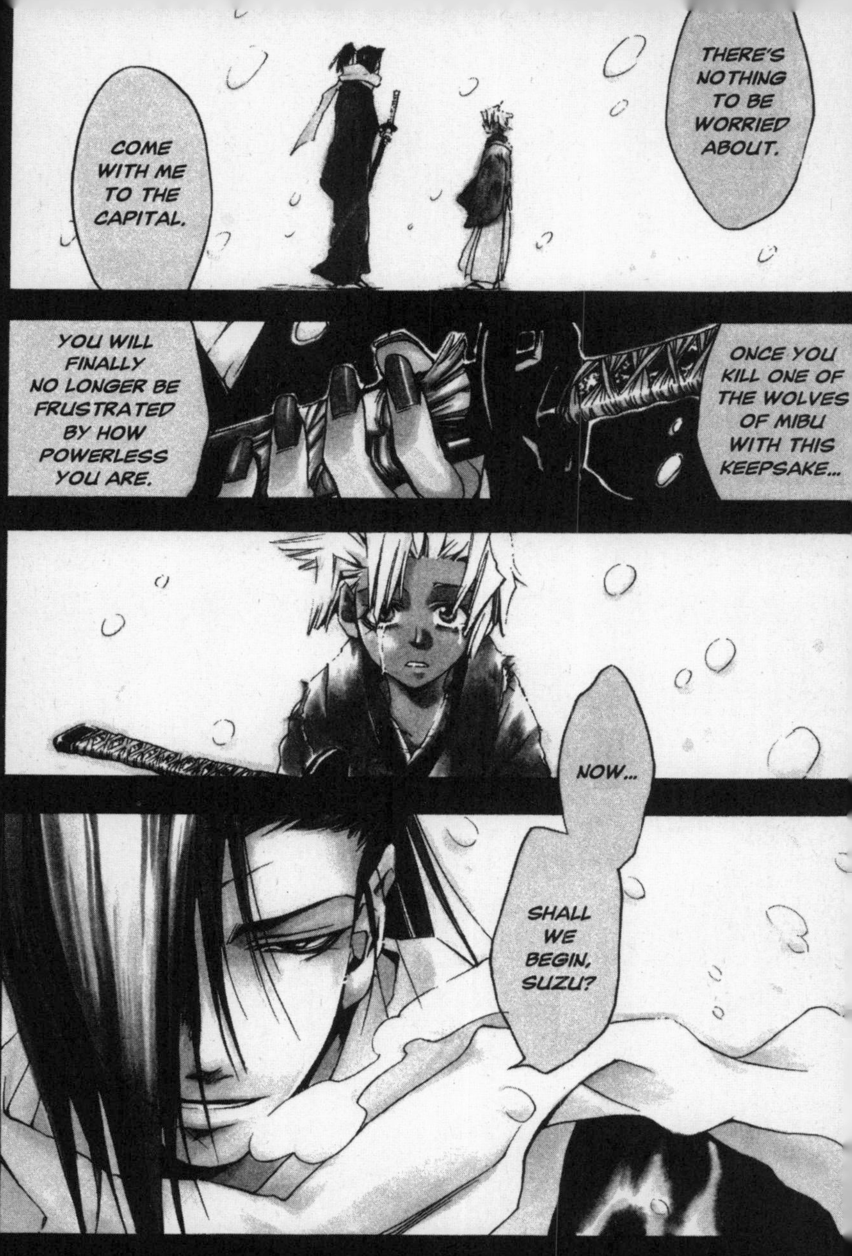
THERE'S NOTHING TO BE WORRIED ABOUT.
COME WITH ME TO THE CAPITAL.
ONCE YOU KILL ONE OF THE WOLVES OF MIBU WITH THIS KEEPSAKE...
YOU WILL FINALLY NO LONGER BE FRUSTRATED BY HOW POWERLESS YOU ARE.
NOW...
SHALL WE BEGIN, SUZU?

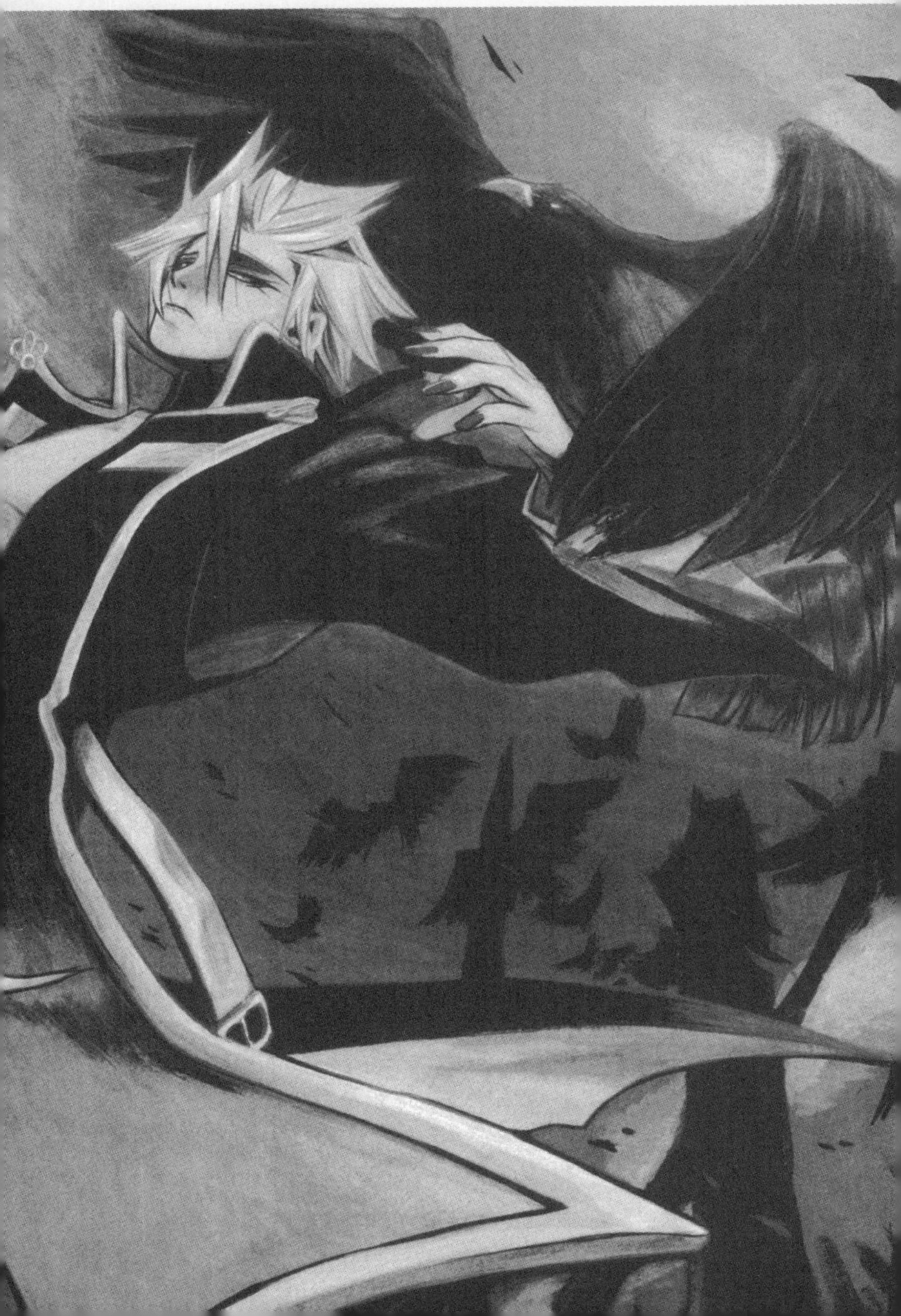

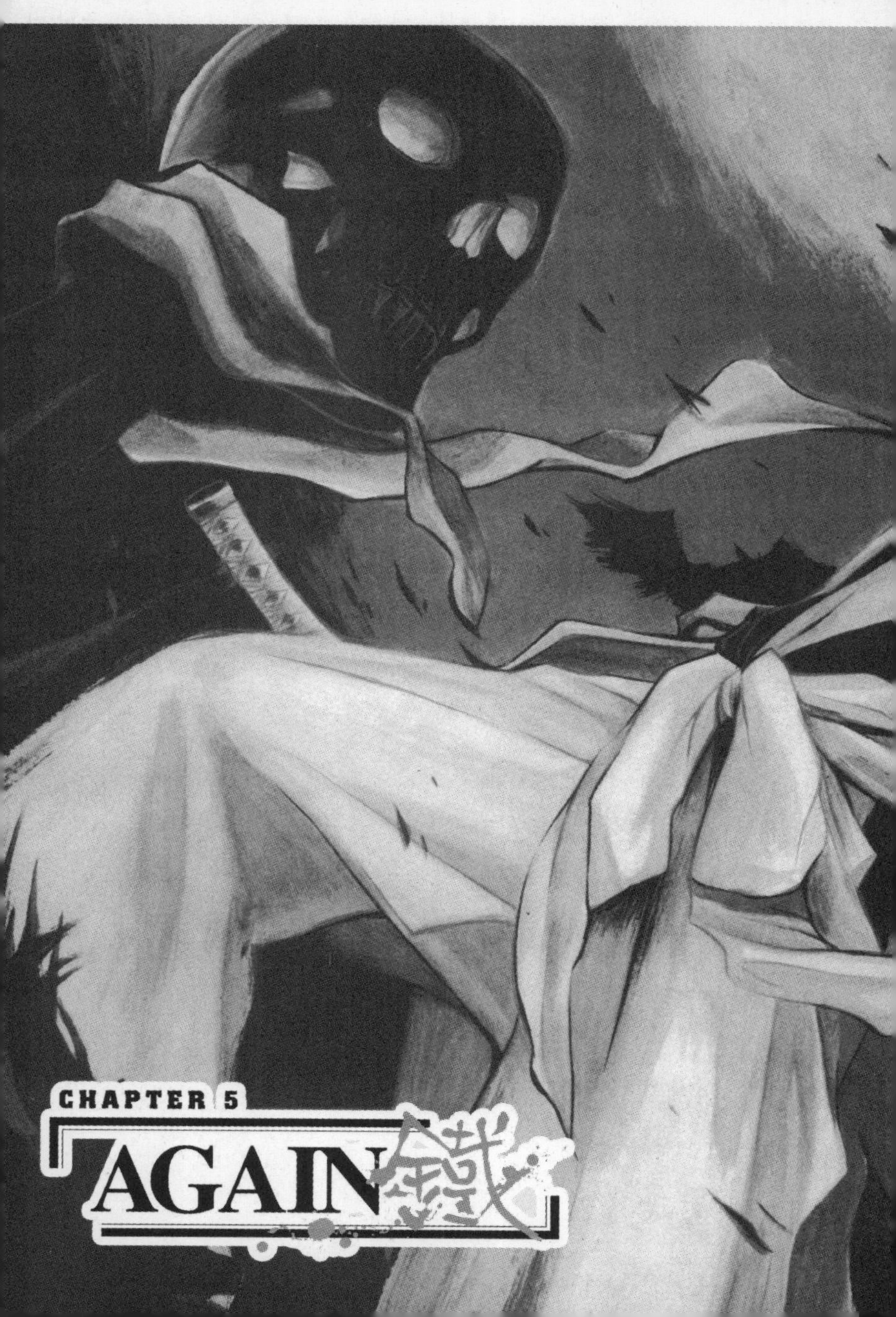
CHAPTER 5
AGAIN

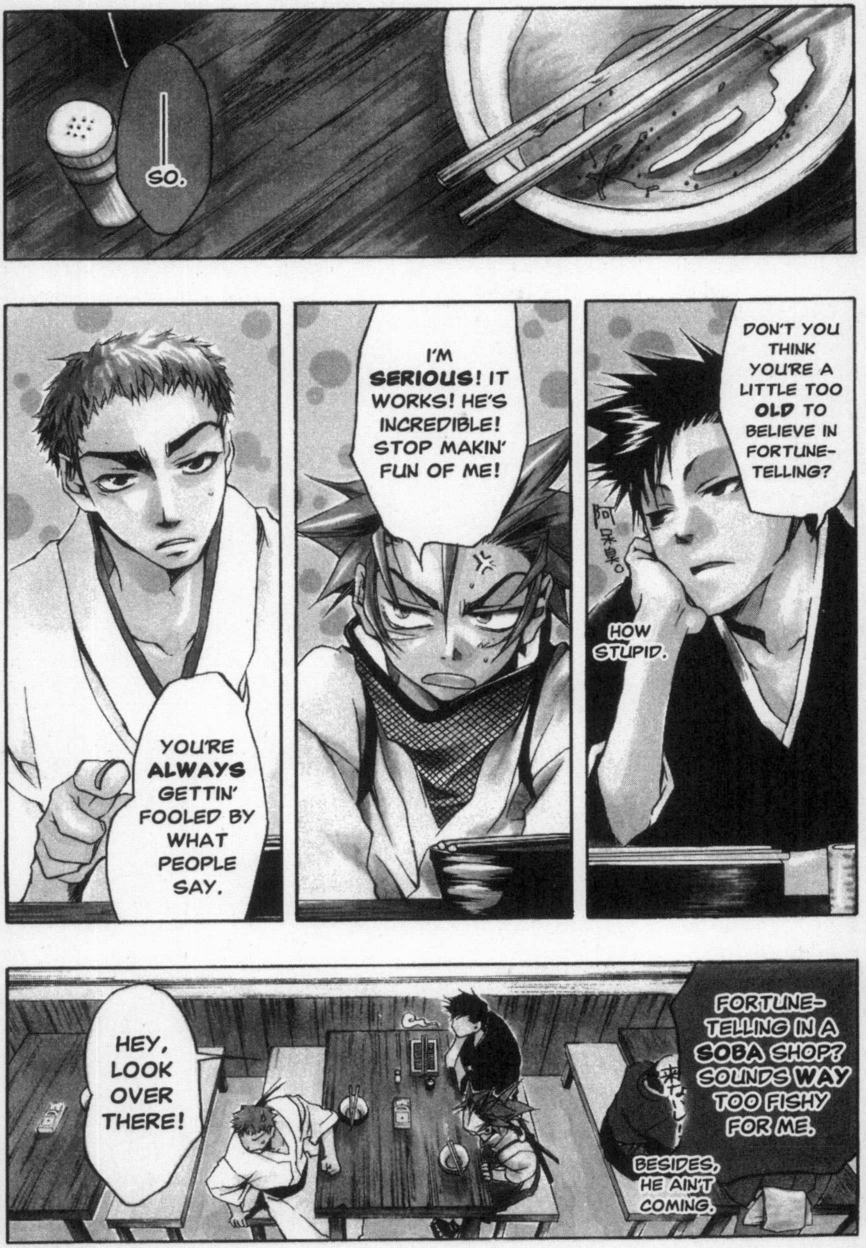
SO.
DON'T YOU THINK YOU'RE A LITTLE TOO OLD TO BELIEVE IN FORTUNE-TELLING?
HOW STUPID.
I'M SERIOUS! IT WORKS! HE'S INCREDIBLE! STOP MAKIN' FUN OF ME!
YOU'RE ALWAYS GETTIN' FOOLED BY WHAT PEOPLE SAY.
FORTUNE-TELLING IN A SOBA SHOP? SOUNDS WAY TOO FISHY FOR ME.
BESIDES, HE AIN'T COMING.
HEY, LOOK OVER THERE!

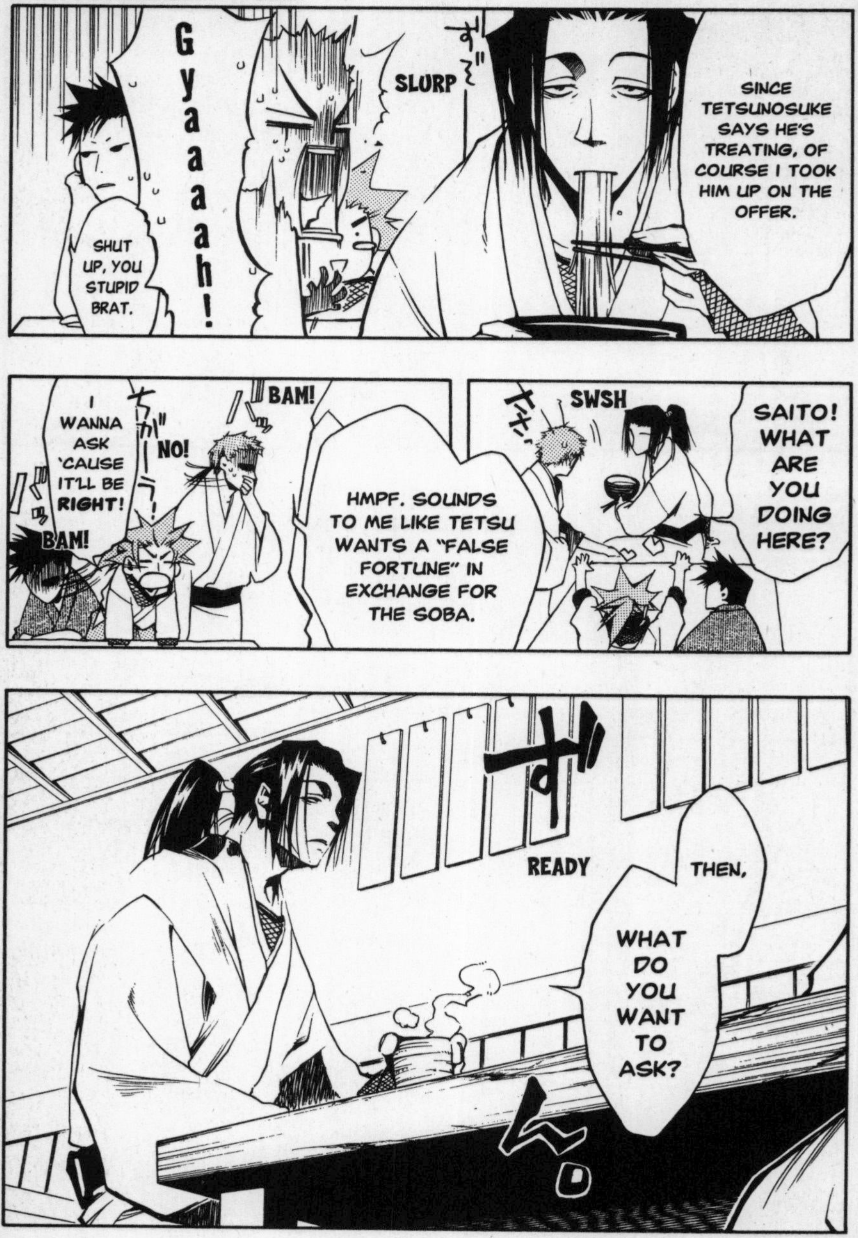
SINCE TETSUNOSUKE SAYS HE'S TREATING, OF COURSE I TOOK HIM UP ON THE OFFER.
SLURP
Gyaaaah!
SHUT UP, YOU STUPID BRAT.
SAITO! WHAT ARE YOU DOING HERE?
SWSH
HMPF. SOUNDS TO ME LIKE TETSU WANTS A "FALSE FORTUNE" IN EXCHANGE FOR THE SOBA.
BAM!
NO!
I WANNA ASK 'CAUSE IT'LL BE RIGHT!
BAM!
THEN,
WHAT DO YOU WANT TO ASK?
READY

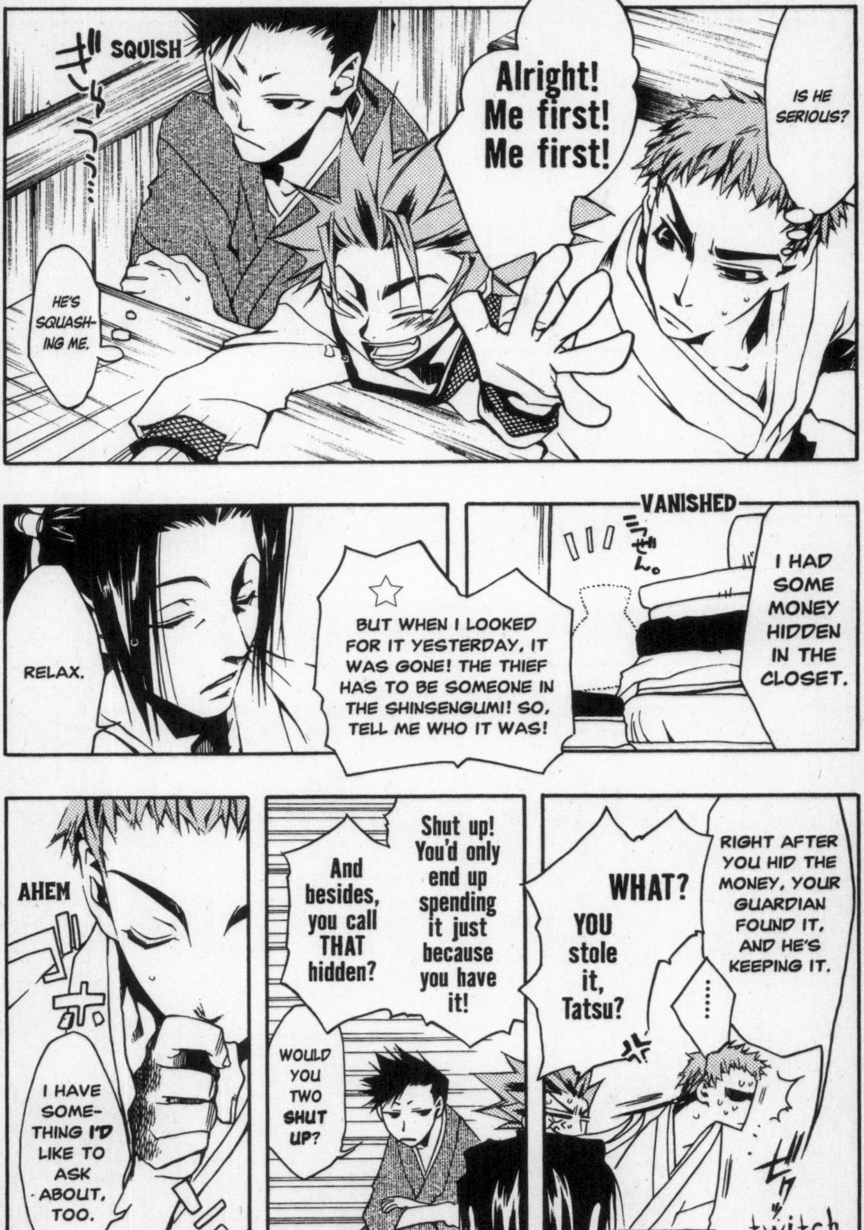
IS HE SERIOUS?
Alright! Me first! Me first!
SQUISH
HE'S SQUASHING ME.
VANISHED
I HAD SOME MONEY HIDDEN IN THE CLOSET.
☆ BUT WHEN I LOOKED FOR IT YESTERDAY, IT WAS GONE! THE THIEF HAS TO BE SOMEONE IN THE SHINSENGUMI! SO, TELL ME WHO IT WAS!
RELAX.
RIGHT AFTER YOU HID THE MONEY, YOUR GUARDIAN FOUND IT, AND HE'S KEEPING IT.
WHAT?
YOU stole it, Tatsu?
......
twitch
Shut up! You'd only end up spending it just because you have it!
And besides, you call THAT hidden?
WOULD YOU TWO SHUT UP?
AHEM
I HAVE SOMETHING I'D LIKE TO ASK ABOUT, TOO.

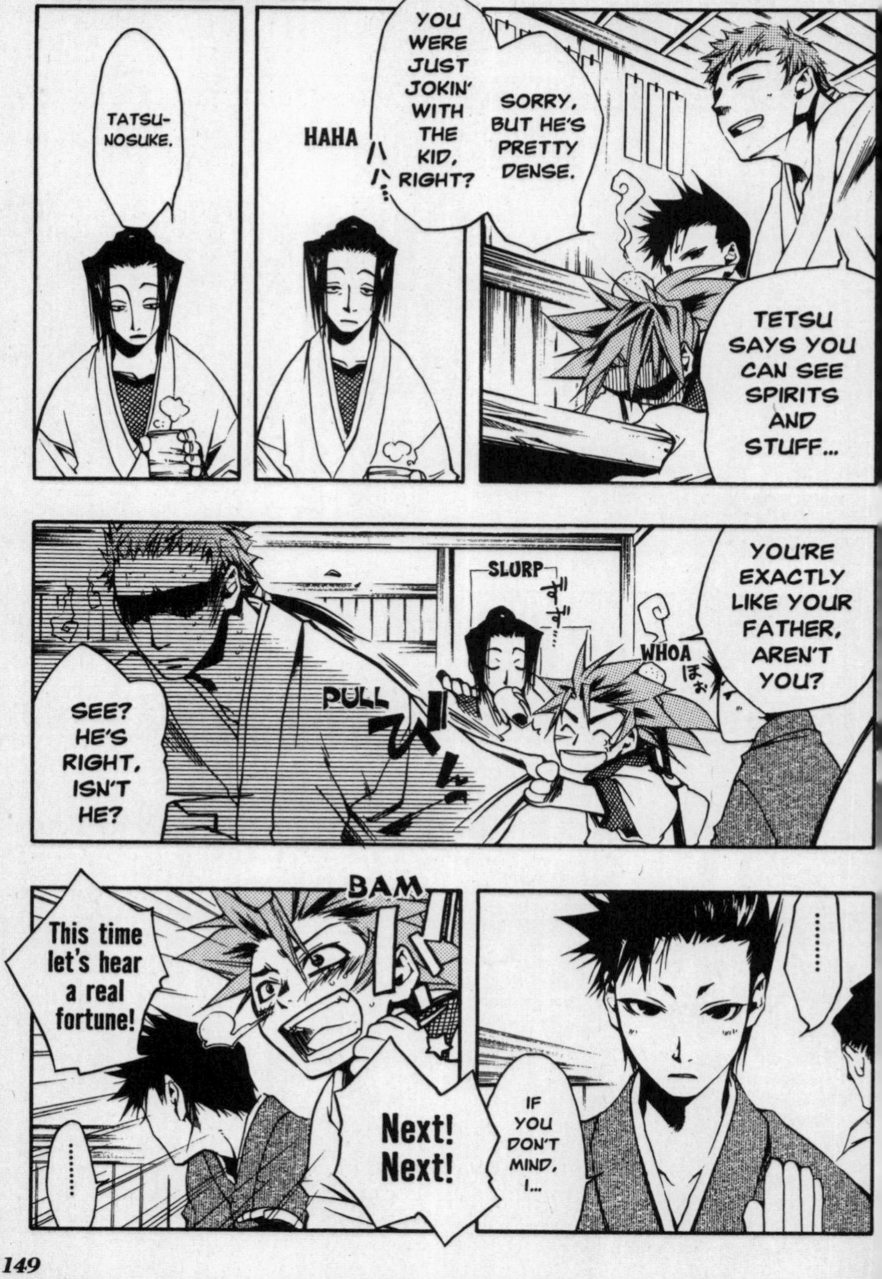
SORRY, BUT HE'S PRETTY DENSE.
TETSU SAYS YOU CAN SEE SPIRITS AND STUFF...
YOU WERE JUST JOKIN' WITH THE KID, RIGHT?
HAHA
ハハ...
TATSU-NOSUKE.
YOU'RE EXACTLY LIKE YOUR FATHER, AREN'T YOU?
WHOA
ほぉ
SLURP
ずず...
PULL
SEE? HE'S RIGHT, ISN'T HE?
......
IF YOU DON'T MIND, I...
BAM
Next! Next!
This time let's hear a real fortune!
......

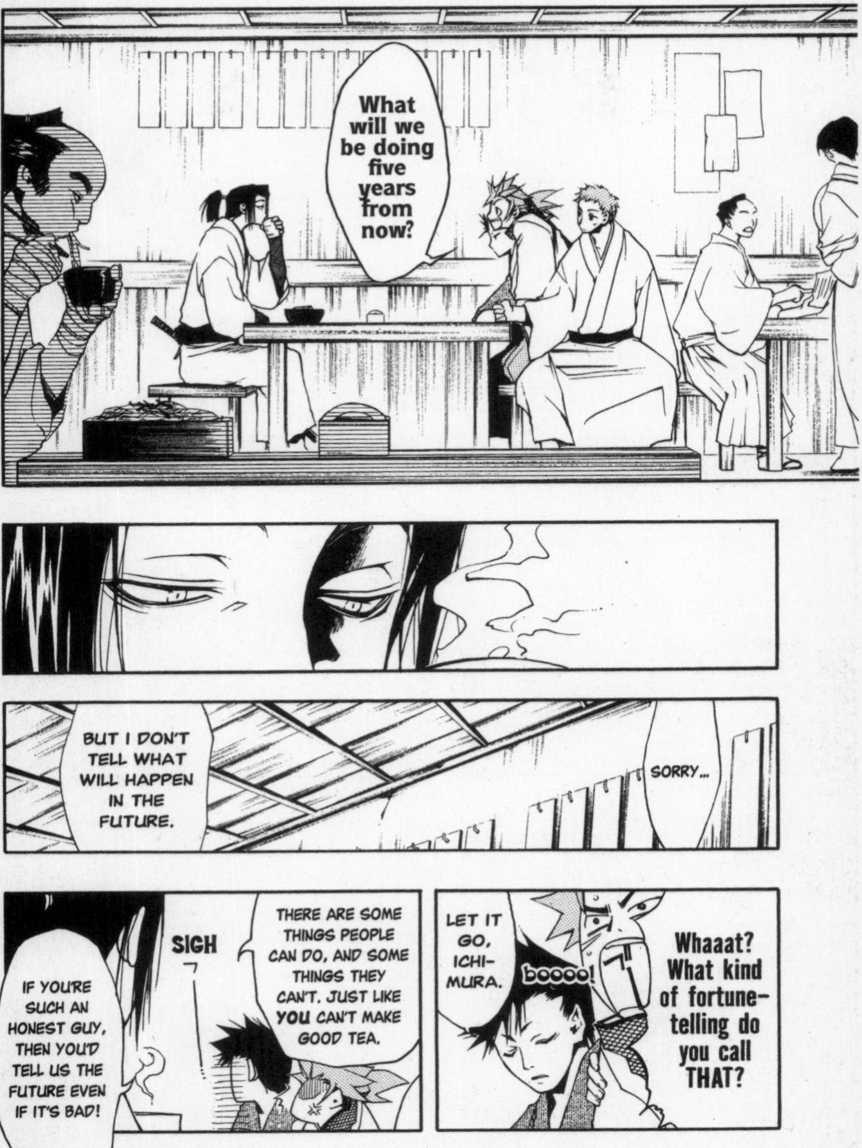
What will we be doing five years from now?
SORRY...
BUT I DON'T TELL WHAT WILL HAPPEN IN THE FUTURE.
Whaaat? What kind of fortune-telling do you call THAT?
booooo!
LET IT GO, ICHI-MURA.
THERE ARE SOME THINGS PEOPLE CAN DO, AND SOME THINGS THEY CAN'T. JUST LIKE YOU CAN'T MAKE GOOD TEA.
SIGH
IF YOU'RE SUCH AN HONEST GUY, THEN YOU'D TELL US THE FUTURE EVEN IF IT'S BAD!

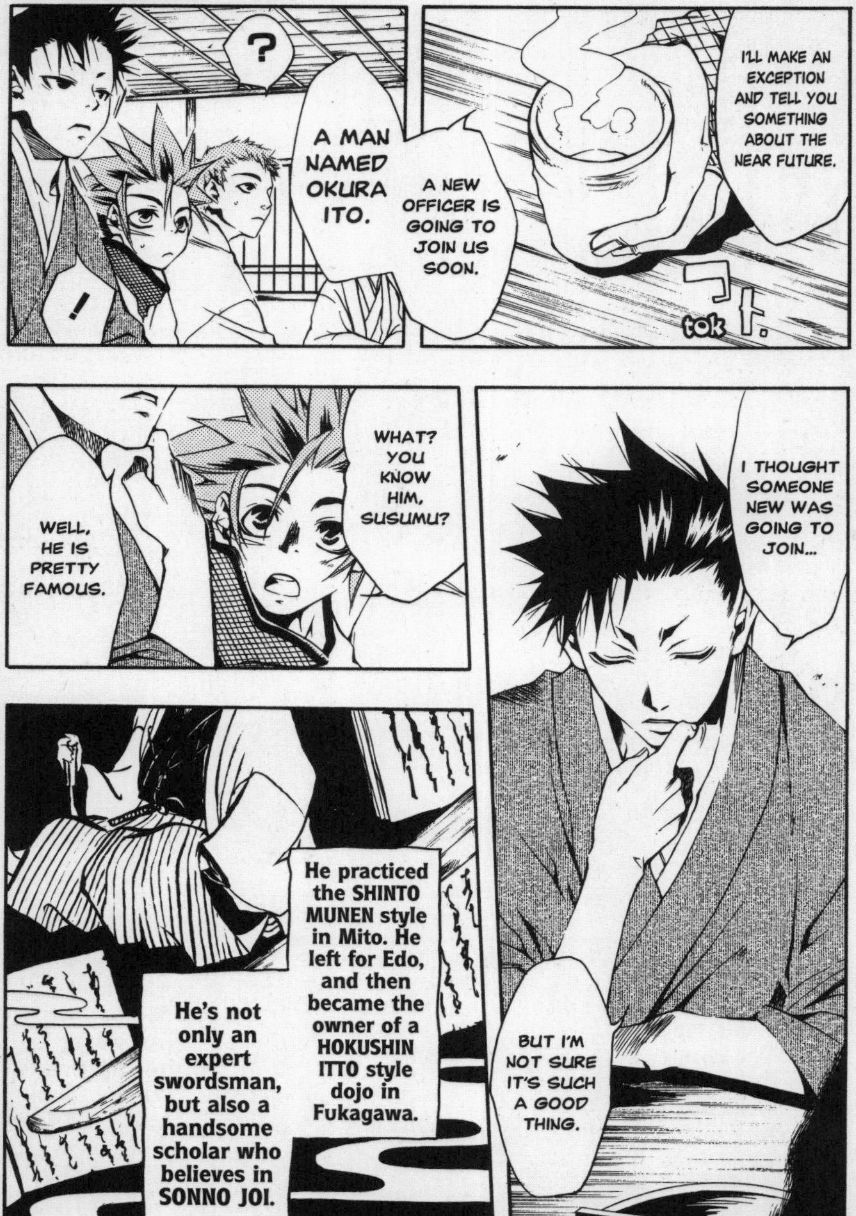
I'LL MAKE AN EXCEPTION AND TELL YOU SOMETHING ABOUT THE NEAR FUTURE.
tok
A NEW OFFICER IS GOING TO JOIN US SOON.
?
A MAN NAMED OKURA ITO.
!
I THOUGHT SOMEONE NEW WAS GOING TO JOIN...
BUT I'M NOT SURE IT'S SUCH A GOOD THING.
WHAT? YOU KNOW HIM, SUSUMU?
WELL, HE IS PRETTY FAMOUS.
He practiced the SHINTO MUNEN style in Mito. He left for Edo, and then became the owner of a HOKUSHIN ITTO style dojo in Fukagawa.
He's not only an expert swordsman, but also a handsome scholar who believes in SONNO JOI.

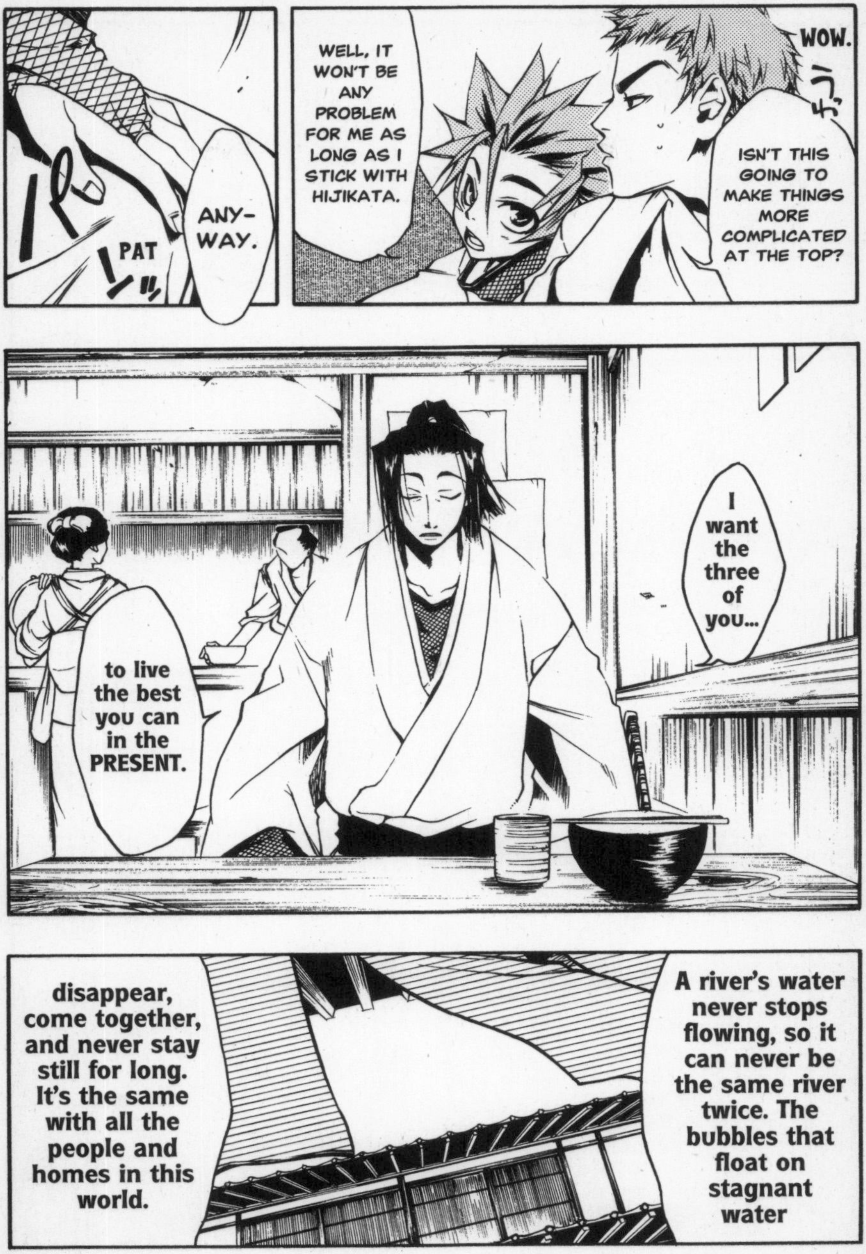
WOW.
ISN'T THIS GOING TO MAKE THINGS MORE COMPLICATED AT THE TOP?
WELL, IT WON'T BE ANY PROBLEM FOR ME AS LONG AS I STICK WITH HIJIKATA.
ANY-WAY.
PAT
I want the three of you...
to live the best you can in the PRESENT.
A river's water never stops flowing, so it can never be the same river twice. The bubbles that float on stagnant water
disappear, come together, and never stay still for long. It's the same with all the people and homes in this world.

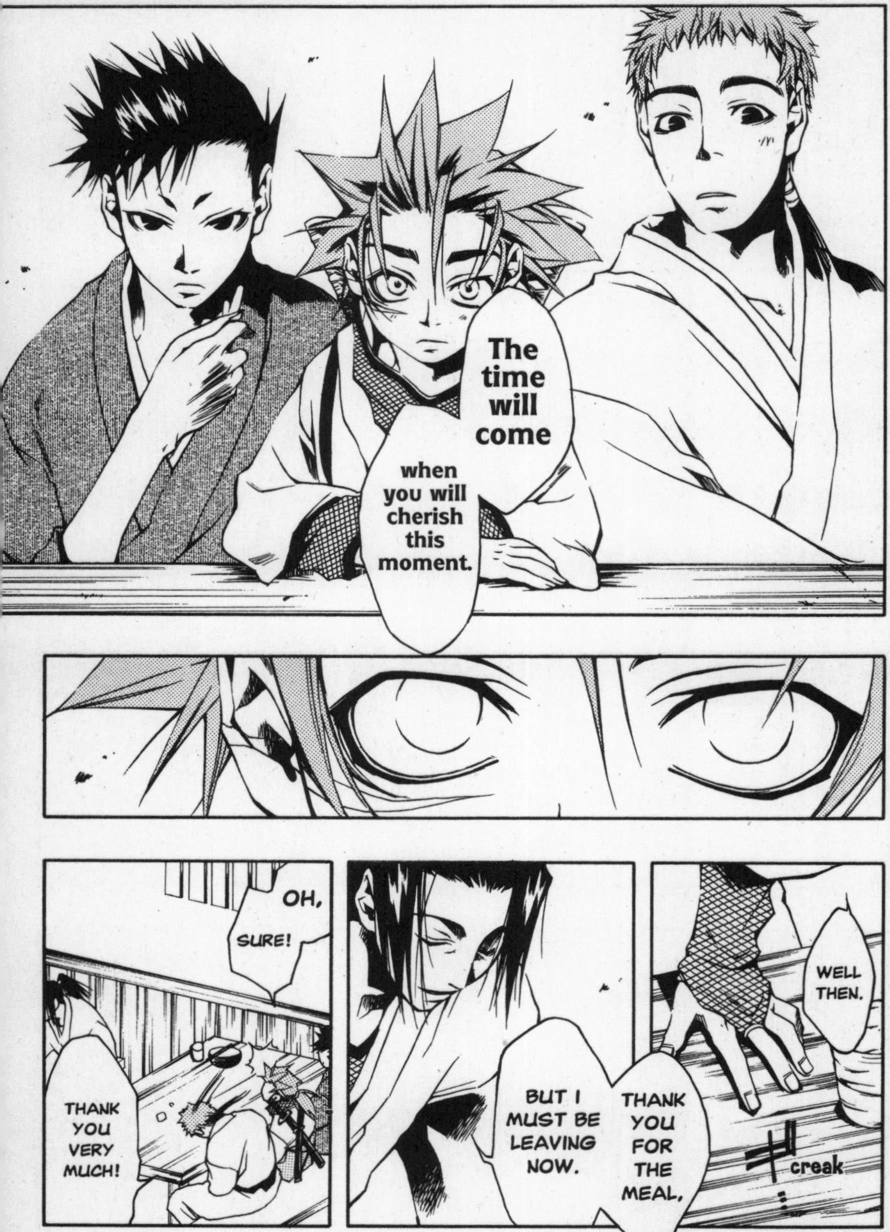
The time will come
when you will cherish this moment.
WELL THEN.
creak
THANK YOU FOR THE MEAL,
BUT I MUST BE LEAVING NOW.
OH, SURE!
THANK YOU VERY MUCH!

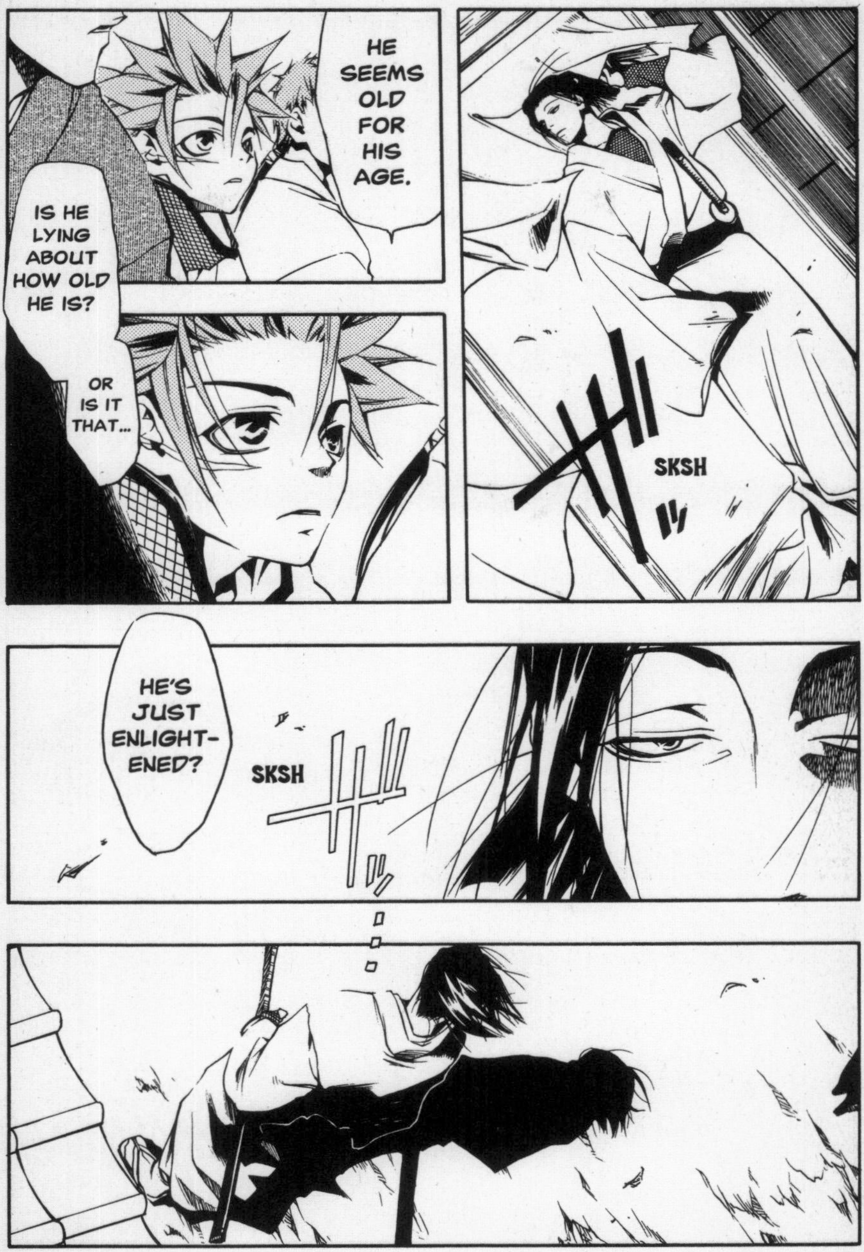
SKSH
HE SEEMS OLD FOR HIS AGE.
IS HE LYING ABOUT HOW OLD HE IS?
OR IS IT THAT...
HE'S JUST ENLIGHTENED?
SKSH

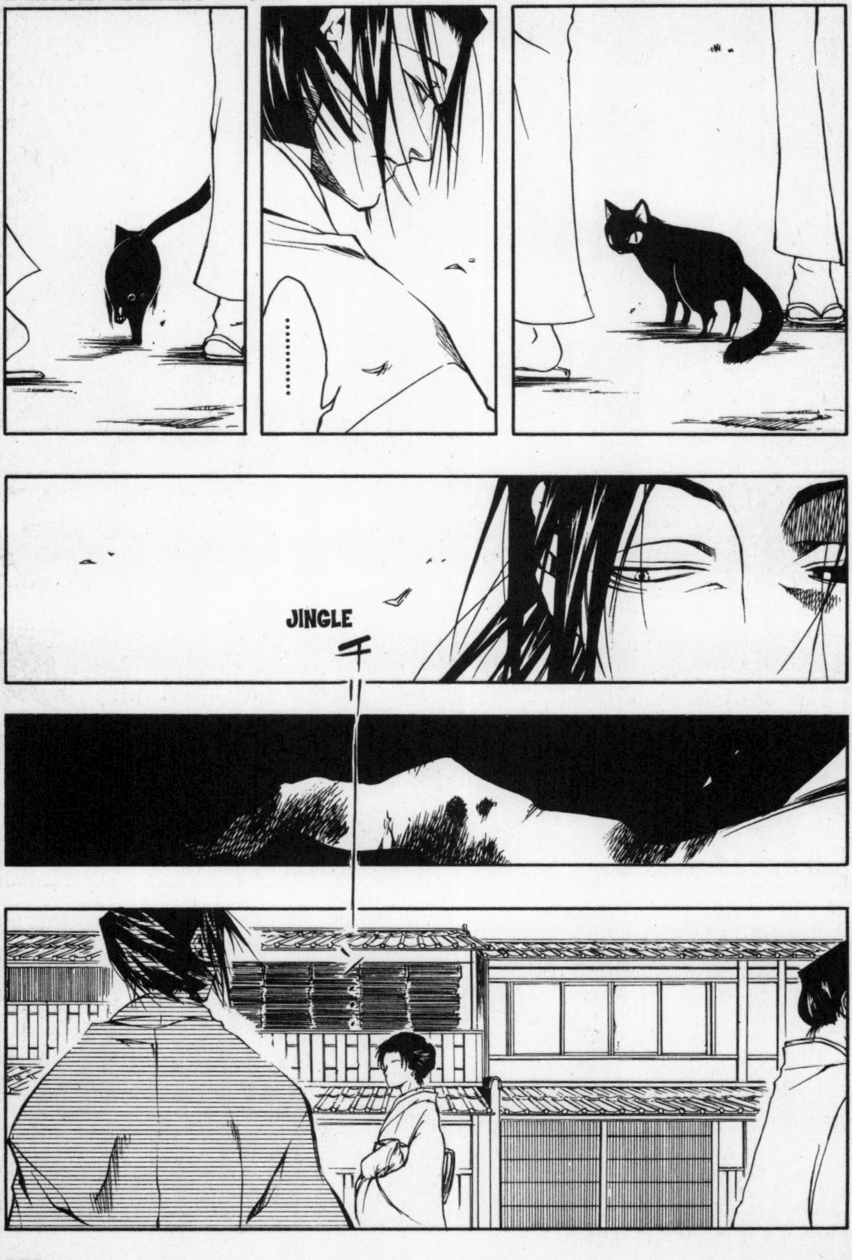
....
JINGLE
チリ

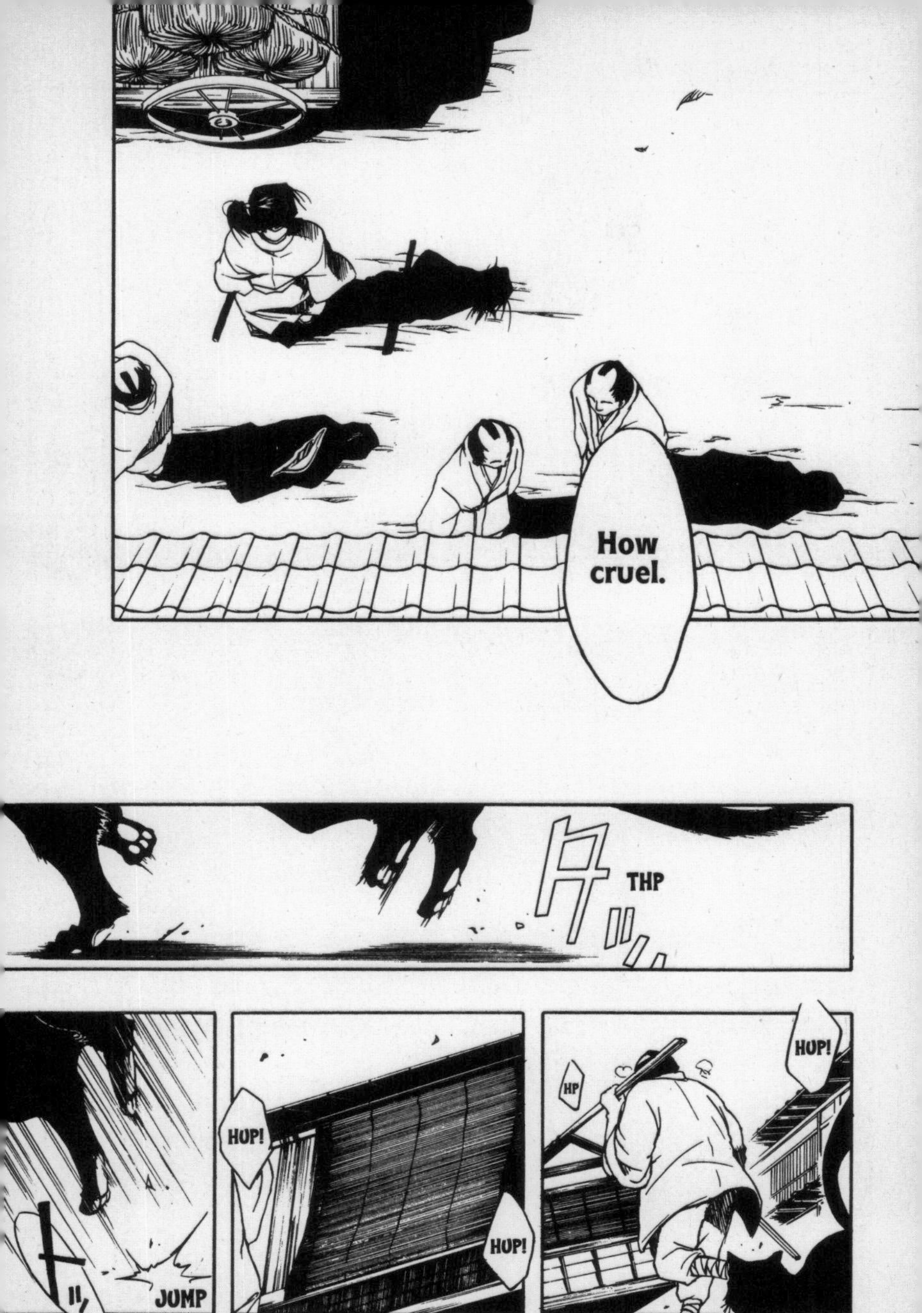
How cruel.
THP
HOP!
HP
HOP!
HOP!
JUMP

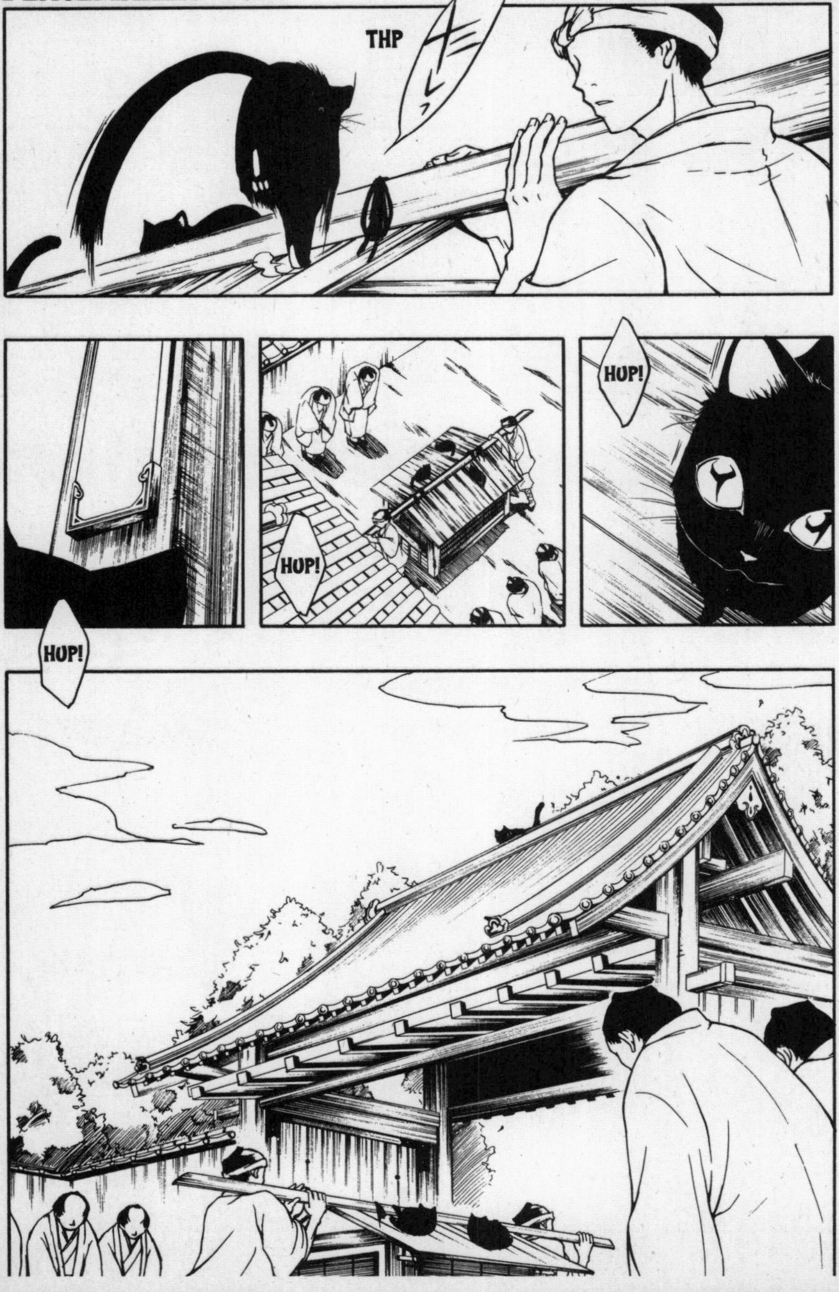
THP
HOP!
HOP!
HOP!

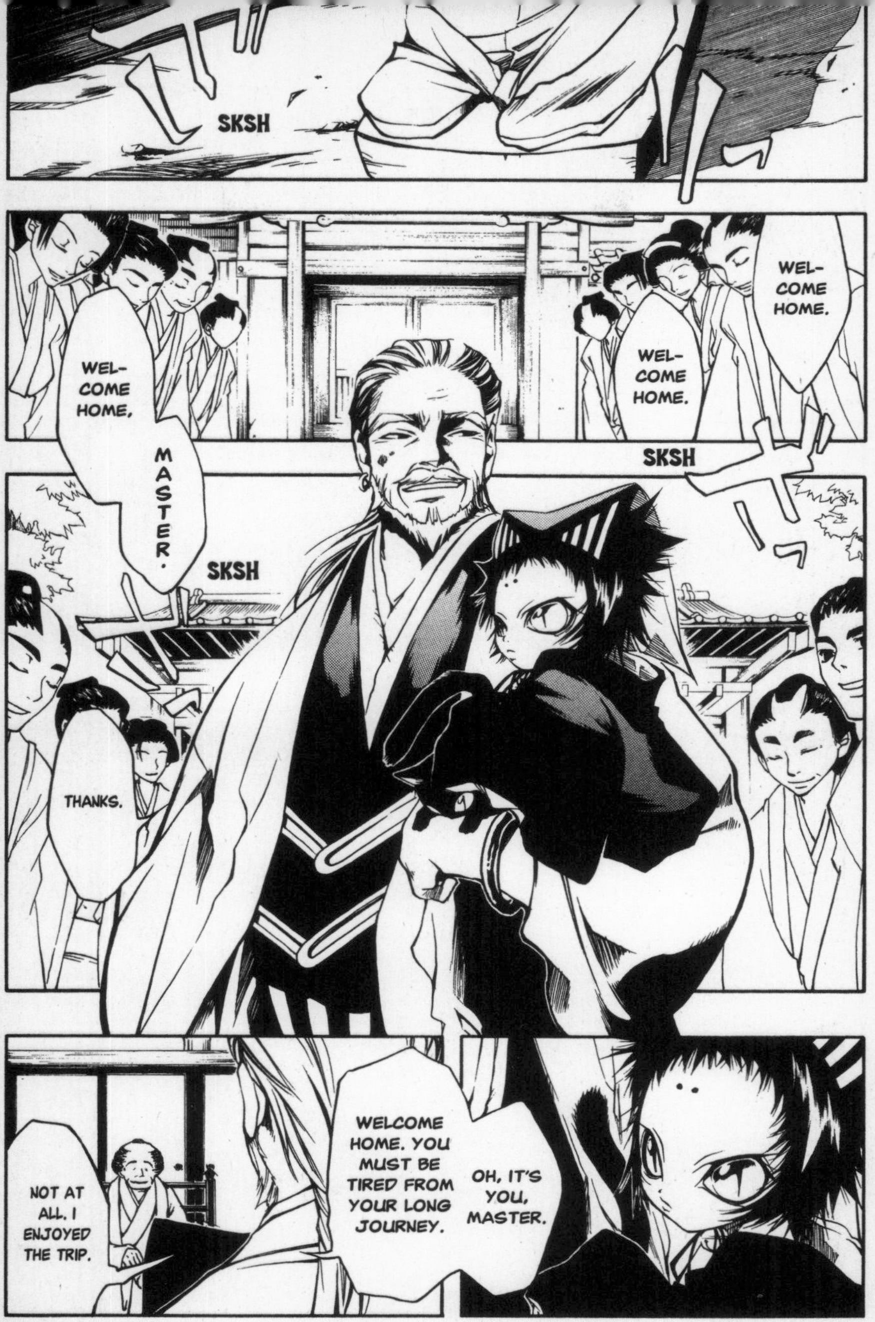
SKSH
WEL-COME HOME.
WEL-COME HOME.
WEL-COME HOME, MASTER.
SKSH
SKSH
THANKS.
OH, IT'S YOU, MASTER.
WELCOME HOME. YOU MUST BE TIRED FROM YOUR LONG JOURNEY.
NOT AT ALL. I ENJOYED THE TRIP.

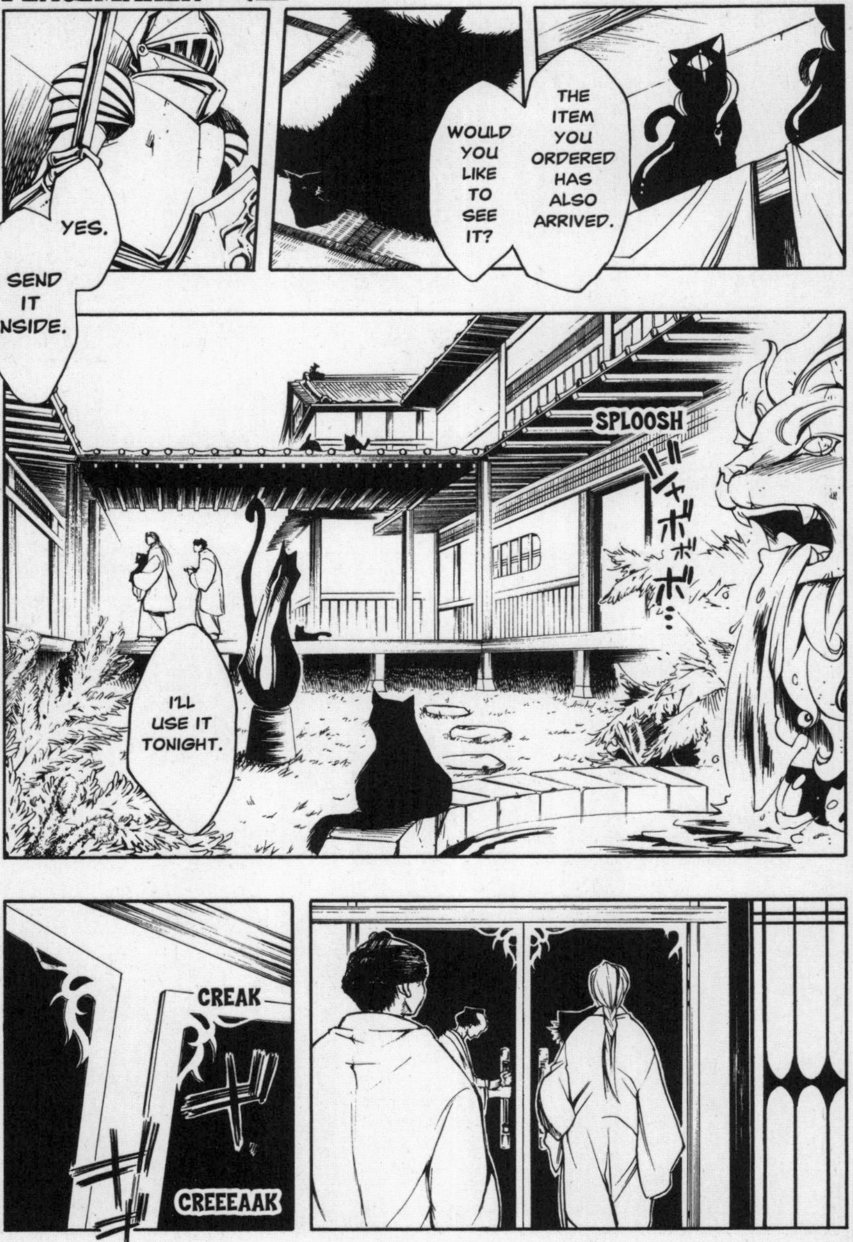
THE ITEM YOU ORDERED HAS ALSO ARRIVED.
WOULD YOU LIKE TO SEE IT?
YES.
SEND IT INSIDE.
SPLOOSH
I'LL USE IT TONIGHT.
CREAK
CREEEAAK

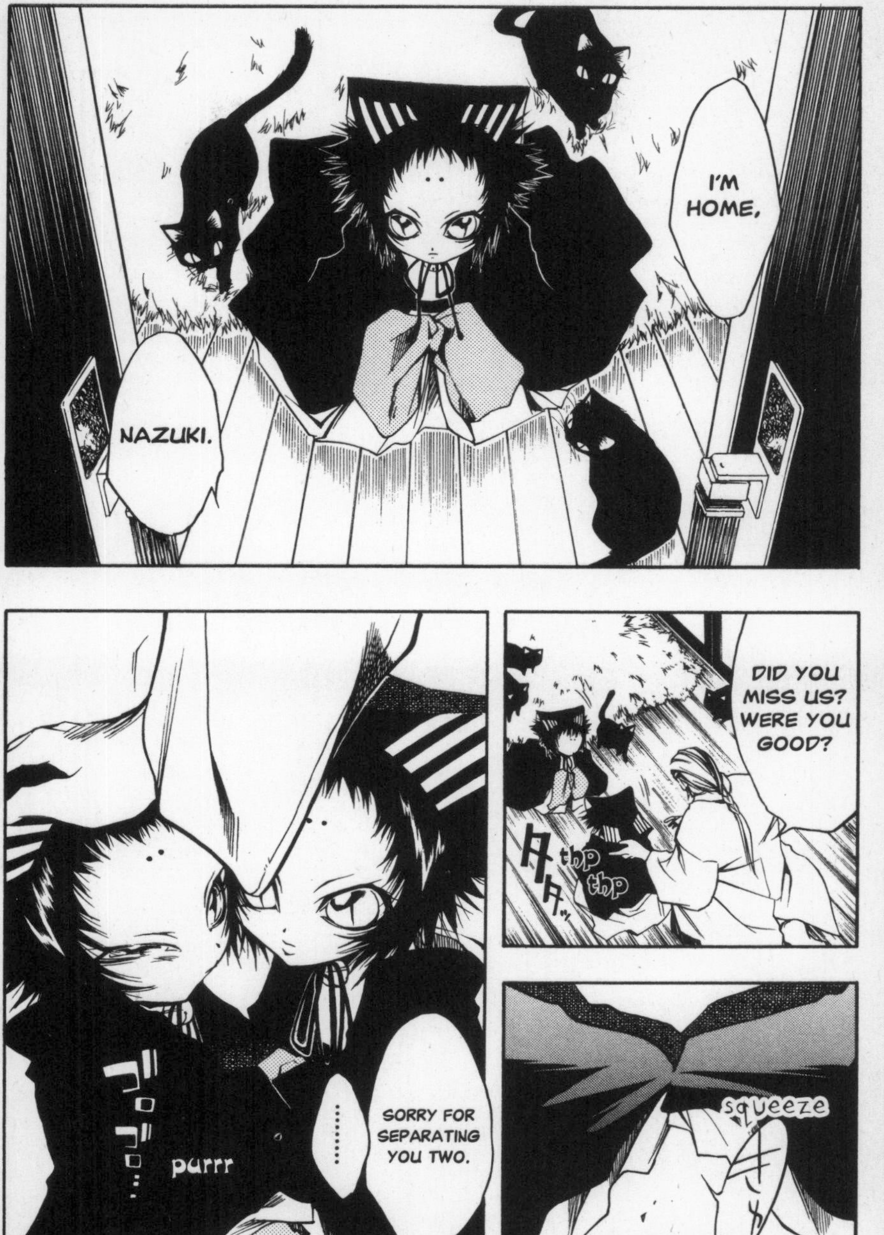
I'M HOME,
NAZUKI.
DID YOU MISS US? WERE YOU GOOD?
thp thp
squeeze
SORRY FOR SEPARATING YOU TWO.
......
purrr

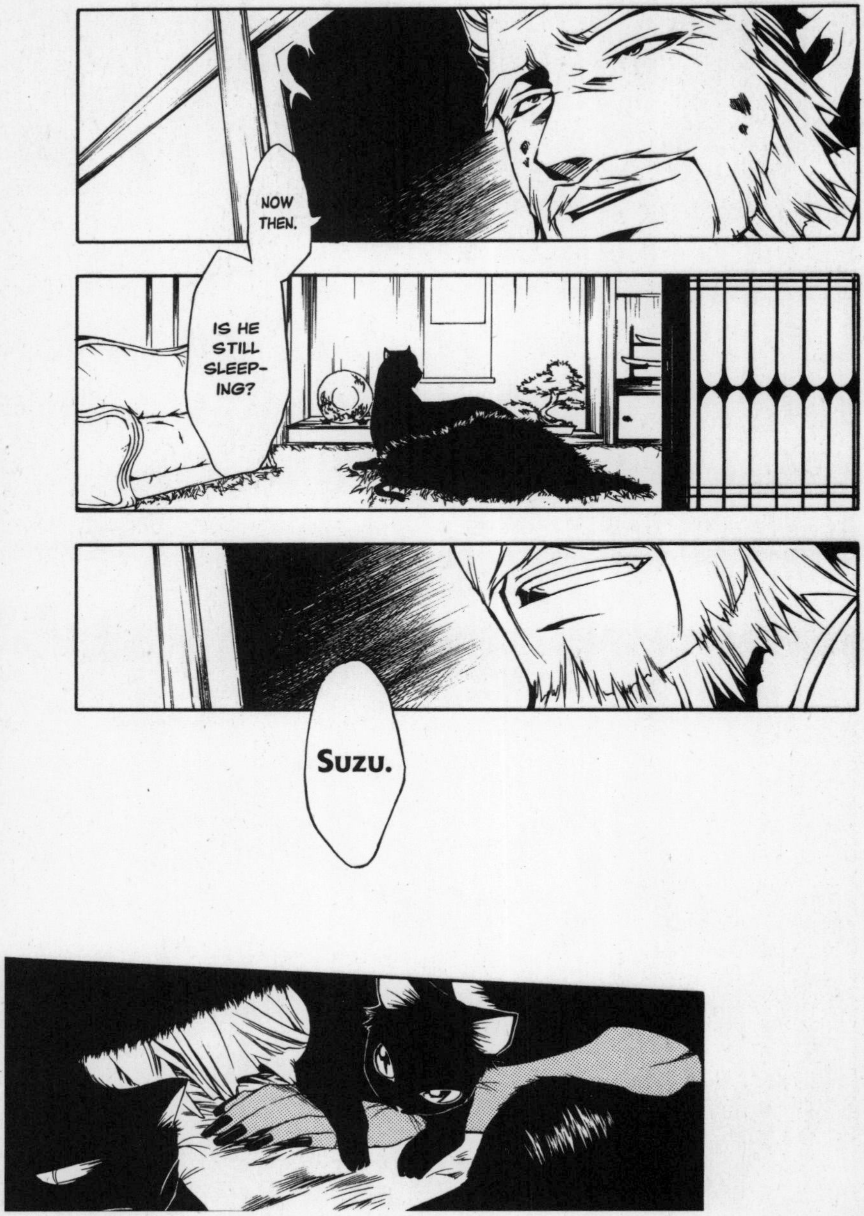
NOW THEN.
IS HE STILL SLEEP-ING?
Suzu.

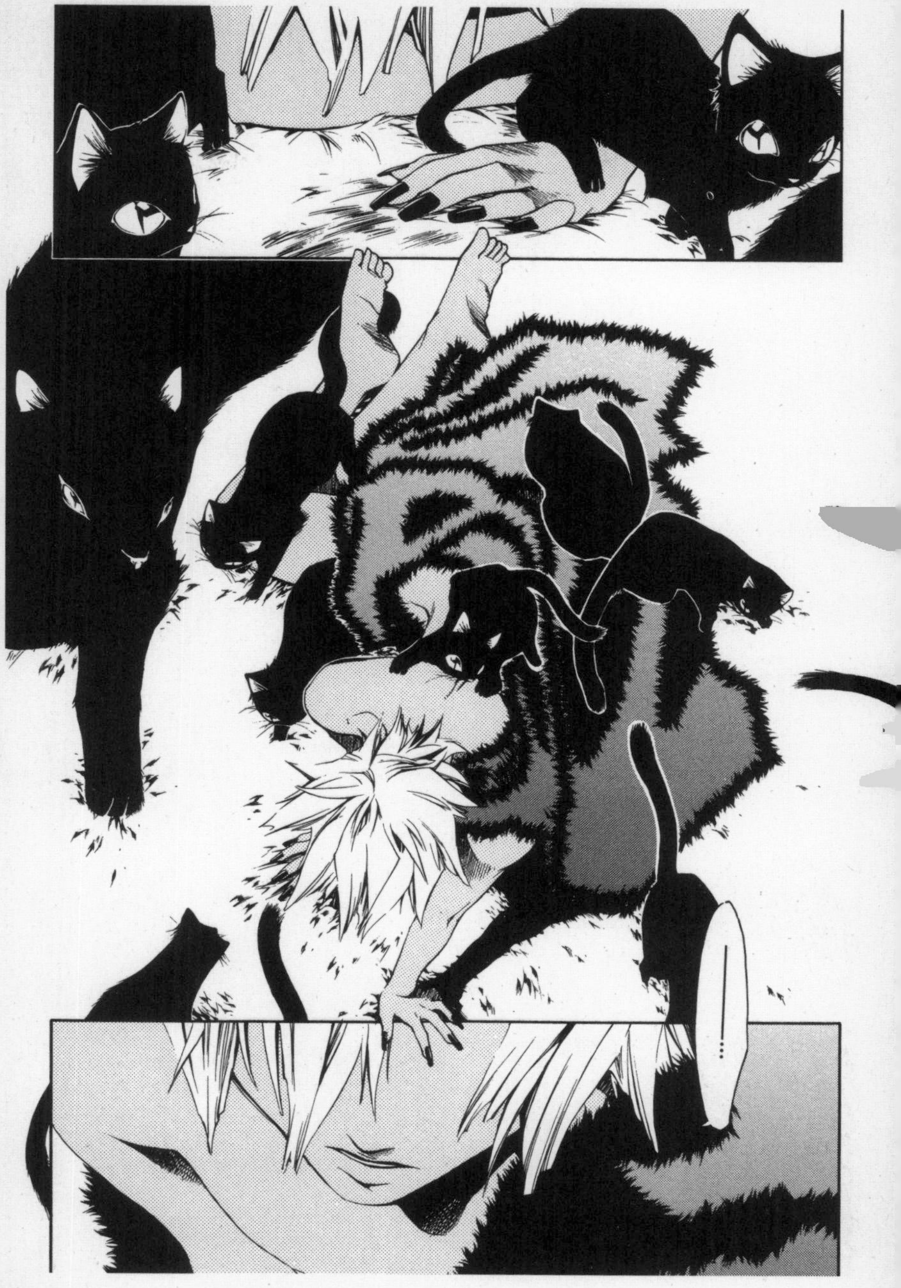
—…

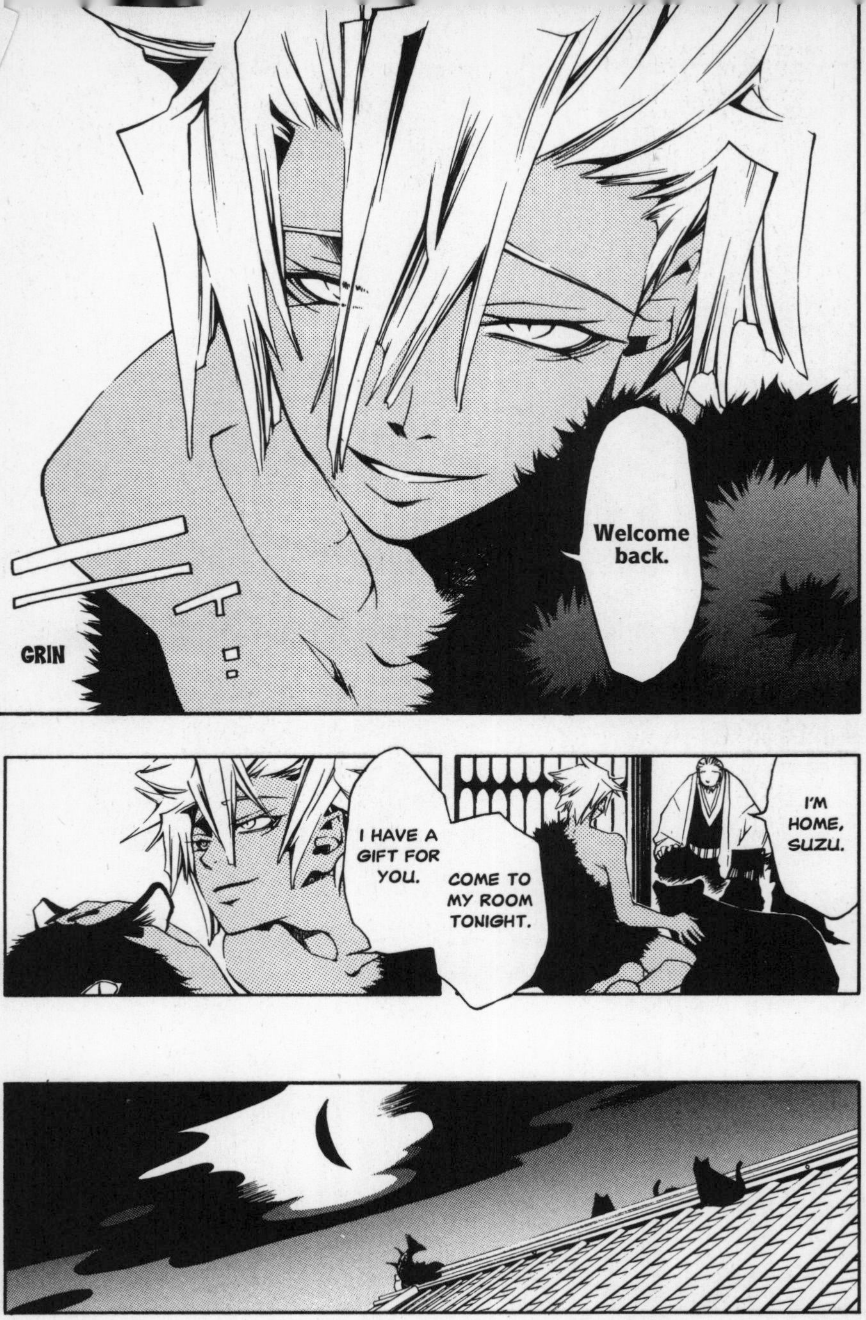
Welcome back.
GRIN
I'M HOME, SUZU.
I HAVE A GIFT FOR YOU.
COME TO MY ROOM TONIGHT.

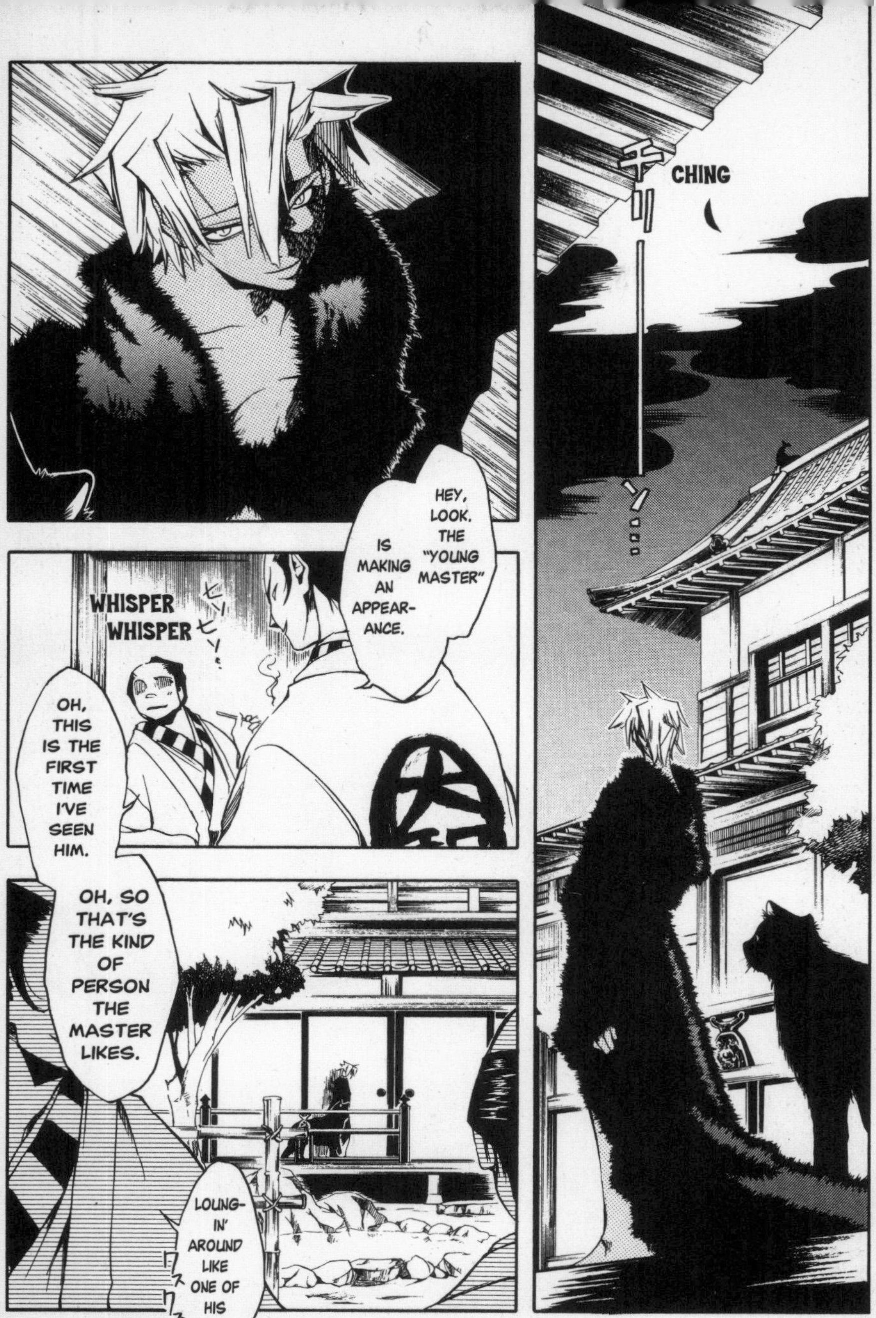
CHING
HEY, LOOK. THE "YOUNG MASTER" IS MAKING AN APPEARANCE.
WHISPER WHISPER
OH, THIS IS THE FIRST TIME I'VE SEEN HIM.
OH, SO THAT'S THE KIND OF PERSON THE MASTER LIKES.
LOUNG-IN' AROUND LIKE ONE OF HIS CATS.
CHUCKLE

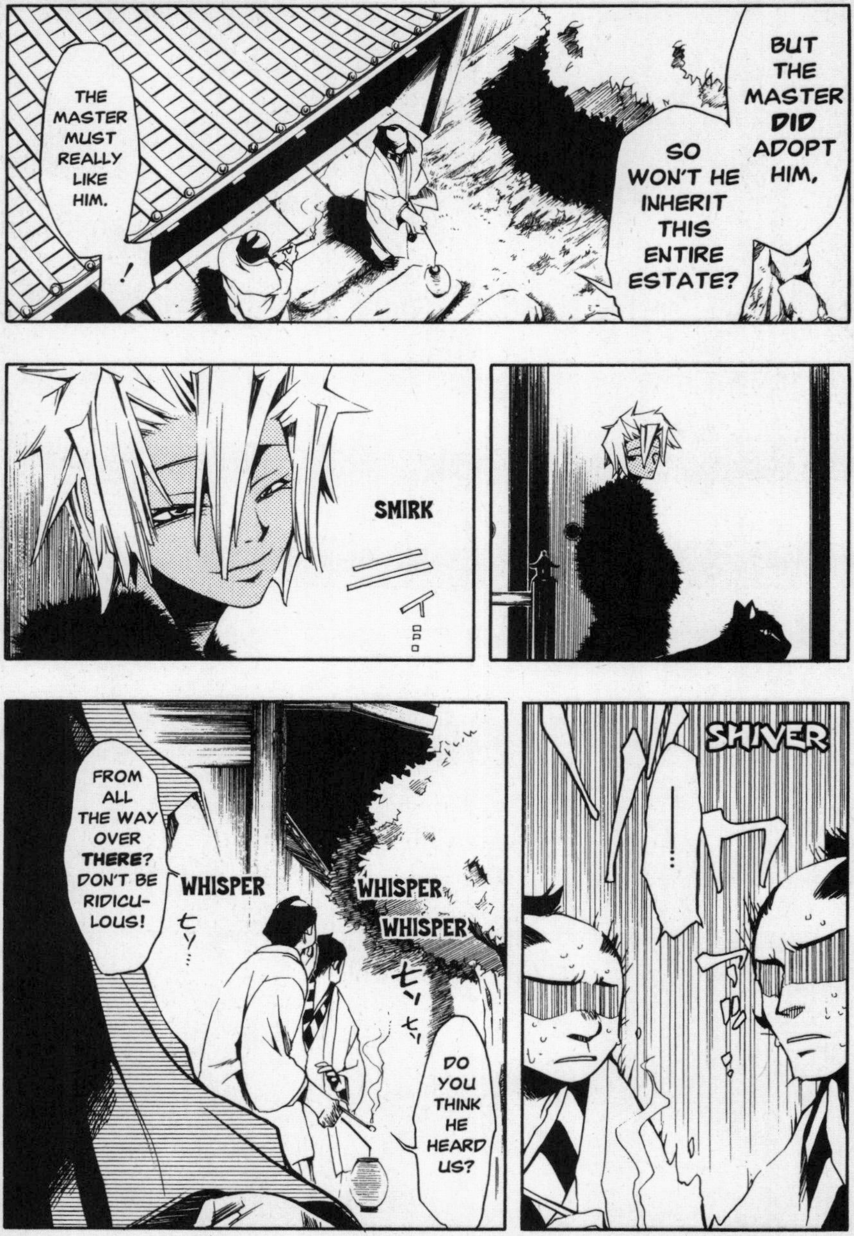
BUT THE MASTER DID ADOPT HIM,
SO WON'T HE INHERIT THIS ENTIRE ESTATE?
THE MASTER MUST REALLY LIKE HIM.
!
SMIRK
SHIVER
DO YOU THINK HE HEARD US?
WHISPER WHISPER
WHISPER
FROM ALL THE WAY OVER THERE? DON'T BE RIDICULOUS!

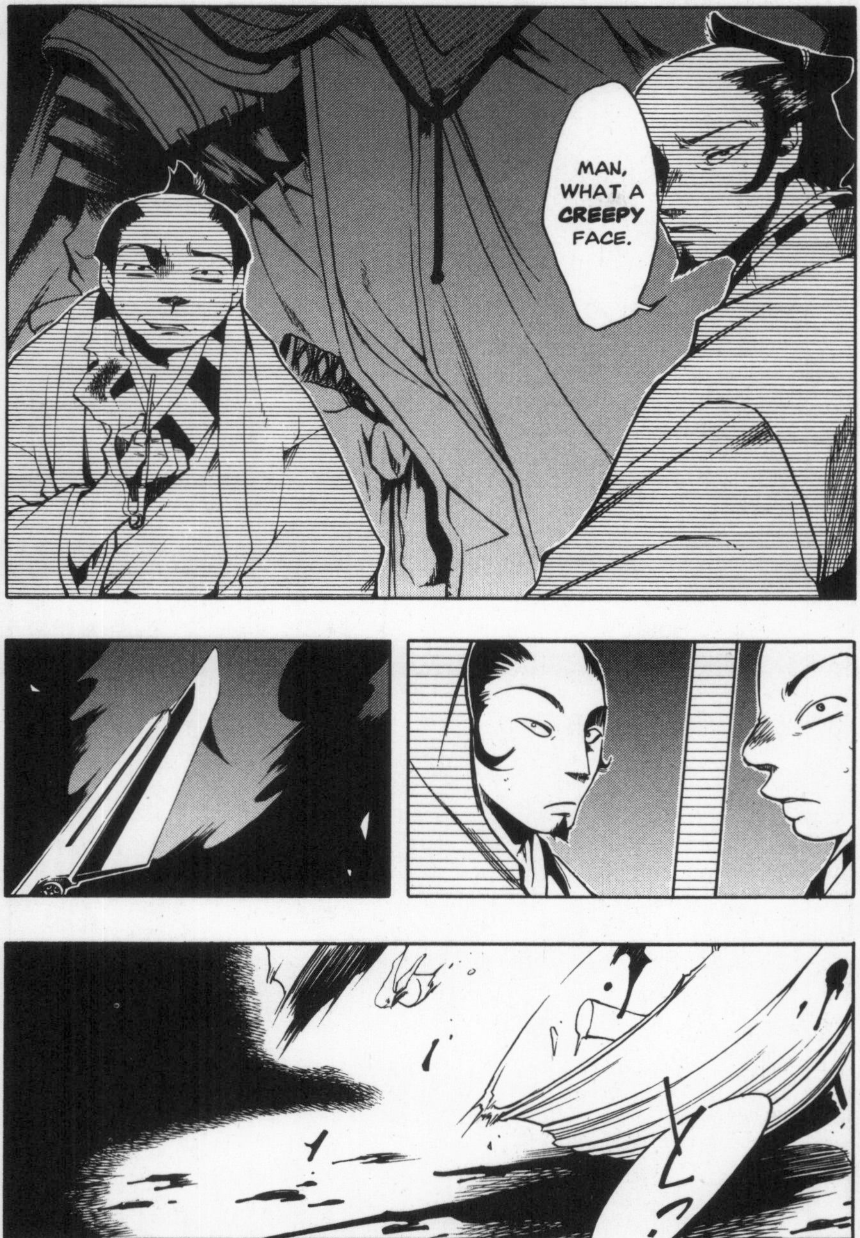
MAN, WHAT A CREEPY FACE.
clunk

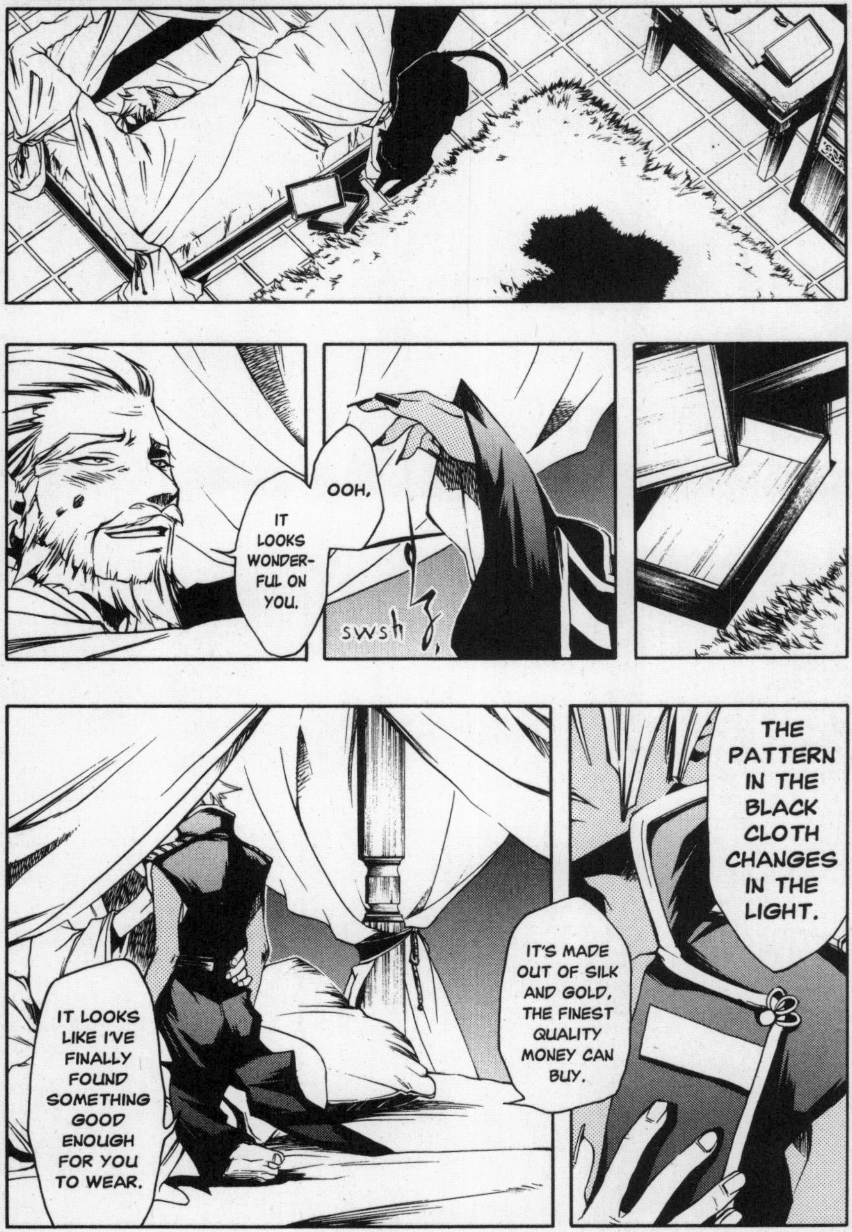
OOH,
IT LOOKS WONDERFUL ON YOU.
swsh
THE PATTERN IN THE BLACK CLOTH CHANGES IN THE LIGHT.
IT'S MADE OUT OF SILK AND GOLD, THE FINEST QUALITY MONEY CAN BUY.
IT LOOKS LIKE I'VE FINALLY FOUND SOMETHING GOOD ENOUGH FOR YOU TO WEAR.

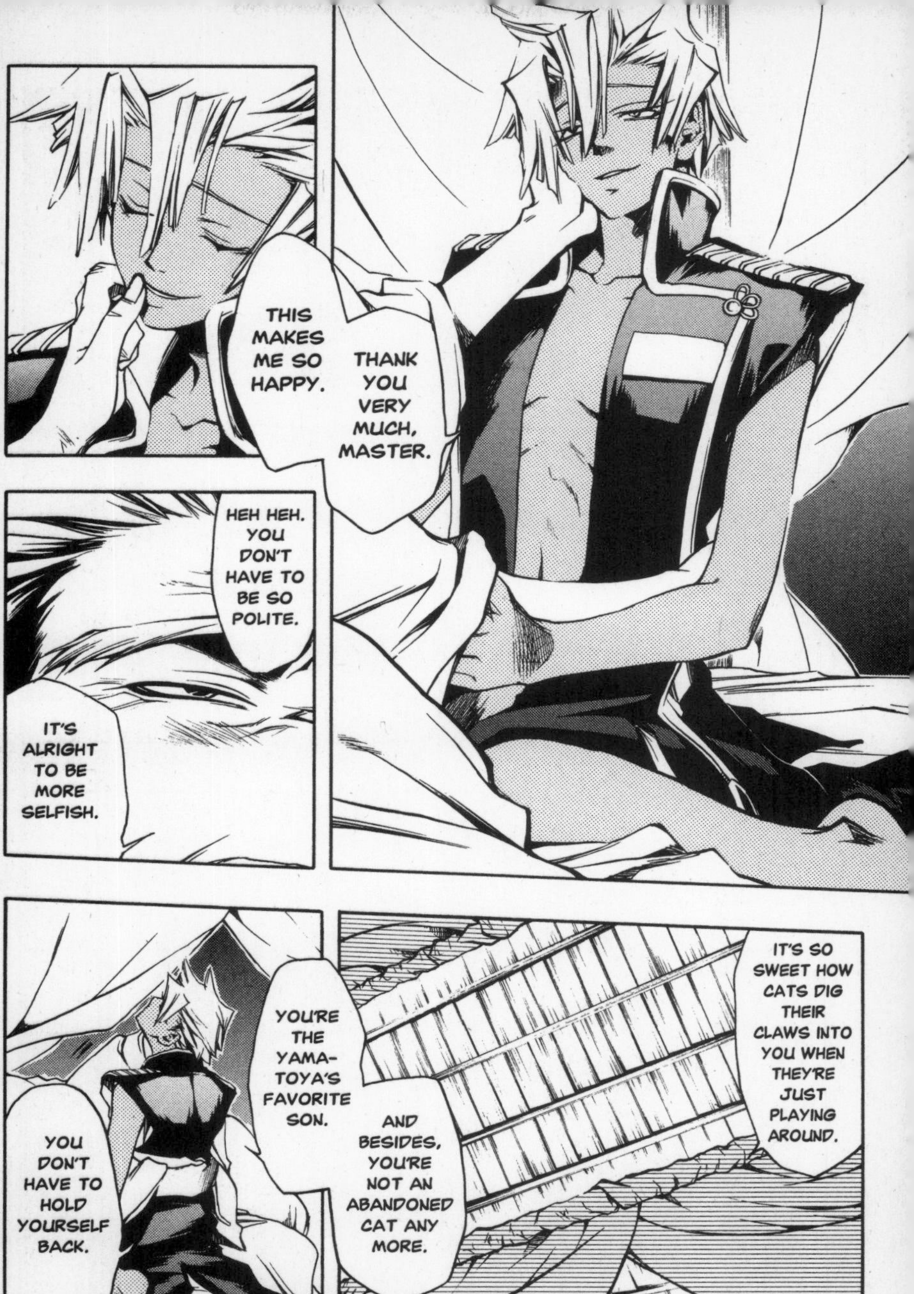
THANK YOU VERY MUCH, MASTER.
THIS MAKES ME SO HAPPY.
HEH HEH. YOU DON'T HAVE TO BE SO POLITE.
IT'S ALRIGHT TO BE MORE SELFISH.
IT'S SO SWEET HOW CATS DIG THEIR CLAWS INTO YOU WHEN THEY'RE JUST PLAYING AROUND.
AND BESIDES, YOU'RE NOT AN ABANDONED CAT ANY MORE.
YOU'RE THE YAMA-TOYA'S FAVORITE SON.
YOU DON'T HAVE TO HOLD YOURSELF BACK.

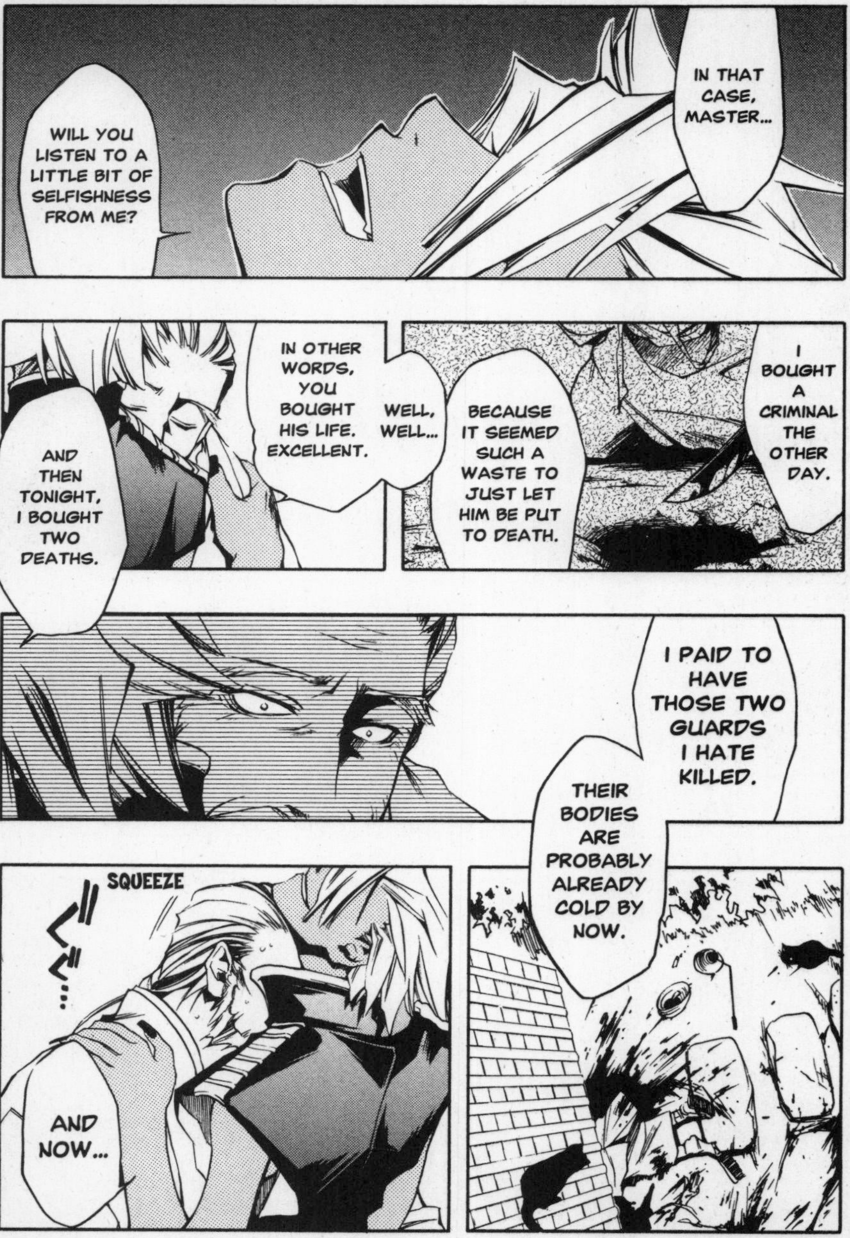
IN THAT CASE, MASTER...
WILL YOU LISTEN TO A LITTLE BIT OF SELFISHNESS FROM ME?
I BOUGHT A CRIMINAL THE OTHER DAY.
BECAUSE IT SEEMED SUCH A WASTE TO JUST LET HIM BE PUT TO DEATH.
WELL, WELL...
IN OTHER WORDS, YOU BOUGHT HIS LIFE. EXCELLENT.
AND THEN TONIGHT, I BOUGHT TWO DEATHS.
I PAID TO HAVE THOSE TWO GUARDS I HATE KILLED.
THEIR BODIES ARE PROBABLY ALREADY COLD BY NOW.
SQUEEZE
AND NOW...

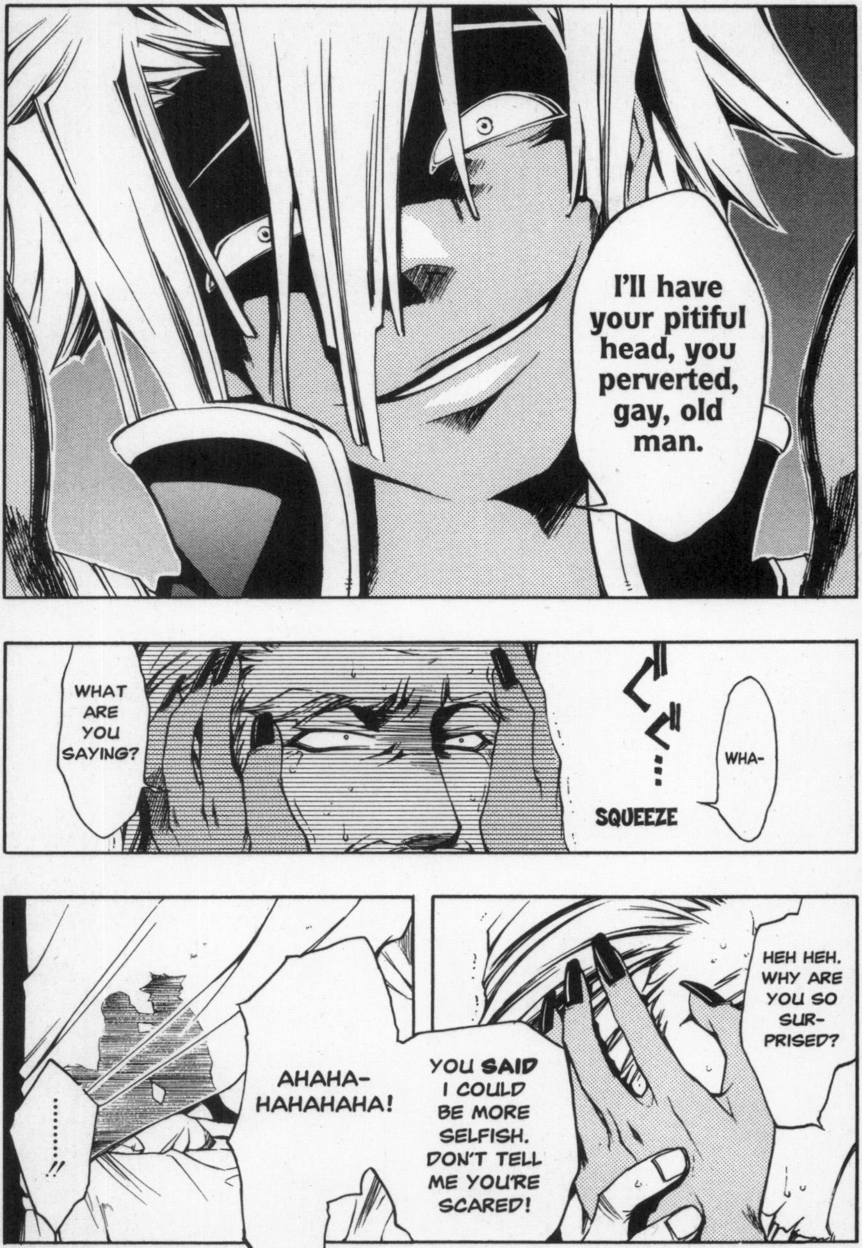
I'll have your pitiful head, you perverted, gay, old man.
WHA-
SQUEEZE
WHAT ARE YOU SAYING?
HEH HEH. WHY ARE YOU SO SUR-PRISED?
YOU SAID I COULD BE MORE SELFISH. DON'T TELL ME YOU'RE SCARED!
AHAHA-HAHAHAHA!
......!!

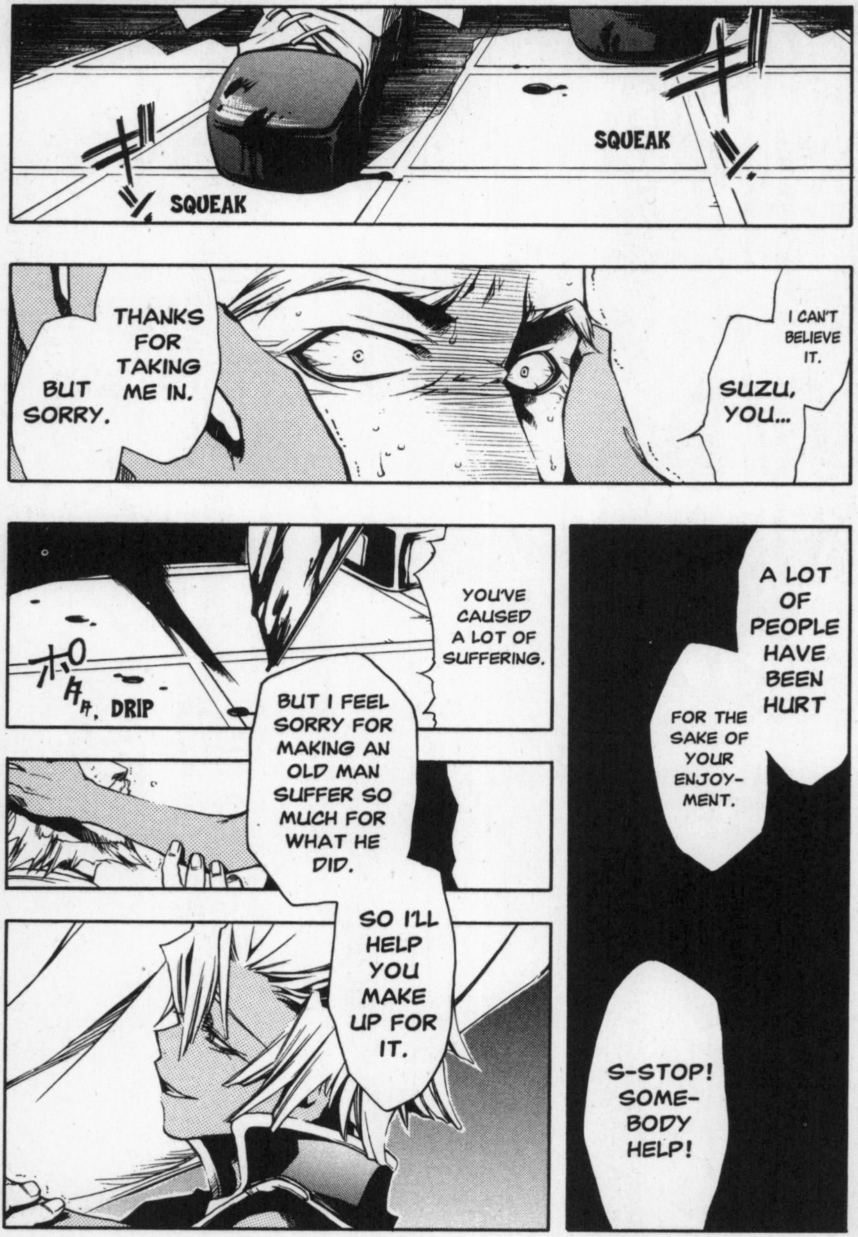
SQUEAK
SQUEAK
I CAN'T BELIEVE IT.
SUZU, YOU...
THANKS FOR TAKING ME IN.
BUT SORRY.
A LOT OF PEOPLE HAVE BEEN HURT
FOR THE SAKE OF YOUR ENJOY-MENT.
S-STOP! SOME-BODY HELP!
YOU'VE CAUSED A LOT OF SUFFERING.
DRIP
BUT I FEEL SORRY FOR MAKING AN OLD MAN SUFFER SO MUCH FOR WHAT HE DID.
SO I'LL HELP YOU MAKE UP FOR IT.

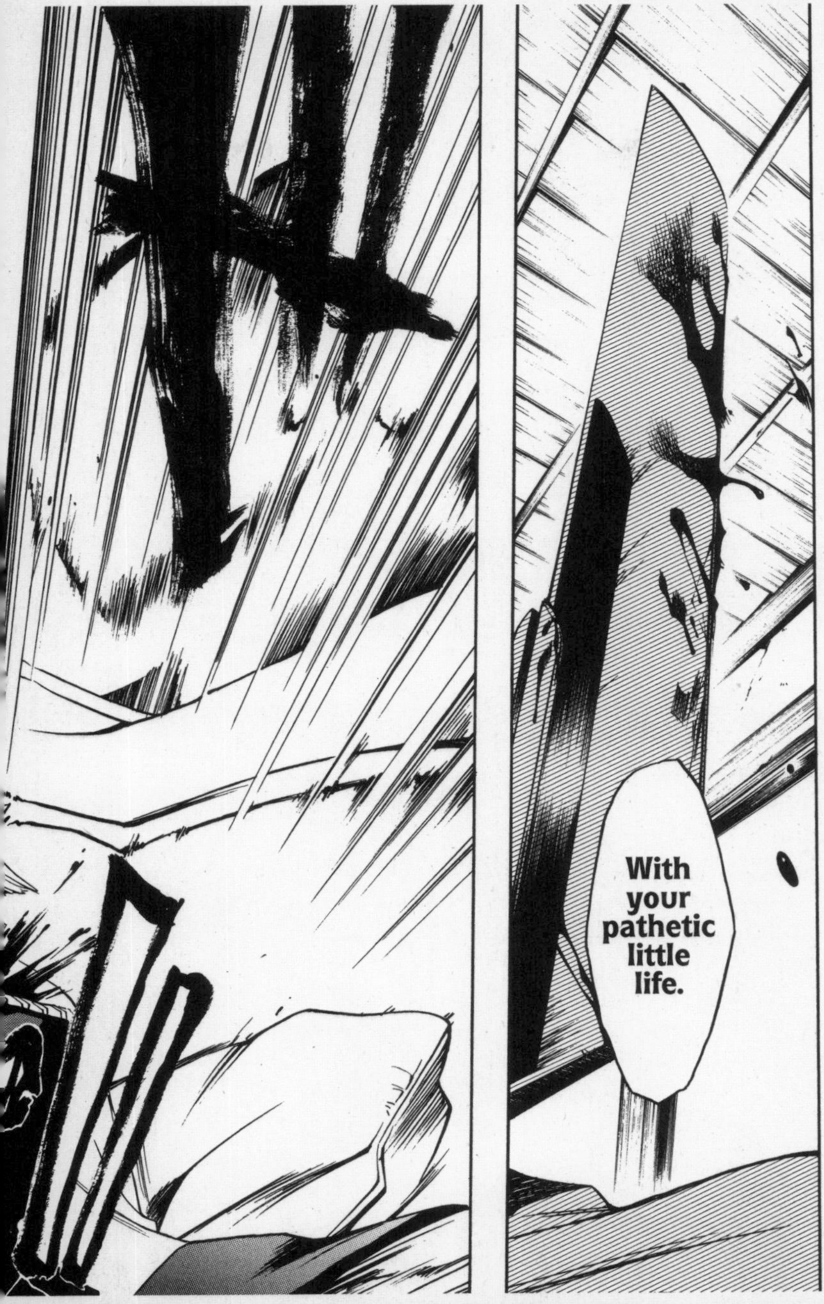
With your pathetic little life.

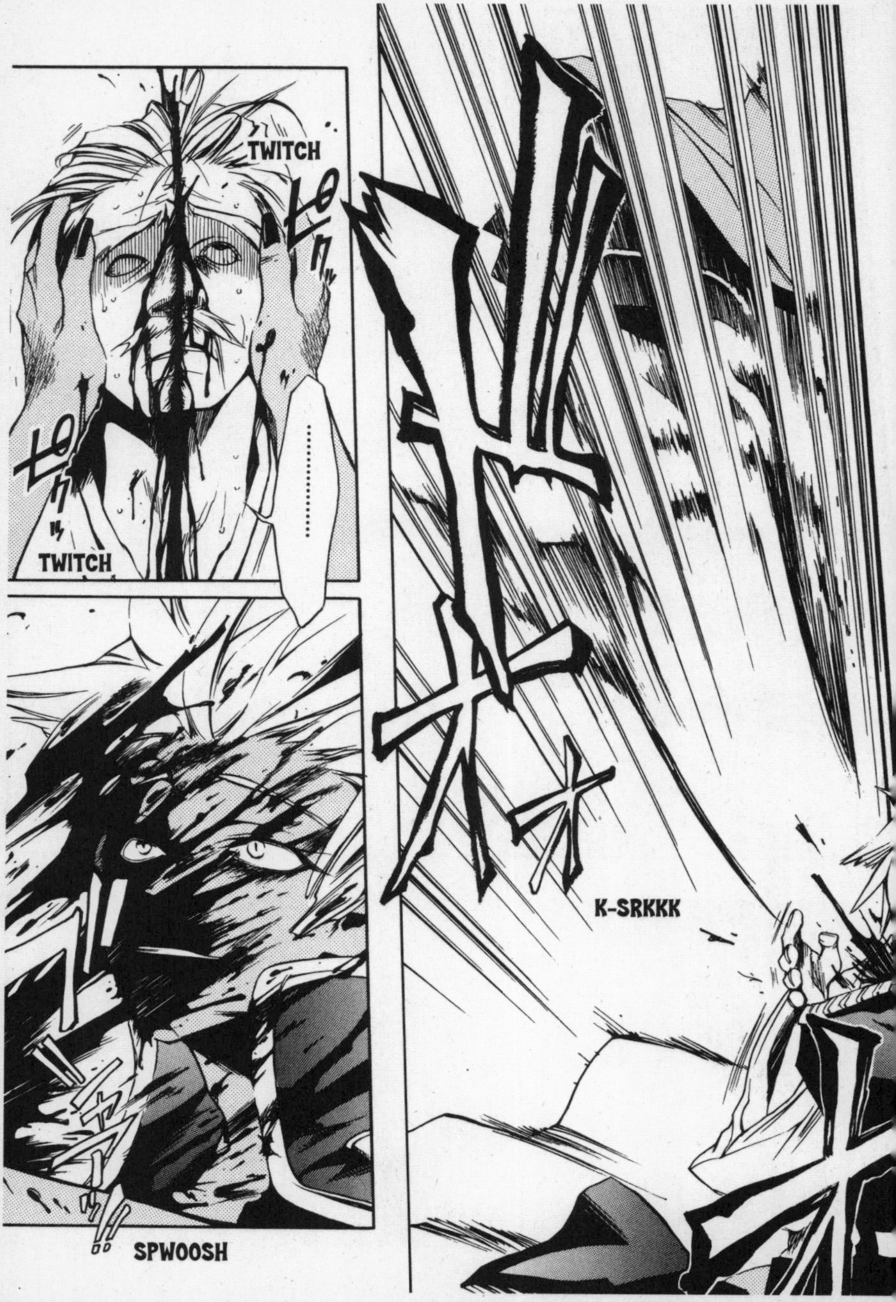
K-SRKKK
TWITCH
......
TWITCH
SPWOOSH

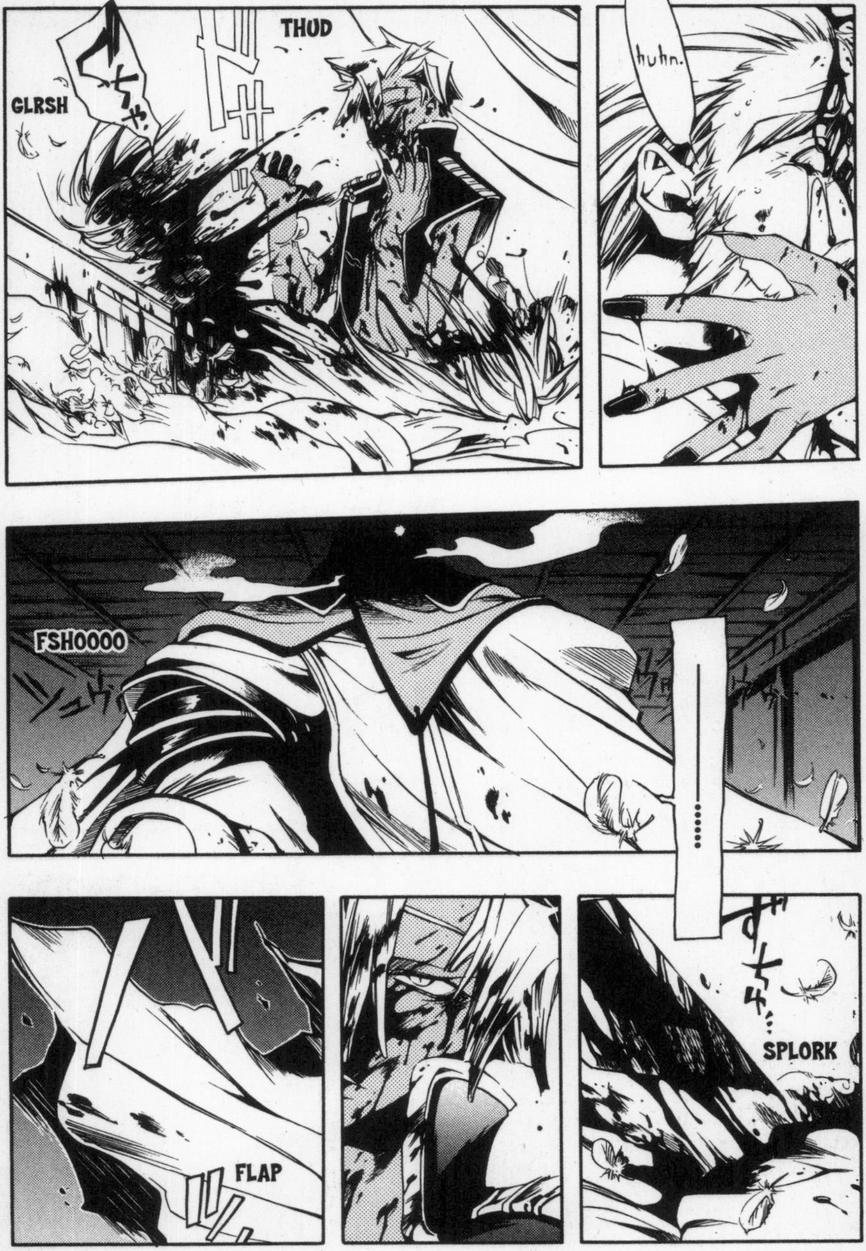
huhn.
THUD
GLRSH
FSHOOOO
—......
SPLORK
FLAP

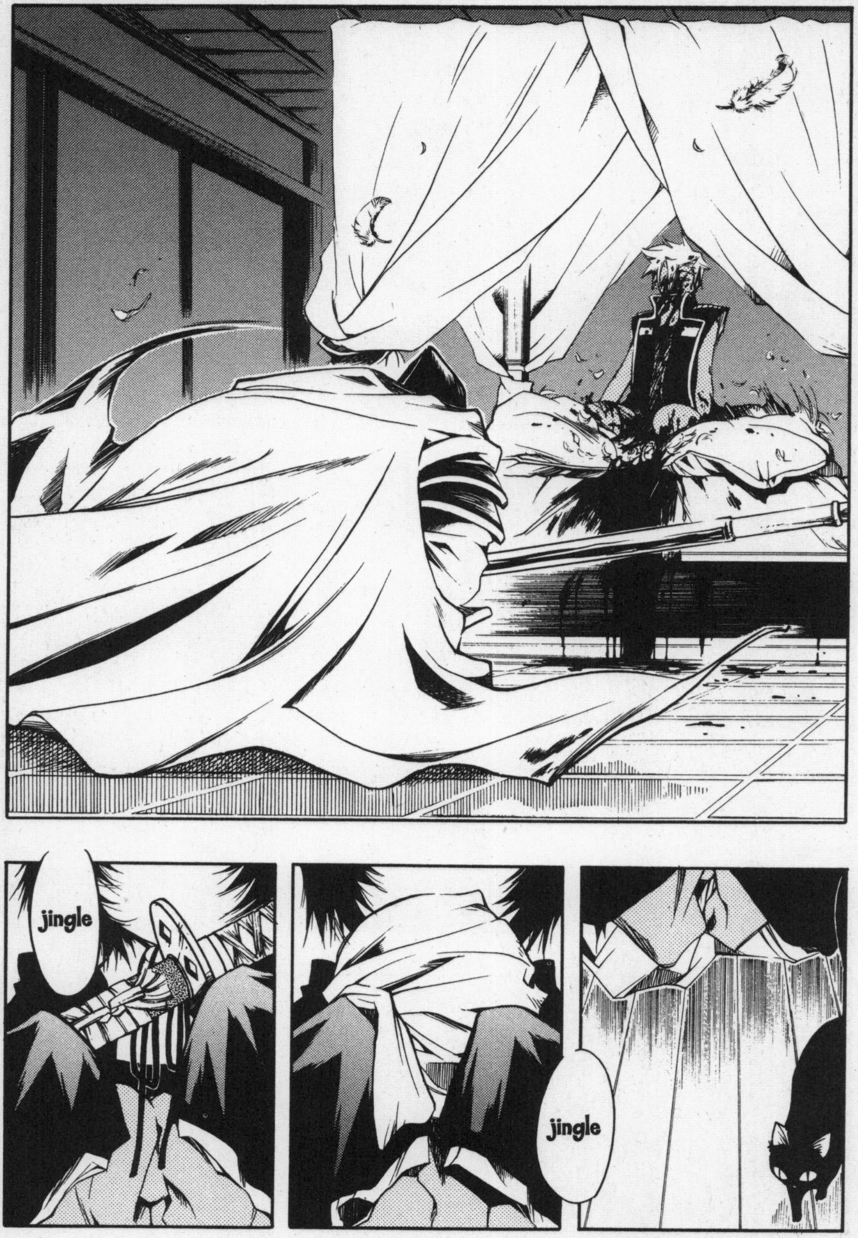
jingle
jingle

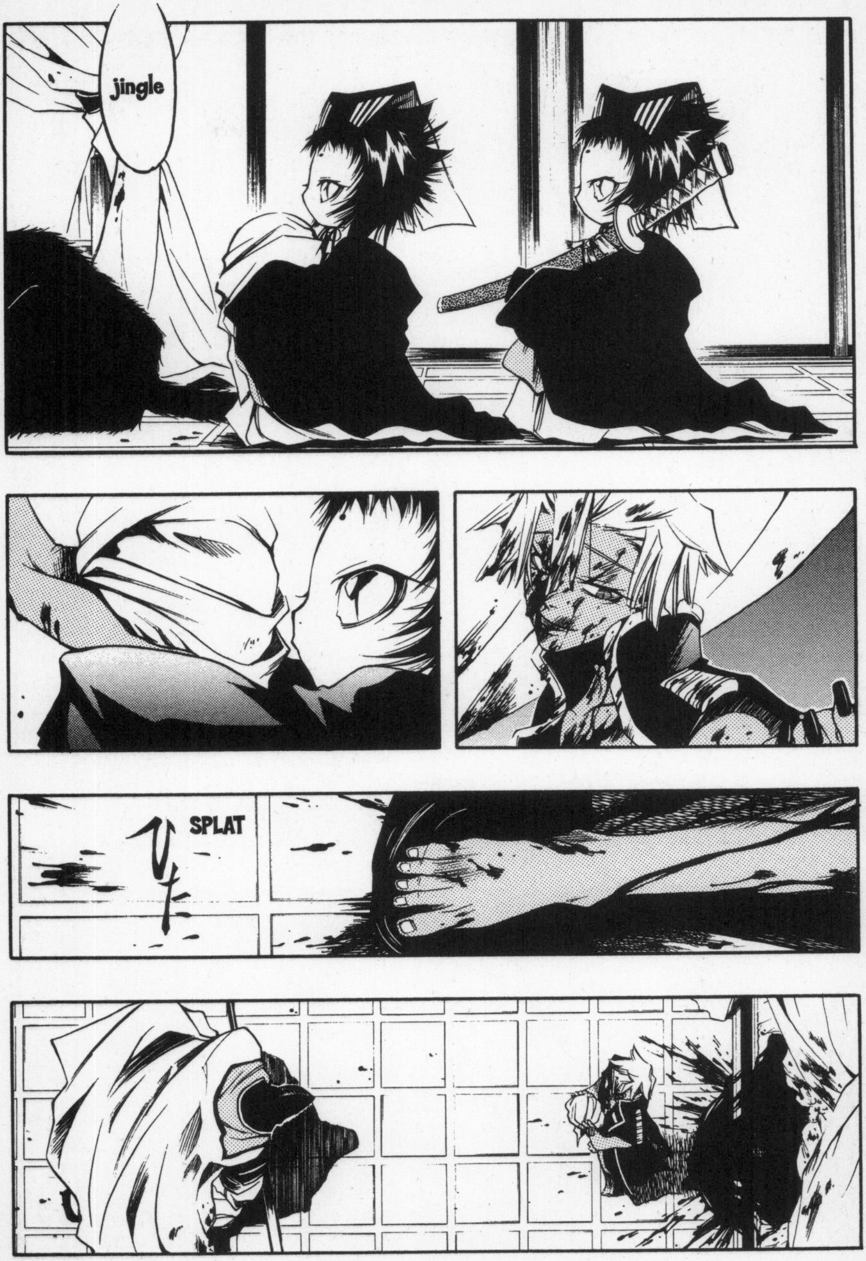
jingle
SPLAT
ぴた

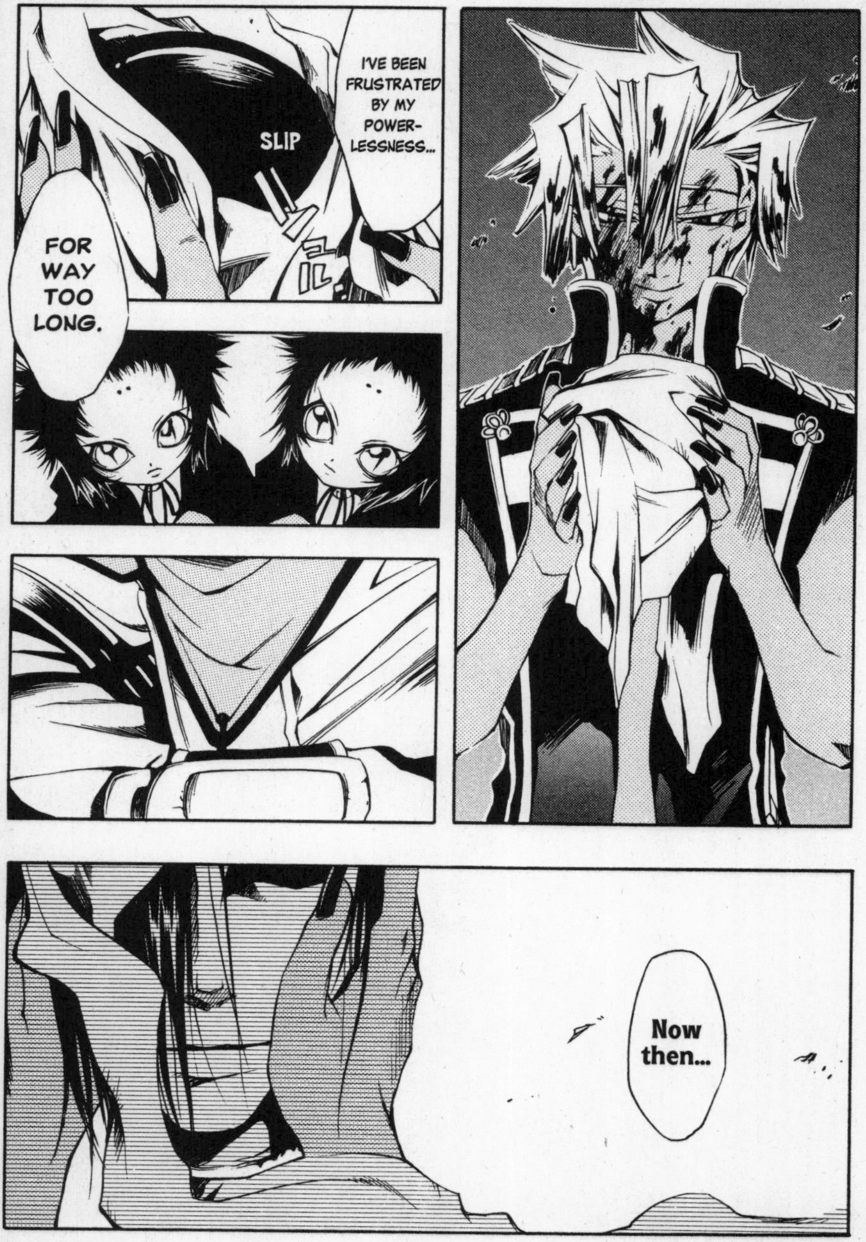
I'VE BEEN FRUSTRATED BY MY POWER-LESSNESS...
SLIP
FOR WAY TOO LONG.
Now then...

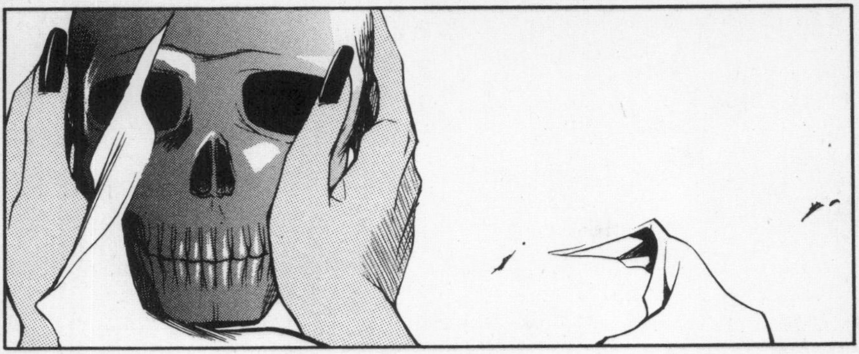

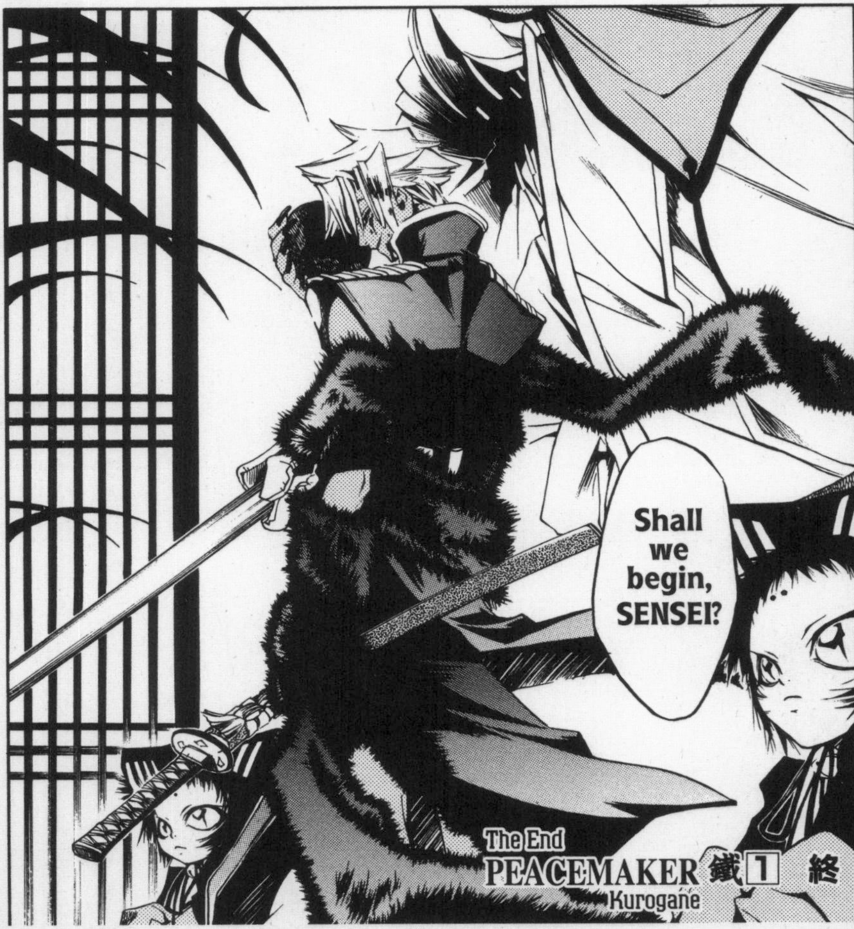
Shall we begin, SENSEI?
The End
PEACEMAKER 鐵 1 終
Kurogane

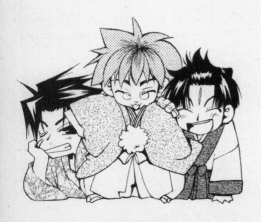

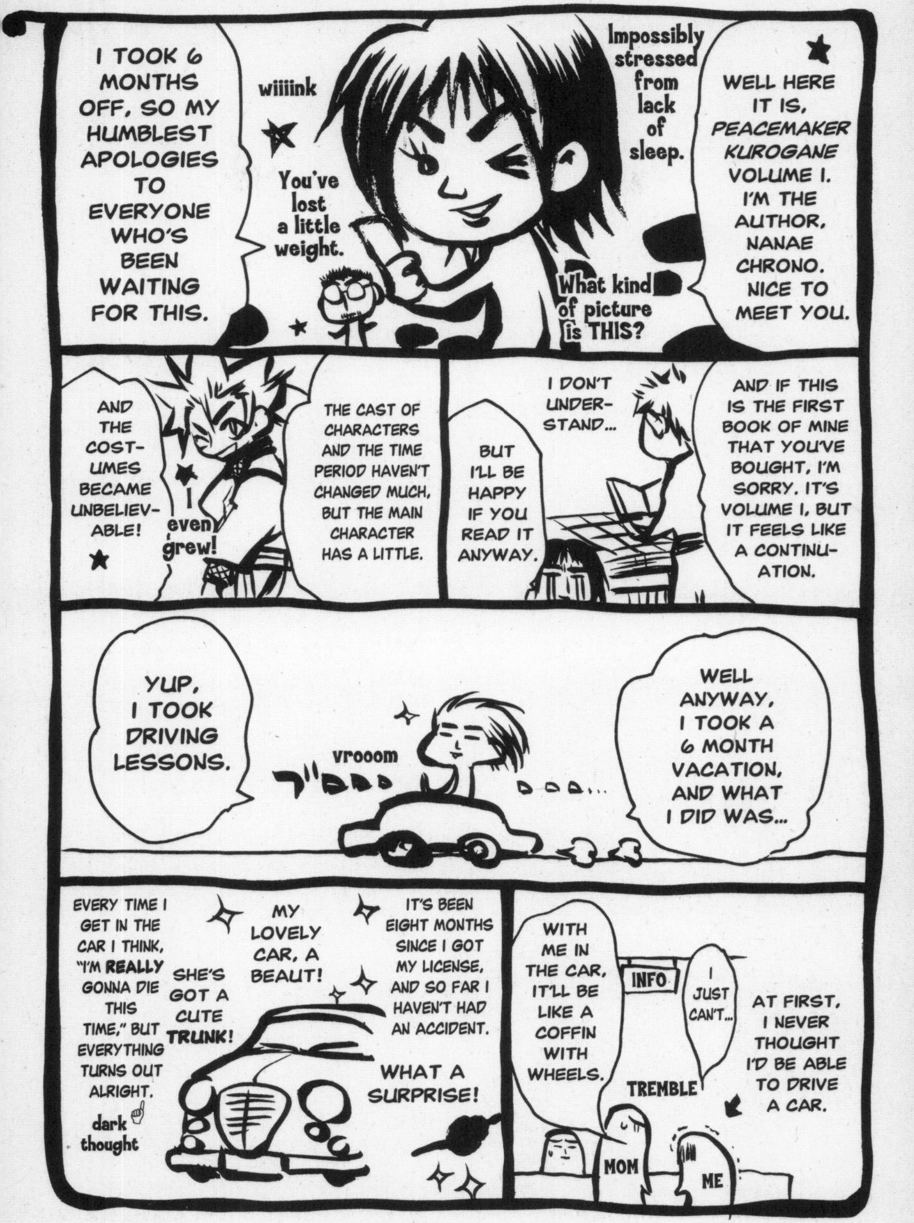
WELL HERE IT IS, *PEACEMAKER KUROGANE* VOLUME 1. I'M THE AUTHOR, NANAE CHRONO. NICE TO MEET YOU.
Impossibly stressed from lack of sleep.
What kind of picture is THIS?
wiiiink
You've lost a little weight.
I TOOK 6 MONTHS OFF, SO MY HUMBLEST APOLOGIES TO EVERYONE WHO'S BEEN WAITING FOR THIS.
AND IF THIS IS THE FIRST BOOK OF MINE THAT YOU'VE BOUGHT, I'M SORRY. IT'S VOLUME 1, BUT IT FEELS LIKE A CONTINUATION.
I DON'T UNDERSTAND...
BUT I'LL BE HAPPY IF YOU READ IT ANYWAY.
THE CAST OF CHARACTERS AND THE TIME PERIOD HAVEN'T CHANGED MUCH, BUT THE MAIN CHARACTER HAS A LITTLE.
AND THE COSTUMES BECAME UNBELIEVABLE!
I even grew!
WELL ANYWAY, I TOOK A 6 MONTH VACATION, AND WHAT I DID WAS...
vrooom
YUP, I TOOK DRIVING LESSONS.
AT FIRST, I NEVER THOUGHT I'D BE ABLE TO DRIVE A CAR.
I JUST CAN'T...
INFO
WITH ME IN THE CAR, IT'LL BE LIKE A COFFIN WITH WHEELS.
TREMBLE
MOM
ME
IT'S BEEN EIGHT MONTHS SINCE I GOT MY LICENSE, AND SO FAR I HAVEN'T HAD AN ACCIDENT.
MY LOVELY CAR, A BEAUT!
EVERY TIME I GET IN THE CAR I THINK, "I'M **REALLY** GONNA DIE THIS TIME," BUT EVERYTHING TURNS OUT ALRIGHT.
SHE'S GOT A CUTE **TRUNK**!
WHAT A SURPRISE!
dark thought

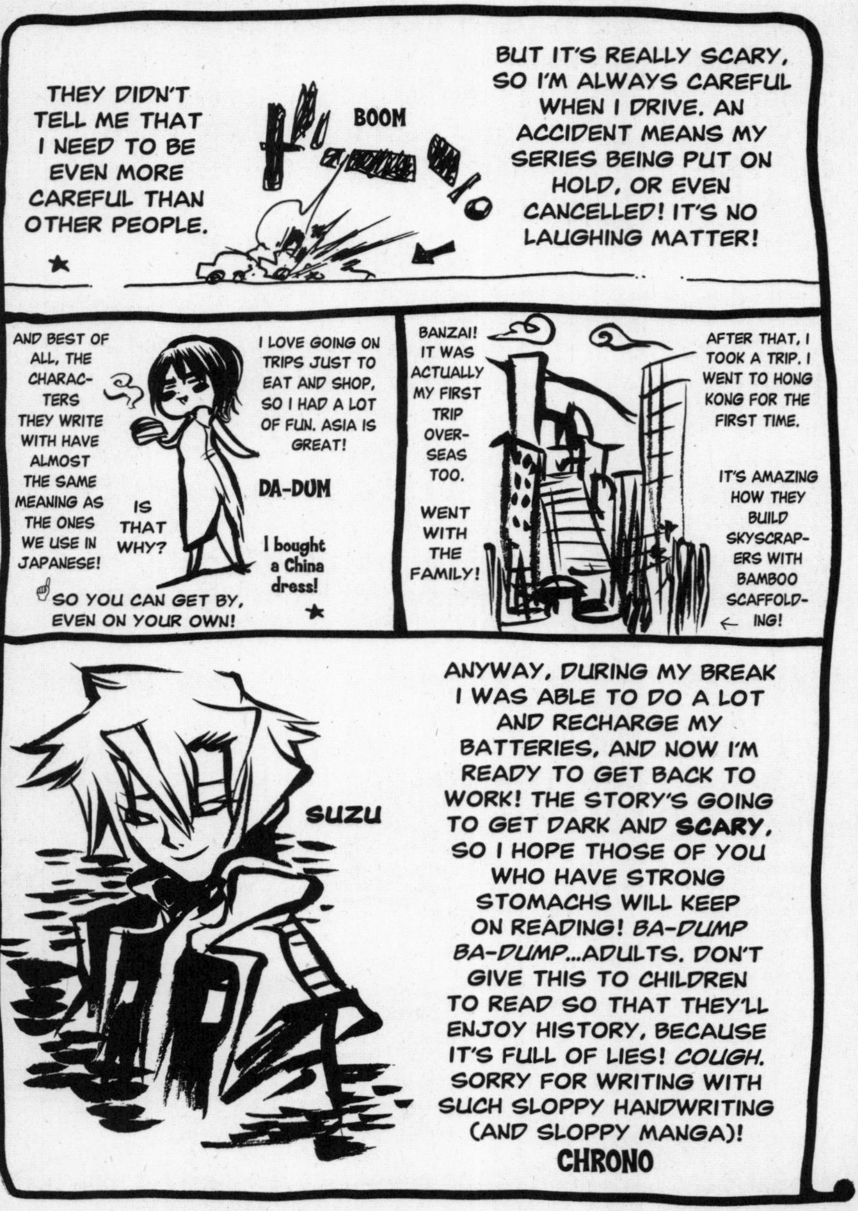

BUT IT'S REALLY SCARY, SO I'M ALWAYS CAREFUL WHEN I DRIVE. AN ACCIDENT MEANS MY SERIES BEING PUT ON HOLD, OR EVEN CANCELLED! IT'S NO LAUGHING MATTER!
BOOM
THEY DIDN'T TELL ME THAT I NEED TO BE EVEN MORE CAREFUL THAN OTHER PEOPLE.
AFTER THAT, I TOOK A TRIP. I WENT TO HONG KONG FOR THE FIRST TIME.
BANZAI! IT WAS ACTUALLY MY FIRST TRIP OVER-SEAS TOO.
IT'S AMAZING HOW THEY BUILD SKYSCRAP-ERS WITH BAMBOO SCAFFOLD-ING!
WENT WITH THE FAMILY!
I LOVE GOING ON TRIPS JUST TO EAT AND SHOP, SO I HAD A LOT OF FUN. ASIA IS GREAT!
AND BEST OF ALL, THE CHARAC-TERS THEY WRITE WITH HAVE ALMOST THE SAME MEANING AS THE ONES WE USE IN JAPANESE!
DA-DUM
IS THAT WHY?
I bought a China dress!
SO YOU CAN GET BY, EVEN ON YOUR OWN!
ANYWAY, DURING MY BREAK I WAS ABLE TO DO A LOT AND RECHARGE MY BATTERIES, AND NOW I'M READY TO GET BACK TO WORK! THE STORY'S GOING TO GET DARK AND SCARY, SO I HOPE THOSE OF YOU WHO HAVE STRONG STOMACHS WILL KEEP ON READING! BA-DUMP BA-DUMP...ADULTS, DON'T GIVE THIS TO CHILDREN TO READ SO THAT THEY'LL ENJOY HISTORY, BECAUSE IT'S FULL OF LIES! COUGH. SORRY FOR WRITING WITH SUCH SLOPPY HANDWRITING (AND SLOPPY MANGA)!
CHRONO
SUZU

The story has progressed a little bit, too. I thought maybe I'd make it a little more dark. Drawing the older Tetsu is so much fun. And he'll be growing up a little more, too! The only thing that really hasn't changed so far is his positive image. I worry about what kind of reaction he's going to get from the readers about him becoming a negative character.

Suzu Kitamura's downfall is, in a certain meaning, the highlight of the new series, so I've thought about it a lot. As a "wanderer," he keeps on his journey. As an assassin, his pride cannot be broken. I think this might be what makes both girls and guys think, "if it was me, I'd absolutely HATE it!" I'm sorry I used such graphic images (maybe there were some I shouldn't have included?), but there were some parts which couldn't have been done any other way, so I just went ahead with them. And I'll keep doing that. [grin]

Well then, it's about time to part. I'm really sorry for writing so sloppily. [sweat] I hope I'll be able to see you again in Volume 2.

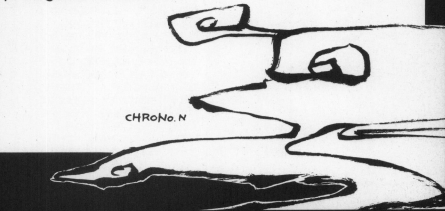

CHRONO. N

Hello. I'm Chrono. I finally released Volume 1! I'm glad you decided to buy this, whether you've been waiting for it, or this is the first book of mine you've bought. I'm experimenting with this size of manga for the first time. I can't wait to see how it turns out! It's not that there was anything WRONG with the size of my previous manga. But I haven't liked it ever since the face of one of my favorite characters from my favorite manga got cut. (As a manga author, I guess there's no better reason.) Does anybody else feel the same way? I hate it when things get cut off.

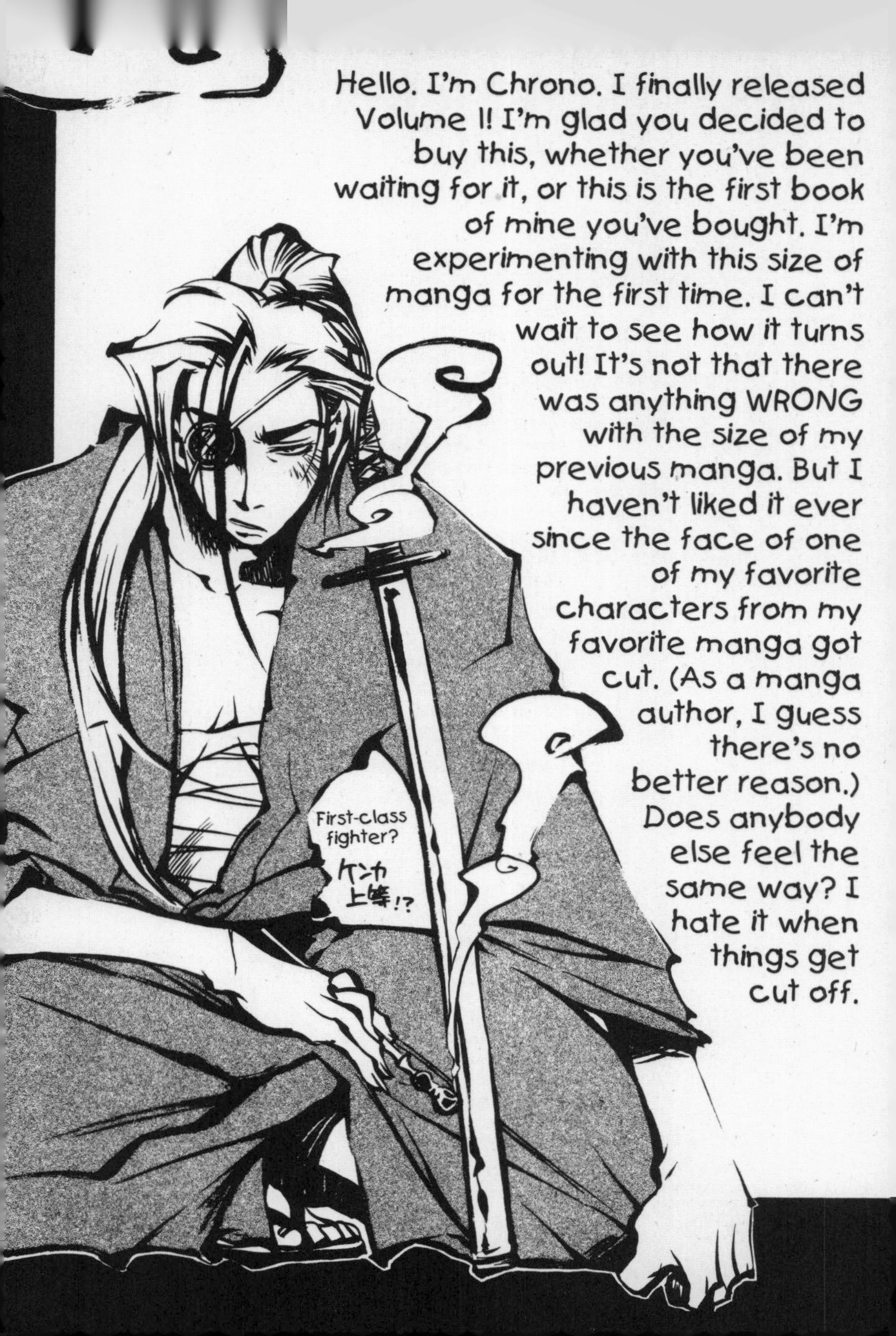
First-class fighter?
ケンカ上等!?

PEACEMAKER KUROGANE
VOLUME 1

© Nanae Chrono 2002

All rights reserved.
First published in 2002 by MAG Garden Corporation.
English translation rights arranged with MAG Garden Corporation.

Translator **AMY FORSYTH**
Lead Translator/Translation Supervisor **JAVIER LOPEZ**
ADV Manga Translation Staff **KAY BERTRAND, JOSH COLE, BRENDAN FRAYNE,
HARUKA KANEKO-SMITH, EIKO McGREGOR AND MADOKA MOROE**

Print Production/Art Studio Manager **LISA PUCKETT**
Pre-press Manager **KLYS REEDYK**
Art Production Manager **RYAN MASON**
Senior Designer/Creative Manager **JORGE ALVARADO**
Graphic Designer/Group Leader **SCOTT SAVAGE**
Graphic Designer **GEORGE REYNOLDS**
Graphic Artists **HEATHER GARY, SHANNA JENSCHKE, AND LISA RAPER**
Graphic Intern **MARK MEZA**

International Coordinator **TORU IWAKAMI**
International Coordinator **ATSUSHI KANBAYASHI**

Publishing Editor **SUSAN ITIN**
Assistant Editor **MARGARET SCHAROLD**
Editorial Assistant **VARSHA BHUCHAR**
Proofreaders **SHERIDAN JACOBS AND STEVEN REED**

Research/Traffic Coordinator **MARSHA ARNOLD**

Executive VP, CFO, COO **KEVIN CORCORAN**

President, CEO & Publisher **JOHN LEDFORD**

Email: editor@adv-manga.com
www.adv-manga.com
www.advfilms.com

For sales and distribution inquiries please call 1.800.282.7202

ADV MANGA™ is a division of A.D. Vision, Inc.
10114 W. Sam Houston Parkway, Suite 200, Houston, Texas 77099

English text © 2004 published by A.D. Vision, Inc. under exclusive license.
ADV MANGA is a trademark of A.D. Vision, Inc.

ISBN: 1-4139-0161-1
First printing, October 2004
10 9 8 7 6 5 4 3 2 1
Printed in Canada

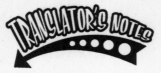

Peacemaker Kurogane Vol. 01

 PG. 6

(1) Shinsengumi Literally, "Newly selected group." A notorious and elite group of exceptionally skilled swordsmen who supported the shogunate. The actual origins of the group go back further, but they were established under the name "Shinsengumi" in 1863. They acted as a sort of police corps to patrol the particularly bloody city of Kyoto (the imperial capital) and "deal with" any revolutionists stirring up trouble.

(2) The Ikeda Inn This is a reference to the infamous "Ikeda Inn incident," which is what spread the name and fame of the Shinsengumi. It occurred on June 5th, 1864. The revolutionists had planned to set all of Kyoto on fire and assassinate important members of the shogunate amidst the chaos. The Shinsengumi got news of this, and when they discovered that the revolutionists were holding an important meeting at the Ikeda Inn, they raided the Inn and killed or arrested most of the revolutionists there. Thanks to this incident, the extremists were able to overpower moderates in the Choshu fief and raise an army in retaliation. They attempted to capture Kyoto, which came to be known as the Hamaguri Gomon Incident.

(3) Toshizo Hijikata: Vice-Commander of the Shinsengumi. He was born in what is now Hino in 1835. He trained in the *Tennen Rishin* style of swordsmanship. He had a reputation for being mean and very strict, earning him the nickname "Demon of the Shinsengumi." He is supposed to be the one who wrote and enforced the harsh rules of the Shinsengumi.

(4) "I offer you thanks on behalf of Kondo." This is a reference to Isami Kondo, commander of the Shinsengumi, and one of its founding members. Born in Tama in 1834, he became the 4th inheritor of the *Tennen Rishin* style of swordsmanship. He was the owner of the Shieikan *dojo*, and had been best friends with Hijikata since childhood.

 PG. 7

Dono This is a term of respect that can be used between people (mostly samurai) of same or similar ranks. It's not used as much today as it was during the time period of *Peacemaker Kurogane*.

 PG. 9

Soji Okita The character laughing with his hand over his mouth is Soji Okita, captain of the first unit of the Shinsengumi. A skilled swordsman from a very young age, and master of the *Tennen Rishin* style. He was one of the first to join the Roshigumi (the group that would eventually become the Shinsengumi), and he took part in every important affair in the group.

 PG. 14

Sama Another term of respect. This is still in common use in modern times, and is sometimes translated as "Master" or "Lady."

 PG. 19

Hamaguri Gomon Incident: Also known as the Kinmon Incident or the Palace Gate Incident. In 1864, in retaliation for the Ikeda Inn incident, Choshu gathered an army and invaded Kyoto. The result was a bloody battle that cost many lives and a huge fire that lasted three days and destroyed a good part of Kyoto. Choshu was defeated and was officially declared an enemy of the Emperor. The Shinsengumi were involved in the defense of Kyoto during this incident.

 PG. 54

"A Choshu spy?" Choshu was located on the western end of Honshu, in what is now Yamaguchi prefecture. It was a center of anti-shogunate sentiment.

 PG. 58

Hajime Saito The infamous captain of the third unit of the Shinsengumi. He was born in Edo. He joined the Shinsengumi at the age of 21 or 22. It's uncertain exactly which sword style(s) he practiced, but one of the most commonly accepted is the *Mugai* style. He joined the sword-wielding police in 1877, and later fought in the Seinan War under the name of Goro Fujita. Late in his life, he worked as a museum guard in Tokyo. He died of a gastric ulcer on September 28, 1915, at the age of 72.

 PG. 67

"It's improper to the path of a samurai!" This is a reference to the dreaded laws of the Shinsengumi. All members were forced to obey these laws on pain of death. They were:
First Article: It is not allowed to deviate from the path proper to a samurai.
Second Article: It is not allowed to leave the Shinsengumi.
Third Article: It is not allowed to raise money privately.
Fourth Article: It is not allowed to take part in other's (other than Shinsengumi's) litigation.
Fifth Article: It is not allowed to engage in private fights.

 PG. 74

"Since he was a wanderer and was new to the capital..." At this time in Japanese history, the capital is Kyoto, not Tokyo. The capital would be moved from Kyoto to Edo (now Tokyo) at the beginning of the Meiji restoration, in 1868.

 PG. 79

(1) *Sensei* Teacher, instructor, or master. This is used for teachers in any field (not just the martial arts), as well as for doctors. It may also be used as a term of respect for someone who isn't necessarily a teacher, but who has gained some level of proficiency or notoriety.

(2) Heisuke Todo Commander of the 8th unit of the Shinsengumi, born in 1844, supposedly as a bastard son of a feudal lord. He studied the *Hokushin Itto* style of swordsmanship in the Genbukan *dojo*, under Shusaku Chiba. However, he left his dojo and joined the Shieikan, which is where he would meet Isami Kondo and other men who would become the core group of the Shinsengumi.

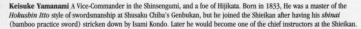

Continued...

PG. 92

Keisuke Yamanami A Vice-Commander in the Shinsengumi, and a foe of Hijikata. Born in 1833, He was a master of the *Hokushin Itto* style of swordsmanship at Shusaku Chiba's Genbukan, but he joined the Shieikan after having his *shinai* (bamboo practice sword) stricken down by Isami Kondo. Later he would become one of the chief instructors at the Shieikan.

PG. 95

(1) Sannan Sannan is another name for Keisuke Yamanami. The characters used to write his family name can be read either Yamanami or Sannan.

(2) *Hokushin Itto* style Literally, "North Star One Sword Style." This is an old style of swordsmanship founded in 1821 by Shusaku Chiba, who was one of the most famous swordsmasters in all of Japan, and very influential in the popularization of *kendo*. This style has been practiced by several notable people, including Ryoma Sakamoto and some of the Shinsengumi.

PG. 97

"The blood that got on it when I killed Kamo a year ago has completely rusted it." This is a reference to the assassination of Kamo Serizawa. Kamo Serizawa was a master of the *Shinto Munen* style, and who was a member of the Shinsengumi from the very beginning, when it was still called the Roshigumi. However, Serizawa was a very proud and hot-tempered man, which caused problems in the group. Almost from the start, he and Isami Kondo were at odds with each other. It eventually reached the point where Kondo, Hijikata, and others plotted to have Serizawa murdered. He was assassinated in a sneak attack at night. There's been some controversy as to who actually killed Serizawa in real life. It is likely to have been four people: Toshizo Hijikata, Soji Okita, and two among Keisuke Yamanami, Sanosuke Harada, Genzaburo Inoue, and Heisuke Todo.

PG. 125

(1) "Hey! Dragon Boy!" "Say hello to Iron Boy for me!" He calls Tatsunosuke "Dragon Boy" because the first character in his name (*tatsu*) means "dragon." And he calls Tetsunosuke "Iron Boy" because the first character in his name (*tetsu*) means "iron."

(2) Ryoma Sakamoto A samurai who would have an important impact on Japanese history. He was born on January 3, 1836 in Kochi, in the Tosa fief, and practiced swordsmanship from a young age. In 1862 he abandoned his fief, becoming an outlaw. He was a leader of the *sonno joi* movement. However, later he realized that Japan needed Western technology, and would eventually pave the way for the modernization of Japan.

PG. 127

(1) "He was recognized as a master in *Hokushin Itto* style" The term used here is *menkyo kaiden*. This is a license of full proficiency. Someone who is *menkyo kaiden* is recognized as having mastered all aspects of the style (physical, mental, and spiritual), and is permitted to teach the style to others.

(2) "...but he's left his fief" The word used here is *dappan*. This literally means "out of the fief." More specifically, it means leaving the fief without previous approval. Thus someone who is *dappan* would be treated as a pariah, never allowed to return to the fief again.

(3) "...he associates with a lot of revolutionists." Revolutionists were those who fought to destroy the shogunate and restore the Emperor to power.

PG. 130

Shamisen The instrument Saya is playing is the *shamisen*. It is a traditional Japanese instrument having three strings. It is played by striking the strings with a large wedge-shaped tool called a *bachi*.

PG. 133

Shimabara This area is the red-light district of Kyoto.

PG. 143

Wolves of Mibu The Shinsengumi were first headquartered in Mibu village (now a district of Kyoto), and thus gained the nickname *Miburo* (Wolves of Mibu).

PG. 151

Sonno Joi Restoring the emperor to power and getting rid of the "barbarians"—foreigners.

PG. 164

"Loungin' around like one of his cats." The original Japanese is a play on words. The Japanese word for cat is *neko*. But in this case, instead of using the correct character for "cat," the author wrote *neko* with the characters for "sleeping" and "child."

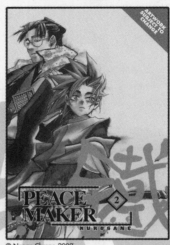

© Nanae Chrono 2002

......AND LEADS DOWN THE
BLOODY BACK ALLEY

Having run off gun-slinging Ryoma Sakamoto, the Shinsengumi seemed to have kept the streets of Kyoto free from trouble; but when self-interest gets out of control and leads down the bloody back alley of murder, then all is not quiet and peaceful. Suzu, formerly a friend of Tetsunosuke, makes a bloody mess of his caretaker, thus putting his self-absorbed plan into motion. How will the Shinsengumi respond to such a blatant disregard for human life? What price, if any, will Suzu pay? The Shinsengumi will discover a harsh vulnerability in their pursuit for justice, as the lawmen of Kyoto continue to patrol the streets in **Peacemaker Kurogane**, Volume 2!

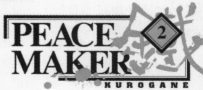

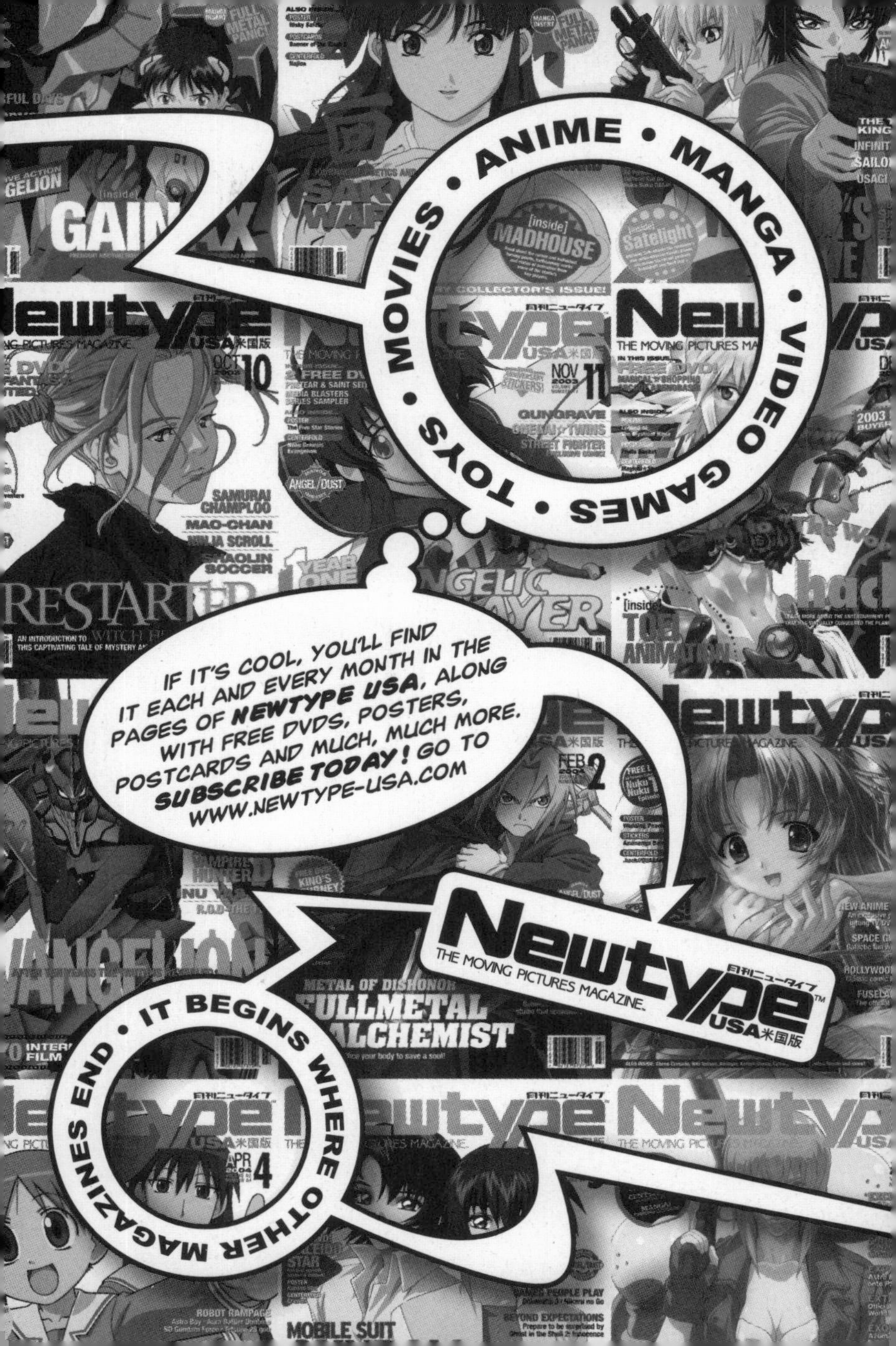
MOVIES • ANIME • MANGA • VIDEO GAMES • TOYS •
IF IT'S COOL, YOU'LL FIND IT EACH AND EVERY MONTH IN THE PAGES OF NEWTYPE USA, ALONG WITH FREE DVDS, POSTERS, POSTCARDS AND MUCH, MUCH MORE. SUBSCRIBE TODAY! GO TO WWW.NEWTYPE-USA.COM
Newtype™
THE MOVING PICTURES MAGAZINE.
月刊ニュータイプ
USA米国版
IT BEGINS WHERE OTHER MAGAZINES END •

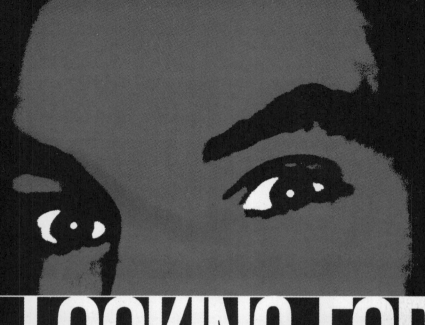

LOOKING FOR ANIME NETWORK?

THIS GUY WAS, THEN HE CALLED HIS LOCAL
CABLE PROVIDER AND DEMANDED HIS ANIME!

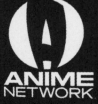

ANIME
NETWORK

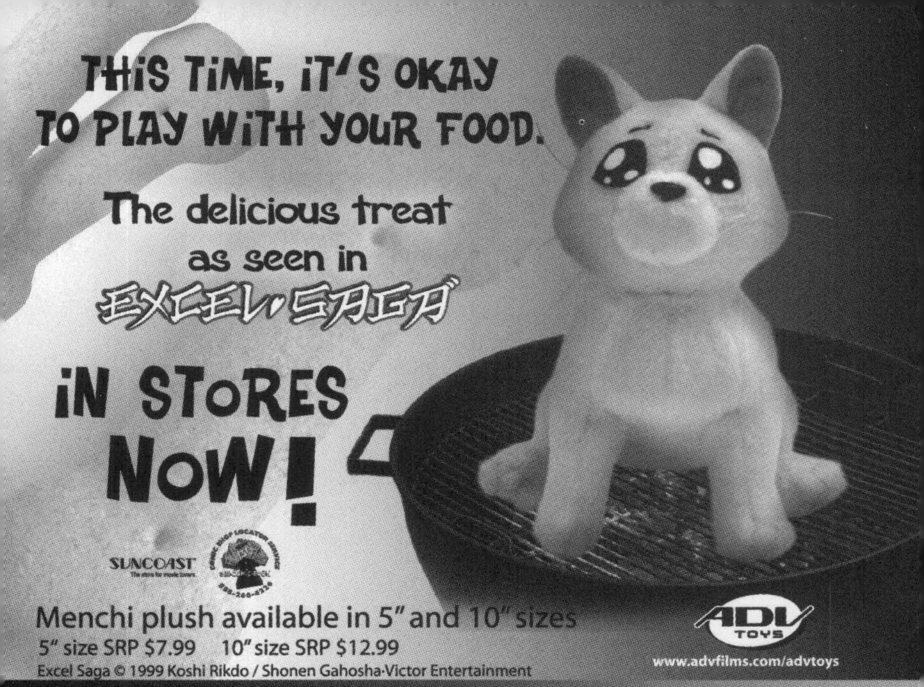
THIS TIME, IT'S OKAY
TO PLAY WITH YOUR FOOD.
The delicious treat
as seen in
EXCEL SAGA
IN STORES
NOW!
SUNCOAST
Menchi plush available in 5" and 10" sizes
5" size SRP $7.99 10" size SRP $12.99
Excel Saga © 1999 Koshi Rikdo / Shonen Gahosha-Victor Entertainment
ADV TOYS
www.advfilms.com/advtoys
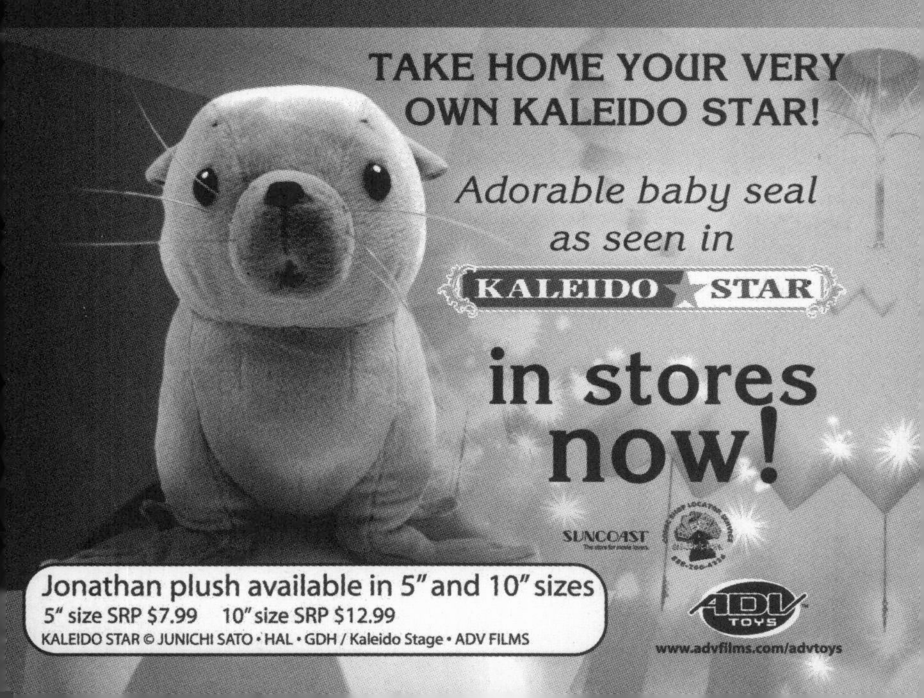
TAKE HOME YOUR VERY
OWN KALEIDO STAR!
Adorable baby seal
as seen in
KALEIDO STAR
in stores
now!
SUNCOAST
Jonathan plush available in 5" and 10" sizes
5" size SRP $7.99 10" size SRP $12.99
KALEIDO STAR © JUNICHI SATO • HAL • GDH / Kaleido Stage • ADV FILMS
ADV TOYS
www.advfilms.com/advtoys

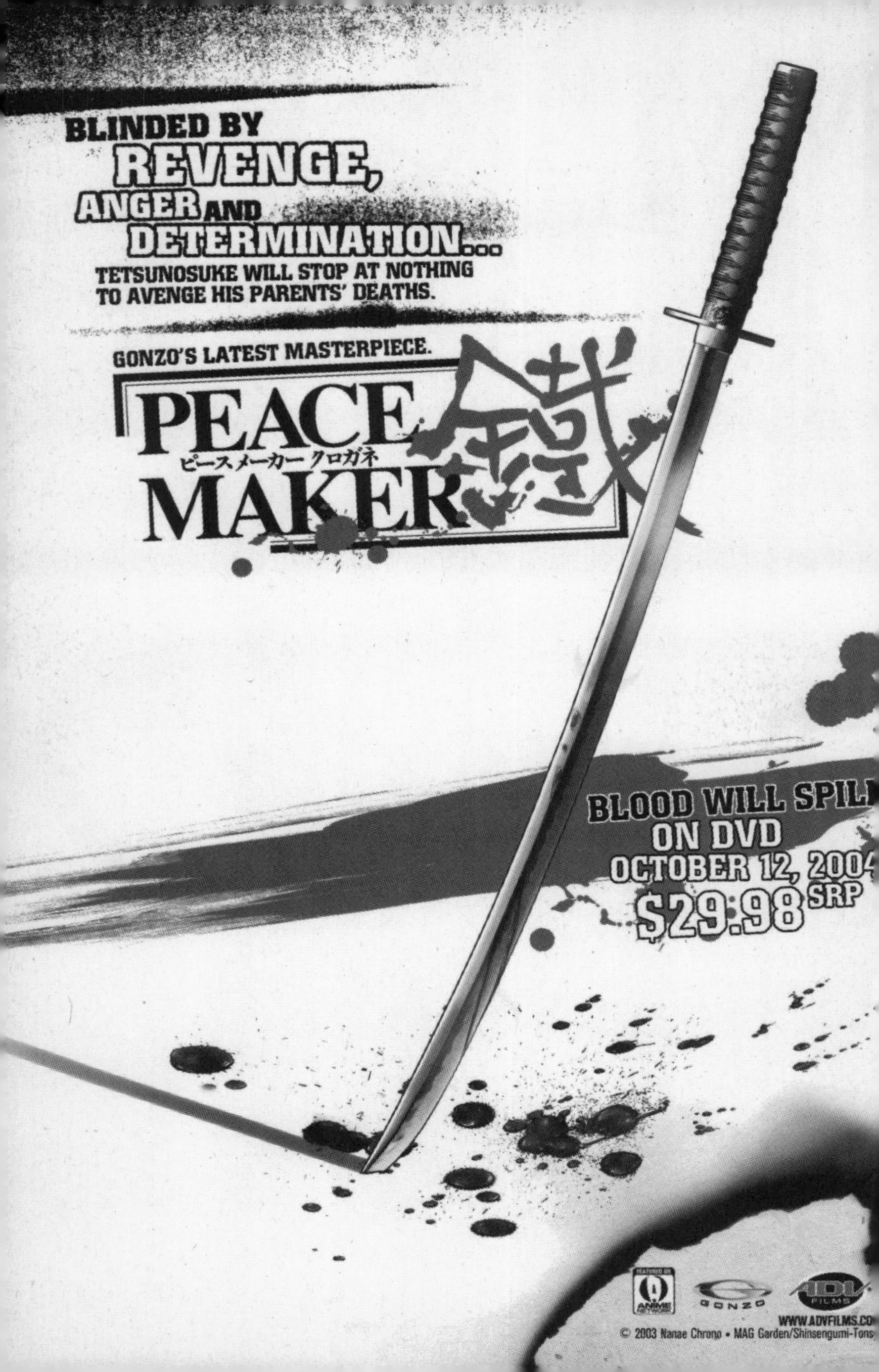
BLINDED BY
REVENGE,
ANGER AND
DETERMINATION...
TETSUNOSUKE WILL STOP AT NOTHING
TO AVENGE HIS PARENTS' DEATHS.
GONZO'S LATEST MASTERPIECE.
PEACE MAKER 鐵
ピースメーカー クロガネ
BLOOD WILL SPIL
ON DVD
OCTOBER 12, 2004
$29.98 SRP
GONZO
FILMS
WWW.ADVFILMS.CO
© 2003 Nanae Chrono • MAG Garden/Shinsengumi-Tons

Mythical Detective LOKI Ragnarok

vol. 1

The **strange** cases of a boy detective who may just be a **god**!

from Sakura Kinoshita, who brought you *Tactics*!

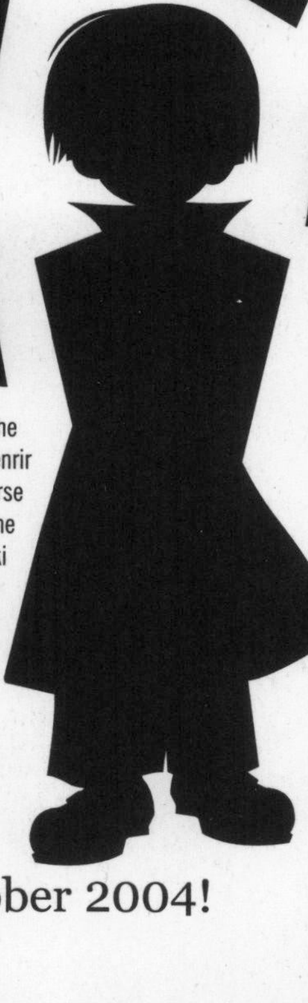

Loki is no normal 10-year-old boy! For one thing, he is a mythical detective. He is also the father of Fenrir the Dog and Yamino. And he may just be the Norse god of mischief! These are the strange cases of the world's strangest detective. In his first case, Loki must help a mute girl he names Spica. Spica has been cursed by Odin—who hates Loki. But does Spica have some other connection with Loki that has been disguised?

In his second case, Fenrir has been kidnapped. Loki is aided in his search by the prophetess Skuld the Norn. But Skuld has her own reasons for separating Loki from his son!

Volume 1 available in October 2004!

Sakura Kinoshita 2002

www.adv-manga.com